THE CRINOLINE CHURCH, EASTNEY BARRACKS

The Story of the Royal Marine Artillery Church,
its Chaplains and its Baptisms,
1866-1905

Dennis Bill

Series Editor
Colonel Brian Carter OBE RM

ROYAL MARINES HISTORICAL SOCIETY

SPECIAL PUBLICATION NO 44

The Crinoline Church, Eastney Barracks

All Rights Reserved

ISBN 978-1-908123-13-8

First published 2016 by the
ROYAL MARINES HISTORICAL SOCIETY
Royal Marines Museum
Eastney
Southsea
Hants PO4 9PX
United Kingdom

Cover, design and layout
Tim Mitchell
www.tim-mitchell.co.uk

Printed and bound in Great Britain by
CPI Antony Rowe Ltd, Chippenham and Eastbourne

This book is dedicated to the unsung heroes of Victorian history – the clerks – their no doubt boring and tedious toil left us with such a wonderful legacy.

Contents

Acknowledgements

I could not have written this book without the help of so many people that it would be impossible to list them all here, even if I knew all their names. The authors of the books and websites listed in the bibliography have all contributed to my knowledge, especially of naval history. I have contacted all the libraries and archives listed in Appendix B either in person or by email and their librarians and archivists have always been unfailingly helpful. In particular I must thank the staffs of Portsmouth City Library Naval and Genealogical Collection and the Portsmouth Record Office, latterly merged as the Portsmouth History Centre, for their help in understanding and searching their collections. And also the Friends of Highland Road Cemetery and the staff of the Portsmouth City Council Cemeteries Office who helped me to locate many of the graves mentioned in the book. Chris Sugg provided valuable information about Victorian gas lighting which would have been unobtainable elsewhere, Sioban Clarke provided the photo of Rev Lloyd's memorial plaque in Greenwich Chapel and Joyce Cummings and Vic Cole of the Cheltenham Local History Society were kind enough to do some research on John Blizard at Cheltenham Local and Family History Centre for me. Colonel Brian Carter and the late Major Alastair Donald of the Royal Marines Historical Society read my draft and prevented some gaffes going any further.

Special thanks must go to Matthew Little who was the Librarian at the Royal Marines Museum for nearly all the time that I was researching there and he gave me crucial guidance on the Museum collections and Naval history generally and also Alison Firth, Curator of Images, and her predecessor John Ambler who gave me invaluable assistance in sourcing photographs.

Regardless of all this expert assistance all errors and omissions are my own responsibility.

Photographs and Images

I have strived to identify the owners of all the photographs and other images that I have included in the book and I hope that I have correctly assigned ownership and sought the appropriate permissions. I would like to thank the following for allowing me to reproduce text and images from their collections:

The National Archives; Royal Marines Museum; Royal Marines Historical Society; Portsmouth History Centre; City of London, London Metropolitan Archives; London Gazette; Illustrated London News/Mary Evans Picture Library; Cheltenham Local & Family History Centre; National Art Library (V&A); The Architectural Review; Cengage (Times Digital Archive); The Greenwich Foundation for the Old Royal Naval College; St Simon's Church; E C Coleman and Martin Edwards.

The origins of the images and photographs are individually acknowledged in the list of sources in Appendix B.

Introduction

I first became aware of the Crinoline Church when I was researching my family history in Portsmouth Record Office. My Wiseman ancestors had moved to Portsmouth from Ringwood, Hampshire, in about 1830, part of the great exodus of farmers and farming labourers from the country to the industrialised towns in the first part of the nineteenth century. Through the second half of the nineteenth century this migration had helped Portsmouth to expand to such an extent that by the end of the century there were upwards of 46 places of worship in the town and this had increased to 60 by the end of World War One. This makes searching for baptisms and marriages quite complicated and I was always getting confused about which churches were operating on a particular date and whether the records had been transcribed or not. So for my own benefit I created an index of all the churches on Portsea Island (it was only after World War Two that Portsmouth spread onto the 'mainland'). The index is arranged in a timeline format, indicating what records are available, where they are held and if they have been transcribed. This Master Index to Portsea Island Church Registers and Indexes is available as a free download from my web site (see Appendix C). Having completed that project it seemed a natural progression to take photographs of all the extant churches and find postcards of those that no longer existed; these are in the Church Photo Gallery on my web site. It was these two projects that made me aware of the story of the Crinoline Church.

I had long been an admirer of Victorian bricklayers, not only for their buildings but also for their bridge and tunnel work. But here was a wonderful example of Victorian carpentry the like of which I had never seen before. I knew that my own family had no connection to the church but I got very excited when, a couple of years later, I found a connection through the outer branches of my family tree; the ancestors of some of my first cousins had been in the Royal Marines, father and son. On my next visit to The National Archives (TNA) I ordered-up the baptism register and to my delight there were the baptisms I was looking for. Not only that but in the eight years I had been researching my family history this was the first time I had actually handled an original church register, having always had to rely on microfiche and transcriptions; it was a special moment.

Like most researchers looking for baptism, marriage and burial records I had relied heavily on the transcriptions of church registers produced over the years by countless volunteers and I was beginning to feel a bit guilty that I wasn't contributing. I decided that when my research reached a plateau I would start to 'put something back'. Handling the Royal Marine Artillery (RMA) baptism register made me think that perhaps this was the transcription project I was looking for. As churches and chapels on military land are not under the jurisdiction of the local diocese it means that they are not subject to the same archive deposit arrangements and so they are archived at TNA rather than the local archive office. This also means that they have largely 'escaped' the microfilming and transcribing projects that have made 'normal' church records so accessible. The only way to access these records is by personal visit to TNA, not a viable option for most researchers. And so I decided this was to be my project for the 2008-9 winter.

My original idea had been to make the baptism data available through my web site as a searchable database but I soon discovered that this would require special software that I had no knowledge of and my internet service provider did not support. The only option was to publish the records in a traditional book format. To accompany the transcriptions a short history of the church was required and so, like a good researcher, I decided to go back to prime sources and create my own version of the story rather than re-hash the information that I had read elsewhere. It wasn't long before I came to realise that there were no easily available prime sources. It appeared that most of the previous histories had been written 'off the back' of earlier ones, the very thing that I was trying to avoid. Hardly any of the 'facts' of the story were easily verifiable. The accepted wisdom seemed to be that the church was originally intended for use in the Crimean War but there is no contemporary evidence to support this story. So what was to be a few days research in the local archives turned into a serious project devouring hours of travel and research time over the course of four and a half years. I hope you find the story interesting.

Part One - The Church

Chapter 1- The Building

This story is about a church with three lives. It began life in 1858 as a temporary church to be used prior to the building of St Bartholomew's in Southsea, a district of Portsmouth, Hampshire. Three and a half years later, after the completion of St Bartholomew's, it was disassembled, moved just over a kilometre and re-erected on a small plot of land adjacent to the site of another new church, St Simon's, that was being built at the junction of St Ronan's Road and Waverley Road also in Southsea. Finally it was purchased by the Admiralty and moved once again and erected a third time on a plot owned by the War Office in St George's Road, just outside the then new Royal Marine Artillery (RMA) Barracks at Eastney. Here it stood for the next 39 years until superseded in 1905 by the 'permanent' RMA church dedicated to St Andrew that was built on the northern boundary of the barracks in Henderson Road.

This 'temporary' wooden church was a truly extraordinary building. It was twenty-sided, 22 metres in diameter and 18 metres high; it could hold a congregation of 600 (later increased to 800); and it was built in 28 days.

The building had a timber frame and the 'sides' were weather-boarded; from these 'sides' the timber-clad roof rose in sections to a circular lantern light, producing a conical shape. It was this overall shape that quickly earned it the nickname of 'The Crinoline Church' after the dress that was all the fashion at the time. The roof sections were covered in asphalted felt sheeting, an early form of the modern roofing felt. Asphalt is a naturally occurring bituminous material that was known and used in the ancient East. In the early nineteenth century it became widely used for road surfacing and, as in this case, as a weatherproof roof covering. The roof covering was produced by saturating a paper or fabric mat with the ashphalt which could then be rolled, transported to site and cut to shape as required.

The church had three entrances, on the north, south and west sides. On the east side was an extension that formed the apse with a small 'lean-to' attachment that was probably the vestry. Above each entrance there were triangular windows and there were five smaller triangular gable windows set into the roof. These together with the roof lantern provided natural light to the interior. In the photographs of the church the triangular windows appear to be translucent and are probably 'Vitreous Cloth' which was cheaper than glass, unbreakable and gave a good diffused light (see Chapter Three – Peter Thompson). A small bell turret was set into the roof above the west entrance. Inside the church seating was provided by conventional wooden pews providing accommodation for 600 people.

All the surviving images of the church were taken during its third life at Eastney. Figure 1 shows the church soon after its erection there in 1867.

Figure 1 - RMA Church, Eastney, 1867 [1]

The clock tower at the entrance to the RMA barracks can be seen to the left and Teapot Row, now like much of the barracks converted to private housing, can be seen behind the church. This photograph is owned by St Simon's Church and is held at Portsmouth History Centre where it is catalogued as "pre 1905". However, evidence from the Admiralty records held at The National Archives (TNA) enable us to date this picture more precisely to May/June 1867 and so this is one of the earliest surviving photographs of the church and shows it as it would have looked in its first two locations. A second photograph taken from Eastney Beach that is in the RM Museum collection also appears to show the church at this early date (Figure 2). All the later images of the church show modifications made by the Royal Marines within about a year of its erection at Eastney – this is discussed later in Third Life - The Last Resting Place.

There are only three images known to exist of the interior of the church. Two are in the RM Museum photo collection and were obviously taken at the same time but from a slightly different position – Figure 3 is one of these. The third was published in the Evening News in 1932 and is at Figure 4. These photographs show the large gas chandelier (more correctly a gasolier) that was supplied by local tradesman William Stevens, who had premises in Hanover Street, Southsea[2]. An enquiry to The

Figure 2 – The church from Eastney beach, 1867 [2]

National Gas Museum led me to Chris Sugg, an expert on gas lighting. Chris's great-grandfather founded William Sugg & Co in 1837 and the company were involved in the design and manufacture of gas lighting and other gas equipment until 1969. It would appear that the Crinoline Church's gasolier is fairly typical of decorative open flame lighting units of the time. The gas jets can be seen pointing upwards about 30 cm apart around the circumference of the fitting.

I had originally thought that the whole gasolier would have had to have been lowered to light the flames; a rope can be seen right of centre in both of the pictures leading up into the roof at an angle and I thought that this was the lowering and raising method. However, Chris tells me that although rubber pipe technology was available at the time it was very fragile and so it is unlikely that the gasolier could be lowered. There are three possible ways that the flames could be ignited without lowering the fitting. If the burners are close enough together then lighting one will 'cross-light' the others; a special 'fantail' design of the burners facilitated this. Alternatively there could be a valve that allowed the gas flow to be reduced whilst the lamplighter walked around the circle lighting each outlet with a lighting torch, increasing the gas flow once all were lit. In the 1850s the so-called 'sun burner' became popular and this had a low setting which acted as a pilot light. The light would have been permanently lit during the dark months with the user turning up the gas supply when lighting was required. We shall never know which of the methods was used or whether Stevens was the manufacturer or just the installer. He is listed

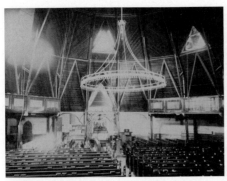

Figure 3 – Church interior, exact date unknown[4]

Figure 4 – Church interior, exact date unknown [6]

in contemporary trade directories as *'brass founder and gas fitter'*[5] so it is quite likely that he would have built the fitting, possibly buying-in the burners from a specialist manufacturer such as Suggs. The gas lights over the entrances, visible in the exterior photograph, were probably also part of the original building.

There is a rumour that some light fittings were salvaged when the church was finally dismantled and were installed in Christ Church at Widley, just outside Portsmouth. I have visited Christ Church and discussed this with Reverend Andrew Wilson but the hanging lights which he thinks are not original to Christ Church are not to be seen in any of the interior pictures of the Crinoline Church and must have come from another source.

At the back of the interior photographs can be seen the altar and the apse extension mentioned earlier. The harmonium and lectern are also clearly visible either side of the apse. Clearly visible in Figure 3 is the internal gallery; this gallery was not part of the original building and was added later by the RMA (see Third Life - The Last Resting Place below).

The second interior photograph at Figure 4 was owned by a Mrs Hughes of 5, Hellyer Road, Southsea at the time it was published in the Evening News in 1932 in an article entitled *"The Church That Went Round And Round"*[6]. It shows the church bedecked for a special occasion probably for Harvest Festival, there are a number of reports of the church being decorated for this festival[7].

The bell turret can be seen above the west entrance in Figure 1. The bell that was used for the

Figure 5 - The RMA Church bell [8]

time that it was the RMA Church still exists and is in the RM Museum collection.

Following the final demolition of the church this bell was utilised in the Sea Training School at the RM Barracks until that building was itself demolished in 1958. The bell is currently in store at the Royal Marines Museum, Eastney. It is not known if this or another bell was fitted in its earlier two 'lives'.

No mention is made anywhere about the flooring of the church but, with it having been erected and able to be used within 28 days, it must either have been wooden or simply compacted earth.

First Life - How it came to Southsea

During the middle part of the nineteenth century Portsmouth was a boom town. From a cluster of buildings around the dockyard area it was gradually expanding across Portsea Island, swallowing up arable land for new housing and industry. An area called Southsea had originally been established as a 'spa' in the early nineteenth century but by the 1840s the need for quality housing for the upper working and middle classes led to the development of what was then called New Southsea. A Norwich auctioneer and land agent called William Butcher was one of the developers. In conjunction with sons Henry and Robert, he had obtained 25 acres of land from the Lowe family and possibly others in 1857[9] (In the 1838 Tithe Map Apportionment Book the owner is recorded as *"William Loe & others"*[10]) and planned a quality development laid-out as what we would now call a 'gated community', with gatehouses at each entrance. It was named Havelock Park after the popular hero of the Indian Mutiny and in particular the Relief of Lucknow, General Sir Henry Havelock. When the development was underway it was described in a contemporary trade directory as being *"laid out as a park, and divided into allotments for the erection of genteel houses, with tasteful gardens, &c."*[11]

William Butcher was a prominent figure in Norwich society having been Mayor, Alderman and Sheriff of the city. It is not clear quite how he became involved in a development in Southsea but much later in 1874 he owned *"a freehold estate in Southsea consisting of several messuages or tenements in Richmond Terrace"*[12] but whether this was the cause or effect of his relationship with Southsea is unknown. Whether the Butchers were short of capital or whether they wanted to give an investment opportunity to some friends is also not known but they agreed to allow a local resident, William Samuel Turnley of Raglan House, Clarence Parade, and presumably his relation Thomas Wesley Turnley, a solicitor of Bedford, to invest £2800 in the scheme in exchange for a third share[9]. In some subsequent reports William Turnley has been described as the owner but this is a misinterpretation of his status as he was probably acting as a project manager or agent for the Butchers. Could it be that there was some family or business relationship between the Butchers and Turnleys that had originally led Butcher to Southsea? William Turnley went on to develop land adjacent to Havelock Park on his own account, giving it the name Nelsonville, although this was not entirely successful.[13]

An integral part of the Havelock Park development was a new church to serve the area, to be dedicated to St Bartholomew, and to be built on a roughly circular plot of land at the junction of what are now Campbell Road and Outram Road (named after Sir Colin Campbell and Lieutenant General James Outram, both heroes of the Indian Mutiny). William Butcher's youngest son Henry was part of the architectural partnership Goodwin & Butcher, operating out of Bedford Row, London, and they were the architects. The building of a new church within an existing parish involved negotiations with the Winchester Diocese and a standard agreement was reached with the Archdeacon of Winchester, Philip Jacob, and the new parish committee that as soon as the church was finished and consecrated the land it stood on would pass to the Ecclesiastical Commissioners[9]. It is not known whether the Butchers or the Diocese initiated the idea of building the new church but the inclusion of the church in the development was of mutual benefit. The Diocese would be able to increase its congregation and the Butchers would have what would be known in today's marketing speak as a USP or 'unique selling point'. In our current secular times it is difficult to fully understand the hold that religion had on society in the Victorian era. Today prospective buyers would be concerned about the availability of public transport, local shopping facilities and the performance of local schools; in the mid-nineteenth century it was the religious facilities that were at the top of the list. The population of Portsmouth vastly outnumbered the church seats available and so the Butchers knew that the local Diocese was bound to back the plans. William Butcher provided a great incentive to the project by donating land and £500 towards the construction of a vicarage[3]; in some reports this act of generosity was attributed to William Turnley, who was just Butcher's agent, as mentioned above. But the Butchers couldn't wait and they needed to sell properties whilst the new church was being built, also the appointed minister, Reverend Nathaniel S Godfrey, previously curate of St Jude's, Southsea, needed to raise money to pay for the new church. The solution was to build a temporary church adjacent to the site of the new church and it is this building that this book examines.

The temporary church was completed in early October 1858 just 28 days after construction began. The first Sunday service was scheduled for 10 October but unfortunately nature was to take a hand and on the previous Saturday night there was a great storm and the church suffered some unspecified damage that prevented the opening service taking place[14]. It was another two weeks before it was ready and the first service took place on 24 October 1858. The Hampshire Telegraph reported it as follows:

St Bartholomew's Temporary Church, Havelock Park, New Southsea. - This church, which was opened by divine service on Sunday last, may be truly denominated one of the wonders of the day. Those of our townspeople who a month since passed along Wish-lane into the Fratton-road saw nothing but a pretty little cottage, which they were told was intended for a lodge entrance to Havelock Park, and a board announcing that a temporary church was to be opened on the 10th of October. They looked about in every direction, but in vain; they saw nothing before them but a field of stubble, dotted here and there with a few white pegs, which indicated an intention on the part of the owners, at some time or other, to sell the ground in lots suitable for building. But how was this scene changed! Timber was carried into the ground – workmen commenced their operations – the sound of saw and hammer and axe resounded through the air – and in one day less than four weeks from the day of commencement Divine service is celebrated in the building by its Minister, licensed thereto by our beloved Diocesan.[3]

The cost to erect the church was £600 plus £100 for the internal fittings.

The local watchdogs were immediately concerned about the health and safety aspects of having upwards of 600 people in a temporary wooden structure. The matter was raised at the October meeting of the Landport and Southsea Commissioners who resolved:

'That the Surveyor do give notice to the owners of the New Church at Southsea that though the Commissioners may not at present interfere with the fact of its being constructed of combustible materials they hold to themselves the right of doing so at any time hereafter whenever they may think proper and that it be intimated that it should only be regarded as a temporary Building.'[15]

Services continued at Havelock Park without interference from the Commissioners until the permanent St Bartholomew's was completed in 1862 and the Crinoline Church became surplus to requirements.

Second Life - A Short Move

Following the opening of St Bartholomew's, the temporary church was advertised for sale in The Times by Henry Butcher from his address in London. The advertisement appeared on Saturday 7 June 1862 and read as follows:

To be SOLD by Private Contract, a temporary WOODEN CHURCH, with Pulpit, Desk and Pewing. The church is polygonal in form, 72 ft in diameter; contains sittings for 600 persons, and is well lighted and ventilated. It has been erected for 3½ years, and is in good repair. The plans of the building can be seen, and all particulars obtained at the offices of Messrs Butcher, 37, Bedford-row, W.C.[16]

The use of 'Messrs Butcher' rather than Godwin & Butcher might imply that the building may have been the property of the Butcher family and not purchased by the church or diocese, and hence it was a private sale by the Butchers. The sale was also advertised in the local Portsmouth Times by the Southsea auctioneers Becks[17]. They didn't really need to go to this bother as a buyer was almost literally 'just around the corner'.

A new church to be called St Simon's was to be built in a development off Waverley Road. The church building committee did not have sufficient funds to purchase the Crinoline Church and so a Mr Marvin agreed to purchase the church on their behalf. He paid £250 for the church and also covered the £100 it was estimated that it would cost to pull it down and re-erect it on the Waverley Road site. He was also to provide the land for it; the land for the 'proper' St Simon's was to be given by Mr Josiah Webb. The intention was for the church to repay Mr Marvin from any surplus monies after the incumbent, the Reverend Baldy, had been paid his stipend and expenses[18]. Figure 6 is an extract from a map dated about 1861 showing the Crinoline Church in this location.

No paperwork appears to have survived of the sale but there is evidence to tell us that the removal and subsequent re-erection of the church on the St Simon's site was carried out by a George Riddett. This information comes from a scrapbook compiled by Riddett's grandson Lewis Edwin Bambury (1876-1966)[19].

George Riddett appears in the contemporary trade directories (in 1863 erroneously as George Riddell) as the publican of the Plough & Barleycorn at 33, St George's Square. In the four census returns from 1841 to 1871 he claims to be in turn a bricklayer, licensed victualler and lastly a builder *'master employing 6 men and 2 boys'*[20-23]. So Riddett clearly had the necessary experience and contacts in the building trade to undertake this contract. It wasn't uncommon for publicans to have a second occupation, in fact this was often the case with the husband nominally holding the licence but the pub being largely run by the wife and family, in this case the pub seems to have been an interlude in his building career.

The architect and builder of the new church were both local men. The architect Thomas Hellyer was born in Emsworth and at the time of this commission was living in Ryde, Isle of Wight. The builder was Henry Laurence. The 1861 census shows that Laurence, born in Guildford, Surrey, was living at 60, Commercial Road, Portsmouth

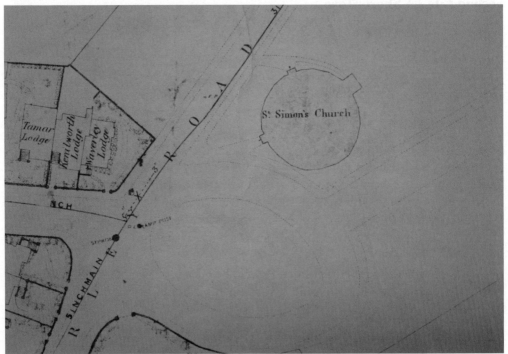

Figure 6 - The Crinoline Church as St Simon's. The feint outline of St Ronan's Road can be seen including the oval that was to contain the permanent St Simon's.[25]

with his wife. At the age of 38 he had a substantial business employing 47 men and 7 boys.[24]

But things did not go smoothly. There were a number of setbacks, the two most serious delaying the opening of the new church and subsequent sale of the Crinoline Church by nearly a year. On 25 November 1865 the Portsmouth Times as part of an article on the recent severe gales reported:

On Wednesday the "principals" of the roof of St Simon's Church ..... were observed to be swaying to and fro owing to the immense force of the wind, and almost immediately afterwards six of the seven "principals", each of which weighed nearly a ton and a half, fell with a loud crash. Several workmen were employed below and their escape was almost miraculous.[26]

But worse was to come. Less than three months later, on 11 February 1866, another storm said to have been the worst for over half a century brought the following report in the Hampshire Telegraph:

A serious accident occurred at St Simon's Church – which by-the-bye appears to be particularly unfortunate. About half-past twelve o'clock the whole gable end of the building was blown into the road, carrying with it the scaffolding &c., the poles snapping like reeds. At the moment of the fall a young gentleman was passing from the temporary church where the service had just closed, to his uncle's house and was completely buried in the debris. [27]

The young gentleman recovered from his injuries but serious damage had been done to the partly-completed building. Two weeks later the trustees placed an announcement in the Hampshire Telegraph which began as follows:

The injury done to St Simon's Church by the storm on Sunday week was so serious that a considerable larger sum than that originally estimated will now be needed to complete the erection. Considering the almost unprecedented character of the storm, the Building Committee have determined to relieve the contractor of his liability to the extent of £200; and they have decided, on the recommendation of the architect, to carry out at once additional works against the north and south walls, with a view to their effectual support. ......[28]

The appeal was for a further £1600 from subscriptions to enable remedial work to be done and the church completed [29]. The church was eventually completed and the first service was held on 19 December 1866.[30]

Third Life - The Last Resting Place

This research on St Simon's left me confused. If the Crinoline Church was still in use at the St Simon's site in December 1866 how was it that the first entry in the baptism register for the RMA Church was on 22 July 1866? Had the St Simon's trustees sold the wooden church before the new church was finished because they were so desperate for funds? When did the Crinoline Church make its final 1.7 kilometre journey to Eastney?

Local research had drawn a blank on the final move and so it was to TNA and the maze that are Admiralty records series ADM 1 and ADM 12 that I had to rely for information. These two series of documents hold an amazing amount of information about the activities of the Admiralty but they are far from easy to search. The pieces

Figure 7 - The Drill Shed, Eastney Barracks [33]

in ADM 12 are an index to the original in-letters and documents that are held in the ADM 1 series. The indexes are in two forms; index listings under the name of the ship or person involved in the correspondence; and a digest that indexes the correspondence under subject headings. The advantage of the digest listings is that they include a brief summary of the document and this is often the only evidence if, as was often the case here, the original documents in ADM 1 have been 'weeded'. The following account has been compiled from the records in ADM 12 digests and the surviving original documents in ADM 1 and the Admiralty Marine Office records.

Although his initial letter has not survived we know from the surviving papers that the Colonel Commandant of the RMA at Eastney, Colonel Alexander, wrote to the Admiralty on 12 November 1866 proposing the purchase of the church for use at the newly completed barracks. He was asked to provide further information and to find out if the church was available for rent rather than outright purchase; this was answered in the negative. On 29 November the Admiralty wrote to Colonel Alexander to say that *"they are not prepared to make the purchase of the wooden church as proposed"* [31]. However, a few days later the Director of Works submitted a report on the suitability of the wooden building and his report, dated 1 December 1866, is worth transcribing in full as it gives an insight into what was in Colonel Alexander's letter and a good summary of the thinking and options being considered at the time.

Eastney
Church accommodation for Royal Marine Artillery
The inconvenience of the present arrangements for the performance of Divine Service at the

Royal Marine Artillery Barracks at Eastney has been strongly represented by the Colonel Commandant. At present services are held in a portion of the Drill Shed temporarily enclosed by canvas screen, but this arrangement could not be continued during the winter months, and it has, therefore, become necessary to provide some other accommodation for the purpose.

It will eventually be requisite to erect a permanent church for the use of the Marine Artillery, and for the wives and families of both officers and men of the Corps, and will be economical for the Admiralty to contribute towards such an object, that so a church might be provided, sufficiently commodious to accommodate both the Marine Artillery and the inhabitants of the locality. Should My Lords approve of this proposal, the Ecclesiastical Commissioners or proper authorities might be communicated with and their wishes and intentions ascertained.

The estimate of cost and amount of contribution by the Admiralty would then be taken into consideration.

In the meantime some temporary place for service must be furnished, and in view of this I submit, for the information of the Board, two courses which have suggested themselves to me, and which I have carefully weighed.

The first is to purchase the large wooden building at Southsea which has been occupied as a church during the building of Saint Simon's.

On personal inspection I found that the roof and other parts of the structure are in bad order; its size is insufficient for the number of men that attend service at Eastney; the cost of procuring, taking it down, removing and re-erecting it would be about £700, and possession could not be obtained for nearly two months.

The second mode, and that which I recommend for adoption, is to fit up the end of the Drill Shed between the officer's and men's quarters as a temporary church. This would meet the present want of a place of worship, to be available for the Adult School, and serve every purpose for the next two years, during which (if my proposal to that effect be approved) the District Church might be erected.

The cost of this fitting up and warming the Drill Shed would be about £500, and to this expenditure, which may be charged to the extension of the Barracks at Eastney, I now request My Lords sanction.

P.S. Since writing the above I have heard that the Admiralty have no intention of purchasing the wooden church to which I have referred. [32]

Could it have been that the Director of Works was building the case for the permanent church in order to provide work for his department? At least the mystery of the early baptisms is solved – they took place in the Drill Shed.

On 6 December a rather different report was made by Mr Henry Wood, the Superintending Civil Engineer, and again it is worth quoting in full.

Eastney Barracks
Purchase of Temporary Wooden Church

Sir,
In obedience to your minute of 5th instant on Boards Order of 4th instant: I beg to report

that I have placed myself in communication with Colonel Alexander the Commandant of the Royal Marine Artillery with reference to the purchase of a wooden church for the use of the Marines: and having examined the wooden church in question, beg to state respecting its condition and capabilities as follows: viz

On the day on which I examined the church the weather was very rainy and I found that the wet was dripping from the roof, thereby shewing that the asphalte felt covering was defective, but under any circumstances the felt covering could not be again used if the church be re-erected.

The framing of the superstructure as well as the internal fittings of the church are in good condition, but portions of the weather boarding covering the sides are defective and in the event of the church being purchased, much of this boarding say 1/3 of the whole will have to be made good with new.

The other portions of the church as far as I could ascertain are in good condition.

As regards the capabilities of the church I find it will accommodate about 600 persons but this number could be much increased by the introduction of a gallery.

During my visit to the church I had an interview with the incumbent, the Reverend Mr Baldy, who informed me that the ediface together with all fixtures, Reading Desk, Pulpit, Pews, stoves, gas fittings (except the meter) could be had for £175, but that all moveable furniture such as the chairs for the Communion would not be in the purchase.

Referring to the last sentence in your minute, I beg to state that this building has been used for a twofold purpose 1st as a temporary church during the erection of the church of St Bartholomew and 2nd it having been purchased by the trustees of St Simon's it has been used for a similar purpose during the erection of that church also; and the cause of it being in the market is that the latter church is now completed.

I was further informed by the Revd Mr Baldy that if the church be purchased by the Admiralty, possession can be obtained about the 20th instant.[32]

Immediately on receipt of this more down to earth report a telegraph message was sent to Admiral Superintendent Portsmouth, Admiral Wellesley, asking him "…to report what would be the cost of purchasing, repairing and putting up at Eastney…". By 7 December Wellesley replied by telegraph:

The cost of the wooden church for Eastney will be as follows, viz,

Purchase £175 – repairing and putting up with the assistance that will be afforded by the Commandant of the Royal Marine Artillery £140 – Making a total of £315.[32]

Finally, in a letter dated 8 December, Wood confirmed Wellesley's telegraph as follows

Sir

In obedience to your minute of this days date:

I beg to report that the cost of purchasing, repairing, and putting up, for the use of the Royal Marine Artillery the wooden building at Southsea, which has been used as a church during the construction of Saint Simon's Church; will be £315 in all that is £175 for the purchase, and £140 for repairs and re-erection, provided the said re-erection be

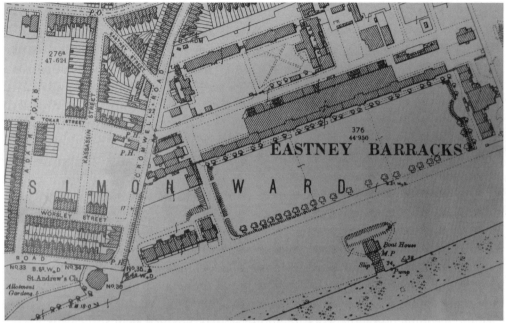

Figure 8 - St Andrew's Church at Eastney, about 1896 [35]

done by the working parties of Marine Artillery as arranged with Colonel Alexander the Commandant of that Corps.[32]

So it was the marines who were to provide the work force not the craftsmen of the Works Department, no doubt under the pretence of good training and exercise. But where was the church to be put? On 16 January 1867 Wood wrote to Admiral Wellesley, saying that he had spoken to the local Commanding Royal Engineer about putting the church *".. on War Department land in rear of the west demi Bastion.."* and had been told that *"..application must be made by the Director of Works to the Secretary of State for War."* [34]. It was subsequently identified that the application to the Secretary of State for War had to be made by the Lords Commissioners of the Admiralty.

The church's position in relation to the barracks can be seen in the extract from an Ordnance Survey 1:2500 scale map at Figure 8, this map is dated 1896 [35].

The exact date of the moving and opening of the church is still not clear. But on 23 May 1867 the RMA Chaplain, Reverend Beal, wrote to the Colonel Commandant, who by then was Colonel Schomberg C.B., as follows:

Sir

I have the honor to call your attention to the insufficient number of sittings about to be placed in the temporary church being built for the use of the Division under your command.

The average number of men attending Church is 840.

The Sunday School children number about 120.

Officers and visitors frequently amount to 50.

The old pews of the Church which they are about to replace in it will not seat more than 760 men.

I beg permission, therefore, to suggest that a gallery be erected at the west end of the Church for seating the children, drummer boys and bandsmen, and that in the place of the old pews, rush-bottomed chairs be used in the body of the Church.

These chairs stand compactly together and are durable, and adapted for Church purposes.

I believe they can be purchased for about 10/- per dozen, so that a grant of £35 would be sufficient to provide enough chairs to seat the whole congregation deducting those accommodated in the gallery.

I have the honor to be

Sir

Your most obedient servant

Saml. Beal

Chaplain [36]

Colonel Schomberg forwarded the letter the same day to Major General Langley, Deputy Adjutant General, Royal Marines, endorsing Reverend Beal's suggestion. On 18th June the Director of Works forwarded the request to the Secretary of the Admiralty confirming that the erection of the gallery by Marine labour would cost £91 and recommending the work for approval, to be charged against the general vote for Eastney Barracks. However, on the subject of the chairs, he pointed out that, if approved, they would be considered Barrack Stores and would not then be provided by his department. He went on to point out that he doubted that the chairs could be obtained for the sum quoted but would be at least *"18/- per dozen"* and that *"..the expense is likely to be nearly double.... say £70."* This last letter is endorsed on the reverse *"Refix pewing erect gallery"* and dated 20 June [36].

Reverend Beal's letter indicates that the relocation of the body of the church was complete by 23 May but the internal fitting-out was still in-hand. There are no further references to the church building in the Admiralty Indexes and Digests after this date and so it remains unclear when the church was first used but we can infer from the date of Reverend Beal's letter that at least the first nineteen baptisms recorded in the Register (in 7 groups from 22 July 1866 to 2 June 1867) and possibly the first twenty-three (the next group was on 7 July 1867) must have taken place in the Drill Shed. The next three baptisms were on 4 August 1867 and must surely have been in the new church. By 20 September 1867 the church was in need of some equipment and the Admiralty agreed that the Storekeeper General should supply the *"articles specified"* [37], but no list of them survives. A few days earlier on 15 September 1867 Colonel Barnard wrote to the Admiralty asking for the appointment of a man to take charge of the temporary church and also act as organist and choir master. The Admiralty refused saying that *"this must be a divisional arrangement"* [38] although much later in 1895 the Treasury did approve the payment of an annual allowance of £10 to an organist [39].

There is no evidence to show if the gallery was added before or after the church was opened but the Marine Office correspondence log for 1867 records that a letter was received dated 1 November 1867 *"requesting that the gallery may be enlarged"* [40], so the gallery was built in two stages, the enlargement definitely taking place after the church was in use. The two existing photographs of the interior (Figures 3 and 4) show that the final gallery extended around a large part of the perimeter of the interior, covering 17 of the 20 'sides' of the building. Access to the gallery was provided by the construction of two new entrances on the north and south sides that incorporated covered stairways.   It may have been that the original gallery joined the two new stairways with the two ends being extended towards the altar at the later date. The new south entrance is shown in the later photographs of the church at Figures 9 and 10; these are typical of a number of images of the church issued as postcards just after the turn of the century. Figure 9 shows substantial growth in both hedge and trees and the title *"Old RMA Church"* suggests that the photo was taken after the new church was built. The reverse shows that the card was posted on 31 May 1907 and we must assume that the card was fairly new then. Figure 10 is a better image and makes the church look newer but the wear of the roof covering is apparent and the shadows cast by the hedge and trees suggest a date not too different from Figure 9

I was mad with myself when I first saw the early photograph (Figure 1) for not realising before that the entrance in these later photos was not contemporary with the original build. With hindsight, it is so obvious in these later images that the stairway was an addition to the original building by the way that it sits uncomfortably with the gable window that would have been above the original entrance. This clash is caused by the fact that the new entrances were built in different positions to the originals, presumably due to constructional constraints. The two original porches at the north and south entrances were removed and the gaps boarded up.

There are far fewer surviving photographs taken from the north side but the one at Figure 11 is a nice example. It shows the new north entrance and also the presence at some point of a triangular window in the end of the apse protrusion which looks as though it has been boarded-up. It could be that what looks like boarding-up is just an effect of the image quality but perhaps it indicates the removal of the Noble Window for it to be reconfigured for installation in the new church - this would date this photo

Figure 9 - The church circa 1907 [41]

Figure 10 - The church circa 1905 [42]

Figure 11 - The church from the North (junction of Cromwell Road & St George's Road) [43]

as 1904/5 (see The Memorials below). This picture also shows that what I assume to be the vestry had an external door. There is another photo taken from the east that also shows this boarding-up of the Noble Window but unfortunately I have only seen it as a reproduction in the Evening News and it is of too poor quality to reproduce here [44].

As the idea of adding a gallery originally came from Henry Wood, the Superintending Civil Engineer, in his report dated 6 December 1866, the design of the gallery and its access might also have come from him but equally it might have come from marines or civilian carpenters employed at the Barracks. On 7 May 1868 and 12 May 1869 Colonel Schomberg received letters from the Deputy Adjutant General approving the employment of a Gunner as a carpenter for a period of three months *"for the purpose of repairing barrack furniture"* [45] so the use of marines on these types of duties was not unusual. The evidence from the Marine Office records indicating that the gallery was built in two stages would seem to support the idea that the majority of the work was done by marines and/or barrack tradesmen. Whoever was responsible the design of the stairways shows some skill and they were worthy additions to the building.

There are no further mentions of the building in the Admiralty records after 1867 but there were matters of an ecclesiastical nature that caused the Admiralty and the War Office some problems.

In December 1867 just six months after the church was opened a letter was sent to Reverend John Cawston (Cawston had replaced Reverend Beal in September 1867) by the incumbent of St James', Milton, (presumably Reverend William Wyke Bayliss) *"which prevents him baptising children or Churching of Women"* [46]. This letter certainly caused a flurry of activity at the Admiralty, especially in the Solicitor's department [47]. The matter was referred to Travers Twiss DCL QC who was then Queen's Advocate General but had previously been at the Admiralty and had knowledge of matters both naval and ecclesiastical. What the Admiralty was not aware of at the time was that the

War Office was having similar problems related to Army chaplains and already had the solution in hand. [48]

The issue of military chaplains officiating in chapels within military barracks had been simmering for some time. The expansion of military establishments during the middle of the nineteenth century was in response to the creation of a standing army and navy; prior to this recruitment had been on a temporary 'as and when needed' basis. These permanent forces had to be accommodated somewhere when not serving overseas and the eruption of barrack building inevitably brought a demand for chapels to serve the religious needs of these home-based forces. Technically these military chapels were built on land that was part of existing parishes and were therefore seen by the local Diocese as coming under their jurisdiction. Military chaplains were appointed by the War Office or the Admiralty and were responsible to them only; they had no official link to the established church. For some time there had been considerable public debate over the status of military chaplains and the fact that they were not accountable to the Archbishop of Canterbury as were all other Church of England priests, placing them outside the established church. From a more practical point of view the local clergy were also upset because the military had previously attended their churches and the drop in attendances had made a dent in the church's income.

By the time that the issue had been raised at Eastney the War Office had already instigated the adoption of an Act designed to clarify and specify the responsibilities for military chapels. The Army Chaplains Act 1868 was the military's response to a judgement passed in the Provincial Court of Dublin in May 1867 upholding objections made by the local incumbent, Reverend Thomas Mills about the chapel in Richmond Barracks, Dublin. What the new Act did was to allow defined areas within military establishments to be designated as "extra parochial" and it gave the Secretary of State the power to appoint chaplains to serve in such districts. The Act was amended at a late stage so that the definition of the term "army chaplain" covered *a commissioned chaplain to Her Majesty's military forces in holy orders of the said church*" (meaning the Church of England) thus covering Naval Chaplains. Much later in 1918 the Act was amended to cover the Royal Air Force [49]. The status of Navy Chaplains with regard to the established church was not resolved until 1902 and this is covered in Chapter 4 – The Naval Chaplain Service. The prohibition letter had little if any effect on Reverend Cawston's activities at Eastney and baptisms at the RMA Church continued in the normal way.

By November 1869 the church was clearly in need of some repair as orders were given by the Director of Works to tar the outside of the building and that other repairs would have to be provided for in the 1870-71 estimates[50]. After that the church appears to have led a quiet life and was no further trouble to the Admiralty or its clerks for the rest of its days.

There is one remaining mystery though, and that is when the church was named. I had originally assumed that it became St Andrew's when the new church was opened in 1905. I was therefore surprised to find the old church annotated as St Andrew's

Church on a 1:2500 scale Ordnance Survey map revised in 1896 [35] (at Figure 8). There is no record of a dedication service in the local press and all references in the Admiralty archives always refer to the church as the 'RMA Church'. The newspaper report on the laying of the foundation stone of the new church in 1904 mentions that the new church *"..as is generally the practice with Admiralty churches will not be consecrated,.."* [52]. So this may explain the absence of a report at this earlier date. A search in the Hampshire Telegraph archive revealed the use of St Andrew's in a report on 8 March 1882 about the church services that offered thanksgiving after the failed attempt to assassinate Queen Victoria on 2 March [53]. Further research has unearthed even earlier uses of the name, the earliest definite appearance being in a directory dated 1879 [54], with a possible earlier mention in a Portsmouth guidebook that is thought to have been published in 1876 [55].

Unfortunately the book recording the authority for the spelling of names shown on the Ordnance Survey map (the Object Name Book) has not survived but it is most likely that the name was collected by the surveyor from a name board outside the church, although there is no sign of one in any of the surviving photographs.

Before the turn of the new century it was clear that there was a need for a larger and more modern church; evidence relating to the memorial window to Major Noble installed in 1898 (see The Memorials below) indicates that it was assumed then that a new church was fairly imminent [56]. However it wasn't until the Navy Estimates for 1903-4 that money was included for the building of the new church [57] with the proviso that 10% of the money must be spent before 1 April 1903 so we can assume

Figure 12 – The Crinoline Church & Teapot Row (undated) [51]

that work commenced early in 1903 [58]. The new church was built on a site adjoining Henderson Road and the Princess of Wales accompanied by the Prince laid the foundation stone on Wednesday 16 March 1904 [59]. The new church was completed in 1905, but the exact date is unknown. Unfortunately Reverend Plant, the chaplain at the time of the changeover, like Reverend Beal at the the time of old church's opening, made no record in the register to indicate when the change actually took place. Nor is there any accurate information in the local press. There was a report published in the Hampshire Telegraph on 21 January 1905 saying that it *"can only be a matter of months before the church is ready"* [60] and then on 9 June the Evening News carried an article titled *"New R.M.A. Church – The Structure Finished"*. In this article it was reported that *"...it is understood that the ceremony of opening will be performed during the visit of the French Fleet to Spithead in August."* [61]. During August there were pages devoted to the programme of formalities and festivities planned for the French visitors and a similar space devoted after the event to reports of what happened; however, the only mention of the RMA was of the barracks hosting a social evening on the Thursday. On Sunday, which would seem a likely day for a grand church opening, the visitors were encouraged to take to the country in the motor coaches that were provided. The church was eventually dedicated on 17 November 1905 by the Bishop of Winchester, Dr Ryle. Also in attendance were the Chaplain of the Fleet, Venerable Archdeacon W Stuart Harris, Reverend A P Hill, then Chaplain at Portsmouth Dockyard and the RMA Chaplain, Reverend A W Plant [62]. On the following day there was an advertisement in the Evening News's Church Notices announcing a recital on the new organ to be given on 20 November [63]. The church placed no other announcements in this column between August and the end of December 1905. So the nearest we can get to an opening date is the dedication ceremony on 17 November.

But the story of the Crinoline Church was not quite over. It had already given nearly 50 years service in three different locations but it still had one more service to provide to the Royal Marines. A note held in the Royal Marines Museum collection tells the story of the church as related by Sergeant Major Beale RMA, who claims to have been the last man to hold the rank of Barrack Sergeant in the Royal Marine Artillery. This infers that he was serving at Eastney about 1923 when the RMA and the Royal Marine Light Infantry (RMLI) were amalgamated. His note is written on a piece of an old "Workmans Lost Time" form which appears to have been printed in the 1920s [64]. The most likely man in the surviving service records is Colour Sergeant Benjamin Peter Beale, DSM, RMA 9515. He was a local man born in Portsmouth on 5 June 1883. He enlisted on 6 May 1901 and completed his service on 5 June 1922. In WWI he served with the RMA Anti-Aircraft Brigade in France and was for a while Acting Quartermaster Sergeant at Base Stores, Dunkirk. He reverted to Sergeant on 22 June 1916 and was eventually promoted to Colour Sergeant on 26 June 1920 [65]. He was awarded the Distinguished Service Medal in 1918 [66] for his work with the RMA Heavy Siege Train and on retirement was recommended for the Meritorious Service Medal. He appears to have died in North East London on 19 May 1968 [67]. It is not unusual for senior NCOs to inflate their rank following retirement, especially if they had spent some time acting in a temporary capacity at a higher rank, so it is quite possible that the Sergeant Major and Colour Sergeant are one and the same.

It is not known when he wrote the story as he could have kept the old form as scrap paper for some years. Most of it is confused and he starts by saying that it *"was originally known as the Circus Church"*, a commonly held misconception (see Chapter Two – The Myth). He then goes on to refer to the new church as St Margaret's instead of St Andrew's and omits any mention of St Bartholomew's entirely. However, we must take note of the closing part of his story:

The Crinoline Church was not demolished immediately on completion of its successor. It was finally broken up somewhere about 1912. The main portions were returned and broken up as firewood for the use of the Barracks. Many of the pews were given to former Colonels Commandant for use as garden seats etc. and portions of the reredos to former Chaplains of the Marines.[64]

So the old church had one last trick up its sleeve – it was recyclable and fuel efficient. I haven't been able to substantiate this by any other source but as this part of the story relates to the time that Sergeant Beale was serving at Eastney it probably has more credibility than the earlier part, and must be essentially a true record. Beale's service record shows that he was serving at Eastney from 1906 to 1915 and so he would have known about this, strengthening the case that he wrote the note.

The picture at Figure 11 suggests that the old church may have been used as the Sunday School well after the opening of the new church, possibly until 1912. There are also suggestions that the old church was used as a library but this has not been confirmed.

I have already mentioned the rumour that some light fittings went to Christ Church at Widley but do any of the pews or parts of the reredos survive? They could well be hidden away somewhere as some family's heirloom. It would be wonderful to locate at least one piece of the old church and what a splendid asset it would provide to the RM Museum collection.

The Memorials

The known survivors from the old building were the many memorials that adorned the walls; in March 1904 the Portsmouth Evening News reported that *"The old Church contains many monumental brasses and other memorials to those of the RMA who have lost their lives in the service of their country. For these spaces have been arranged in the arcades of the new church"* [52]. When the new church was converted to housing in 1997/98 as many of the memorials as possible were removed and only those permanently fixed to the building were left. Most of these were subsequently plaster-boarded over and remain behind the interior walls of the houses. Those that were removed are stored in the RM Museum with the exception of one plaque relating to 1940 that is known to have been moved to Stonehouse Barracks in Plymouth [68]. The following are the memorials that, from their dates, we must assume were in the old church. There are mini-biographies of the Marines that appear in both these memorials and in the list of baptisms later in Part Two – The Biographies.

Egypt Campaign

The inscription reads:

In memory of the officers NC officers and men Royal Marine Artillery killed in action died of wounds or from effects of climate &c during the Egyptian Campaign 1882-3-4

Lieut E S Hickman
Lieut W D Marshall
Col Sgt Lonsdale Clarke
Sgt John Fairchild

Bugler Freeland Lovett
Gunners:
John Adams
John Vase
W J B Neeve
Robert Craddock
Frank Hall
George McClarne
J A Wann
James Catley
Fred. Cox
Thomas Tustin
Thomas Davis
John Gilbert
Charles Lester
Cornelius Baker
Joseph Broad
Thomas Colston
William Osborne
James Jenkins
H E Newton
John Gilkes
Thomas Rogan
Samuel Sutton
Edward Free
W Steans
Colour Sergeant Clarke and Gunner

Baker are described in more detail in Part Two – The Biographies.
Sources: 69

RMA – South Africa & China

The inscription reads:

In memory of the officers and men who were killed in action or died of wounds or disease 1899–1902

South Africa
Capt Guy Senior	25 Nov 1899
Gunners	
Alfred Bennett	25 Nov 1899
W H Hughes	28 Mar 1900
Frank Winning	29 Mar 1900
William Holloway	8 May 1900
P G Jefferies	5 Jan 1902

China
Capt H W H Beyts   23 June 1900
Gunners
J T Yates   23 June 1900
Ernest Lunn   23 June 1900
W J A Horne   11 Sep 1900
WM McNicoll   27 Jul 1900
J J Fleetwood   8 Jan 1901
Sources: 70

HMS Captain

The inscription reads:

De profundis ad te clamavi – Sacred to the memory of .... HMS Captain September 7th AD 1870

This plaque records all 28 marines who were lost.

Gunners	W Caseley
W Morris	G Davis
R Oswald	A Durkin
F Pitchfork	T Hoskett
B Porter	J Gordon
J Redrup *	S Grove*
J Rogers	J Hammond
J Rowan*	D Hughes
F Savin*	G Jones*
D Smart	J Knowles
G Turner	F Lock*
J Turner	H Misson
F Weston	Captain R A Gorges
W Wilson	Sergeant J Francis
Bombardiers	Corporal G Morse

The significance of what appear to be asterisks after some of the names is unknown, perhaps it could be related to bodies recovered.

There was a separate memorial to Captain Gorges (see below). Sergeant John Francis and Gunner John Hammond are also commemorated in a plaque that was in the former Methodist Central Hall in Eastney but is now in the Portsmouth City Museum.

Gunner Porter, Bombardier Hughes and Corporal Morse are included in Chapter 9, The Lucky, the Unlucky and the Musical.

HMS Captain foundered during her sea trials on 7 September 1870. She was something of a cause celebre. Her designer Captain Cowper Phipps Coles had been

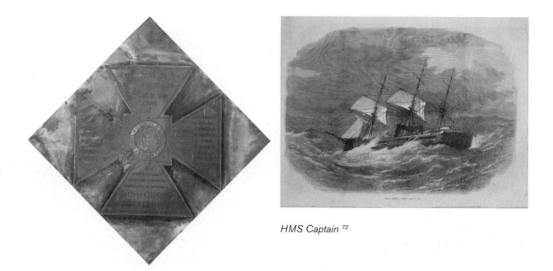

HMS Captain [72]

arguing publicly with the Admiralty for many years over his revolutionary design that included mounting the ship's guns on rotating turrets so that the ship could fire in almost any direction regardless of the direction in which it was travelling. In short, Coles decided to go it alone and convinced Birkenhead shipbuilders Lairds to build the ship, Britain's first privately-built warship. One point of dispute had been *Captain's* low freeboard (the height of the sides above the waterline) which was originally to be 8 feet (2.4 metres). This was considered to be dangerously low by Edward Reed the Chief Constructor of the Admiralty and it was made worse by an error in construction to such an extent that when the ship was built the freeboard was only 6 feet 7 inches (2 metres). The result was inevitable and during a storm while on its trials in the Bay of Biscay the ship capsized with the loss of 482 men out of a crew of 500 including the designer Captain Coles and the son of Hugh Childers, the First Sea Lord.

Sources: 71-72

HMS Victoria

The inscription reads:

De Profundis Ad Te Clamavi - Sacred to the memory of..., HMS Victoria lost off Tripoli, Syria 22 June AD 1893

The loss of Admiral Tryon's flagship *Victoria* in the Mediterranean on 22 June 1893 is one of the Royal Navy's most notorious disasters, all the more so because it was self-inflicted. The full story can be found in many Naval histories and the subsequent enquiry can be seen at TNA. Admiral Tryon was a bullish, overbearing commander and few dared to question his judgement. Having left Beirut after a spell of leave ashore he decided to put his Mediterranean fleet through its paces and ordered the ships to form into two columns six cables (1097 metres) apart. He then instructed them to turn 'inwards' and reverse direction. His initial command that the columns should be six cables apart was, somewhat courageously, questioned by his Staff Commander and he agreed to change the instruction to eight cables (1463 metres). However he wrote six cables on his written instruction and when this was queried he refused to alter it. Admiral Markham, leading the second column in *Camperdown*, delayed his turn as he was sure that a mistake had been made but after a further command from Tryon he had to obey. The result was inevitable and the *Camperdown* rammed the *Victoria* which sank within ten minutes. The event was so unbelievable that vital minutes were lost in giving the

command to abandon ship and, even though the rest of the fleet had launched boats, 357 officers and men plus Admiral Tryon himself were lost. There were 103 marines on board of which 68 were lost including 31 from the RMA who are recorded on the memorial.

R Savage	J R Scambler
A Baker	W Ferguson
F W Franklin	J Humphries
A E Jones	E Farley
A W Butt	J G Matsell
C Lane	J Bowling
T Gibson	F W Ballett
P Vernon	W Ellis
J J E Moore	F Cole
A Featherstone	G Marsh
J L Kent	R I Peters
A Bancroft	C W H Cox
H Lodge	W Brown
J Williamson	Bomb. Henry Weeks
H S Duck	Bugler H Langford
F Sheldrake	

This is not Admiral Markham's only link with the RMA memorials. It was he, as Commander Markham, who buried Gunner George Porter during the Arctic Expedition of 1875-76, see below.

Sources: 73-76

HMS Thunderer

The inscription reads:

Ad Majorum Dei Gloriam

In memory of Lieutenant Edward Daniel and Corporal Thomas Bolton Royal Marine Artillery, who were killed by the bursting of a 38 ton gun on board HMS Thunderer in the Sea of Marmora on the 2 January AD 1879

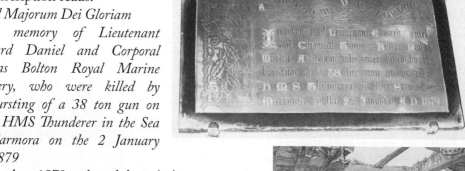

In the 1870s the Admiralty's conservative attitude towards ship design meant that ships were still being built with muzzle-loading guns when the safer breech-loading system had been available for some years. *Thunderer* was one such ship and whilst at gunnery practice in the Gulf of Ismid, off Turkey, the barrel of one of her huge 12-inch muzzle-loading guns exploded whilst it was being loaded. It is thought by many that the charge had been loaded twice. The barrel blew apart and caused carnage, two officers and nine men were killed and 35 others seriously wounded. One of the wounded was Gunner James Innoles – see Chapter 8. As a result of this accident the Admiralty quietly changed its mind and huge muzzle-loading guns were consigned to history. Less than three years

Inside the gun turret of HMS Thunderer after the explosion [79]

earlier one of *Thunderer's* boilers had exploded during trials off Stokes Bay, killing 45 officers and men including her commanding officer.

Sources: 77-79

Lieutenant Edward DANIEL

He was born on 29 January 1857 and started at the Royal Naval College as a probationary Lieutenant on 1 October 1874. He was initially earmarked for the Royal Marine Light Infantry (RMLI) but after obtaining his 1st Class Certificate he was offered the option of further study for appointment to the RMA. He accepted this opportunity and was formally transferred to the RMA on 1 July 1876. He was at Eastney until 6 May 1878 other than for a few months at *HMS Excellent* in 1876 where he passed the Torpedo course. He then had short periods of service in *Valiant* and *Warrior* until on 15 October 1878 he was moved to *Thunderer* in an exchange with another Lieutenant. This was to prove a fatal move as less than three months later he was killed, four weeks short of his 22nd birthday. The official report said that he was found dead from *"Skull and Chest crushed in"*. The officer he had exchanged with was Lieutenant Arthur Bucknall Shakespear later to become Brevet Lieutenant Colonel RMA (see Chapter 8). On 2 January 1879, the very day of the accident, the *Times*, in a report from Constantinople (Istanbul) dated 17 December, reported that on 2 December 1878 there had been a sports day to mark the Princess of Wales's birthday and that Lieutenant Daniel had won *"A hurdle race – 100 yards, with eight flights."* Lieutenant Daniel was buried in the Armenian Burial Ground at Ismid along with the other eleven fatal casualties. This was the third tragedy to hit the Daniel family. On 11 November 1856, their eldest son, Lieutenant Edward Daniel of the Royal Engineers, was killed as a result of being thrown from a taxi-cart near Guildford Barracks.

A year later on 16 November 1857 another son, Midshipman Martin Abbot Daniel, was killed during the Relief of Lucknow. He had been part of the Naval Brigade from *HMS Shannon* under the command of Captain William Peel and his name appears on the Shannon memorial on Clarence Parade, Southsea.

Sources: 78, 80-86

Corporal Thomas BOLTON

Corporal Bolton's service register has not survived and so we know virtually nothing about him. He is almost certainly the Gunner Thomas Bolton whose two children, Charles John and Harry, were baptised in the Crinoline Church on 25 August 1872. These boys with the addition of another boy and girl are with mother Susannah Bolton in the 1881 Census. Susannah is shown as a widow and the youngest child, Frances Ann, is 3 years old and so could be Corporal Bolton's daughter.

The official report stated that as a result of the accident his injuries were a *"Fracture of base of skull and burns"* and that he died two hours later. Like Lieutenant Daniel and the others killed in the accident he was buried in the Armenian Burial Ground at Ismid.

Sources: 78, 82 & 87

Honorary Major General George BRYDGES

The inscription reads:

In memory of Major General George Brydges late Colonel Commandant RMA, died Jan 29th 1896 Aged 64 years. This brass is erected by his widow

He was born in Winchcombe, Gloucestershire, on 15 December 1831, the son

of Lieutenant Thomas Brydges RN. He started at the RN College on 30 December 1848, was appointed to the RMA on 9 January 1850 and was promoted to Lieutenant on 13 December 1852. Interspersed with periods at Eastney he served in *Royal George* and *Russell* in the Baltic Sea during the Crimea War, commanding a mortar vessel at the Bombardment of Sweaborg for which he was mentioned in despatches. The *Seahorse* (1856) took him to the Mediterranean and Home Stations followed by postings to Plymouth, Eastney and Plymouth again during which time he was promoted to Captain (13 July 1860). He then served in *Orion* in the Mediterranean (1860-61) and was subsequently transferred to *Exmouth* (1861-62) before being invalided home to Eastney on 27 March 1862. On 2 August 1866 he was posted to *Ocean* on China Station. Here he led marines ashore in Japan during the revolution of 1868, including the pursuit and dispersion of the rebels after their occupation of the foreign settlement at Kobe. As a result of these actions he was *"invalided home for the preservation of life"* and recommended for Brevet Major by Captain Stanhope RN, which was declined by the Admiralty. He was appointed Gunnery Instructor at Eastney on 14 December 1870 and subsequently was appointed Brevet Major on 6 April 1873. Over the next ten years at Eastney he had promotions to Lieutenant Colonel (1 October 1877), Colonel (1 October 1881), Colonel 2nd Commandant (3 July 1883) and Colonel Commandant (3 September 1883). He was made an Honorary Major General on his retirement on 3 September 1886 and at the same time purchased the discharge of his groom and manservant. He moved to a house in Cheltenham where he spent his winters whilst in summer he somewhat eccentrically *"travelled around the country in a gypsy van"*. In September 1889, at the age of 58 he married the daughter of the Rector of Dowdeswell, Gloucestershire and they subsequently moved to Weston-super-Mare where their house was named 'Eastney'. He died there after a long illness on 29 January 1896.

Sources: 88-93

Colonel George Stephen DIGBY

The inscription reads:

In memory of Colonel George Stephen Digby, Commandant Royal Marine Artillery, Companion of the Bath, Knight of the Legion of Honour and of the Medjidie, who after a distinguished career died on 19 March AD 1877 aged 55 years. This memorial is erected by his brother officers as a mark of their affectionate esteem

He was born in Newry, Northern Ireland on 7 July 1821; his father was Lieutenant Everard Digby RN. He joined at Chatham on 16 August 1842 and after a couple of months in *Camperdown* at Sheerness, he was posted to Ireland on 1 January 1844. On return he served first in *Excellent* and then at Eastney and Woolwich before being appointed permanently to the RMA on 1 July 1846. After sea service in *Dragon* (Ireland & Mediterranean, 1847-50) he returned to Eastney in June 1850 and was made Adjutant on 24 February 1854 and subsequently promoted to Captain on 27 December 1854. On 30 April 1855 he embarked for the Crimean War campaign in the Black Sea serving in *Rosamond* and *Odin* and he was Senior Officer of Marine Artillery in the Mortar Boat flotilla. He was mentioned in dispatches for his part in the bombardment of Sebastapol and mentioned again for the action at Kinburn after which he was appointed Brevet Major. He returned to Eastney on 2 October 1856 and on 2 January 1857 he was appointed a Companion of the Bath (CB). On 9 November 1861 he was appointed to the Battalion in Mexico and was in command of the RMA Battery there. Whilst in Mexico he was appointed Laboratory Instructor. He returned to Eastney on 31 March 1862 *"in a shattered state of health"* but was subsequently promoted to Lieutenant Colonel in 1863, Brevet Colonel in 1868, Colonel 2nd Commandant in 1870 and Colonel Commandant on 3 May 1876. Less than a year later on 19 March 1877 he died in London while on leave. He was buried in Highland Road Cemetery, Southsea four days later on 23 March 1877. His tomb is heavily overgrown with ivy and the inscriptions are badly eroded. His scientific expertise led to him developing the Digby Laying Calculator which was designed to *"enhance the accuracy of plunging fire in the overcoming of fortresses by seaborne guns"*. The Portsmouth Cemetery Office registers record his grave as being next to the position occupied by Major Douglas (see right) but in fact it is two rows

away. This area of the cemetery was hit by a land mine in WWII and much damage was done. There is rumour that some of the gravestones may have been restored to the wrong position, but this cannot be confirmed.

Sources: 89-90 & 94-98

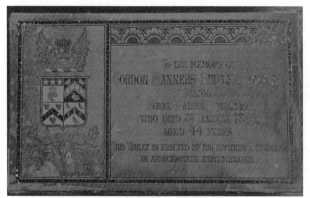

Major Gordon Manners Shipley DOUGLAS

The inscription reads:

To the memory of Gordon Manners Shipley Douglas, Major, Royal Marine Artillery, who died 8 January 1892 aged 44 years. This tablet is erected by his brother officers in affectionate remembrance

He was born in Southsea in 1847 and was the son of Commander William M Douglas, RN. He began his studies at RN College as a Qualified Cadet on 27 June 1864 and was appointed Lieutenant on 5 August 1867. He was posted to *Northumberland* (Channel) on 1 September 1868, returned to Eastney on 25 August 1872 and was promoted to Captain on 9 August 1876. He stayed at Eastney for another three years until being appointed to *Achilles* (Mediterranean & Channel, 1879-82). He returned to Eastney on 4 January 1882 for five and a half years during which period he was appointed Brevet Major (27 June 1885) and a couple of months later Gunnery Instructor; and on 23 March 1886 he was promoted to Major. On leaving Eastney on 20 June 1888 he was appointed to *Northampton* for two months before moving

to *Alexandra* (Mediterranean, 1888-89) via the troopship *Himalaya*. He returned to Eastney for a few months before being posted back to the Mediterranean in *Camperdown* on 19 December 1889. Seven months later he was invalided home from

Victoria having been diagnosed at Malta Hospital "*to be suffering from melancholia*". When he returned to England on 29 July 1891 he was admitted into the RN Hospital at Plymouth and he later died in Brighton, Sussex on 8 January 1892 at the age of 43, apparently without returning to duty. He was buried in Highland Road Cemetery, Southsea with full military honours in a service conducted by Chaplain Samuel Kenah. See the comments on his grave position under Colonel Digby above. His wife Elizabeth who lived on to the age of 85 was buried with him in 1935.

Sources: 81, 96-101

Major General Sir Francis Worgan FESTING, KCMG, CB

The inscription reads:

In memory of Major General Sir Francis Worgan Festing Esquire, Royal Marine Artillery KCMG CB Knight of the Legion of Honour who died on the 21st November AD 1886 aged 53 years. Erected by his brother officers "Thanks Be to God which gives us the victory (through) our lord Jesus Christ"

He was born in 1833 in High Littleton, Somerset, the second son of Commander Benjamin Morton Festing RN. He joined as a Gentleman Cadet and was appointed to Eastney as 2nd Lieutenant on 3 July 1850. By 1854 he was serving as 1st Lieutenant in the Crimean War, firstly in the Baltic Fleet and then in the Black Sea where he served in the mortar boats at the Bombardment of Sebastapol and the Capture of Kinburn. For this he was mentioned in despatches on 22 September 1855 and was subsequently appointed a Knight of the Legion of Honour (French). After a year back at Eastney he was sent to China for shore service as Adjutant but soon found action again. He had many exploits around China and was mentioned in despatches on 5 March 1858 where he was described as "*...that indefatigable and talented young officer..*". Then as senior RMA officer he commanded a Rocket Division at the action of White Cloud Mountain on 2 June 1858 and later commanded the 9th Field Battery at the Capture of Canton in December 1858 (mentioned in despatches again). After returning to Eastney he was promoted to Captain and six weeks later on 22 April 1862 to Brevet Major. It was during this spell at Eastney that he was involved in the rescue of the crew of the *Ocean*, a schooner that had gone aground on the shingle bank off Hayling Island in a "*fearful hurricane*". After an unsuccessful attempt by the steam tug *Comet*, Major Festing took the RMA cutter and with a crew of fishermen from Hayling Island managed to rescue three of the crew of the stricken vessel who were clinging to the rigging. For this he was awarded the Silver Medal of the Royal National Lifeboat Institution and

a Silver Medal from the Board of Trade.

He then spent three years in *Achilles* (Channel, 1865-68) before returning to Eastney in October 1868. On 24 October 1872 he was appointed Brevet Lieutenant Colonel and continued to serve at Eastney until May 1873 when he was sent to the Gold Coast (now Ghana) where he served for the duration of the Ashanti War. He arrived in Africa with 110 marines equipped with two mountain guns and 200 rockets. He conducted all the military operations including the Bombardment of Elmina and was repeatedly mentioned in despatches, including when being seriously wounded whilst attempting to rescue the mortally wounded Lieutenant Wilmot RA. He was thanked for this campaign by Her Majesty and received the rare acclamation of being mentioned in both Houses of Parliament at the conclusion of the war. He was also considered for a Victoria Cross but instead he was made a Companion of the Bath on 31 March 1874 and was appointed a Knight Commander of the Order of St Michael and St George (KCMG) by the Queen at a naval review at Royal Clarence Victualling Yard, Gosport, on 23 April 1874. This review was to honour the Naval Brigade that had served in the Ashanti War and involved 112 officers and men of the RMA. Colonel Festing's appointment was a surprise to all and it was not gazetted until 8 May 1874.

On return to Eastney he was appointed Laboratory Instructor and, after a year as Assistant Adjutant General in the Royal Marine Office at the Admiralty, he returned to Eastney HQ and there followed a series of promotions over the next seven years, with him becoming Colonel Commandant on 3 September 1886. In 1879 he was appointed as Aide-de-Camp to Her Majesty The Queen. He relinquished the post of RMA Colonel Commandant after just four weeks on being made Major General on 5 October 1886. Sadly he held this rank for just six weeks before dying suddenly at Newbury on 21 November 1886. He was buried with full military honours on 25 November 1886 in Highland Road Cemetery, Southsea.

His name lives on in Southsea; Festing Road (1881), Festing Grove (1898) and the Festing Hotel (1894) having been named in his honour.

Sources: 89-90, 96-97 & 102-111

Captain Richard Archibald GORGES

The inscription reads:

In memory of Capt R A Gorges RMA, aged 30, Lost in the foundering of HMS Captain, Sept 7 1870, RIP, "He shall send down from on high to fetch me, and shall take me out of many waters"

Captain Gorges was part of the RM detachment on board *Captain* when she sank on her sea trials – see the memorial to all the 28 marines lost above.

Richard Gorges had joined as a Gentleman Cadet on 4 February 1858. As a 1st Lieutenant he served in *Orestes* (Cape of Good Hope & East Coast of Africa, 1861-65) before being promoted to 2nd Captain on 1 December 1867. He served at this rank at Eastney for just under two years before more sea service in *Minotaur* (Channel, 1867-68). He then served another 15 months at Eastney before embarking on his fateful service in *Captain* on 30 April 1870.

Captain Gorges death had a major effect on his young family as in the 1871 census his Prussian-born wife Louise was a *"German Governess"* in Ellesmere, Shropshire, whilst her four young children, Richard, 3, Edmond, 2, Louisa, 1, and Archibald, 3 months, were living at Shanklin Lodge, Clarendon Road, Southsea with their Irish-born aunt, who was also a widower. Second son Edmond, who was born on 23 November 1868, was baptised in the RMA Church on 6 January 1869, the only one of the family to have been baptised there. Young Edmond at least did not let the early loss of his father and the partial break-up of the family affect his chances in life – see Chapter 8 – The Gallant and The Irreproachable.

Sources: 112-116

Quartermaster William Kay HEALEY

The inscription reads:

To the memory of William Kay Healey, Quarter Master in the Royal Marine Artillery who died 12 October 1876 aged 59 years. This monument is erected by his brother officers to mark their estimation of a long and honourable career of 41 years and as a token of affection and sincere regard.

His only surviving service register begins on 1 November 1859 when he was granted his commission as Quartermaster. This sparse document has just two entries; one recording that he was granted a pay increase of 1 shilling and 6 pence (7½ p) a day for

completing 12 years as Quartermaster, and the other that he was discharged dead on 12 October 1876. From census returns we find that he was born in Woolwich, Kent. We can only speculate about his early career from the facts that he was awarded the Long Service & Good Conduct Medal in January 1857; this confirms the inscription on his memorial which infers that he enlisted in 1835. He also held the Naval General Service Medal with Syria bar (1840), and the Turkish Medal for Acre (1840). He must also have seen action in the Crimean War as he was awarded the Meritorious Service Medal (MSM) on 31 October 1857 for *"Good service before the enemy at Sweaborg"* (Baltic Sea) even though he had not served the 24 years that was normally required for the award of this medal. (Note: as he had no children baptised in the RMA Church he does not appear in the MSM list in Chapter 8). He was a Sergeant in 1851 and Sergeant Major when awarded the MSM in 1857. He died in Portsmouth on 12 October 1876, aged 59, leaving his widow Caroline, a son and three young daughters. He was buried on 17 October 1876 in an unmarked grave in Highland Road Cemetery, Southsea. His son, William L Healey, joined the Navy after his father's death and became a Naval Instructor.

Sources: 96, 112 & 117-123

Captain Charles James KINSMAN

The inscription reads:

Sacred to the memory of Charles James Kinsman Captain RMA, Died on Christmas Eve 1873 at Bermuda when serving in HMS Bellerophon, aged 34, "What I do thou knowest not now but thou shalt know hereafter"

Born at Dartmouth on 23 August 1839, he was the son of Lieutenant James Byrne Kinsman RN. He joined as a Gentleman Cadet in 1856 and was appointed to the Artillery Company at the RN College in July 1858. His first ship was *Tartar* (1860-65), which served at Pacific Station up to September 1863 and then at China Station. This led to him being involved in an important action against the Japanese. On 5 September 1864 *Tartar* was part of the engagement with the Japanese batteries at Shimonoseki and on the following day he was ashore fighting with the Marines Battalion.

Two days later on 8 September 1864 he took part in the capture of more land batteries and that same day the rebel forces surrendered. After a spell at Eastney and two years recruiting in Belfast and Lincoln he was promoted to Captain on 4 August 1873. On 14 October 1873 he joined *Bellerophon*, Flagship for West Indies Station. It was whilst in the West Indies that he died, aged 34. His service register states very precisely that he died at 6:36 AM on 24 December 1873 in the RN Hospital, Bermuda.

Sources: 112 & 124-125

Major Evelyn James Wheelock NOBLE

The inscription as far as can be interpreted from the photograph reads:

This Window Is ?? By The Officers ?? Royal Marines To The ?? Evelyn James Wheelock Noble Of The ? Royal Marines, Died 5 October 1896, Aged 47 Years

Following Major Noble's death his brother officers were intent on providing a suitable memorial to him. Subscriptions were quickly forthcoming but there was a delay in deciding what form the memorial should take and, having decided on a window, in getting approval from the Admiralty to install it in the Crinoline Church. The window was designed and made by Lavers and Westlake of London, one of the most celebrated stained glass window designers and manufacturers of

the Victorian period. The window was finally installed in 1898 and had been designed so that it could be installed in the triangular format of the old windows but could *"easily be removed when the new church is built"*. The designer clearly did a good job as it was indeed moved to the new church and re-assembled in the format shown above. Beneath them was set a plaque which stated that *"The above window was formerly in three triangular lights in the chancel of the round wooden RMA Church"*.

Major Noble was born in 1848 in Honiton, Devon, the son of Captain Jeffery Wheelock Noble RN. He joined the RMA as a 2nd Lieutenant on 8 December 1866 and became full Lieutenant on 3 August 1867. He served in *Ocean* (1869-72, China) and was due to return to the RN College, Greenwich for further studies but this was cancelled to enable him to join the Staff of Observers of the Transit of Venus (across the Sun) in the Sandwich Islands (Hawaii) in December 1874.

He returned to Eastney on 28 July 1875 but was evacuated with recruits to RMLI headquarters at Gosport on 3 November 1875 following an epidemic of enteric fever (typhoid) at Fort Cumberland. On 2 January 1877 he was appointed to *Alexandra* (Flagship, Mediterranean) and on 21 June was promoted to Captain. He returned to Eastney on 17 August 1877 and for the next five years alternated between Eastney and Staff College. On 30 June 1882 he was posted to the Mediterranean Battalion in Egypt

where he was present at the actions at Mallaha Junction (reconnaisance), El Magfar, Tel-el-Mahuta, Kassassin and Tel el-Kebir. He was mentioned in despatches for his actions at Kassassin where his horse was killed under him. He was back at Eastney at the beginning of November and appointed Brevet Major on 18 November 1882 in recognition of his services in Egypt. He received his Egypt medal with Tel el-Kebir clasp from Queen Victoria at Windsor Castle on 21 November 1882. He also received the Khedive's Bronze Star and the Order of the Medjidie 4th class.

On 1 December 1882 he was appointed to Special Police Duty in Dublin to be assisted by Captains Morgan and Boyd-Hamilton of the RMLI. On 6 May 1882 Lord Frederick Cavendish, on his very first day as Chief Secretary for Ireland, and Thomas Burke his Under Secretary were walking across Phoenix Park to their residencies when they were assassinated by a group calling themselves the Irish National Invincibles. The search for the assassins was led by Superintendent John Mallon of the Dublin Metropolitan Police. The subsequent atmosphere in Dublin was febrile and the local police under-resourced for such a major investigation and so a contingent of 300 specially selected Royal Marines was sent to assist them. This was no normal posting though; the marines, all volunteers, were to operate in plain clothes; some reports suggest that they were 'undercover' but there was no real pretence about their presence, which must have been obvious to the local

population. The first group arrived in Dublin on 3 December with the others following in groups over the succeeding days. Before they left home the marines were given £5 5s (£5.25) to purchase plain clothes and an overcoat and on arrival they were sworn-in as constables and issued with a waterproof cape, baton and revolver. The volunteers were given 30 shillings (£1.50) a week in addition to their normal pay from which they had to provide their own food. The weekly wage for a Gunner at the time was about 10 shillings and this extra payment was regarded by the Chief Secretary to the Treasury, who had not been consulted in advance, "to have been somewhat lavishly conceived". They were accommodated in a number of houses and empty hotels and established a complex but secret patrol system throughout the city. Revolvers were a new weapon for the majority of marines and Captain Noble organised target practice in an underground corridor in one of the hotels. This proved to be unnecessary as no shots were fired in anger during their six month stay; the only casualties being one fatality due to an accident with a revolver and one death from tuberculosis. Their presence and the assistance they gave to the local police were acknowledged as vital to the capture and prosecution of the Invincibles. Their behaviour throughout the assignment was impeccable with just a few instances of drunkenness, not surprising given that they probably had more disposable income than they had ever had in their lives.

In January 1883 twenty-three Invincibles were arrested and in May and early June five were hanged and the remainder sentenced to long prison sentences. Most were secretly shipped back to England on board the *Valorous* and were landed unannounced at Chatham and marched to the nearby prison before hardly anyone knew that they were there. This plain clothes assignment was probably the most unusual deployment for the marines up to that time.

Captain Noble returned to Eastney in July 1883 having been promoted to Staff Captain whilst in Dublin and was later promoted to Major on 1 August 1886 and then on 28 September 1887 to Military Instructor. On 28 September 1892 he retired at his own request due to problems with a long standing illness. He died at his home in Pelham Road, Southsea, on 5 October 1896, aged 47. His coffin was carried to the Crinoline Church and then to his burial place in Highland Road Cemetery by six RMA Sergeants. His grave is overgrown and the cross and its plinth laid flat, most probably like many in the cemetery for health and safety reasons.

Sources: 81, 96-97 & 126-136

Lieutenant Colonel John POORE

The inscription reads:

In memory of Lt Col John Poore RMA who died April 4 1880 aged 49 years.

He was born in Andover, Hants, in 1830; his father was Lieutenant John Poore, RN. He joined as a Gentleman Cadet and was appointed to the Royal Marine Artillery on 10 May 1847. In addition to service at Eastney Barracks, Portsmouth, he served in *Retribution* (Particular

Service, 1850-52) and then in the Baltic Sea during the Crimea War in *Duke of Wellington* (1853-56). His *"exertions and precise firing"* were noted and he was mentioned in dispatches for his part in the Bombardment of Sveaborg. He returned to Eastney on 20 August 1856 and took up the post of Adjutant on 22 December 1856 and was promoted to Captain on 19 January 1859. His next ten years involved further service at Eastney and recruiting in St Albans and Reading (1860-62). His ship appointments during this period were *Resistance* (Channel, 1862-63), *Black Prince* (Home, 1864-66) and *Ariadne* with HRH the Prince of Wales (1868-69). He returned to Eastney and was subsequently appointed Brevet Major and served for a time as Gunnery Instructor. On 20 March 1877 he was promoted to Lieutenant Colonel and posted to recruiting duties in Derby before returning to Eastney on 1 April 1877. He died at Eastney from a brain haemorrhage on 4 April 1880 and was buried in Highland Road Cemetery, Southsea, in a service conducted by Chaplain E A Williams. In addition to his RMA Church memorial he is remembered in a family memorial window and plaque in his home town church of St Mary's, Andover. His Baltic Medal is in the RM Museum collection.

Sources: 89, 96-97 & 137-142

Gunner George PORTER

The inscription reads:

In memory of George Porter Gunner RMA who died 10 June 1876 while in the performance of his duty in a sledging party in the Arctic Expedition of 1875 & 1876. Erected by the officers Non Com Officers and men of his company

The Arctic Expedition of 1875-76 set out from Portsmouth on 29 May 1875 amid great celebrations. Two specially prepared ships, *Alert* and *Discovery*, were to follow in the footsteps of earlier expeditions northwards through Baffins Bay and Smith Sound and, when ice prevented them from travelling further, the ships were to be used as base camps for exploration by sledge, including an attempt to reach the Pole. Winter conditions were appalling and beyond anything experienced by anyone other than the native Inuit. The lowest temperature recorded during the expedition was -77°F (-60°C) and the mean temperature during February 1876 was -38°F (-39°C) causing the mercury in the thermometers to be frozen for eleven consecutive days.

George Porter was a crew member in *Alert* and a servant to Lieutenants Aldrich and Parr. He was selected to be a member of the sledge team under Lieutenant Parr, the whole party being under the command of Commander Markham. Their route from *Alert* was extremely difficult with continuous ice hummocks and ridges and progress was painfully slow. Ten days after leaving *Alert* one of Markham's men complained of aching joints and over the coming days and weeks more men began suffering from what Markham and Parr realised was scurvy. The effects became so bad that some men could hardly drag themselves along behind the sledges, and eventually some had to be carried on the sledges, thus greatly increasing the efforts required of the others. Forty days out and with only thirty days rations left Markham realised that the game was up and that they must start the return journey. But not before he and the

eight remaining fit men pushed on a mile or so to reach 83° 20' 26", the northernmost point reached by western man at that time. The return journey was even more difficult with more men being incapacitated by the terrible disease. Eventually in desperation Lieutenant Parr volunteered to set off alone to summon help from the *Alert*. He heroically achieved the 27 mile return journey to the *Alert* in 24 hours and within 50 hours of his leaving the sledging party the first help had arrived, but too late for George Porter who passed away just hours before their arrival. Commander Markham's journal includes the following moving account:

Poor Porter is no more! He expired at ten minutes past noon. He was very sensible to within a few minutes of his death, and his end was calm and quiet.

With the ensign at half mast, and the Union Jack as a pall, the funeral procession, attended by all but the four very bad cases, started at nine and the burial

Burial of George Porter [144]

services being read, the remains were consigned to their very last resting place in this world. Improvising a crude cross, formed with a boat's oar and a spare sledge batten, it was placed at the head of the grave, with the following inscription

"Beneath this cross lie buried the remains of Geo. Porter, RMA. Thy will be done"

Of all the melancholy and mournful duties I have ever been called upon to perform, this has been the saddest. ....During the service all were more or less affected, and many to tears.

Unknown to them at the time all the sledging parties were suffering the same fate. It was Captain Nares decision not to include lime juice in the provisions of the sledge parties that set him up as the scapegoat at the subsequent inquiry. However, experienced arctic explorers knew that this accusation was unfair as even if the sledges had carried lime juice they had no real fuel-effective means of de-frosting it. Another factor, unknown at the time, was that lime juice is far less effective against scurvy than lemon juice and had been supplied by the Admiralty as a result of commercial pressures from the growers in the West Indies.

George Porter's service record has not survived so we know nothing of his career or personality but he must have been an exceptional character as competition for places on the expedition was intense. One of the questions asked of the volunteers was if they could sing, dance or otherwise entertain as their forced incarceration in the ships during the 142 dark days of winter put the strongest of characters to the test and self-made entertainments were a major contribution towards keeping the men sane.

Three other men died during the expedition, they were Able Seamen James J Hand and Charles W Paul, and the Danish Eskimo (Inuit) interpreter, Neils Christian Peterson, who died from the after effects of frostbite after being ill for three months.

In addition to Porter the RMA men in the expedition were; Sergeant William C Wellington and Gunners Elias Hill, Thomas Oakley, Wilson Dobing, John Crope and Elijah Rayner. Wellington, Dobing and Oakley feature later in Part Two – The Biographies.

Following their return to England, Captain Nares was knighted and Commander Markham was promoted to Captain. This is not Markham's only link with the RMA memorials. It was he, as Admiral Markham, who was commanding *Camperdown* when she collided with *Victoria* in 1893, see above.

Sources: 143-147

Major George Dalhousie Churchill RAITT

The inscription reads:

In memory of G D C Raitt Major Royal Marine Artillery, Born 7 Nov 1854, Died 15 June 1897, erected by his brother officers.

George Dalhousie Churchill Raitt was born on 7 November 1854 in London. He was attached to the RMA on 15 July 1872

whilst at the RN College and subsequently posted to Eastney on 24 October 1873. He saw sea service in *Achilles* (1876, Coastguard Rockferry) and *Resistance* (1877) before returning to Eastney on 11 May 1878. On 4 June 1879 he joined the troopship *Jumna* for special service in South Africa. He was encamped ashore for 14 days before returning to the UK. He was then appointed to the Mediterranean Station in the flagship *Alexandra* (1880-83) and took part in the Bombardment of Alexandria and was ashore with the marines from 13 to 20 July 1882. He later returned to the Mediterranean in *Temeraire* (1887-91) until returning to Headquarters on 19 June 1891. He then spent nearly six years at Eastney, the last three and a half years as Musketry Instructor. During this period he was appointed Brevet Major and on 6 August 1894 promoted to Major. On 1 February 1897 he was moved to Naval Intelligence but returned to Eastney on 20 April that year due to ill health. He died on 15 June 1897 at St Thomas' Home in South London, aged 42.

Sources: 81, 131 & 148-150

Major John LeCocq ROBILLIARD

The inscription reads:

In memory of Major John Le Cocq Robilliard, Royal Marine Artillery, who was drowned at Port Jervis Sydney NSW on 11 Sep 1887 whilst serving in HMS Nelson

John Robilliard was born in Alderney, Channel Islands, in 1848, the son of Commander John Robilliard, RN. He began his service at Woolwich on 26 June 1866 and after study at the RN College was allocated to the RMA at Eastney on 19 December 1867. His first ship posting was on 13 August 1869 to the ironclad *Caledonia* (Mediterranean). He returned to Eastney on 25 September 1872 and was

appointed Adjutant there on 10 April 1874 and promoted to Captain on 16 June 1877. He returned to the RN College and obtained a *"3rd Scholarship"* and *"Hon. Certificate"* before withdrawing from the College on account of ill health in February 1879. He was at Eastney for eighteen months before being posted to the Antrim Artillery Militia (2nd/3rd North Irish Division, Royal Artillery) as Adjutant on 25 September 1880. He was removed from this post on 7 June 1883 for *"improperly drawing Forage Allowance to*

which he was not entitled under the Regulations" and returned to Eastney on 27 June 1883.

On 11 April 1885 he was posted to the armoured cruiser *Nelson* (Australia) and promoted to Major the following year on 3 July 1886. On 11 September 1887 *Nelson* was at anchor in Jervis Bay, New South Wales, Australia, about 60 miles (100 km) south of Sydney. Major Robilliard had set off from the ship in a whaler with three other officers and a boy sailor with the intention of sailing to a small settlement at the other side of Jervis Bay. They were about two miles from the ship when a sudden squall capsized the boat and threw them all into the water. They attempted to cling to the hull but the boat kept rolling over in the choppy conditions and after being in the cold water for some time and being a poor swimmer Major Robilliard's strength gave way. His comrades tried to save him especially the young boy sailor George Beer who struggled to keep him afloat at some danger to himself. Eventually Beer could keep him up no longer and had to release his hold, Major Robilliard then disappeared and was seen no more.

George Henry Beer, Boy 1st Class (RN 132961), was awarded the Royal Humane Society's Bronze Medal *"for his determined, though unsuccessful, attempt to save the life of Major Robilliard"*. He was 17 at the time of this incident and shortly afterwards on his 18th birthday he signed for 12 years; he ended his service as a Petty Officer 1st Class (Gunner) in 1900.

Major Robilliard is also commemorated by this plaque in St Jude's Church, Southsea.

Sources: 81 & 151-157

Lieutenant Alfred Bertie ROMBULOW-PEARSE

The inscription reads:

In memory of Lieut A B Rombulow-Pearse, RMA, of HMS Ramillies. Born 8th April 1873. Died at Malta 30th September 1897

He was born on 8 April 1873 in Little Parnden, Essex, the son of Captain W A Rombulow-Pearse, RN. He joined the RMA as a 2nd Lieutenant on 1 September 1890 and was made full Lieutenant on 1 July 1891. His initial training was not spectacular, he 'passed unsatisfactory' in an examination in Torpedo with a mark of 74 out of 280 but obtained a 2nd class certificate for getting 160 out of 200 six months later. He also claimed a 2nd class pass in gunnery at *HMS Excellent* and subsequently passed two examinations for promotion and one in Military Law. He was appointed to Eastney on 21 July 1892 where he stayed

until being appointed to *Ramillies* on 7 October 1895. His assessments showed him to be a promising officer with an ability to draw and he was *'of good physical qualities'*, but he fell ill whilst in *Ramillies* and died on 30 September 1897 from *'peritonitis and cardiac failure'*. He was buried on 1 October 1897 in the Naval Cemetery near the Hospital in Bighi Bay, Malta.

Sources: 158-160

Captain Humphry Weston SPURWAY

The inscription reads:

In memory of Captain H W Spurway, RMA. Born 1st February 1875. Killed by a gun accident on board HMS Royal Sovereign, 9th November 1901

He was born on 1 February 1875 in Exeter, the son of Charles Spurway, Surgeon, Army Medical Corps. He was appointed full Lieutenant on 1 July 1893 and successfully completed his training with 2nd class passes in Gunnery, Torpedo and Military Law. By 1900 he had also passed three examinations for promotion to Captain. He was also fluent in Italian, having spent much of his early life in Rome. He was appointed to Eastney on 1 July 1894 and then on 4 July 1896 began his sea service in *Majestic* (1896-98, Flagship Channel) where his Italian was fully utilised during the visit of the Italian fleet to Portsmouth in 1895. He was promoted to Captain in June 1898 and then returned to Eastney on 23 December 1898. On 27 April 1899 he was appointed to *Royal Sovereign* which was part of the Mediterranean fleet. He married on 1 November 1900 in Malta but the marriage was to be a short one.

On 9 November 1901 the *Royal Sovereign* was off the Greek coast. At 11:15 hours Captain Spurway was taking part in gunnery target practice when he was killed in an accidental explosion. It was the second day of target practice and Captain Spurway was *'marking for deflection'* during firing of the Starboard After 6-inch Casemate Gun. There was no need for him to be near the gun but he was in the casemate to support Lieutenant James who had only been with the ship a few weeks and had very little experience with the 6-inch gun. A subsequent enquiry chaired by Admiral Lord Charles Beresford concluded that, after a number of mis-fires, the breech had been closed with the percussion striker extended and a charge already loaded, the mis-fires using electric firing having instigated a change to percussion firing. This resulted in the charge exploding before the breech was fully closed. The shell travelled about 400 yards (366 metres) but the rearward explosion through the partially open breech caused the deaths of Captain Spurway, the Chief Armourer, two Petty Officers, an Armourer and a Leading Seamen. Captain Spurway sustained horrific injuries but survived for about and hour and three-quarters before dying. A further 19 men were wounded including five RMA Gunners, three RMLI Privates and a RMLI Bugler. It was intended to return the bodies to Malta for burial but due to the massive injuries sustained decomposition had begun quickly and on the Surgeon's advice the men were buried at sea.

Captain Spurway's wife Eleanor never re-married and died a widow, aged 81, in Hertfordshire in 1952. Captain Spurway is also commemorated on a memorial in Victoria Park, Portsmouth. The monument commemorates not only those who died in the explosion but nine others who died during the commission (1899-1902).

Sources: 158 & 160-164

Captain Frederick Napier TEMPLER

The inscription reads:

In memory of Capt F N Templer, Royal Marine Artillery, Born 5 August 1865, Died 9 February 1896, erected by his brother officers

He was born on 5 August 1865 at Lindridge, Bishopsteignton, Devon and was educated at Marlborough College. He started as a probationary Lieutenant at RN College on 1 September 1883 and was appointed to the RMA on 1 July 1885. His first ship was *Shannon* (Ireland) from May 1887 to June 1889 after which he returned to RMA Division. On 3 August 1893 he was posted to *Esquimalt* (RN Dockyard, British Columbia) *"for submarine mining duties under Colonial Government"*. It was there that

on 1 September 1894 after eleven years service he was appointed Captain. He was a keen cricketer and his assessments record that he had *"good physical qualities"* and was *"of active habits"*, but in October 1894 he was granted four months leave in Honolulu to try and effect a cure for his *"bronchial catarrh"*. Whether he returned to *Esquimalt* or the UK is not clear but he was then granted twelve months sick leave and went to South Africa hoping that the climate there would aid his recovery from what was now realised was tuberculosis. He died of phthisis (tuberculosis) at Bloemfontein on 8 February 1896 at the age of 31.

Sources: 158 & 165-167

Captain John Edward THOMAS

The inscription reads:

Virtus invicta gloriosa

In memory of Captain John Edward Thomas Royal Marine Artillery, who died 20 August 1881 aged 32 years

He was born at Milford Haven in 1848, the son of Surgeon David Thomas, RN. He was attached on probation to the RMA when starting at RN College on 6 December 1867. He moved to Eastney on completing his studies on 30 June 1869 and was posted to his first ship *Inconstant* (Channel & Detached Squadron) on 15 February 1871. He returned to Eastney from 18 October 1872 to 7 July 1873 and was then appointed to Coast Guard duties (Southampton, 1873-75) in *Hector*. On 29 September 1875 he

returned to the RN College, Greenwich for further studies. The following year he was discharged back to Eastney at his own request *"being unable to complete examination on account of ill health"*. Admiral Fanshawe, Director of the College, reported that Lieutenant Thomas was *"one of the most distinguished students at the College"*. A year later in June 1877 whilst he was serving at Eastney he passed his examination for Captain and was promoted on 1 October 1877. He died at Haslar Hospital on 20 August 1881 from acute bronchitis at the age of 32 and was buried in Highland Road Cemetery, Southsea in a service conducted by Chaplain W V Lloyd. He lies next to Lieutenant Colonel John Poore.

Sources: 81, 96-97 & 168

Corporal Arthur WALL (RMA 5631)

The inscription reads:

In memory of Corporal Arthur Wall, Royal Marine Artillery, who lost his life in a boat accident at Genoa on 11 November 1902 while serving in HMS Implaccable. Erected by his shipmates in affectionate remembrance

Corporal Wall was on board one of the steam pinnaces belonging to *Implaccable* when it was 'run down' by a tug in the inner harbour at Genoa on 9 November 1901. He sustained injuries that necessitated the amputation of both legs and he died in the early hours of the following morning. He was born on 20 February 1877 in Chatham and had enlisted in London on 13 August 1895. On 14 February 1897 he was posted to *Centurion* (China Station) during the Boxer Rebellion, returning to Eastney on 13 November 1898. He was promoted to Corporal on 24 June 1899 and had passed for Sergeant on 29 November 1900 but had yet to be promoted when he was posted to *Implaccable* on 10 September 1901.

Sources: 169-171

Colonel William Davis WELCH

The inscription reads:

In memory of Colonel William Davis Welch 2nd Commandant Royal Marine Artillery who died at Eastney May 18th 1891. Erected by his widow and children

He was born in London on 2 July 1839. A Gentleman Cadet he started at Woolwich HQ on 24 June 1857 and was allocated to the RMA on 1 July 1858. On 15 July 1859 he was appointed to his first ship the brand new *Clio* (Pacific), where he took on the post of Gunnery Lieutenant for the last three of his four years on board. He then spent fourteen years at Eastney first as 2nd Captain, then a period as Adjutant before being promoted to Captain on 4 August 1873. On 2 January 1877 he was appointed to *Alexandra* (Mediterranean) and then to *Hibernia* (Malta Dockyard). He was made Staff Captain on 17 September 1877. Following his return to Eastney he was promoted to Major on 2 October 1879 and appointed to *Hercules* (First Reserve, Portland then Coast Guard Greenock, 1880-82). His newspaper obituary notes that he landed at Panama on 27 September 1880 to assist in suppressing the rebellion although there is no sign of this on his service record. He returned to Eastney on 22 December 1882 and then on 24 June 1885 was made Brevet Lieutenant Colonel and posted to London for recruiting duties, being made substantive Lieutenant Colonel within days. Three years later on 21 May 1888 he was promoted back to Eastney as Colonel 2nd Commandant. He died of pneumonia at Eastney on 18 May 1891 after a long illness and was buried in Highland Road Cemetery, Southsea, in a service conducted by Chaplain Samuel Kenah. The detailed report in the Hampshire Telegraph is worth quoting at length as it tells us a lot about the respect in which

Colonel Welch was held and also gives us a glimpse of how many of the other officers' funerals described in this book were conducted.

"...The weather was cold and dull, with occasional showers. Yet notwithstanding this drawback there was a strong muster of the general public, both within the Cemetery and along the line of route from the barracks through Highland Road. The occasion was marked throughout Eastney and the neighbourhood by the general lowering of blinds, the closing of shutters, and other forms of respect, while the whole of the public houses and beer houses in the immediate vicinity of the barracks closed while the funeral cortege passed. A firing party, consisting of 400 rank and file of the Royal Marine Artillery, with three rounds of blank ammunition per man, under the command of Lieutenant-Colonel Poore.......formed up on the ground facing the Field Officer's quarters........The funeral guard passed with slow and measured tread from the spot where they had been paraded to the entrance of the barracks, to the accompaniment of a solemn roll of muffled drums from the band of the Corps. The bands of the 1st Battalion Yorks Regiment, the 1st Battalion of the Royal Inniskilling Fusiliers, the Royal Marine Light Infantry from Gosport, and the Royal Marine Artillery, fell in immediately in the rear of the firing party in the order named, and jointly broke forth with the strains of Beethoven's beautiful funeral march, which was continued until the cemetery was reached. Following the bands came the remains of the deceased, contained in a handsome polished oak coffin, bearing a brass plate, inscribed with his name and date of death. The coffin was born upon a gun carriage, drawn by six horses, supplied by the officer commanding the

Royal Artillery at Hilsea, and was covered by the Union Jack, surmounted by a large number of beautiful wreaths and crosses, which nearly hid the deceased's helmet and sword. By the side of the gun carriage walked a number of sergeants, who carried wreaths, which it was impossible to place on the gun carriage, and which had been sent by old friends in all departments of the corps and others. Immediately following came the deceased's charger, with the deceased's boots reversed, and led by the groom. Next came the chief mourners, and then the rest of the corps, every available officer, non-commissioned officer, and man off duty being present. The end of the procession was made up of naval and military officers from every ship in port, and regiment and corps in garrison, the Duke of Connaught, Sir Edmond Commerell VC, and Colonel Crease bringing up the rear, the latter being attired in deep private mourning. At the cemetery gates the procession was received by the Chaplain; who recited the opening sentences of the Burial Office. The approaches to the cemetery and the line of the route from

the gates to the mortuary chapel and to the grave were lined by strong detachments of the Yorkshire Regiment, the Royal Marine Light Infantry and the Inniskilling Fusiliers. The service at the grave being concluded the customary three volleys were fired and the troops returned to their respective quarters."

Colonel Welch's grave is sadly overgrown and broken.

Sources: 96-97, 112 & 172-175

Captain Walter John WHIFFIN

The inscription reads:

In memory of Captain W J Whiffin RMA of HMS Goliath, Born 6 October 1865, Died in the Red Sea, 28 June 1900

Walter John Whiffin was born on 6 October 1865 at Dovercourt, Essex; his father, John G Whiffin, was Paymaster-in-Chief, RN. He started at the Royal Naval College on 1 September 1883 and later that year was appointed to the RMA. In July 1887 he was appointed to his first ship *Raleigh* (Flagship Cape of Good Hope and West Africa) where he stayed for over three years. In 1892 he was appointed as Assistant to the Professor of Fortification at the RN College, Greenwich serving five years there during which time he was promoted to Captain. He returned to Eastney in 1897 for just over a year and was then posted to the Mediterranean in *Caesar*. For some private reason he sought an exchange and on 27 March 1900 he was appointed to *Goliath* which set-off for China

Station. It was on the way to China that he died from *'heat apoplexy'* at Aden on 28 June 1900 at the age of 34. Apart from being weak in French he was clearly a promising officer, the word zealous is used six times in his assessments. His physique and physical strength are also mentioned twice, so his early death must have been a shock to all.

Sources: 158 & 176-179

The Artefacts

Among the photographs held in the RM Museum archive are pictures of a number of church artefacts whose whereabouts are unknown and history unrecorded. It is most likely that they were removed to be used elsewhere following the closure of the 'new' St Andrew's but neither the RM Museum at Eastney nor RM Stonehouse nor the Royal Navy Chaplains Service has any knowledge of their whereabouts and an appeal through the Retired Navy Chaplains Association has also drawn a blank. My research suggests that the following items are of a date that would place them in the Crinoline Church.

Processional Cross

This photograph is annotated *"Ven Harris and his wife"* which is presumably taken from the inscription on the cross. Reverend William Stuart Harris was chaplain at Eastney from 1896 to 1901 and a year later became Chaplain of the Fleet and was inducted as the very first Archdeacon of the Royal Navy (See Chapters 4 and 5). As the description refers to *"Ven Harris"* this dates it to after his induction on 23 October 1902. There were two obvious opportunities for Archdeacon Harris to present the cross; at the time he became Archdeacon in 1902 or when he officiated at the dedication of the new church in November 1905. The former would link it to the Crinoline Church, the latter would not.

Sources: 180-181

Silver dish

Inscribed *"Sunday School 1900"* and *"Freely Ye Have Received Freely Give"*
The caption to this photo in the RM Museum photographic archive states that this plate was in the Vestry and was connected to the Children's Sunday School 1900. The source for this information is unknown but could possibly be from an inscription or label on the reverse.

Source: 182

Memorial Sundial

The old church has its own memorial in the shape of a sundial.

The pillar bears a plaque inscribed:

This sundial marks the site of the old "Crinoline" church which was built as a hospital for the Crimea. After being brought to England it was purchased by the Admiralty, erected at Eastney and accommodated 800. In 1905 the church of St Andrew's took its place

This plaque with its erroneous history no doubt contributed to the Crimea myth. The pillar was originally on the site of the old church but was moved when the land was developed for housing in about 1970 and now stands in the private gardens belonging to the residents of the converted Married Officers' Quarters known as Teapot Row.

Source: 183

Other Denominations

Although outside the scope of this book it is worth noting that other denominations were also served at Eastney. In 1868 it was estimated that there were approximately 126 Roman Catholic marines in the barracks not counting their families. Up until that time they had to travel to the chapel in Prince George Street, a distance that prevented most of the wives and children making the journey. Following an application from Reverend Horan, the RC priest at the chapel, the Admiralty agreed that the library could be used for the weekly Catholic service and agreed to pay £12.00 for the necessary fittings but did not approve the payment of his travelling expenses[184]. In later years the barracks had its own Roman Catholic chaplain. Presbyterians and non-conformists were not catered for in the barracks but were allowed to go to the appropriate churches or chapels in the town for their weekly service.

Chapter 2 - The Myth

Unfounded Stories

Over the years various myths became attached to this singular building. The most popular being that it was originally a military building, probably a hospital, and that it had been built for or used in the Crimean War and, either being surplus to requirements or having come back from the Crimea after use, it was available as a ready-made and cheap option for a temporary church. I even promulgated a version of this story myself in a short item about the church on my web site. But when I began to investigate the sources for this story it became evident that it was a myth and that the truth was to be much more elusive.

The story had obviously become a well-entrenched urban myth by the turn of the century as in a report in the Portsmouth Evening News about the laying of the foundation stone of the new St Andrew's in 1904 there is a denial of the truth of the story.

Unfounded Stories

If hearsay was only to be believed, the quaint old structure would be one of the most interesting buildings in existence, but in this instance hearsay has erred, and erred tremendously. With many it is a popular theory that the building was originally used as a hospital hut during the Crimea, while another curious story is that its origin was a circus in Fountain-street, Landport – an opinion which, although prevailing at Whitehall, is equally fictitious.[1]

The *"circus in Fountain-street, Landport"* referred to was the equally extraordinary Circus Church. This building off Edinburgh Road had once been the home of an indoor circus but was taken over by an evangelical church in 1857 and was used as such until the church moved to new premises in 1864. It is not surprising that these two churches should have become confused as the Crinoline Church looks very much like a circus big top. The reference to Whitehall presumably refers to some statement by the Admiralty. It wasn't only the Admiralty that was confused about the origins of the church; one local guidebook recorded that the church was *"known, from its shape, as the "Crinoline Church" or "Umbrella Church", which was originally built for a theatre."*[2]

I consulted both the Army Medical Museum and the Army Chaplains Museum but neither had any knowledge of such a building. The most important source on Victorian prefabricated buildings is a book by Gilbert Herbert[3], now Professor Emeritas at Technion, Haifa, Israel. He does not mention the church building in his book even though he devotes a chapter to the use of prefabricated structures in the Crimea and he has indicated to me that he has no knowledge of any building resembling the Crinoline Church[4]. This, together with the Evening News's rebuttal of the story, is supported by the absence of any mention of a Crimean connection in any contemporary reports in newspapers, guidebooks and local histories. Portsmouth's most famous historian, William Gates, mentions the church in many of his publications but never once mentions a Crimea link. In fact the 1904 Evening News article is the earliest mention in print of the Crimean story. So if the church had no relationship with the Crimea how did this erroneous story come about?

Origins of the Myth

The Crimean War – or Russian War as it should be known as it involved actions in the Baltic and Pacific as well as the Black Sea – is chiefly remembered for three things; Florence Nightingale, the Charge of the Light Brigade and the incompetent strategic and logistical management of the British Army.

When the allied British and French forces left for the Black Sea the initial object was to prevent the Russian Army crossing the Danube and threatening Constantinople (Istanbul). Although there was a realisation that eventually the allies would have to move on to the Crimea and take Sebastapol in order to disable the Russian Black Sea fleet, there was no invasion plan at that time. And even if they were to move on to the Crimea there was no realisation that there would be a long conflict. The allied armies, the British in particular, were unprepared for a long campaign and certainly not equipped to survive the Crimean winter.

This was a time when army officers bought their commissions and regardless of ability there was no prospect of a soldier, however capable, rising through the ranks. There had been no major conflict for forty years and many of the officers, although capable of performing well on the parade ground, had little or no battle experience. The prolonged peace had, as is always the case, tempted the Government to reduce spending on the military and as a consequence the British Army was under-manned, poorly equipped and inadequately trained. Amazing as it seems now the provision of stores and transport was not controlled by the army or the Secretary for War but was under the jurisdiction of civil servants in the Commisariat, a department of the Treasury. The staff of the Commisariat were even more inexperienced in the needs of an overseas war than were the army. The stories about the ineptitude of the British logistical support are legendary; for example, left and right boots were sent in separate ships, and one of those sank in a storm; the sourcing of 100,000 pairs of woollen socks that turned out to be childrens' sizes; the shipping out of oil lamps and wicks, but no oil; the list is endless.

The most telling statistic about the Crimean War is that the number of men who died of disease was more than three times the number who died in action or from wounds sustained in action. Out of approximately 111,300 British officers and men sent to the Crimea 2,755 were killed in the fighting with a further 2,019 dying later of their wounds; however a massive 16,323 succumbed to disease (mainly typhoid and cholera), not counting those who died later at home. It must be said though that the other combatants, French, Sardinian, Turkish and Russian, fared little better.

It was mid-September 1854 when the allies eventually landed near Eupatoria in the

Crimea and within weeks they were suffering from the extreme conditions, first rain and mud and then deep snow. The lack of proper clothing and food and deficiencies in the medical support combined with the atrocious conditions allowed diseases to develop and spread. News soon reached Britain about the conditions under which the troops were operating and the perceived failures of their commanders. For the very first time the public were being kept informed of the situation thanks to the ground-breaking work of Irish-born journalist William Howard Russell. Russell was what is known in 21st century jargon as 'embedded' with the troops; he had a pass for the trenches and was given a virtually free hand by the generals. His reports to The Times initially took ten to fourteen days to reach London but later when the new technology of the electric telegraph reached the war zone his reports were almost instantaneous. Being unrestrained by censorship Russell did not pull his punches and his reports created a public and political outcry that put the Government under severe pressure to take urgent remedial action. In mid-November it was obvious that the campaign was going to extend through the increasingly harsh winter and that one of the more urgent requirements was for some kind of transportable barrack accommodation.

There had long been a tradition of sending simple prefabricated buildings to the colonies along with the emigrants and it was to one such supplier, William Eassie of Gloucester and his associate company Price & Co, that the Government issued a contract for 500 huts. It was Richard Potter of Price & Co who is supposed to have first suggested the use of pre-fabricated huts and effectively lobbied the Duke of Newcastle (Secretary of State for War) to obtain the initial contract [5 & 6].

Another contract for a similar number of huts was let to Luke Camwell, a building contractor of 1, St Mary's Street, Portsmouth [3 & 7]. Previously the military had shipped out the necessaries to build huts, timber, nails, and so on, if they could not be obtained locally but this was the first occasion when they used pre-fabricated kits of parts that were packaged *"like the parts of a steam engine, all numbered, jointed and ready for erection"* [8]

The huts were ordered on 18 November 1854 [9] and within a couple of weeks there were completed hut kits accumulating in Portsmouth awaiting transport ships. On 29 November 1854 two of the huts, almost certainly Camwell's, were erected in a demonstration by the Royal Engineers in their yard at Milldam Barracks in Portsmouth and *"attracted considerable curiosity"* [10]. The Royal Engineers connection didn't end there as contingents of sappers were sent to the Crimea with the hut kits to assist with assembly in the field [11]. On 3 December the first shipment of huts left from Southampton and were almost certainly those produced by Eassie [12]. Three days later The Times reported that the transport ship Cumberland had departed with the first load of huts to be shipped from Portsmouth, presumably Camwell's [13].

The huts varied slightly in size depending on the contractor but were typically 28 feet by 16 feet (about 8.5 metres by 4.8 metres) and intended to house 20 or so men when used as barrack accommodation. Initially just over 1000 huts were ordered giving potential accommodation for 20,000 troops and more were ordered later in 1855.

By 18 December a further seven steamers had left England carrying huts bringing the total to 694 huts with the remaining 330 huts due to leave on four ships just before Christmas [9]. However, on 5 January The Times reported that there was *"a considerable quantity"* of British huts lying in Southampton waiting for transport ships [14]. When the final shipment of huts left Portsmouth in the transport ship *Rajah* on 25 January 1855 included in the cargo was *"a good moiety of the contributions from private sources for the troops, sent from Messrs Hayter and Howell and Fortnum and Mason's"* [15]. The first two shipments of huts from Portsmouth in the *Cumberland* and the *John Bowes* reached Gibraltar on 15 December but wasted no time before setting off on the final stage of their journey to Balaclava [16]. At the same time troops leaving England were being given instruction in the erection of the huts by the Royal Engineers at Milldam Barracks in Portsmouth [17].

Although they provided a great improvement in accommodation for the troops the huts were not an unqualified success. The specifications had been a little 'loose' and the quality of some of the buildings was not good. When William Eassie jnr. saw some of the British huts at Balaclava he thought that they had been poorly erected, especially those made in Portsmouth [5].

Things were better organised for the 1855-56 winter and a further 1000 huts were supplied, the contractors being: Cubitt & Co; Hayward & Nixon; Myers, Piper, Jackson, Locke and Nesham and Lucas Brothers, all of London; Edmund Smith of Woolwich; Eassie of Gloucester and Luke Camwell [18]. This second tranche of huts were more sophisticated and varied in size and design than the first, with at least four different models being shipped [19]. By 25 August 1855 Camwell had already *"deposited a considerable proportion of the 300 his contract has been taken for"* [20].

Altogether there were about 2400 of these timber prefabricated buildings sent to the Crimea for use by the British army as stores, medical facilities and so on as well as barrack accommodation. The specifications of the British huts were amended for the 1855 contracts and included windows and improved ventilation but they were still simple structures much like a larger version of the modern garden shed and wherever they are mentioned, whether in newspaper reports, the proceedings of Parliamentary committees or other contemporary or more recent studies, these units are always described as 'huts'. By no stretch of the imagination could the Crinoline Church be described as a hut. In summer 1856 when British troops embarked for home at the end of the war some of the huts returned with them but what became of them is unknown [21].

The cost of the huts for troops was estimated as £54,800 for the 1854-55 financial year with another £31,301 being spent on hospital huts and stable huts for horses, but these figures will presumably include shipping and so on [22].

In 1856 when hostilities had ceased a Board of Officers visited the camps in the Crimea and produced a report assessing the different types of hutting that had been used during the war. A paragraph that must relate to Camwell's huts reads:

"The Portsmouth Small Hut, of the pattern first issued, with feather-edged boards, is easily transported, and can be moved bodily for short distances. It is also easily ventilated,

but it will not bear being taken to pieces and trans-shipped without great loss; and, being single boarded, must be completely covered with felt or other material to be rendered weather-proof." [23]

Unfortunately no drawings of Camwell's huts seem to have survived but there are a number of other surviving drawings relating to the inquiry including that for Eassie's 'Small Gloucester Hut' that was regarded as the most successful [24].

Emperor Napoleon III was also concerned about barrack accommodation and William Eassie's associate, Richard Potter, went to Versailles to demonstrate their huts. The result was a contract to supply 1,850 to a modified design for the French Army, which were all shipped through Southampton [5].

There was one important exception to these simple huts and that was the trend-setting military hospital built at Renkioi in Turkey [25]. Much to the disgust of many of the Army medical staff Florence Nightingale had been sent to the war zone by Sidney Herbert, Secretary at War, in response to public and political concerns about the welfare of British troops. Today we know that cholera and typhoid are mainly the result of contaminated drinking water but this was not really understood at that time. The general understanding, and that includes by Florence Nightingale, was that these diseases were miasmic (carried in the air). The more progressive medics supported Florence Nightingale and understood that the wounded needed space, clean air and most importantly good sanitation to aid recovery. They may not have understood the exact reason for the spread of these diseases but their solution was largely correct. Unfortunately the buildings being used as hospitals at Smyrna (on the south coast of the Black Sea) and Scutari (on the opposite bank of the Dardanelles to Constantinople) were totally unsuitable; they were overcrowded and were disgustingly dirty and foetid. William Russell's reports about the prevalence of disease and the awful hospital conditions endured by the troops forced Sidney Herbert to turn for help to one of the great heroes of the age.

On 16 February 1855 Herbert asked Isambard Kindom Brunel to design a new war hospital. Brunel quickly accepted the challenge and in his usual workaholic style had finalised the design for a prefabricated timber building complex and built a prototype in just over four weeks. His proposal was equally as quickly accepted and by September 1855 construction was underway well behind the lines at Renkioi, on the southern shore of the Dardanelles. The design consisted of 60 self-contained huts (or wards), each with its own toilet and washing facilities. Each hut was set at right-angles to the long covered walkways or corridors that formed the 'spine' of the layout. Most of the huts were made by William Eassie of Gloucester and William Eassie jnr actually went to Renkioi to supervise the build. The basic layout designed by Brunel was so ground-breaking that it remained the accepted layout for hospitals and government buildings into the next century. In fact I worked in a similarly designed building in the late 1960s. It had been hurriedly built for mapmakers Ordnance Survey during WWII after their main buildings in central Southampton had been badly damaged by bombing. It was constructed of brick but laid-out on the same lines as Brunel's hospital, with long covered corridors and offices leading off at right angles. One legend has it that it was built to this design so that it would appear to be a hospital on German reconnaissance photos and so be 'off limits' to their bombers but it may just have been a proven cheap and simple way to provide the necessary replacement office accommodation.

The hospital at Renkioi was a great success but had never accommodated its full complement of patients by the time the war ended in 1856. Although the intention had been to repatriate the hospital this never happened and it was sold locally and broken up[25].

Some of the wooden huts sent to the Crimea were used as churches but although they may have gained a small spire or bell tower they were still based on the rectangular hut[26].

Wooden huts were also being used as temporary troop accommodation at home. The initial build of Aldershot Garrison was of wooden huts and similar huts were erected at Colchester. These latter pre-fabricated huts, 275 of them, had been intended to house the German Legion troops when they got to the Crimea but the war ended before they were shipped. The German Legion stayed put and the huts were erected at Colchester as their barracks. A more permanent wooden building was also erected at Colchester at this time, this was the Garrison Church. It was a large building much taller than the accommodation huts and it was fitted with tall church-style windows. It remained in use until 2007 but being Grade II listed has been saved and was recently converted to a Russian Orthodox Church. Co-incidentally this church also has an erroneous myth that claims that it was intended as a hospital in the Crimea but was rejected by Florence Nightingale[27]. There were also huts erected for the German Legion in Heligoland (then in British hands) which was a recruiting post, but none of these barracks and camps included a building anything like the Crinoline Church.

Although the reports of the war from William Russell had created a furore there was never any diminution in the desire to see the Russian bear defeated. There had been enormous support for the war from the outset and nothing showed this better than the public reaction to the Grand Naval Review prior to the departure of the Baltic fleet in March 1854. Thousands of people descended upon Portsmouth to see the spectacle and to see Queen Victoria lead the fleet out past St Helen's in the temporary Royal Yacht *Fairy*[28].

With this level of interest in the war there is no doubt that Portsmouth's links with the prefabricated huts would have been well-known to local residents. The barrack huts and Brunel's hospital were extensively reported in both national and local newspapers. The involvement of a well-known local businessman, Luke Camwell, must have also been widely known.

Born in Coventry about 1813, by 1841 Camwell had become the clerk of the works for the building of Beaumanor Hall, a new stately home being built at Woodhouse, near Loughborough[29 & 30]. This must have been quite an achievement for a man in his twenties. In addition to being a more than competent builder he must have been a good man-manager, literate, numerate and honest as he was also paymaster for the project. The main building work was largely completed by 1850 and by the time of the 1851 census Camwell had moved south to Portsmouth [7]. He must have established his business quite quickly as he was already employing 18 men and had that same year won a contract for work, including new buildings, for the South Coast and South Western Railway between Landport and Cosham [31]. Another of his known contracts (1854) was to build a new Police Station *"on the site of Tollervey's Pond"* [32] which was approximately at the southern end of Guildhall Square where it meets Commercial Road. His work at Beaumanor Hall clearly gave him high aspirations as he also built two large houses in Queen's Crescent and Queen's Road in Southsea amongst Thomas Owens' fine work[33]. At the time he was building the huts for the Crimea he was operating from 1, St Mary's Street, just a stones throw from the Gunwharf.

Camwell, who was a bachelor, was also socially and politically active and regularly contributed to local causes [34 & 35]. He was a churchwarden of St Thomas's [36] and a guardian of the Poor House and he was part of the committee that organised a grand banquet for the officer heroes of the Crimean War in September 1856[37]. Also in 1856 he put himself forward for election to the City Council [38] and he was elected a councillor for St Thomas's Ward on 2 November 1857 [39], but his service was cut short by his untimely death on 20 April 1859 at the age of 46. He was thrown from his dog cart whilst travelling *"at a brisk rate"* when it hit a fixed stone marking the corner of what are now St Edward's Road and Pelham Road, Southsea. He suffered a compound fracture to his right leg which was not of any great concern to the attending surgeon but two days later he died from *"constitutional irritation"*, presumably shock or trauma [40]. He was buried on 25 April 1859 in Highland Road cemetery [41, 42].

The shipping of the Crimean huts from Portsmouth and Camwell's involvement in their construction over a period of about a year must have been well-known around the town and it is easy to see how the story, without him being around to contradict it, could easily have been distorted over a couple of generations and been retrospectively associated with the Crinoline Church (which had appeared in Portsmouth just a couple of years after the end of the war). With no other obvious alternative this seems to be the most likely source of the Crimean myth but unfortunately it is a theory that can never be proven.

Chapter 3 - The Architect

The London Link

If the church did not have a link to the Crimea conflict then where did it come from? The architects for St Bartholomew's church were Goodwin and Butcher of Holborn and the contractors that originally built the temporary church were Rowland and Herniman, from Islington [1], so these were the first leads to follow.

The Goodwin in Goodwin & Butcher was Edwin (sometimes Edward) Goodwin. He had previously been in partnership with Henry Coe (1826-1885). Coe had trained with the Scottish architect Sir George Gilbert Scott and is probably best known for designing the marvellous Agricultural Hall, Islington (1861-62 with F Peck) [2]. Coe & Goodwin had originally operated from Old Jewry, London and made their first mark by winning the competition for Holy Trinity, Bracknell, Berkshire, in 1849. Later, in 1852, they won a competition to build the Infirmary in Dundee, which led to a number of other contracts in that city. Unfortunately their use of Caen stone for dressed work in these buildings soon backfired as it was not able to stand the Scottish climate and so ended the partnership's promising future in Scotland. At the time that they were winning the Dundee contract both were subject to bankruptcy procedures and at one point they were both in prison [3]. They had done some work in west Wales before the partnership ended some time after 1856 and subsequently Goodwin concentrated on business in that area, eventually moving to Laugharne, near Tenby in about 1867. He again became bankrupt after losses in a development at Burry Port about 1874 but continued to work up to 1895 [4].

The Butcher in Goodwin & Butcher was Henry Butcher, son of William Butcher and part of the family team developing Havelock Park. He has left a very small footprint as an architect, his partnership with Goodwin appears to have been a short one and I can find no trace of their records in the various London archives. It must be assumed that he became a partner with Goodwin after the dissolution of the partnership with Coe in about 1856. Goodwin & Butcher are listed in the London trade directories up to 1861 and Butcher appears in that year's census lodging at Finsbury [5]. The partnership does get a couple of mentions in the records of the Incorporated Church Building Society for work on some churches in Norwich, Butcher's home town, but I have been unable to find much more about them [6]. There is no trace of where Henry Butcher trained nor are there any surviving business records of the Butcher family in the Norfolk Record Office. By the time of the 1871 census Butcher had abandoned architecture and returned to the family business in Norwich as an auctioneer [7]. He then appears to have taken over a *"family and commercial hotel and posting house"* in Norwich called The Royal [8]. Ten years later

Henry was married and living as a 'gentleman' in Heigham, Norfolk[9]. He may have been short of income as by 1891 he was still in Heigham but once again as a Hotel/Pub proprietor[10]. He died in 1898[11].

The history of St Bartholomew's published in 1934 and assumed to have been written by the then incumbent Reverend C F Aspinall provides what may be an interesting insight into Butcher's capability as an architect. Reverend Aspinall criticises the design and the *"...construction of the cheapest and most barn-like quality. A huge expanse of roof constructed of nothing but deal, rests its weight solely upon the outer walls."* He also refers to notes in the parish magazine by Reverend AGM Meugens recording that the original font was crudely made of bricks plastered over and that the high altar was *"equally cheap, paltry and un-worthy. It was very roughly made of the cheapest deal, and it would have been an insult to a carpenter as a bench."* This history also claims that the vicarage was bought from Mr Butcher for £850 in 1864 indicating that whilst Butcher senior may have donated the land he owned the vicarage built on it. By 1893 the Diocesan Surveyor considered it to be of such poor quality that it was not worth repairing. How much all this reflects poor initial design and construction or poor maintenance is unclear. The vicarage was sold for £650, a loss of £200 in just under 30 years. By the outbreak of WWI the congregation was trying to raise money to keep a *"jerry-built"* church from falling to pieces and the effort seems to have had an adverse effect on the health of more than one vicar. Reverend Aspinall's opinion of the quality of design and construction had further confirmation in 1924 when it was found that the west gable was twelve inches (30 cm) 'out of plumb' and the west end of the church had to be rebuilt[12]. All this provides more than circumstantial evidence that Henry Butcher was not the greatest of architects and may have had some bearing on his abandoning the profession and returning to the family business. With all this evidence one is left thinking that Henry Butcher's architectural ambitions were ill-founded and probably only supported by an indulgent parent.

The Rowland of Rowland and Herniman was almost certainly Edward Rowland of Coleman Street, New North Road, Islington[13-15]. He was for some years associated with a Thomas Evans and they traded as Rowland and Evans. The partnership was listed in the London Post Office Directories from 1853 to 1856 but there is earlier evidence of its activity in the lists of tenders published in The Builder in the early 1850s[16]. Rowland appears on his own in the directories from 1858-1861[15]. This change was due to the partnership being declared bankrupt at the end of 1856[17 & 18].

Hernimann has been more difficult to find. In the 1851 census there is a George Herniman, carpenter, born in Bath, living at Broad Street (near the old Covent Garden), but I have been unable to find him in the censuses before or since[19]. It is a surname that can easily be misinterpreted or mis-transcribed but even allowing for variations in spelling he is still not to be found. Circumstantially he is probably the Hernimann linked with Rowland in 1858 and it may have been a one-off association for this contract. Interestingly the Hampshire Telegraph mentioned in one report that the site foreman in Portsmouth was a Mr Evans, so could this be the Thomas

Evans previously in partnership with Rowland? – this must remain conjecture [1].

Despite this research into both partnerships I could find no connections to link Goodwin, Butcher, Rowland or Hernimann to any other temporary church buildings. There were, however, two architects/builders that were involved in producing 'circular' wooden temporary churches during this period.

John Blizard

John Blizard was born about 1821 in Cheltenham, Gloucestershire. His father, Thomas Blizard, was a builder and in the 1841 census, at the age of 20, John is living with his father and described as an architect [20]. By the next census in 1851 John was in business for himself, described as *"Manufacturer employing 9 Men"* [21]. In 1856 he is listed in the Post Office Directory as *"timber, slate & cement merchant, & sawing planing & moulding mills"* [22].

On 13 December 1854 under the heading *"Wooden Huts for the Crimea"*, the Cheltenham Examiner reported that a delegation from the French Government had visited Gloucester in connection with the supply of modified huts to the French Army by William Eassie, as described earlier. It went on to say that John Blizard's steam sawing mills had entered into *"a contract to saw 300,000 feet of timber for other houses about to be constructed at Gloucester"* [23]. The use of the word *"houses"* is confusing but this may imply that that Blizard was supplying sawn timber for Eassie's huts.

Blizard was also manufacturing pre-fabricated houses about this time and we know that he exported at least ten *"portable houses recommended for colonists"* to Australia in 1853 [24]. Three years later Blizard produced a pre-fabricated wooden church for use in north London [25]. It was a temporary building to serve as St Luke's, Holloway, whilst the permanent building was under construction. It was 84 feet (25.6m) in diameter and 50 feet (15.2m) high and could accommodate 1000 persons. The roof was in one span supported on 24 principals which were framed and braced together and covered with boards that were felted on the outside. The church was lit by eight side windows and a circular skylight surrounding the central bell turret [26]. It sounds and looks very similar to the RMA Church but there were some differences.

If the quoted measurements are correct then Blizard's church was slightly wider and lower than the Crinoline Church and its 24 principle supports gave it extra 'sides' compared to the Crinoline Church. The positioning of the

St Luke's Temporary Church, Holloway [27]

windows was also different, being set in the 'sides' rather than the roof.

The permanent St Luke's opened in1861, three years after the first appearance of the Crinoline Church. Sadly John Blizard died in 1857, aged 37, and as the Butcher's did not purchase land for Havelock Park until November 1857 it seems unlikely that they had contracted Blizard to design the church before his death [28].

George Truefitt, FRIBA

George Truefitt was born on 14 February 1824 and built a substantial architectural portfolio through the second half of the nineteenth century including 16 churches and chapels, 7 schools, 13 banks and 170 houses and mansions [29]. He was also an accomplished artist and spent much of his spare time and holidays sketching and painting. As a young man he published *Architectural Sketches on the Continent* (1847) [30] and *Designs for Country Churches* (1850)[31]. In addition to his many individual contracts he was surveyor to the Tufnell Park Estate for over 25 years and through this association came to design a wooden church in Upper Holloway [32].

The church was erected in 1858 the same year as the RMA Church and was described as being 84 feet (26 m) in diameter and 72 feet (22 m) high. The roof span was 64 feet (19 m), just 2 feet (0.6 m) less than Westminster Hall. The outer uprights were 9 inches by 3 inches (23 x 8 cm) and 16 feet (5 m) high and well braced together. They were boarded inside and out and the gap filled with sawdust. The principal rafters were 59 feet (18 m) in length and joined into an iron ring 60 feet (18 m) from the floor. Above the ring was a lantern for ventilation with 10 feet (3 m) of glass below it to admit light to the interior. The Ecclesiologist magazine was impressed and credited Truefitt as having *"contrived a singular and picturesque structure, which would be thoroughly suitable for Cushing's American Circus"* [33]. Unfortunately the temporary church was initially built in the wrong place and had to be dismantled and moved a matter of metres to ensure it was wholly within the Tufnell Park estate [34]. This wooden church was eventually replaced in 1861 by a permanent structure to a design by Truefitt said to be based upon a medieval church in Salonica [35]. This building still stands and was for some time a theatre but is now a Nigerian church and is being refurbished. In 1890 George Truefitt retired from his practice and moved to Worthing where he died on 11 August 1902 [4].

Truefitt's wooden church was larger and apparently more sophisticated in its design and construction than the RMA Church but clearly Truefitt could easily have produced the design for the RMA Church but there are no apparent links between him and the Butcher family or any other wooden churches. Intriguingly the contractors for the building of his wooden church were *"Messrs Evans"* [32]. Truefitt also had a connection with Southsea – he designed the memorial to Lord Frederick Fitzclarence that stands at the junction of Pembroke and Gordon Roads [36].

Throughout my research another name related to wooden temporary churches kept cropping up and that was the name Peter Thompson, the most prolific supplier of temporary churches in the London area.

Peter Thompson

Thompson has a colourful history. He was born in Earsham, Norfolk about 1800 (there is a baptism register entry for a Peter Thompson at All Saints, Earsham on 26 November 1797 but this has not been positively confirmed[37]) but by 1828 he had moved to London and made his first appearance in London trade directories as a "carpenter and builder"[38]. By 1830 he was also listing himself as a "bookseller", more of this later in the story[39].

He was a man who had high opinions of his own capabilities and a gift for self-promotion and this is made clear as early as 1836 when he submitted plans to the competition for the design of a new House of Commons, much of which had been irretrievably damaged in a fire in 1835. Not only did Thompson submit plans to the Committee of Taste who were in charge of the competition but he also sent copies of his submission to The Times. This publicity ploy backfired somewhat by instigating an article in the edition of 4 March 1836 in which the author mocks Thompson's plans, his flowery preface to his designs and his insistence that he is a *"mere carpenter"*[40]. The fact that Thompson had not complied with the rules of the competition and had planned for the destruction of Westminster Hall, the Law Courts and other buildings saved from the fire did not work in his favour. Suffice to say that Thompson's design did not get onto the long list let alone the short list for the contract.

Little is known of his activities over the next six years although he was involved in projects in Norwich[41] and also in some government contracts including one on the *"Isle of Portland"*[42]. He was also promoting his prefabricated houses and churches for export to the colonies, including in at least one instance sending a 12-room, two story house to India[43]. None of this, however, could have been enduringly profitable as by 1842 his creditors were nervous enough to instigate bankruptcy procedures and on 3 November 1842 his financial and business affairs were placed in the hands of trustees[44].

Desperate for money to get his creditors off his back, Thompson saw what appeared to be a great business opportunity. He had watched building developments in the city and was aware of the pressure to build more churches for the masses; churches were seen as essential in the regeneration and 'gentrification' of the slum areas of London and could not be built fast enough to meet the demand. Thompson realised that he could use his colonial church experience to design and manufacture a cheap temporary church that could be partly prefabricated in his workshops at Limehouse, thus reducing costs and building time. Such a building would enable the church authorities to raise both a congregation and the funds to pay for the permanent church as it was being built.

His first such church was erected in September 1844 in Kentish Town as a precursor to the building of the permanent church dedicated to St John the Baptist. Thompson immediately wrote to the influential magazine The Builder trumpeting his design and how it could provide a very cost-effective method to provide a simple place of worship. The editor commented that the church building authorities should look closely at Thompson's church and that, if it started a trend for wooden churches, then it would create employment opportunities for many craftsmen [45].

Thompson's design was certainly taken seriously and a year later he was sub-contracted by architect Thomas Little to provide a temporary church as part of his commission to build All Saints' Church in Finchley Road, St John's Wood. Unfortunately in the meantime the forerunner of local authority planning departments, the Metropolitan Buildings Office (MBO), had been created and building in London was now under severe scrutiny [46]. The MBO were particularly nervous about the fire risk attached to Thompson's wooden buildings and didn't like his first proposal at all. They insisted on a simpler structure with brick walls and other restrictions which must have reduced the cost-effectiveness of Thompson's design [47].

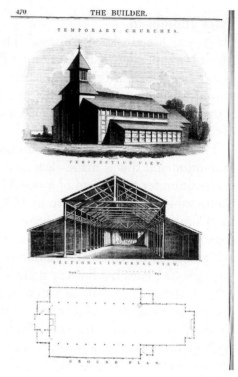

A Thompson design, 1844 [45]

Thompson did, however, build a number of other temporary churches at sites in London, including Hamptead, Camden Town, Agar Town, South Lambeth, Westminster, Maida Vale and St Pancras [48-50].

In 1845 his designs were somewhat unfairly criticised by The Ecclesiologist magazine who did not seem to be aware of the restrictions placed upon Thompson by the demands of the MBO. When there was a second criticism of his designs two years later Thompson was swift to respond with a little self-publicity in which he states that he was leasing some if not all of the temporary churches, the church paying a deposit and rent. He suggests that on completion of the permanent church his 'temporary' building could become a school, although I have found no evidence to suggest that this actually happened [48].

Between these projects, in 1847, he built a large wooden church for Eton College, to be used whilst the college chapel was being altered and improved. The temporary church, which could accommodate a congregation of nearly 1000, was built on an island in the Thames that was owned by the college [51-52]. This was presumably a straightforward project for Thompson because it was, like his first wooden church in Kentish Town, geographically outside the jurisdiction of the MBO.

Thompson's designs and construction methods were quite sophisticated for the time and the advantage of being able to dismantle and re-erect the building, enabled by his modular construction system, was proved by an advertisement that appeared in *The Times* in September 1845:

CHURCH for SALE, complete with nave, side aisle, chancel, recessed communion, robing rooms, tower with belfry, two side lobbies, fittings of pulpit, and seats for 800 persons. Price 300 guineas. Has been in use 12 months, during the re-building of Kentish-town Chapel. See a specimen belonging to Sir T. M. Wilson, Bart., Belsize-lane, Hampstead. – Peter Thompson, builder, Limehouse. Churches built complete, suitable for town and country, and let on hire for any period. See specimen for town – All Saints Church, St John's-wood, Rev. E. Thompson; and St Mark's Church, Maida Vale, Rev. A. B. Haslewood. [53]

Whether his Kentish Town church was purchased for one of the locations mentioned earlier, or whether it went elsewhere is not known. Nor is Thompson's relationship, if any, to Reverend E Thompson. If Reverend Thompson was not a relative then he must have been impressed with his temporary church as he lobbied the Chaplain General of the Army, Reverend Gleig, about adopting Thompson's design for use by the army. Gleig in turn wrote to Sidney Herbert, Secretary at War, pushing for the adoption of numerous wooden temporary churches for the army rather than spending the budget on just one or two more permanent chapels; but this seems to have come to nothing [54].

Thompson's business of providing prefabricated buildings for the colonies was presumably still operating as in the 1851 census his occupation is listed as *"Colonial Architect"* [55], but a successful business it was not; in June 1849 he was officially declared bankrupt [56]. Over the next couple of years his creditors managed to get two dividends, one of nine shillings (45 pence) in the pound and another of twopence (1 pence) in the pound [57-58].

Although he was still advertising his wooden churches into the 1850s [59] Thompson clearly needed another money spinning idea and in his desperation utilised his considerable artistic talent in the production and sale of forged drawings and prints. From his early days in London he had operated as a bookseller from his home in Osnaburgh Place, near Regents Park, in addition to his architectural and building enterprises.

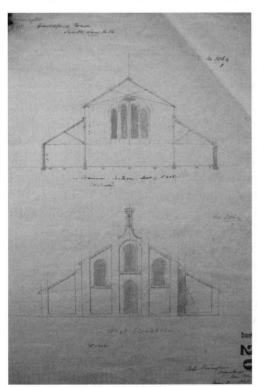

Thompson's sketch for a church at South Lambeth [50]

Presumably it was through this business that he became aware of the optimism and gullibility of collectors and antiquaries. In March 1852 he offered for sale engravings of what were claimed to be drawings of London's fortifications at the start of the Civil War, said to have been drawn by a Captain Eyre of Cromwell's army[60]. A number of sets of the engravings were sold at £2 12s 6d (£2.65) two of which are held in the Guildhall Library, London[61]. The sale also attracted the attention of William Salt, a wealthy young man and a partner in the family bank, who was a great collector and a Fellow of the Society of Antiquaries. We can be sure that it wasn't serendipity that Thompson just happened to have other seventeenth century drawings for sale, including some related to Staffordshire, where Salt had family interests. In spite of advice to the contrary Salt purchased a number of drawings which other experts were very dubious about at the time. Unfazed, Thompson placed an entry in Notes and Queries in June 1853 offering for sale *"Shakespearean Drawings"*, three said to be by Hollar, and three by Capt Eyre[62]. They included exterior and interior views of Shakespeare's house in Clink Street, and the Globe Theatre before it was burnt down. Thompson was proposing to sell engravings of the three Hollar drawings for 1 guinea (£1.05) providing that there were 60 subscribers. There were many experts at the time who were dubious about the authenticity of Thompson's drawings and this had a great effect on sales. The drawings in the William Salt Library[63] and the prints held at the Guildhall Library and the London Metropolitan Archives[64] are now acknowledged to be forgeries and the work of Thompson. No doubt as is often the case in art fraud the embarrassment of the 'experts' prevented Thompson's prosecution and he escaped to return to more familiar business. Later that year he was back to advertising his wooden churches but seemingly the market and probably his reputation prevented much activity in this direction[59].

Throughout this period Thompson had also tried his hand at designing housing for the working class and other projects including the publication of a periodical, The Oil and Colourman. These activities are outside the scope of this research and I would refer readers to Ida Darlington's article, Thompson Fecit, published in the The Architectural Review, for more details of his colourful career[60]. At the end of her article Darlington notes that Thompson was a contemporary of Charles Dickens and speculates whether they might have met. On the evidence that we have of Thompson's life and character; carpenter, architect, artist, forger and irrepressible opportunist; he could certainly fit quite easily into one of Dickens' tales.

One odd thing about Thompson's career is that although he was the pre-eminent designer and supplier of prefabricated buildings throughout the first half of the nineteenth century he was not involved in the contracts for the Crimea huts when you would have thought that he was the obvious man to go to. I can only assume that his reputation had been tarnished by the forgeries scandals and also perhaps by an earlier dispute with the Admiralty[42] to make him persona non grata with the Admiralty and War Office. In 1871 he was living with his son in Harrow and presumably died there in 1874[65-66].

Whodunnit?

The primary candidates must be the architects of St Bartholomew's, Edwin Goodwin and Henry Butcher. Clearly, as a working architect, Goodwin would have had the experience and ability to design such a building but there is nothing in his history to suggest that he had done anything like this before or after and there is no clear evidence that he did any work in conjunction with Butcher. As mentioned before Butcher has left little evidence of his architectural career. Besides the poorly designed St Bartholomew's, which we must assume was Butcher's work, he was involved in a couple of improvement projects to churches in Norfolk but beyond that no evidence remains. And what are we to make of Butcher's subsequent career? First he returns to the family auctioneering business in Norwich, then a spell living off his savings before finally becoming a hotel proprietor/publican. Was he a failed architect, a failed businessman or both?

John Blizard certainly designed a church of very similar style to the Crinoline Church but I can find no other mention of him building temporary churches elsewhere and he died young nearly a year before the Crinoline Church was built.

George Truefitt is undoubtedly the most accomplished of the candidates and had already designed a similar church. But he was a prominent architect and his career has been chronicled in some detail, so surely if he had been involved in the RMA Church it would have been common knowledge and his involvement would have been publicised, especially by the Butchers who would surely have grasped the opportunity to promote the involvement of a top architect in their project.

Then there is Peter Thompson. His history makes him a much more convincing candidate but where is the proof? Sad to say, there are no hard facts, just circumstantial evidence and speculation. The prefabricated churches that he did

Water colour by Peter Thompson [60]

build were of a simpler design than the Crinoline Church; mainly it must be said due to the restrictions placed upon him by the MBO. However, one example of his work does show that he had ideas for much more complex structures. When asked by Thomas Little to provide the temporary church for All Saints, Finchley Road, his first submission was a flight of fancy that must have caused raised blood pressures at the MBO. There is a 'thumbnail' picture of this design, an ink and watercolour, in Ida Darlington's article in the The Architectural Review mentioned earlier. Unfortunately the original drawing seems to have disappeared and extensive searches by myself and London Metropolitan Archives staff have failed to uncover it.

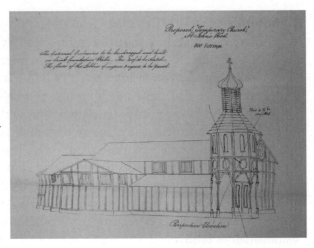

There does exist though a simpler sketch by Thompson in one of Little's letters to the MBO which has the tower crossed-out and the annotation *"This is to be omitted"* [67]. This sketch forms part of what became increasingly

Sketch by Peter Thompson for a proposed church at St John's Wood [67]

tetchy correspondence between Little and the MBO about his and Thompson's plans for the temporary church [47].

The concept for the tower in Thompson's design does show a certain familiarity with the multi-sided shape of the Crinoline Church, but this is as far as this circumstantial evidence goes.

An even more tenuous link is the use of vitreous cloth for the church windows. I noted in Chapter 1 that the photos of the Crinoline Church seem to show that the windows were glazed with this material which Thompson was known to favour in his temporary buildings. One more important factor with respect to Thompson is his birth in and links to Norfolk. He was born in the village of Earsham near Bungay, no more than twelve miles from Norwich, home and business base of the Butchers [37]. And between 1832 and 1842 he was involved in several building developments in Norwich, mostly in partnership with another local auctioneer Samuel Lovick, so it is most likely that he was known to the Butchers from this time [41]. Could it be that the Butchers turned to someone they knew and who had experience of supplying prefabricated churches when they needed one? Also we must assume that Thompson knew about the churches built in London by Blizard and Truefitt and his history suggests that he might not be averse to 'poaching' someone else's design.

What other candidates are there? Luke Camwell, the Portsmouth-based supplier of huts for the Crimea can surely be dismissed as there would be stronger local evidence linking him to the project and no need for the Crimea myth to have arisen. Also he would have used his own workforce to erect the building not contractors from London. One of the earliest contractors to provide prefabricated building to the colonies not previously mentioned was Thomas Manning and his family [68], but they appear to have no links to temporary church building at this time.

As mentioned earlier (Origins of the Myth) the firm of Eassie of Gloucester were major contractors and manufacturers of prefabricated buildings and in addition to being the main contractor for Brunel's hospital at Renkioi they also supplied huts for both the British and French armies. Later they had a design for a hospital hut in their catalogue and became a prominent supplier of prefabricated metal (corrugated iron) churches, but there is nothing to link them to this project; their church designs were simpler and again it is unlikely that they would have used London contractors to erect the building if it was delivered from their workshops in Gloucester.

So I believe the most likely candidates to be either Goodwin and/or Butcher (although there is no evidence of their involvement with similar buildings and a big question mark over Butcher's competence) or Thompson. I will honestly admit that I want it to be Thompson. He's the sort of colourful character that any family historian would love to discover in their family. If this were a crime mystery then Goodwin and Butcher are the ones with the proven connection with the 'crime scene' but Thompson is the suspect with 'form', but we can only judge on hard evidence and that is in very short supply. I leave the reader to decide and, hopefully perhaps, time to tell.

Part Two - The Biographies

Chapter 4 - Introduction and Historical Background

Introduction

Whilst transcribing the baptisms I was drawn into looking at the careers of the Navy Chaplains that served in the Church. Some of them had particularly interesting careers that I thought were worth recording as part of the Church's story. And so I decided to produce mini-biographies for each of the Chaplains who performed baptisms in the Church during its lifetime. The resulting biographies are in Chapters 5 and 6.

Although my research into the lives of the chaplains had taken me way beyond my area of expertise it had also made me realise that if non-combatant chaplains could have such interesting histories there must be many great stories hidden among the 2000 plus front line marines who had their children baptised in the Church. And in addition to the fathers the majority of the sons baptised in the church could have served in WWI or WWII and possibly both. But opening up the research as wide as this was a daunting prospect, I had to draw the line somewhere and my research needed achievable goals.

Those men recorded on the church's memorials clearly had to be included and also those who had lost their lives in the various wars. Beyond that I decided to restrict my research to those who had been awarded gallantry medals and, because John Bilcliffe's book made it achievable, those NCOs who had been awarded the Meritorious Service Medal[1]. The memorial to George Porter gave me the excuse to include the other RMA marines who were part of the expedition and so received the Arctic Medal 1875-76. And the memorials to those lost on *HMS Captain* and *HMS Victoria* and the ships ledger for *HMS Vanguard* (1879) gave me further scope to include some lucky survivors. I was now straying somewhat from my original criteria and realised that I could be accused of being arbitrary. Such an accusation is strengthened by other anomalies. For example, Sergeants Jenvey, Lambert, Mathieson, Russell, Saddon, Seabright, Sears and Trowbridge are well-known to RM historians for their contributions to the Nile Campaign and subsequent receipt of the Distinguished Conduct Medal. But Lambert, Russell and Sears do not appear in my biographies because they never had any children baptised in the church, worthy as their service was and even though they probably attended the church regularly when at home. Not only that but my criteria led me to include men who were not marines but who were the sons of marine officers and had distinguished careers in the Army and Navy. However, the most difficult omission of all is of Brigadier General Frederick William

Lumsden, VC, CB, DSO (3 bars), the Corps most decorated officer. Although he was awarded all his medals during WW1 and was killed in action on 8 June 1918, he does not qualify for inclusion in Chapter 7 – The Fallen as he never had any children baptised in the church. But as this book is supposedly about the RMA Church and those connected to its baptisms I believe I can justify these and other exclusions and omissions even though it may upset some historians.

I anticipate that many readers of this book will be family or local historians like me and not necessarily experts in naval history. To place the biographies that follow into context I have included the following: some small sections to give an overview of some of the organisational, technological and social changes that took place in the Royal Navy in the years covered by this book; a background to the Naval Chaplain Service; a brief outline of the history of the Royal Marines; and an outline of the breadth of operations of the Navy and Royal Marines during the period 1840-1918. I would recommend that naval historians go straight to the biographies lest they are offended by the omissions and sweeping generalisations I have made to try and encapsulate nearly a century of Royal Navy history into a few paragraphs. More competent and definitive histories will be found among the books listed in the Bibliography.

The Victorian Navy

This was a period of radical change for the Royal Navy as well as for society at large. The scientific and technological changes brought by the industrial revolution had a profound effect on the Royal Navy. The most senior of the RMA Church chaplains, James Stuart Robson, enlisted in 1848 and his early ships were wooden sailing ships that would not have been out of place in Nelson's navy; and this would apply to many of the marine fathers who appear in the earlier years of the baptisms list. The first ships utilising steam power were introduced in the 1850s but they still retained sail rigging and the first mastless warship did not appear until 1871. The production of cast iron and later steel enabled wooden ships to be armour plated giving rise to the term 'ironclad'. *HMS Iris* the Royal Navy's first all-steel warship followed in 1875. Steam assisted ships moved quickly from being paddle-driven to screw-driven and by the time that the least senior of our chaplains, Arthur William Plant, was serving at the RMA Church (1905), the massive, powerfully armed and steam turbine-driven *Dreadnought* was about to revolutionise naval technology.

The introduction of steam power provided much more than just propulsion. Having directly or indirectly produced power on board changed the life of the crew. Nearly every visitor to *HMS Warrior* in Portsmouth is astounded by the size of her laundry machines, but this was not all. Power allowed refrigeration which meant an end to salted meat; it also facilitated the distillation of fresh drinking water and freshly baked bread replaced hard biscuits. This improved diet led to improved health which was also helped by the disappearance of bilge water following the transition from wooden to iron/steel ships.

Power also allowed the fighting ability of the ships to advance apace. With hydraulic power available to manoeuvre much larger guns and to handle their projectiles, some massive weaponry was developed. For example, by WWI the larger guns (up to 18-inch or 45cm bore) could throw a one and a half ton (1500 kg) projectile over 20 miles (32 km). An indication of how the accuracy and power of naval gunnery had increased is that at the Battle of Trafalgar 'point blank range' meant exactly that with ships just a few yards apart and ships rarely engaging beyond 100 yards (91.4 m) whereas by the end of WWI the normal range for opening an engagement was about 10 miles (16 km) with anything under 3 miles (5km) considered close-range.

There was a price to pay though for all these advances; steam engines needed coal in substantial quantities and when the ships bunkers needed to be replenished it was "all hands on deck". After the coal had been craned on board from the dockside or collier ships it had to be manhandled into the bunkers and it could take two days to fully coal a large ship. To give an idea of the scale of this task the *Invincible*-class battlecruisers launched in 1914 had bunker space for 3000 tons (2952 tonne) of coal. This was an exhausting job in a normal climate but close to the Poles or in the Tropics it was a true test of strength and stamina. And the job didn't end there, the act of coaling created an awful mess with the whole ship covered in coal dust which had to be cleaned down before the job was considered done, which left the men themselves to clean-down before normality could be resumed. And a couple of weeks later, or sooner if the ship was moving at speed, the whole process began again.

The replacement of 'handraulics' with hydraulics went along with the decline of traditional seamanship and saw the replacement of the straw-hatted and barefoot bluejacket with a more modern technically-trained sailor. The speed of this technological change must have been bewildering to many of the senior ranks; Sir William Laird Clowes in his history of the Royal Navy (see Bibliography) notes that the best ship of 1877 would have been a close match for the entire fleet of 1867 but was itself obsolete by 1890 [2].

This period also saw a great change in the organisation of the Navy. The lack of a proper career structure and retirement system had led to a situation in 1840 where there were 41 Admirals of whom 33 were over 70 and 1 over 90, the average age being about 76. Fifteen years later at the time of the Crimean War there were senior captains aged over 60 who had never previously commanded a ship in action [2]. The situation was little better with the seamen. They were 'contracted' for one voyage or commission at a time and the press gang was a necessary facility to ensure that ships put to sea with the required complement, as ill-trained as they might be. A major improvement came with the introduction of a system of 'Continuous Service' in 1853 which gave sailors long-term job prospects and the possibility of a pension after 22 years service, making it a much more attractive career. The technological changes brought the need for good training and to an extent, specialisation, which also added to job security. Following the introduction of continuous service came the abolition of flogging as a means of maintaining discipline and the 'stick' was replaced by the 'carrot' of Good Conduct Badges and their accumulating financial rewards. The daily rum ration was made optional and the sailor could opt for payment in lieu. In addition clothing, food and accommodation all improved substantially for the Victorian sailor.

At the time of writing, one section of the Royal Navy Museum's website is titled *"The Paintwork versus Gunnery Controversy"*, a reference to the fact that in a time of comparative peace an obsession with smartness had been taken to extremes, so much so that the officers would buy paint and other materials out of their own pockets to ensure that their ship was in pristine condition for an Admiral's inspection. Gunnery practice splattered the ship's superstructure with cordite and was avoided if at all possible! It was Percy Scott, one of the junior officers present at the Bombardment of Alexandria (see Rev W S Harris's biography below), who was later to have a major influence in bringing the Navy's gunnery standards up to scratch. The Navy never did lose its obsession with paint though. In 1915 the *Agamemnon* was involved in the ill-conceived 'forcing of the Dardanelles' and was bombarding the Turkish forts with its starboard guns and taking fire in return. Midshipman Denham recorded that whilst this exchange of heavy fire was taking place the Commander *"was trying to get the disengaged side painted, but the men were not very willing and I cannot blame them"*[3]. And neither can I. The situation was no better twenty years later – a third-hand story passed to me by an ex-RN Chief Shipright Artificer neighbour relates that at one point in the 1930s the X and Y turrets on a ship of the Mediterranean fleet were found to be inoperable due to a heavy encrustation of paint which had to be labouriously chipped-off by the shipwrights before the guns could be elevated properly.

The Royal Marines

The true origin of the Royal Marines dates from the inception of the Admiral's Regiment in 1664, but the structure of the corps that was in place for the period covered by this history dates from 1802 when the title Royal Marines was adopted.

The Marines non-combatant role was initially to help maintain discipline on board ship. This was a period when Captains often had to resort to the press gang to 'recruit' sufficient crewmen for a commission and the introduction of non-sailors on board inevitably brought discipline problems. Their combatant role was to provide small-arms fire when the ship was involved in close combat. In addition they provided an infantry capability for on-shore operations, often as part of a naval brigade with their bluejacket (RN) colleagues. Prior to 1804 it was the Royal Artillery that provided the crews to man the mortars in the bomb vessels used to support amphibious operations, but this was often problematic in that they were not under the direct command of the Navy and on occasions refused to accept orders from Naval officers. As a direct result of this the Navy decided to dispense with the Royal Artillery crews and instructed the Royal Marines to take over the mortars in the bomb vessels. Incidentally it was Lord Nelson himself who suggested the formation of an "Artillery Force" within the Royal Marines; they became the Marine Artillery Companies within the Royal Marines in 1804 and in 1862 the Royal Marines officially split into the Royal Marine Light Infantry (RMLI) and Royal Marine Artillery (RMA). The RMLI who had performed with such good effect during the Crimean War adopted the red coats worn by the Army infantry and as a means of identification the RMA adopted blue coats.

The RMA certainly came to regard themselves as the elite of the Royal Marines and only those officers showing above average capabilities, especially in science and mathematics, were appointed to the RMA. This 'selection of the best' also applied to the NCOs and rank and file and as a result both officers and men were paid more than their RMLI equivalents.

The RMA was initially based in barracks adjacent to the Gunwharf in Portsmouth and later occupied Fort Cumberland at Eastney but by the 1860s it had become necessary to improve and increase the accommodation and Eastney Barracks was built for this purpose, opening fully in 1867. The Portsmouth RMs continued to utilise Fort Cumberland until 1973. It was a few years beyond the scope of this history in 1923 that the RMA and RMLI were merged into a single corps, the Portsmouth Division RMLI marching from Forton Barracks in Gosport to join the RMA at Eastney.

By the early part of the nineteenth century the Marines had built a reputation for discipline, fearlessness and first-class fighting prowess in all conditions around the world. Their achievements were so considerable that when they adopted new colours (flag) in 1827 a list of 106 potential battle honours was presented to the King from which he found it impossible to make a selection due to the great number of glorious deeds that had been performed over the years by the Marines. Eventually the King decided on the radical selection of just a single battle honour, "Gibraltar". In addition to the new colours the motto "Per Mare Per Terram" (By Sea, By Land) was adopted and a new Corps insignia was made up from a globe encircled by a laurel wreath. The King also insisted that regardless of which Monarch was on the throne his cipher (GR IV) was always to remain part of the badge. This cipher remains part of the Corps insignia on the Regimental Colour to this day.

The Victorian era was one of comparative peace and is often referred to as the 'Pax Britannica' (British Peace). The main reason for this 'peaceful' century was that the Royal Navy were the undisputed masters of the seas and it was not until the build-up of the German fleet prior to 1914 that their superiority would be challenged. Just because Britain was not involved in a war with her immediate European neighbours didn't mean that the Royal Navy had nothing to do. The Empire had to be policed and protected (and in some cases increased) so there was plenty of action for the navy and the marines around the globe. The following timeline list shows the main places and actions in which the 91 marines and 23 naval chaplains whose mini-biographies are included in this book were involved. Their service stretches from about 1830 to 1947 and it includes a good majority of the significant wars, actions and incidents in which the Royal Navy was involved up to the end of WWII.

1840   Eastern Mediterranean
Including actions along the Syrian coast, the bombardment of Beirut and the bombardment and capture of Jean d'Acre (Healey)

1844   Ireland, the Great Famine (Digby)

1854-56   The Crimean or Russian War
In particular, the bombardments of Sveaborg, Sebastapol and Kinburn. (Reverends Robson & Williams and Brydges, Digby, Festing, Healey, Hetheridge & Poore)

1857   Indian Mutiny
Naval Brigade (including marines) from *HMS Pearl* involved in 18 actions across northern India, the most important being at Oudh, Amorha and Tirhoot. (Reverend Williams and Oborn)

1856-60   Second China War
Action at White Cloud Mountain and the Capture of Canton (Festing)
River action and subsequent capture of junks at Escape Creek (Reverend Beal)

1861-62   Mexico
Sabre-rattling and attempted debt-collection by Britain, Spain and France prior to the outbreak of the French-Mexican War, 1861-67. (Reverend Cawston & Digby)

1863-65   Japan
Bombardment and capture of the forts at Shimonoseki (Reverend Rutherford and Kinsman)

1868   Japan
Relief of Kobe (Brydges)

1873-4   Ashanti War (Ghana)
Including participation in the Naval Brigade ashore and the Bombardment of Elmina (Reverend Kenah and Cheetham & Festing)

1875   Loss of *HMS Vanguard* (Burgess Fidler, Knight, Smith & Venner)

1880   Panama
Suppression of rebellion (1880, Welch)

1882   Egypt
Bombardment of Alexandria (Reverends Cox-Edwards, Harris, & Hill and Cheetham, Crook, Newport, Raitt, Wellington snr, Yardy)
Mediterranean Battalion ashore (Innoles, Lappin, Raitt)
Landing at Aboukir (Cheetham)
Tel el-Kebir (1882, Harding, Noble, Puddick)
Kassassin (Baker, Noble)
Actions at Mallaha Junction, El Magfar & Tel-el-Mahuta (Noble)

1882-83   Dublin

	Police duties following the Phoenix Park Murders (Noble)
1883-85	Egypt
	Including actions at Suakin (1884, Bunn, Crook, Puddick & Wheaton), El-Teb (1884, Crook), Tamaii (1884, Crook & Puddick)
1885-7	Third Burmese War
	(Sparrow)
1893	Loss of *HMS Victoria* in the Mediterranean (survivors Blackman, Bunn, Cullimore & Perkins)
1894	The Gambia
	(Trayfoot & Wilton)
1896-9	Sudan
	Including the actions at Dongola (1896, Jenvey & Mathieson), Khartoum (1897, Jenvey), Hafir (1897, Jenvey), Gedaref (1897, Jenvey), The Atbara (1898, Jenvey & Seabright), Nile Expedition (1898, Mathieson, Saddon & Seabright), Rosieres (Rosaries) (1899, Trowbridge)
1899-1900	South African War (Boer War)
	Actions at Belmont, Cape Colony, Graspan, Lodden River, Modder River, Paardeburg, Dreifontein, Johannesburg, Diamonds Hill, Belfast, Wittebergen (Broadbent, Carter, Coen snr, Cullimore, Gasson snr & Trayfoot)
1900	China
	Boxer Rebellion (Wall)
1902	Malaya
	Secondment to Johore Forces (Cullimore)
1914-18	World War I
	Expedition to Ostende (1914, Chapman, Dadd, Jenvey, Mathieson, Phillips, Rayson, Stevens & Wheaton)
	Expedition to Dunkirk (1914, Dadd, Jenvey & Mathieson,)
	Battle of Heligoland Bight (1914, Heaton, Gasson jnr)
	Battle of the Falklands Islands (1914, Heaton, Gasson jnr)
	Invasion of German West Africa (1914, Jenvey)
	Sinking of *HMS Goliath* in the Dardenelles (1915, Dickerson)
	Loss of *HMS Natal* in Cromarty Firth (1915, Harper)
	RMA Anti-Aircraft Brigade, France (1915, Chapman, Dadd & Mathieson)
	Royal Garrison Artillery South African Contingent, France (1915, Dacombe)
	RMA Howitzer Brigade, Belgium & France (1915-17, Dadd, Heaton, Lumsden & Wellington jnr)
	Singapore Mutiny (1915, Cullimore)
	Sinking of *HMS Invincible* at the Battle of Jutland (1916, Gasson jnr & Mann)
	Battle of Jutland (1916, Dix & Weston)

RM Battalion in Gallipoli (1916, Nuttytcombe)
RN Siege Guns, Belgium (1917, Coen snr)
RMA Heavy Siege Train (1917, Mathieson & Saunders)
1939-45   World War II
Norway (1940, Coen jnr)
Arctic Convoys (1943, Coen jnr)

Ceremonial also had its place in promoting the Empire and so two royal tours should be mentioned, they were to:

India by HRH Prince of Wales (1875-6, Reverend York), and

Australia by Duke of York and Duchess of Cornwall, the future King George V and Queen Mary, (1901, Dix)

And the RMAs contribution towards polar exploration shouldn't be forgotten either:

RN Arctic Expedition, 1875-6 (Dobing, Oakley, Porter & Wellington snr)

Whilst this list is very selective, relating only to the men mentioned in this book, it shows just how vital the marines were to the Empire and in both the World Wars. Their amphibious flexibility gave commanders more options and they were used to the full. Marine NCOs were not only experienced fighters but were often used in a training capacity with 'local' troops and their heavy-weapon skills were often used well away from the sea. This was no better demonstrated than when two batches of RMA NCOs were seconded to the Egyptian Army in June 1896 and July 1897 to work on the Nile gunboats as part of Kitchener's campaign to recapture Sudan; six of them appear in the biographies in Chapter 8. The first nine NCOs included Corporal Jenvey and Bombadier Mathieson[4] and they served on the Nile from June to November 1896 when all but Jenvey returned to the UK. The second detachment of eight NCOs including Mathieson, Saddon, Seabright and Trowbridge departed on 1 July 1897[5] and returned in 1899-1900 except for Seabright who stayed until 1905.

Their expertise with the new Maxim machine guns and other rapidfiring guns was crucial to the success of this campaign and their main task was to command the artillery pieces on the gunboats, the guns being operated by native gun crews. There were already a number of gunboats that had been operating on the Nile for some years and to these were added some new boats that were built in the UK and shipped out in parts for assembly on the river. Whilst there were RN and other officers present for much of the period in times of non-combat the marines were often left to command the boats, and their mainly native

Eight RMA NCOs in tropical dress at Eastney prior to embarkation for Egypt & Sudan 1897[7] (far right standing is Sergeant Trowbridge & centre sitting is Corporal Muller)

crews; for example, at one point the then Sergeant Trowbridge was 'acting captain' of the *Melik* for at least a month until joined by Colour Sergeant Saddon who then took command[6]. The contribution to the campaign by these detachments was rewarded by the award of a number of promotions and Distinguished Conduct Medals, including a double award (bar) to Seabright.

A Sergeant of the RMA superintending the fire of a Nile Gunboat[8]

As a further example of their versatility I must make special mention of the marines plain clothes duties in Dublin in 1882-83 which stands as one of the most unusual deployments in the Corps history (see Major Noble's biography in Chapter 1).

The Navy Chaplain Service

The chaplains posted to the RMA Church were part of the Royal Navy Chaplain Service. Applicants wishing to become chaplains had to be ordained priests of the Church of England. This meant that they all had a university-level education and with few exceptions were at least middle class. About 1828 the Duke of Clarence, then Lord High Admiral, went one step further and decreed that only holders of university degrees could become chaplains; at that time this effectively meant only graduates of Oxford, Cambridge or Trinity College, Dublin, would be accepted. A test case in 1835 led to the newly-formed Board of Admiralty accepting William Bowman as a chaplain, much against the wishes of the Supervisory Chaplain of the Fleet, Samuel Cole, because he 'only' had a MA from Lambeth. This elitism was not confined to the Royal Navy and in the middle of the nineteenth century it was still unusual for anyone schooled outside the triumverate of Oxford, Cambridge and Trinity, Dublin, to be admitted as a priest, even though these elite universities issued no degrees in theology. Of the forty-two British and Irish priests whose biographies are listed below only four are not from these three universities and of the thirteen permanent chaplains appointed to the RMA Church there were just three from 'outsider' universities; Robson of Durham and Cawston and Atherton of Lampeter. Even by 1902 out of 120 serving chaplains only 10 were from outside the 'triumverate'[9].

It is indicative of the attitudes at the time when we see that in 1853 the very first entry in Reverend John Cawston's service record states *"Not a graduate of Oxford, Cambridge or Dublin."* Some traditionalist eyes must have been raised in 1876 when Cawston was appointed Chaplain of the Fleet.

For many years it had been unclear what the chaplains' status was in relation to the other officers, were they the equal of commissioned officers or warrant officers and what was their chain of 'command'? It was not until 1859 that the Senior Chaplain of

Greenwich Hospital was formally recognised as head of the Naval Chaplains, given the title Chaplain of the Fleet and the equivalent rank of Rear Admiral. At the same time the chaplains were divided into four grades and given equivalent rank status as follows:

Fourth	Chaplains under 10 years service	- Lieutenants
Third	Chaplains above 10 years service	- Commanders
Second	Chaplains above 15 years and under 20 years service	- Captains under 3 years
First	Chaplains above 20 years service	- Captains above 3 years [10]

This clearly shows that seniority was everything, as it was for all officers in both the Navy and Army at that time; it was to be well into the next century before a meritocracy existed in the armed forces. However, this 'ranking' of the chaplains was soon abandoned and subsequent regulations stated somewhat ambiguously that *"Chaplains shall not hold any Naval rank but shall retain, when afloat, the position to which their office would entitle them on shore…"*[11]. It did though have some benefits for the chaplains as it was subsequently decided that they should be allowed to have servants like the officers and there is also evidence that it pushed them up the pecking order when it came to picking cabins onboard ship.

It's not difficult to appreciate that even though their status on board ship had been resolved their responsibilities were ambiguous. Did they serve the Navy or the Church? Did their responsibilities lie with their superior officers or with the crew (their flock)? This conflict of loyalties came to a head in 1867 when Captain Chamberlain of *Resistance* had reason to reprimand one of his midshipmen for inattention during morning prayers and gave him what he probably thought of as the lenient sentence of attending service every day. He then instructed the chaplain, Reverend Frederic Emanuel Gutteres, to let him know if the midshipman failed to appear. This Gutteres refused to do claiming, quite rightly, that he would be regarded as the officers' spy if he did. The maintenance of discipline was everything in the Navy and the refusal of an order was not a trivial action. The captain was livid and re-issued the order and again Gutteres refused. Eventually after a lot of posturing and arguing the Admiralty backed Captain Chamberlain but almost immediately issued an instruction that prevented chaplains being put into such a position again; Gutterres had won an important moral battle for the chaplains[12].

The chaplains did have one very obvious form of independence in that they had no uniform and wore their normal clerical attire. In 1874 Chaplain O'Callaghan wrote to the Admiralty through Admiral Hornby, Commander in Chief of the Nore, suggesting the adoption of a uniform, using as part of his argument the fact that army chaplains now had an agreed uniform. But his letter also suggests that vanity was partly behind his proposal as he mentions that on more than one occasion he had been refused entry to areas open *"to the most junior officers"* because the policeman did not recognise his status and that when visiting other ships chaplains were not received *"in a manner becoming their position"*[13]. Admiral Hornby gave the proposition his full support and Lord Gilford even devised a series of uniforms but their Lordships at the

Admiralty shelved the proposal. Later Queen's Regulations stated that *"…a Chaplain shall wear a clerical collar or stock or a collar and white tie, and shall be dressed in other respects in such a manner as shall clearly indicate his profession."*[14]. It was not until after the life of the Crinoline Church, in 1918, that the Chaplains were given a bronze badge to indicate their occupation. Whilst some of the senior officers probably saw the introduction of a uniform as a step towards making the chaplains more 'navy' than 'church' and thereby lessen their independence, the Admiralty clearly understood the need for chaplains to be seen as apart from the officers so as not to restrict their freedom to serve their flock. An amusing footnote to the uniform story is that later, in 1887, the pompous sounding Reverend O'Callaghan was accused of living an immoral life but unfortunately papers relating to the charge have not survived[15].

The ambiguity of the chaplains' role and status showed itself in other ways that are reflected in some of the correspondence in the Admiralty records. There are a number of clashes recorded between chaplains and their superiors over the contents of sermons, three such are mentioned below in the biographies of Reverends Rutherford, Smith and Williams. It would seem that some Captains saw their relationship with the chaplain as the same as a squire to his curate. The chaplains themselves seem to have courted a lot of this opposition by open displays of independence. In 1886 the Commander in Chief, Portsmouth called attention to the non-observance of the regulations in regard to beards and moustaches by chaplains and a circular letter was issued directing chaplains to conform strictly to the regulations[16]. On another occasion, in 1884, Colonel Bland Hunt, then Colonel Commandant at Eastney, wrote to the Admiralty asking whether chaplains should salute him within the precincts of the barracks. We must assume from this that Reverend Davies, the incumbent at the time, had refused to do so and had invoked the Colonel's ire. The Admiralty's response can only be seen as a 'put down' to the Commandant - *"my Lords do not think it necessary to define the exact description of the mark of respect due and disapprove of the question having been raised by Col. Bland Hunt"*[17]. Not only does the raising of the subject tell us a lot about Colonel Bland Hunt but perhaps the response also shows the Admiralty's reluctance to get involved in a dispute with chaplains and some senior officers that they knew was simmering under the surface.

It was only after a lot of campaigning by the Church Times and others that the Admiralty eventually agreed that with the appointment of John Cawston in 1876, the Chaplain of the Fleet would have a new important addition to his job description, he was to be responsible for the selection of candidates for the post of Navy Chaplain, something, like all officer appointments, that had previously rested with the Admiralty and relied as much on who you knew as what you knew – so this was one small step towards a meritocracy. However, Cawston soon found that there had been no revolution; he still had no say over the postings and careers of his chaplains; that remained with the Admiralty.

There was still much concern that the chaplains had no links to the Church of England. Although they had to be ordained in the Church of England in order to become a chaplain, once in the service they had no links with the established church. This problem was eventually solved following the appointment of William Stuart Harris as Chaplain of the Fleet in 1901. The following year an Order in Council determined that the Chaplain of the Fleet was to be given the same ecclesiastical status as an Archdeacon[18]. Harris was formally inducted as Archdeacon of the Royal Navy by the Archbishop of Canterbury later the same year. The chaplains now had a designated managerial and ecumenical hierarchy. On appointment chaplains were to receive a special ecclesiastical licence from the Archbishop of Canterbury and this was done retrospectively for all 120 chaplains serving at the time[19].

It was common for chaplains to qualify as Naval Instructors and use much of their time on ship in the technical instruction of midshipmen and also to provide literacy coaching for other ranks that requested it. The chaplains and schoolmasters certainly had plenty on their hands. In 1865 a survey of over 30,000 petty officers, seamen, marines and boys showed that; between 16% (POs) and 30% (boys) could only read indifferently and between 2% (boys) and 23% (marines) could not read at all. From 23% (POs) to 30% (boys) could only write indifferently and between 2% (boys) and 27% (marines) could not write at all[20]. The Chaplains' responsibilities for overseeing the work of the School and schoolmaster were later enshrined in King's Regulations[21].

Becoming a Naval Instructor involved taking an examination in the following subjects:

Practical Navigation
Theory of Navigation
Use of Nautical Instruments
Outline of Surveying, Laying down Positions and Soundings
and Use of Charts
Prevailing Winds, Currents, etc.
Name and use of the parts of the Steam Engine and Boiler
The elements of Mechanics and Hydrostatics
French

The two navigation sections were worth 200 points each and the other subjects 100 points each. To get a first class certificate the candidate had to score a minimum of 900 out of a 1000 or 750 points for a second class certificate.

During the time covered by the transcriptions in this book, in excess of thirty-nine years, there were thirteen permanent chaplains. I have granted Reverends Harris and Atherton permanent status as they filled the void between the retirement of Reverend York on 1 October 1898 and the appointment of Reverend Hill on 30 May 1901. Reverend Harris acted at Eastney whilst attached to Haslar Hospital and Reverend Atherton was posted temporarily to Eastney between service on *Majestic* and *Urgent*. Reverend Harris performed 185 baptisms in over 2 years and Reverend Atherton 19 baptisms over 3 months, so I think they deserve to be considered part of the RMA Church's permanent staff.

These permanent chaplains were augmented by another thirty-one priests acting as deputies. Twenty of these deputies were civilian ministers. The deputies performed the chaplain's duties, including baptisms, for short periods, presumably whilst the incumbent was sick or on leave and many appear in the register for just one day's baptisms.

There is one Chaplain who falls into neither of these categories. Reverend Thomas Ashe's service record and related correspondence from the Admiralty to the RMA states that he was appointed to RM Artillery, Eastney, in place of Reverend Cawston on 24 July 1871 but then as of 9 August he was to take up an appointment at Chatham Dockyard in place of Reverend James Robson who was to take the appointment at Fort Cumberland in Ashe's stead[22-23]. Reverend Cawston's service record shows him appointed to Portsmouth Dockyard as from 17 July 1871 so there appears to be a three week window where Reverend Ashe was theoretically at Eastney, but he performed no baptisms during this time. Reverend Cawston performed two baptisms at Eastney on 26 July and 19 August and between these there were five baptisms performed by Reverend Sheperd on 6 August. This would infer that Reverend Ashe was not at Eastney during this period. It seems most likely that this was a 'phantom' appointment and he never actually made an appearance at Eastney and for this reason I have omitted him from the biographies below.

The table at Appendix A shows the date range of the baptisms performed by each chaplain or minister in chronological order, arranged under the thirteen permanent chaplains. The names of the chaplains and ministers do not appear in the transcriptions in Part Three but they can be established by referencing the date of the baptism in the transcriptions against the dates in this table.

Chapter 5 - Permanent Chaplains' biographies

T he following paragraphs provide short biographies of the thirteen permanent chaplains to the RMA at Eastney during the period of the Crinoline Church. They are listed alphabetically by surname. In addition to the sources listed in Appendix B editions of Crockford's Clerical Directory, the Clergy List and Navy List (various dates) have been used throughout.

ATHERTON, William Bernard

Born 28 February 1867 at Taynton in the Forest of Dean, Gloucestershire, he was the son of Charles B Atherton, *"Landed proprietor"*. He was educated at St David's College, Lampeter where he graduated with a BA. He was ordained a deacon on 1 June 1890 and a priest on 24 May 1891. He served as curate of King's Norton (1890-91), Churcham with Bulley (1891-93) and Atherstone (1893-99), before joining the Navy Chaplain Service on 6 March 1899.

His first posting was to *Majestic* (Channel). Two years later he was temporarily appointed to the RMA Church on 18 February 1901 (see *The Navy Chaplain Service* above). At the end of May 1901 he was appointed to *Urgent* (Jamaica, including RN Hospital, Port Royal). Whilst in Jamaica he married Eva Whitworth on 12 March 1903. He returned to UK in June 1903 to serve in *Hawke* (Home). In 1905 he spent four months in *Boscawen II*, a training ship at Portland. He then moved to the Mediterranean in *King Alfred* for just a couple of months before returning to home waters with *Antrim* (1905-07) and then *Prince George* and *Jupiter* (Channel, 1907-09). In June 1909 he joined *Albemarle* (Atlantic) and completed his service in *London* (Atlantic) in 1911. The comments in his service record include; *"preaches deadly dull sermons"*, *"amiable and exemplary"* and *"perhaps somewhat deficient in energy"*. This last comment is perhaps unfair because the most telling comment of all reads *"much handicapped by severe sea sickness"*, which may explain a lot. It may also explain why he only served 12 years. He was initially placed on the retired list on 1 May 1911 but this was cancelled and he was *"granted half pay on retirement instead of retired pay to which entitled"*. Once back on dry land he first became rector of Holford and then in 1912 he moved to Coberley with Colesbourne in Gloucestershire where he remained until his death in Cheltenham General Hospital on 27 July 1937.
Sources: 1-3

BEAL, Samuel

Reverend Beal was the first and in many ways the most unusual minister to serve the RMA Church. He was born at Devonport on 27 November 1825, the son of a Weslyan minister, and he entered Trinity College, Cambridge as a sizar on 12 January 1843. A sizar was an undergraduate who was expected to carry-out some menial tasks in the College in return for financial help and this would indicate that his father, like many Weslyan ministers, was not a wealthy man. He got his BA in 1847 and soon after became Headmaster of Bramham College in Yorkshire (1848-50). He was ordained as a deacon on 10 November 1850 and as a priest on 23 November 1851 and after short curacies at Brooke in Norfolk and Sopley in Hampshire he became a navy chaplain on 19 November 1852.

His first postings were to the Mediterranean; he served for just over seven months under sail in *Queen* and then transferred to the paddle-driven *Terrible*, the latter with the dual role of Chaplain and Naval Instructor. On 18 August 1853 he was appointed to the sailing ship *Sybille*, again in the dual role. It was this posting that changed the course of his life as *Sybille* was immediately sent to China Station. It is probably unlikely that he had heard or seen a word of Chinese before this but he obviously had an inborn talent for language and during the course of his appointment he became proficient in both written and spoken Chinese. His incentive to learn the language was his desire to gain an understanding of Buddhism from the original Chinese texts but, with the onset of the Second Chinese War, his private study became an invaluable naval resource and he was used as a front line interpreter at the famous river action at Escape Creek (a branch of the Canton River), which led to his being 'gazetted' on 1 August 1857. Commodore Elliot, in his report of *'Operations Against Mandarin Junks Etc., Up The Escape Creek'* , an action in which about 40 junks were destroyed between 25 and 27 May, includes the following:

"I beg here to mention the very great assistance I have received from Rev. Samuel Beal, Chaplain of this ship, who was good enough at my request to accompany me each day as Chinese Interpreter; to his aid the successes of the expedition are in a great degree due, as I had failed to obtain an Interpreter from Hong Kong." [10]

The action, conducted in terribly hot conditions, was a great success with only two men wounded from enemy fire but many more suffering from sun and heat stroke.

After what must have been an exciting and illuminating five years he left *Sybille* on 13 May 1858. Following short periods in *Royal Albert* (Mediterranean), *Pylades* and *Shannon* (both Channel) he was nominally appointed to *Victory* (Flagship,

Commodore Elliot leading the attack on Chinese junks in Escape Creek, 25 May 1857 [4]

Portsmouth) on 4 August 1863. He was actually designated for service with the RMA at Fort Cumberland and later became the first minister to conduct a baptism in the RMA Church. Unfortunately, as discussed earlier in Chapter 1, the exact date of his first baptism in the church is unknown. His last baptism at Eastney was on 1 September 1867 and he was then appointed to Pembroke Dock on 17 September 1867. He was superseded at Pembroke on 6 April 1872 and spent about a year as chaplain of St George's, Portsea, before being appointed to Devonport Dockyard on 21 July 1873. He didn't complete his full five years at Devonport and was appointed to Chatham Dockyard on 21 July 1877, to serve his remaining months before being placed on the retired list.

On retirement he was appointed Rector of Falstone in Northumberland and three years later moved to Wark, also in Northumberland, where he served as Rector until 1888. Both of these livings were in the gift of Greenwich Hospital. Finally he moved to Greens Norton in Northampton where he died on 20 August 1889.

Throughout his service and retirement he had continued with his oriental studies and in 1877 he was appointed Professor of Chinese at University College, London. He published a number of books including *"The Travels of Fah-Hian and Sung-Yun"*, *"A Catena of Buddhist Scriptures"* and *"A Life of Buddha by Asvaghosha Bodhisattra"* all translated from the Chinese. In 1885 he was awarded an honorary degree (DCL) by Durham University and he is the only one of the Crinoline Church's chaplains to merit an entry in the Dictionary of National Biography.

Sources: 4-11

CAWSTON, John

He was born in Flempton, Suffolk, in 1824 but he spent his teenage years in Great Torrington, Devon, where his father Abraham had a post as a schoolmaster. His birth date is not recorded in any of his service records but was about 1824. After graduating from St David's College, Lampeter as a 'prizeman' in 1848 he was curate of St Paul, Newport, Monmouth, and Great Torrington, Devon before joining the Navy Chaplain Service in 1853. He served in *Bellerophon* (1853-55, Mediterranean) and was present at the Bombardment of Sebastapol; *Centaur* (1855-56) which was part of Admiral Dundas's Baltic fleet during the Crimean War; and *Edinburgh* (1858-59, Coast Guard, Scotland) before being appointed to *Mersey* (1859-62, Channel then North America & West Indies) as a joint Chaplain & Naval Instructor. During this latter appointment he served ashore during the civil unrest in Mexico. He then served in *Sutlej* (1862-67, Pacific) earning high praise from Admiral Denman before moving on to the *Duke of Wellington* (Receiving ship, Portsmouth) in August 1867. In September 1867 he was made 'additional' to *Victory* for service with the RMA at Fort Cumberland, Eastney. His first baptism in the Crinoline Church was on 6 October 1867 and his last on 19 August 1871. On 17 July 1871, he was appointed to Portsmouth Dockyard where he served until promoted to Chaplain of the Fleet on 23 October 1876. He served at Greenwich in this capacity until his retirement in September 1882. Just prior to his retirement the following note was added to his service record; *"Satisfaction expressed to him at manner in which he has performed duties."* This doesn't read like overwhelming praise but it is the only such mention in any of the earlier chaplains' records I've looked at, so presumably it is greater praise than it sounds. In 1877 he was awarded the degree of Doctor of Divinity by the Archbishop of Canterbury for his services to the Church in the Navy. In June 1888 he was given another honorary appointment, Chaplain to the Queen. He died suddenly at his home in Blackheath Park, South London on 3 March 1900.

Sources: 12-17

DAVIES, Frederick

He was born in Bristol in January 1830 and entered St John's College, Cambridge as a sizar (see Samuel Beal above) in 1853. He was 20th Wrangler when getting his BA in 1857 and he was then appointed as curate of Cautley and Dowbiggin in Yorkshire (1857-60). In addition to his curacy he was an Assistant Master at Sedberg School (1857-60) and was also studying for his masters degree which he obtained in 1860. On 7 March 1860 he qualified for entry to the Navy Chaplain Service and the following month he passed for a Naval Instructor. His first posting was to the warm waters of the Pacific in the steam-augmented *Bacchante* (1860-64). His next ship was *Conquerer* (1864-66, China) which had just taken part in hostilities against the Japanese at the Straights of Shimonoseki. He then joined *Pallas* (1866-69, Channel), a nearly-new ironclad corvette. Next came a technological step backwards to the *Valorous* (1869, North America & West Indies), a wooden paddle ship, and then to *Trafalgar* (1870-72) a sea-going cadet training ship. Here he received *"Their Lordships approbation … at the way in which he has worked out and corrected the observations of the cadets."* His next ship was the *Pembroke*, then Flagship, Commander in Chief at the Nore (1872, Sheerness) but his duties were with the Royal Marines at Deal. He then had two years in *Narcissus* (1872-74) which was the flagship of a so-called 'Flying' or 'Detached Squadron'. In order to cut costs Government policy at the time was to reduce the number of ships on overseas stations and in their place form squadrons of ships that would 'fly the flag' around the world and at the same time provide good training. They were never involved in hostilities but their movements were sometimes used for political purposes. Following this tour he was nominally appointed to *Fisguard* at Woolwich but was actually Chaplain & Mathematical Instructor at the Royal Naval College, Greenwich (1874-79). In 1879 he requested a change of post and was appointed to the training ship *St Vincent* (1879-82, Portsmouth). He was then appointed to the RMA, Eastney where he served from 2 January 1882 to 20 April 1885. His last posting was to *Duke of Wellington*, Flagship of Commander in Chief, Portsmouth. He retired on 22 March 1888 and was living at Lee, Kent, at the time of his death at Hooton, Cheshire on 13 January 1894. He had gone to Neston, Cheshire, with his wife to see their daughter before she left for Burma (Myanmar). They stayed-on in Neston for a few days with their niece before the three of them left on the 11:50

train for Birkenhead. Apparently they had to hurry to catch the train and as soon as the train left the station Reverend Davies became unwell. Despite the attentions of a nurse and a St John's Ambulance-qualified guard he failed to recover and after being carried into the waiting room at Hooton was pronounced dead by the local doctor. An inquest was held at the Greenland Fishery Hotel, Neston, on 15 January where witnesses gave evidence of recent breathlessness and a weak heart. The jury's verdict was death from natural causes.

Sources: 3, 7 & 18-22

HARRIS, William Stuart

Born in Edgbaston, Birmingham on 11 April 1853 he was another chaplain from a modest background as he too was a sizar at Trinity College, Cambridge (see Samuel Beal above). He matriculated in 1873 and obtained his BA in 1877. In between these successes he found time to play at the relatively new game of Association Football. He was good enough to earn his 'blue' and he played in the very first varsity match against Oxford at Kennington Oval on 30 March 1874, which Oxford won 1-0; he was described as being *"a fine goalkeeper"*. He then played in the two subsequent matches in 1875; the first finished 2-0 to Cambridge when he was said to have had *"a good game"* and in the second a much weakened Cambridge side lost 4-1. Cambridge University also played eight FA Cup fixtures in these three seasons and so it is almost certain that he played in some if not all of these as well, but unfortunately no team sheets have survived. After graduating he was ordained as a deacon in 1876 and a priest in 1877. He held the curacies of New Shildon and Staindrop, both in Durham, before joining the Royal Navy as a chaplain on 23 July 1879. His first posting on 19 August 1879 was to *Crocodile* (Indian Troopship) then on 26 April 1880 he was appointed to *Revenge* (Queenstown) until moving to *Euphrates* (troopship) on 31 July 1880 where he earned a warm recommendation from his captain. During this time (1880) he obtained his MA. On 12 August 1881 he was posted to the ironclad *Temeraire* in which he served until 9 July 1886. In July 1882 the *Temeraire* was part of the Mediterranean fleet commanded by Admiral Sir Frederick Seymour that bombarded the forts guarding the entrance to Alexandria harbour in Egypt in what William Laird Clowes in his *The Royal Navy, A History* describes as *"The most serious naval operation in which British men-of-war were engaged during the last quarter of the nineteenth century"*. Serious it might have been but Geoffrey Regan in his *Guinness Book of Naval Blunders* tells how it wasn't quite the success that the Royal Navy claimed.

The eight British battleships involved in the bombardment fired 3,000 heavy shells of which only 10 hit their targets, an indictment of the poor state of naval gunnery at the time. Chaplain Harris was awarded the Egypt Medal with Alexandria Clasp and the Khedive's Bronze Star for this action as were the other seven chaplains in the fleet which included John Cox-Edwards in the flagship *Alexandra* and Arthur Price Hill in *Inflexible*. After this excitement he was paid off from *Temeraire* on 9 July 1886 and married Ellen Emily Twelves on 29 July 1886, a marriage that was to bring him two sons and a daughter. He was then nominally posted to *Royal Adelaide* at Devonport for 68 days leave before joining *Indus* also at Devonport (1886-88). He returned to the Mediterranean in *Alexandra*, flagship of the Duke of Edinburgh, on 6 June 1888 until July 1889 during which period he was judged to be *"..a most excellent Chaplain, a good friend to the Mess, strongly recommended"*. On 29 August 1889 he joined *Iron Duke* (Channel) for about a year and then moved to *Anson* (Channel) in May 1890. On 5 May 1891 it was back to the Mediterranean again, this time as Chaplain to Malta Dockyard and Hospital. His five years there were broken only by a month's loan to *Hawke* in 1894. In July 1896 he returned to England and Haslar Hospital in Gosport. His service record shows him there for five years but an article entitled *The Chaplains' General* in the Navy and Army Illustrated of 28 May 1910 states that he left Haslar for the RMA at Eastney after two years, which ties-in with his baptism records that start in September 1898. Whichever, he completed this appointment at the end of February 1901 and moved nominally to *President* whilst serving at the Admiralty until on 1 March 1901 he was promoted to Chaplain of the Fleet and Inspector of Naval Schools.

This appointment marked a significant development for the Chaplain Service as he was the first holder of the office to be granted the ecclesiastical dignity of Archdeacon. This was conferred by Order in Council on 11 August 1902 and his institution by the Archbishop of Canterbury took place at Lambeth Palace Chapel on 23 October 1902. Meanwhile he had returned to the RMA Church to officiate at a baptism on 9 July 1901 deputising for Chaplain Hill. He gained a further honour by being appointed as Honorary Chaplain to King Edward VII on 26 June 1902 and Honorary Chaplain to King George V on his accession in May 1910, a post he held until his death twenty-five years later. In 1903 he was made an Honorary Doctor of Divinity by

Aberdeen University. He retired from the Navy on 6 October 1906 and became successively; Rector of Deene, Northants (1906-10), Rector of Etwall in Derbyshire (1910-13), Rector of Bucknell in Oxfordshire (1913-18) and curate of Holy Trinity, Brompton, London (1918-20), before being appointed Chaplain at the Church of the Resurrection in Brussels in 1920 where he served until 1923. On his return to the UK he was Chaplain at Smiles' Home for Invalid Ladies at Woking until 1926. He eventually retired to Beene Cottage, Crescent Road, Chandler's Ford in Hampshire where he died on 23 May 1935. He is buried in Peel Road Cemetery, Chandler's Ford, where his grave is unfortunately in a very poor state.
    Sources: 7 & 23-33

HILL, Arthur Price

Born on 26 March 1854 in Canada he was the son of a minister, the Reverend Arthur Hill. He was educated at Sherborne and Westminster Schools before entering Trinity College, Cambridge. His service record tells us that he went to Trinity as a Westminster Exhibitioner (scholarship) and whilst there achieved a 3rd Class in the Classical Tripos and was 1st with honour in a previous exam, but oddly none of this is mentioned in Cambridge Alumni 1261-1900. He graduated with a BA on 22 March 1877 and was ordained as a deacon by the Bishop of Salisbury the following year and as a priest in 1879. He was curate of Downton, Wiltshire (1878-80) before entering the Navy as a chaplain on 14 December 1880. He was commissioned as chaplain *"but subject to conditions contained in a letter of 15 Dec 1880"*. This letter and the conditions imposed on him remain a mystery but presumably are related to his later problems, see below. His first posting was to *Defence* (Coast Guard, Cheshire) where his *"very good knowledge of Latin & Greek"* was acknowledged. This knowledge of the classical languages was also noted during his next posting to *Inflexible* of the Mediterranean Fleet, on 26 July 1881. *Inflexible* was the first Royal Navy ship to be fitted with compound armour and it was on this posting that he saw action at Alexandria, earning the Egypt Medal with Alexandria Clasp (see William Stuart Harris above). On 8 March 1884 he was ordered to Malta Hospital *"to be surveyed ...in accordance with conditions accepted on entry"*. His subsequent medical report stated that *"none of his complaints render him unfit for the duties of a Chaplain now, nor are they likely soon to do as far as we can judge at present"*. He was, therefore, confirmed as Chaplain on 27 March 1884. However, the medical judgement may have been a little hasty as on 13 July 1884 he was apparently invalided as *"beyond control"*. He was 'surveyed' several times before being declared fit and posted to *Repulse* (Coastguard, Hull) on 12 December 1884. There followed postings to *Rupert* (also Coastguard, Hull) on 12 August 1885 and *Monarch* (Channel) on 26 September 1885. Whilst serving on *Monarch* he married Constance Julia Hill (a cousin perhaps) on 17 May 1887 in Worcestershire. On 4 November 1887, less than six months after his marriage, he was appointed as 'additional' initially to *Flora* and later to *Penelope* (both Receiving ships at Cape of Good Hope) for service at Ascension Island (nominally a tender to *Flora/*

Penelope). Presumably he was judged to have made a complete recovery before he was sent to such a remote location. It is not known if his new wife went with him. Before leaving for Ascension Island he officiated at an adult baptism at Eastney on 14 August 1887, deputising for Chaplain Morton, presumably he was on leave after his marriage and awaiting embarkation for the south Atlantic.

He arrived back in England on 17 December 1890 and was given 42 days leave on full pay whilst on the 'strength' of *Duke of Wellington* in Portsmouth. His next posting was to *Northumberland* (1st reserve ship) but less than three months later, on 8 March 1891, he was transferred to *Alexandra* (Coastguard, Portland), where he was judged *"a most excellent Chaplain"*. On 18 August 1893 he was moved to Haslar Hospital where he served for nearly three years before being posted to the Dockyard & Hospital at Cape of Good Hope on 7 April 1896. On his return to England on 30 May 1901 he was appointed to the RMA Church at Eastney and performed his first baptism there on 9 Jun 1901. He was well-regarded by Colonel Campbell who first commented that he was *"Regular in visiting the school & sick and of great assistance in reporting cases of distress requiring help from local funds"* and then later *"Excellent and has great influence with the men"*. On 1 March 1903 he baptised his own daughter Enid Price Hill. At the beginning of August 1905 he moved across the city to the Dockyard where he served for five years until his retirement on 1 August 1910. Just prior to his retirement he had been given permission to accept the post of Chaplain to the Legation at Vienna. He served two periods in Vienna the first from 1910 to 1914 and the second from 1920 until his death there on 28 November 1924.

Reverend Hill's medals (Egypt Medal, Alexandria clasp; Queen's South Africa Medal, Cape Colony clasp & Khedive's Star) are in the RM Museum collection.

Sources: 7 & 34-35

KENAH, Samuel

Born in Cork on 26 December 1840 he was the son of William Kenah, a surgeon. Initially educated at Queen's College, Cork, he entered Trinity College, Dublin as a sizar (see Samuel Beal) in June 1860 and graduated as *"First Honour Man and First Respondent"* in the BA degree examination in 1863 and subsequently gained an MA. He became a deacon in 1864 and was ordained as a priest in 1865. He held the curacies of Kildallon, County Cavan, Ireland, 1864-65; Bradford, Yorkshire, 1865-66; St Luke, Sheffield, 1866 and St John the Baptist, Nottingham, 1866-67, before enlisting as a Chaplain and Naval Instructor in 1867 when he gave his address as 37, King Street, Cork. His first appointment was to *Bristol*, Commodore Hornby's flagship for the west coast of Africa (1867-68). He then served in *Defence*, *Northumberland* and *Volage* all in home waters before returning to warmer waters in 1870 to serve in *Rattlesnake*, the flagship for the Cape of Good Hope and west coast of Africa (1870-74). He saw active service during this posting in the third Anglo-Ashanti War, 1873-4, for which he was awarded the Ashanti Medal. In 1874 he joined *Narcissus* which was part of a six ship flying or detached squadron (see Frederick Davies) whose itinerary for the next three years was Gibraltar, Madeira, St Vincent, Montevideo, Falkland Islands, Cape of Good Hope, St Helena, Ascension and back again to Gibraltar. Following this tour of the Atlantic he was granted a well earned six weeks leave before being appointed to *Ganges*, a boys training ship at Falmouth, on 17 July 1877. He was then appointed to *Alexandra*, flagship of Vice-Admiral Seymour in the Mediterranean (1879-1882) before returning to Dartmouth and the cadet training ship *Brittania* (1882-88). In 1888 he moved to Portsmouth for the training ship *St Vincent*, before being appointed to the RMA, Eastney on 29 August 1889. He spent five years at Eastney until on 1 October 1894 he was appointed Chaplain of Greenwich Hospital and School where he served until retirement on 5 October 1899. He lived the rest of his years in south London, first at Lewisham and then at Blackheath, were he died on 23 October 1911.

Sources: 36-39

LLOYD, William Valentine

Born on 14 February 1825 and educated at Trinity College, Dublin, he moved to Canada shortly after graduating and was later ordained as a deacon by the Bishop of Montreal and, on 15 June 1851, as a priest by the Bishop of Quebec. In 1850 he married well, to the Hon. Caroline Amelia Sophia Aylmer, a descendant of Barons and Lords Aylmer, her eldest brother became Baron Aylmer in 1867. He returned to England to join the Navy Chaplain Service in 1858. His first posting was to *Blenheim*, serving coast guard duties off Portland (1858-59); he then moved to the cadet training ship *Brittania* (1859-60) followed by *Melpomene* of the Channel Fleet (1860-63). In 1860 he had failed his first attempt at the examination for Naval Instructor but passed on his second attempt. In March 1863 he was appointed to *Emerald*, also Channel Fleet, just too late for the excitement of welcoming Princess Alexandra of Denmark to London for her marriage to Prince Albert Edward (later King Edward VII), but he was in time for some experimental trials of new screws (propellers) in the Solent, including numerous speed trials over the measured mile in Stokes Bay. On 1 October 1863 his career took him away from England for the first time as a chaplain, and he couldn't have gone much farther; his new ship *Scylla* was bound for China Station. On 27 November 1866 he was invalided (cause unknown) and by 8 January 1867 he was on his way back to England with the extra responsibility of looking after a group of Japanese students for the Foreign Office. On arrival, presumably because of his health, he was 'lent' to the Foreign Office to direct the studies of the Japanese students for the two years they were in England. This duty ended in December 1868 with a strong recommendation from the Foreign Office, but this didn't stop the Admiralty refusing for this time to count as full pay towards his pension. He was then appointed to the gunnery training ship *Cambridge* at Devonport (1869) and then to *Royal Adelaide*, flagship of the Admiral, Devonport (1869-72). He moved back to Portsmouth for service in *Duke of Wellington* and then *St Vincent* (training ship, 1873-75). On 15 March 1875 he was appointed to *Sultan*. In February 1878 *Sultan* was part of Admiral Hornby's squadron that 'forced' a passage through the Dardanelles contrary to the London Straights Treaty which restricted such passage in peacetime to ships of the Ottoman Navy. This flaunting of the Treaty was a British reaction to the Russo-Turkish War. On 8 May 1879 *Sultan* was back in Malta Dockyard where her crew was transferred to *Black Prince* due to the former's boilers being worn out. *Black Prince* was a state-of-the-art warship and sister ship to *Warrior* and the captain of both *Sultan* and *Black Prince* was the then Duke of Edinburgh, Prince Alfred Ernest Albert, Duke of Saxe-Coburg and Gotha, second son of Queen Victoria and Prince Albert. The *Black Prince* although nominally part of the Channel Fleet in 1878 was actually serving in the Mediterranean.

Reverend Lloyd and his royal captain must have hit it off as in addition to becoming the Duke's private chaplain Lloyd was granted leave in October 1878 to *"..christen the Duke of Edinburgh's child"*. The child was Princess Alexandra of Hohenlohe-Langenburg, who was born on 1 September 1878 in the family castle of Rosenau, Coburg, Germany; so presumably Reverend Lloyd made the considerable journey to northern Germany and back to the Mediterranean on his 'holiday'. On 20 May 1880 he was to be posted nominally to *Duke of Wellington* for duty at the RMA Church, Eastney, but this was cancelled and he was given a Warrant appointing him directly to Eastney Barracks. All subsequent Chaplains were posted directly to Eastney rather than a nominal posting to *Duke of Wellington*, *Victory* or Portsmouth Dockyard as had previously been the custom. He must have been a keen horseman as almost immediately he applied for a forage allowance but this was denied. His last baptism at the RMA Church was on 25 December 1881 and he formally retired on 31 December that year and became Rector of Hazelbeach, Northampton. He died in Leamington Spa on 17 June 1896, aged 71.

Sources: 3 & 40-45

MORTON, Thomas Fitzhardinge

He was born on 28 September 1837 the son of Edward Morton of Hyde Park, London. He arrived at Christ's College, Cambridge from King's College, London in 1858. However, his BA (1862) and MA (1865) were awarded by Trinity College. In the meantime he had been ordained as a deacon in 1861 and a priest in 1862. He held curacies at Doncaster, followed by St Michael's, Handsworth in Staffordshire and Brightstone, Isle of Wight, before joining the Navy Chaplain Service on 16 June 1868. He immediately set off for North America and the West Indies in *Constance*, the first Royal Navy ship to be driven by a compound steam engine, and then returned to British waters for duty in *Valiant* (1869). In 1870 he was off with *Ocean* to serve at the China Station and eighteen months later transferred to *Princess Charlotte* at Hong Kong where his duties included being chaplain of the naval hospital ship *Melville* (1871-74). He then returned to home waters serving in *Penelope* (1874-76) and then he returned to the North America and the West Indies station with the newly recommissioned *Bellerophon* (1876-78). This posting ended in the autumn of

1878 when he was invalided for three months before joining *Revenge*, the flagship of the Port Admiral, Queenstown, Jamaica (1878-80). In April 1880 he was appointed as chaplain to Malta Dockyard and Hospital where, although showing some signs of a delicate health, he stayed until the end of February 1883. He then returned to England for a posting to the Royal Marines, Chatham Division for two years during which period he was involved in a dispute with the Colonel Commandant of sufficient severity to warrant a Court of Inquiry. Unfortunately the relevant papers have not survived but the incident may well have prompted his transfer to the RMA Church, Eastney on 10 April 1885. On 29 August 1889 he moved across Portsmouth Harbour to the Royal Marine Division at Forton for a few months before becoming chaplain of Portsmouth Dockyard, where he served until retiring on 20 December 1895. He died a bachelor in Naples on 11 November 1902.

Sources: 7, 35 & 46-48

PLANT, Arthur William

Born on 19 September 1858 in Lincoln, the son of Thomas Plant, he was educated first at Surrey County School in Cranleigh and then at Magdalene College, Cambridge where he gained his BA in 1882 and his MA in 1886 according to *Cambridge University Alumni 1261-1900* but 1881 and 1885 respectively according to his Service Record. He returned to Surrey and Cranleigh School for five years as an Assistant Master (1881-1886). Meanwhile he was ordained as a deacon in 1883 and a priest in 1885. He moved from Cranleigh to become curate of St Michael and All Angels, Southsea from 1886-1888 and joined the Chaplain Service on 18 December 1888. His first posting was to *Colossus* of the Mediterranean fleet in February 1889 but he was invalided home and three months later joined the Channel fleet to serve in *Northumberland* (1890) and *Howe* (1890-1892) before joining *Defiance* (June 1892). *Defiance* was then the Torpedo and Mining School at Plymouth but in 1861 had been the last wooden battleship to be launched in Britain, although she was never fitted for sea service. He then served in *Nile* (1893-96) of the Mediterranean fleet before moving to the cadet training ship *Brittania* at Dartmouth on 1 September 1896 where he served until January 1902. He then went overseas again to Malta Dockyard and Hospital until returning to England and the RMA Church at Eastney on 1 August 1905. He was the last chaplain to officiate in the Crinoline Church and the first in the new St Andrew's in Henderson Road. Unfortunately he made no reference in the baptism register indicating which were the last and first baptisms and we can only speculate from other sources that the change took place about November 1905 (see Chapter 1, Third Life – The Last Resting Place). In November 1909 he left Eastney for Sheerness Dockyard, serving there until 1910. Whilst at Sheerness he married Eva Coelina Valentine in London, they were both in their 50s. He then moved to Portsmouth Dockyard for four years until 13 February 1914 when he was placed on the retired list at his own request. At this time he was living in St David's Road, Southsea. However, the declaration of war against Germany on 4 August 1914 changed his retirement plans and he returned in September 1914 to serve at RN College, Dartmouth for a year and then RN Barracks, Devonport, until finally retiring on 22 August 1916 at the age of 65. He then became chaplain at Little Berwick, Shropshire before becoming vicar of Bayford, Herts, until finally retiring in 1921. In 1911 he had been appointed as Chaplain to the King, a post he held until his death. He had been living at Hyde Park, London when he died in Notting Hill on 3 June 1938, aged 79.

Sources: 3, 7, 35 & 49-51

ROBSON, James Stuart

He was born on 23 February 1815 at Holdacres, Yorkshire and although it was transcribed onto his last Service Register that he gained his BA at "University College, Dublin" he was in fact an alumni of Durham.

He was ordained as a deacon on 23 July 1843 and as a priest on 30 June 1844 and became assistant curate at Corsenside, Northumberland. He became a Navy chaplain on 31 January 1848 making him the most senior of all the Crinoline Church's chaplains. His first posting was to *Prince Regent* (1848-49, Channel), a first-rate sailing ship originally launched in 1823. He was then nominally posted to *Ceylon* (receiving ship Malta) in order to serve at Malta Hospital (1849-54). This he did for over four years before moving to Malta Dockyard. In 1854 he joined the fourth-rate sailing ship *Leander* at his own request. This move was to ensure that he had sufficient 'sea time' for his pension and took him to the Black Sea during the Crimean War, where he saw action off Eupatoria and was awarded the Order of the Mejidie, 5th Class, from the Ottoman Empire. This Order was awarded to many British officers who served during the conflict.

Following his return from the Black Sea on 25 July 1856 he was allowed to take the position of chaplain to the Government Convict Establishment at Bermuda; this entailed him accepting half-pay (7 shillings and six pence, or 38p, a day) as being nominally retired from the Navy, but this would have been in addition to his stipend at Bermuda. He then returned to the UK and was appointed to *Asia* (1860-62, Portsmouth). He was then appointed to the living of Thorneyburn where he stayed for six months before returning briefly to *Asia*. Then on 7 November 1866 he was appointed as 'additional' to *Wellesley* at Chatham Dockyard for service with Chatham Marines. In March 1871 it was recorded that he *"represents that he cannot carry on duties alone unless helped by Mr Schon who is consequently to be retained."* Reverend James Frederick Schon was chaplain of Melville Hospital in Chatham and so he must have been assisting Reverend Robson in addition to his own duties. Reverend Robson's appointment had been for five years but on 9 August 1871 he was moved to *Duke of Wellington* at Portsmouth for service with the Royal Marine Artillery. Three months after his posting to Eastney he was granted permission to reside in Field Officers' Quarters in the Barracks ousting Lieutenant Colonel Alexander onto the 'lodging list'. Reverend Robson was also provided with an official issue of furniture;

so perhaps he had some infirmity. Infirmity or not he was able to perform 220 baptisms at Eastney before his retirement in 1875. After retiring from the Navy he went on to be chaplain of Malling Union in Kent for five years and finally curate of Ash, Sevenoaks until 1881.

He returned to the RMA Church to perform a single baptism on 26 November 1881. At that time he was staying with his wife at the Royal Beach Mansions Hotel in Southsea, presumably on holiday. He died in Maidstone, Kent on 30 January 1891.

Sources: 3, 35 & 52-59

WILLIAMS, Edward Adams

His service records state that he was born in 1823 but his entry in *Who Was Who* gives his birth date as 26 March 1826 which ties-in with the inscription on his headstone. He graduated from Trinity College, Dublin (ultimately becoming a MA) and went straight into the church, being made a deacon in 1849 and ordained as a priest on 22 September 1850. He was a curate at Lye near Stourbridge and at Calne, Wiltshire before becoming a naval chaplain in March 1854. His first posting was to the first-rate sailing ship *St George* which was part of Lord Napier's Baltic fleet in the Crimean War and he was present at the Bombardment of the Forts at Dunamunde, near Riga (Baltic Campaign medal). Then, after six months on the gunnery ship *Excellent* at Portsmouth, where he passed as a Naval Instructor in November 1854, he was posted to *Hawke* (1855-56, Coast Guard, Queenstown). On return from Queenstown he was appointed to *Pearl*. It was with this posting to *Pearl* on 3 May 1856 that his big adventure began. *Pearl* was the first of a new class of converted wooden 21-gun corvettes and she was due to join the Baltic fleet. However, the Crimean War ended before she was ready to sail and she was re-allocated to the South America and Pacific station. She left Portsmouth on 30 May 1856 and did not return until 6 June 1859, making a circumnavigation that was broken by about eighteen months spent in Calcutta whilst Reverend Williams was part of a Naval Brigade that fought important actions during the Indian Mutiny. The voyage and the Indian actions were recorded by Reverend Williams in his journal which was published soon after he returned to England as *"The Cruise of the Pearl, with an account of the operations of the Naval Brigade in India, 1857-1858"*. This evocative account has been reprinted in facsimile and is essential reading for anyone interested in Victorian military history.

The story in outline is as follows. After setting off from Portsmouth the *Pearl* called at Rio de Janeiro, passed through the Magellan Straits and steamed up the west coast of South America before setting off across the south Pacific to Honolulu, arriving there in May 1857. By this time war had been declared against China and *Pearl* was sent to reinforce the China Station fleet, arriving at Hong Kong on 19 June 1857. However, before *Pearl* could play any part in the war against China news came through about the atrocities of the Indian Mutiny and *Pearl*, along with *Shannon*, was immediately dispatched to Calcutta. At Singapore *Pearl* took on board troops of the

90th Regiment and arrived at Calcutta on 11 August having lost three days waiting at the mouth of the Ganges for a pilot. *Pearl* was at Calcutta for about a month before a Naval Brigade under Captain Sotheby consisting of 158 seaman and marines and some artillery, set off up the Ganges and then on up the Gogra (now Ghaghara). They embarked on an old steamship called the *Chunar* on 12 September 1857 eventually reaching the fort at Buxar on 10 October and then moving on to Chupra Ghat by 26 October. Here the men, artillery, ammunition and baggage were landed. For the next year or so the *Pearl's* naval brigade was criss-crossing northern India in pursuit of the rebels, often marching upwards of 20 miles a day in temperatures of 40°C. They fought many actions both large and small with the main campaigns known as Oudh, Amorha and Tirhoot. Reverend Williams and his compatriots all earned the India Medal for these actions. Although reinforced by a regiment of Gurkhas and a troop of the Bengal Yeomanry Cavalry they were still often outnumbered ten to one or more but throughout the campaign lost just one officer out of nineteen from the *Pearl's* brigade. At Amorha the brigade and its associates, consisting of 1261 men and four guns, was attacked by 14,000 men with ten guns, but suffered just one killed and 15 wounded.

Reverend Williams' account is very self-effacing and none of it is written in the first person but is related as a description of what happened with only one mention of his personal action, that of him performing burial rites for some of the killed. Although he admits that some of the account is drawn from the reports of others, it is clear that this probably relates to some of the skirmishing actions that took place away from the main body of troops and that in fact he was very close to, if not among, the action for most of the time. His commanding officer, Captain Sotheby, mentioned him in his despatches in the London Gazette on more than one occasion, specifically how he helped the surgeon to deal with the wounded.

After being paid-off from *Pearl* he joined *Emerald* (Home) on 24 June 1859 for over a year; there then followed spells in *Royal Adelaide* (1860-62, Plymouth/ Devonport) and *Impregnable* (1862-65, Plymouth Harbour) before he was sent to North America & West Indies in *Cadmus* on 28 February 1865. In 1868 he returned to Portsmouth and the gunnery ship *Excellent* as Chaplain & Naval Instructor. On 1 August 1873 he was appointed to the training ship *St Vincent* but this was cancelled and on 18 December 1873 he was nominally appointed to *Nankin* for service as chaplain to Pembroke Dockyard. During the period 1872-75 he was also Associate Secretary of the Church Missionary Society. On 6 March 1875 he moved to *Duke of Wellington* at Portsmouth for service with the RMA at Eastney where he stayed until May 1880. In June 1875 he was granted six weeks leave and permission to travel to the Continent due to the ill-health of his wife. After leaving Eastney he had service at Sheerness (1880-81) and Portsmouth (1881-86) Dockyards until he retired on 5 March 1886. It was in 1885 while at Portsmouth Dockyard that he upset the Admiral Superintendant, Rear Admiral Herbert, by deliberately denouncing the misbehaviour of some trainee engineers from the pulpit. A report was made to the

Admiralty but their Lordships were *"not prepared to censure the conduct of Mr Williams in the circumstances referred to."*

He retired in 1886 and moved to London to live at Westbourne Place, Eton Square, but about 1891 he returned to Southsea to live at 5, Queen's Gate, and he died there on 13 April 1913, aged 87. He is buried in Highland Road cemetery with his wife, Jane Ann, who died, aged 57, on 15 November 1907. In 1898 he was appointed as Honorary Chaplain to the Queen, and following Queen Victoria's death, Chaplain to King Edward VII and finally to King George V with effect from the date of his accession, 30 May 1910.

Sources: 3, 31, 35 & 60-68

YORK, Charles Edward

He was born on 16 February 1842 the son of Samuel York a prosperous linen draper of Penzance, Cornwall. He passed matriculation at Pembroke College, Oxford at the age of 18 and gained a BA in 1864 and a MA in 1867. He held the curacies of Charlbury, Oxford (1871-2) and Bembridge, Isle of Wight (1872) before qualifying as a Chaplain and Naval Instructor on 20 August 1872. He was appointed to the Indian troopship *Crocodile* on 14 October 1872 and then in April 1874 to *London* at Zanzibar, but this was cancelled for some reason and he was appointed temporarily to *Pembroke* for service with the Royal Marine Division at Chatham. This appointment only lasted six weeks

and he returned to *Crocodile* (1874-75). The Indian troopship, *Serapis*, was his next posting on 26 July 1875. *Serapis* led the squadron that took the Prince of Wales on a grand tour of India and had been specially adapted to carry her royal passenger. The internal amendments to the ship included a 'state' bedroom and stabling and a treadmill-like exercise machine for the Prince's horses.

A picture of the ships officers that appeared in the Illustrated

HMS Serapis returns: coming alongside the jetty at Portsmouth, 1876 [69]

London News of 9 October 1875 shows Chaplain York sporting a very substantial beard. The Captain, The Honorable Henry C Glyn, clearly took a liberal view of Queen's Regulations that demanded that beards be *"kept well cut and trimmed, and not too long for cleanliness."* Also in the picture are RMA Captain Walter Lambert (later Lieutenant Colonel) who was among the first recipients of the DSO for his services in Burma (Myanmar) during 1885-86, and, as a junior Sub-Lieutenant, His Serene Highness Prince Louis of Battenburg.

Officers of HMS Serapis with the ghostly presence of the Prince of Wales in the background. Chaplain York is unmistakable. The Royal Marine Artillery officer to the left of centre is Captain Walter Lambert. At the extreme left of the front row is Sub-Lieutenant His Serene Highness Prince Louis of Battenburg.[70]

Following his royal tour in June 1876 Chaplain York joined *Monarch* (Mediterranean). In August 1877 he was appointed to the paddle ship *Temeraire* which was part of the squadron that Admiral Hornby (in *Alexandra*) took through the Dardanelles in February 1878 (see Chaplain Lloyd above). On 14 November 1878 he was lent to Malta Dockyard and Hospital. He returned to *Temeraire* in February 1879 but was invalided home on 10 April 1880 arriving in England on 2 June. The nature of his invalidity is not recorded and on 17 December 1880 he was appointed to be Chaplain of Greenwich Hospital School *"at a salary of £200 a year with an official residence but no allowances"*. Although originally appointed for a period "not to exceed 5 years" he wasn't posted again until 1 October 1889 when he moved to the Royal Marine Division at Forton, Gosport. Five years later, on 1 October 1894, he was moved to RMA Eastney where he stayed until retiring on 1 October 1898. He stayed on in Southsea, living at 16, Clarence Parade, until he died at the age of 66 on 19 December 1908.

His legacy to the Chaplain Service was his *Handbook for Naval Chaplains*, published in 1904 after he retired. The book, which was written in consultation with many of his fellow chaplains, covered everything that a chaplain needed to know and even included twenty-five nautical songs, presumably with the 'official' lyrics only! The Admiralty refused to issue the book officially but had no objection to Reverend York issuing it as a private work at his own expense. Unfortunately

I have been unable to locate a surviving copy.

In 1911 his navy and civilian friends installed a commemorative window in his honour in the Memorial Chapel of the Chapel of St Peter and St Paul at the Old Royal Naval College, Greenwich; the subject was the crucifixion. The window was destroyed in WW2 but the

Plaque in the Memorial Chapel of the Chapel of St Peter and St Paul at the Old Royal Naval College, Greenwich [77]

plaque that was fixed under it survives. His widow Amelia Annie lived to the age of 90 and died on 18 May 1938. They are buried together in Highland Road Cemetery, Southsea.

Sources: 3, 33 & 69-77

Chapter 6 - The Deputy Chaplains' Biographies

These ministers, civilian and military, fall into several categories. There are those who were living locally, either active or retired; there are those who were performing the ceremony for a family member; and there are several baptisms that were performed elsewhere, including overseas, and added to the RMA Church register at a later date. I have tried to identify why the particular priest was a stand-in but on a number of occasions I could find no obvious relationship between the priest, the family or the RMA to explain their appearance in the register. I have looked at their published church careers, census returns and sometimes birth, marriage and death registers but if I haven't found the link by those processes then I have left it for other researchers to find. No doubt in some cases a family researcher will know the link.

ADAM, Stephen Condon

Reverend Stephen Condon Adam was almost certainly the brother of the father, Fleet Surgeon William Hogarth Adam. Fleet Surgeon Adam was living in the RMA Barracks with his family at the time of the 1881 census. Reverend Adam had studied at St John's College, Cambridge and graduated in 1858 and got his MA in 1861. He was ordained as a deacon in 1858 and was curate of Holy Trinity, Sheffield (1858-59). In 1859 he was ordained as a priest and became the Associate Secretary for the Irish Church Mission. In 1869 he became the vicar of St Jude, Wolverhampton, and was still serving there at the time of this his only baptism in the RMA Church.

Sources: 1-4

ALLCOCK, J

There are two baptisms on 27 January 1884 attributed to J Allcock, for the children of Sergeants Thacker and Hartnall, so this would seem to rule out a family connection. There is only one J Allcock in Crockford's Clerical Directory and The Clergy List about this time and that is John Allcock, who was listed as being at Baddegama, Ceylon (Sri Lanka) in 1884 and 1888; so it is conceivable that he was travelling through Portsmouth in 1884. The register entries were made in the hand of Reverend Davies, presumably when he returned, and so we must consider the possibility that he miss-spelt the name. There are six J Alcocks in the clergy listings at this time, but none of them living in the vicinity or having any obvious link with the RMA or Southsea. If he was on holiday in the area then he was staying in modest accommodation or with friends or family as there are no visitors called Alcock or Allcock mentioned in the *"Southsea Visitors"* column of the Hampshire Telegraph. His identification remains a mystery.

ANDERSON, Thomas W

Mr Anderson is an imposter here but through no fault of his own. He was not a minister at all but a retired grocer who was also Registrar for the Woolwich Registration District. It would appear that Gunner Butler and his wife Amelia registered their daughter's birth in Woolwich and then, possibly believing that registration and baptism were one and the same, had the event added to the RMA Church register on 16 December 1895. The entry is not in his hand but why Chaplain York didn't put them right when he saw it and insist on a proper baptism is a mystery.

Sources: 5-6

BARBER, William Davin

The three baptisms attributed to Reverend Barber all took place at St Saviour's, Victoria West, British Columbia, Canada. Reverend Barber was Rector of St Saviour's, which served as the local garrison church for the RN Dockyard at Esquimalt. He graduated from St John's College, Manitoba with a 1st in Modern Languages and became a deacon in 1887 and was ordained as a priest in 1888. He served in the Diocese of British Columbia from March 1890 until October 1904 when he resigned due to ill health.

Source: 7

BAYLISS, William Wyke

Born 9 January 1834 in Shropshire, he was educated at St John's College, Cambridge where he gained a BA in 1859 and a MA in 1862. He was ordained as a priest in 1860 and held a number of incumbencies including being curate and later vicar of St James's, Milton, Portsmouth, from 1865 to 1877; during which period he officiated at the RMA Church. It was in 1867 that he served a letter on Reverend Cawston forbidding baptisms in the RMA Church; this was eventually resolved by the Army Chaplains Act 1868 (see Chapter 1, Third Life – The Last Resting Place). In 1877 he moved away from Hampshire before returning in 1884 as Rector of the Church of the Blessed Mary, Upham, Bishop's Waltham. He died at Upham, age 55, on 5 December 1889 and is buried in the churchyard there along with his wife and two of their five children.

Sources: 8-9

BISHOP, Frederick William Freemantle

He was born about 1860 in Grazeley, Berkshire, where his father Reverend Freeman Bishop was the incumbent. He studied at Trinity Hall, Cambridge, graduating in 1881 and gaining a MA in 1885. He was ordained as a priest in 1884. He was the curate at Roath, Cardiff when he officiated at the RMA Church on 10 July 1885 at the baptism of his brother's daughter. His brother was Lieutenant Charles Lewis Nepean Bishop, RMA; they had been at Charterhouse School together.

Sources: 8 & 10-11

BOYCE, Wilfred Anderdon

He was born on 22 September 1849 in Godalming, Surrey, the son of Reverend Edward Jacob Boyce, later rector of Houghton, Hants. He graduated from Trinity College, Cambridge in 1872 and was ordained as a priest at Winchester in 1874. After a period as curate of St Mark's, Surbiton, Surrey, he returned to Hampshire where he remained for the rest of his life. Firstly he served as curate at Shalford from 1876-84, then as vicar of Ecchinswell with Sydmonton from 1884 to 1918. He then moved a few miles to become Rector of Litchfield, a post he held until his death there on 23 December 1935 at the age of 87. We must presume that he was on holiday in the Southsea area from late April to the end of May 1887 when he deputised at the RMA Church, although he doesn't appear in the *"Southsea Visitors"* column of the Hampshire Telegraph between those dates.

Sources: 8

CLARK, Charles

He was born on 18 June 1831 at Chichester, Sussex and was educated at King's College, London. He became a deacon in 1862 and was ordained as a priest by the Bishop of Winchester in 1863. He joined the Navy Chaplain Service in 1865 and subsequently qualified as a Naval Instructor. He saw service in *Resistance* (1865, Mediterranean), *Cumberland* (1867, Sheerness), Malta Dockyard, Prison & Hospital (1868), *Jumna* (1870, Indian Troopship, Portsmouth), *Glasgow* (1871, Flagship East Indies), *Jumna* again (1871), *Hector* (1874, Coastguard), Hong Kong Hospital (1877) and *Revenge* (1880, Queenstown). In March 1881 he took the post of chaplain to Haulbowline Hospital also in Queenstown (Cobh), Ireland, but a year later he was off to the naval establishments at Cape of Good Hope. In August 1885 he came home to the post at Haslar Hospital until July 1886 when he was appointed to the Admiralty living of Greystead and placed on the retired list. However, this was rescinded at his own request and he later took up the post of chaplain to Lewes Prison in Sussex until he finally accepted retirement and the living at Greystead in June 1891. For some reason he was only at Greystead for three months until he resigned the appointment. He was then without a living until becoming vicar of Kimmeridge in Dorset in 1893. A year later he was appointed Rector of Cowthorpe, near Wetherby, where he served until 1902. It was not until 1901 that his marriage to Matilda Botwood at Craig Flower, Vancouver Island, Canada, was added to his service record even though the marriage had taken place on 7 August 1856. He died in Ipswich on 23 January 1907.

At the time of his baptisms on 28 September 1873 he was 'between ships' having been paid off from *Jumna* on 30 June 1873.

Sources: 12-15

CORBETT, Richard Alfred

Born in Ireland about 1846, he was educated at Hertford College, Oxford, gaining a BA in 1870 and a MA in 1876. Meanwhile he was ordained a priest in 1871 and after a short spell as a curate he joined the Army Chaplain Service later the same year. He served in the Ashanti War of 1873-4 (Medal); the Zulu War of 1879 including the engagement at Ulundi (South Africa Medal with clasp); and the Egyptian War of 1882, being present at the battle of Tel el-Kebir (Medal with clasp and the Khedive's Star). He also served at Aldershot, Portsmouth, Woolwich, Dublin and London. He was chaplain at Cairo from 1886 to 1888 when he retired and became rector of Astbury, Congleton, Cheshire. He was made the Rural Dean of Congleton in 1904 and died in Astbury on 30 August 1912.

At the time he performed his baptisms in the RMA Church (May 1871) he was stationed at Army Barracks in Portsmouth.

Sources: 9 & 16-18

COTESWORTH, Gilfillan

Born in 1857 in Walthamstow, London, he achieved a MA at Cambridge (Trinity College) and was ordained as a priest in 1881. He held various curacies including St Jude's, Southsea (1879-82) and was later vicar of Farnborough in Hampshire (1896-1903). The parents of the child he baptised on 26 April 1905 were Major Herbert Slessor and his wife Winifred Mary. They were married in December 1902 and her maiden name was Cotesworth, so she was certainly a relative, possibly a cousin.

Sources: 8 & 19-20

COX-EDWARDS, John

Born in Market Bosworth, Leicestershire on 17 January 1839, he was educated at Emmanuel College, Cambridge gaining a BA in 1861 and a MA in 1864. He held several curacies before joining the Navy Chaplain Service in 1871. His postings included the newly completed *Iron Duke* (1871, China) then, *Vanguard* (1874, Coastguard Ireland), *Sapphire* (1875, Australia), *Royal Adelaide* (1879, Devonport), *Alexandra* (1882, Mediterranean), *Ganges* (1883, Falmouth), *Impregnable* (1883, Devonport) and Portsmouth Dockyard (1886). During his spell on the flagship *Alexandra* he saw active service at the Bombardment of Alexandria where he went ashore with the Naval Brigade; for this he was awarded the Egyptian Medal with the 'Alexandria' Clasp, and the Khedive's Bronze Star. In 1888 he was appointed Chaplain of the Fleet

and Inspector of Naval Schools in which capacity he served until retiring in January 1899. Ironically he had only qualified as a 2nd class Naval Instructor in 1871, falling seven marks short of a 1st class pass due to a poor showing on the *"Name and use of parts of the Steam Engine and Boiler"* and *"The Theory of Navigation"*. In March 1896 he was appointed as Honorary Chaplain to Queen Victoria and continued to serve in this role with her successors King Edward and King George until 1910. After retiring in 1900 he became Rector of Ecton near Northampton until 1908. Much later in about 1925 he returned to Southsea and lived at 11, St David's Road and he died there on 25 March 1926, aged 87. He was buried at Christ Church, Widley and his unmarried daughter Maude was buried with him there in 1929. Originally John Cox Edwards he adopted the hyphenated form in 1882.

He was between postings (*Valorous* & *Sapphire*) when he stood-in for Reverend Williams in July and August 1875.

Sources: 8, 21-25 & 48

EVANS, Edward William

Born in Denbighshire, North Wales in 1852 he studied for a Licentiate of Theology at Durham and became a deacon in 1878 and a priest in 1879. He was Rector of Beverston, Gloucestershire at the time of his baptisms in the RMA Church. The register is annotated *"Retd. Chaplain"* and he was, according to Crockford's Clerical Directory, an "acting chaplain to the Forces" for the period 1890-1896 whilst vicar of Maker, near Plymouth. As he does not appear in the Navy service records or in the Navy Lists he was presumably a civilian priest administering to the Navy at Plymouth. There is no clear reason why he performed the baptisms at Eastney in August and December 1899.

Sources: 26-27

FALWASSER, John Frederick

Born in 1831 in Florence, Italy, (his father was in the Army) he was educated at St John's College, Cambridge, gaining a BA in 1854 and a MA in 1858. He was ordained as a priest in 1856 and held a number of curacies before becoming vicar of Holy Trinity, Privett, near Alton, Hampshire, in 1873. He died there on 6 March 1890 and is buried in the churchyard. There is no obvious link with the family whose child he baptised on 25 August 1878 but at the time he was staying at 'Cairnleigh', Alhambra Road, Southsea, with his wife, presumably on holiday.

Sources: 8 & 28-29

GOOD, Edward Henry

Born on 12 December 1862, he attended Brasenose College, Oxford from where he graduated in 1885 and gained a MA in 1889. He was made a deacon in 1885 and was ordained as a priest in 1886. He held curacies at Stamfordham, Newcastle upon Tyne; St John, Hackney, London, and St Stephen, Westbourne Park, London, before he joined the Navy Chaplain Service on 27 February 1893. He had a varied career serving in a succession of ships and shore establishments including *Edgar* (1893-96, Mediterranean), *Warspite* (1896-97, Queenstown, Ireland), *Howe* (1897, Queenstown), *Calliope* (1897, Home), *Collingwood* (1897-98, Coastguard, Ireland), *Pembroke* (1898-1900, Chatham), Hong Kong Dockyard & Hospital (1900-02), *Vernon* (1903-04, Portsmouth) and RN Engineering College, Keyham, Devonport (1904-06). He married Winifred Amy Aylen in St Stephen's, Birkenhead on 10 August 1905 before further postings to Cape of Good Hope Dockyard (1906-11), *Defence* (1911-12, Home), RN Barracks, Devonport and *Actaeon* (Nore) both in 1912 and finally Devonport Dockyard (1912-13). His service record includes the following comment from Captain Bruce (1912); *"In every way what a Naval Chaplain should be"*. He was placed on the retired list on 1 July 1913 and he then became Rector at Stoke Bruerne with Shutlanger in Northants, a living in the gift of his alma mater Brasenose College; he served there until 1927. He retired to Angmering-on-Sea in Sussex where he died on 25 December 1931.

It was during his posting to the RN Engineering College at Devonport that he deputised for Reverend Hill on 10 April 1904, so he must have been in Portsmouth on leave or official business at the time.

Sources: 9, 16 & 30-31

HARVEY, William J

Born in Portsmouth in 1859 his father was an accountant/cashier in the Dockyard. He attended St John's College, Cambridge were he gained a BA in 1882 and a MA in 1888. He was ordained as a priest in 1883. In 1884 when his baptisms were recorded he was moving from being curate of St Patrick's, Hove, Sussex, to Great Amwell, near Ware, Hertfordshire. His immediate family had moved to Sheerness (1881) and then to Woolwich (1891), so he must have either been on holiday or visiting other relatives in Portsmouth when he officiated at the RMA Church.

Sources: 8 & 32-33

HUGHES, Octavius Rutherford Foster

He was born on 15 December 1864 in Bangor, Wales and was educated at Exeter College, Oxford where he gained a BA in 1890 and a MA in 1892. He was ordained as a deacon in 1890 and as a priest in 1892. He joined the Navy Chaplain Service on 23 June 1892 and, after an initial posting to *Iron Duke* (Coastguard, Firth of Forth), on 21 November 1892 he left for China Station in *Mercury*. In nearly thirty years he held a number of further appointments on ship and shore including Haslar Hospital (1896, Gosport), *Colossus* (1896-97, Coastguard Holyhead), *Renown* (1897-99, North America), *Melampus* (1899-1901, Coast Guard), *Vernon* (1901, Portsmouth), *Majestic* (1901-02, Channel), *Collingwood* (1902-03, Coastguard), *Resolution* (1903, Holyhead), *Edgar* (1903-04, Holyhead), *Euryalus* (1904-06, Australia), *Indus* (1906-08, Devonport) and *Euryalus* again (1908-09, Mediterranean). On 28 December 1908 a massive earthquake struck Sicily and the Calabria area of Italy and the Mediterranean fleet was sent to help. It was estimated that up to 100,000 people lost their lives. Reverend Hughes,

along with 639 of his Euryalus shipmates were later awarded the Medaglia Commemorativa Terremoto Calabro-Siculo 1908 (The Messina Earthquake Medal) by the Italian Government. Altogether 3463 medals were awarded to the Royal Navy fleet of eight ships that went to help. His service continued at Hong Kong Dockyard & Hospital (1909-11), *Renown* (1911-12, Portsmouth), RN Barracks (1912-13, Portsmouth), RMLI Barracks, (1913-17, Forton, Gosport), Chatham Dockyard (1917) and Pembroke Dockyard (1918) until he retired on 1 January 1921. He became Rector of Bradenham, Bucks in 1923 and died there on 23 December 1938. When he performed his single baptism for the Butfield family he was between being paid-off from *Mercury* after the voyage to China and his posting to Haslar Hospital, Gosport.

Sources: 9, 16 & 34-35

HURDON, John Nott Dyer

Born in Launceston, Cornwall on 24 December 1841, he was educated at Christ's College, Cambridge gaining a BA in 1865 and a MA in 1871. He was ordained as a deacon in 1865 and a priest in 1866. He held several curacies, latterly at Sowton, near Plymouth, Cornwall. He has no obvious relationship to the Langleys whose three daughters he baptised on 19 June 1898 but from 18 June 1898 to August 1899 he was staying with his wife at 7, Southsea Terrace, Southsea, presumably on holiday.

Sources: 8 & 36

KIRKPATRICK, James

He was born in Richmond, Surrey in 1809 and was educated at St John's College, Cambridge, gaining a BA in 1830 and a MA in 1833. He was ordained as a deacon in 1833 and a priest in 1834. He initially served as curate at Southery, Norfolk and then in 1838 he took-on the two curacies of Cudham, Kent and Catherington, Hants. The Cudham curacy he relinquished in 1848 but he continued to serve at Catherington until 1873. His two baptisms at the RMA Church were of his grand-daughters, his daughter Katherine Georgiana being the wife of Brevet Major (1874) and later (1876) Lieutenant Colonel Richard Turbervill Ansell.

Sources: 8 & 37-38

MACGACHEN, Nicolas Howard

He was born in Edinburgh and graduated from Pembroke College, Oxford with a BA in 1848. The baptism that he performed on 16 August 1867 is recorded out of sequence in the register and entered in a strange hand sometime between 5 January and 7 February 1868. The baptism had taken place at St Mary's Church, Portsmouth where he was curate from 1858 to 1868, just prior to him being appointed vicar of St Mark's, North End, Portsmouth.

Source: 16

PARRY, William Warner

He was born on 13 December 1832 in Birmingham and graduated from Worcester College, Oxford with a BA in 1857 and a MA in 1859. He was ordained a deacon in 1859 and a priest in 1860. He held curacies at Waverton, Cheshire and Hulme, Manchester before joining the Navy Chaplains Service on 28 March 1866. He also qualified as a Naval Instructor and his first posting was to *Malacca* (1866-69, Pacific). This was followed by service in *Defence* (1869-72, Mediterranean) then *Thetis* (1873, China), *Iron Duke* (1873-75, China), *Excellent* (1875-78, Portsmouth), *Iron Duke* (1878-80, China) again, *Impregnable* (1881-82, Devonport) and *St Vincent* (1882, Portsmouth), until retiring on 16 April 1885. There is one blot on his record – he was censured for *"carelessness and neglect of duty as Auditing Officer in passing Mess accounts of Lt Sandham"* - related to his second spell on *Iron Duke*. He retired to Southsea and so was handily available to deputise in February 1886. In 1891 he was living at Denbigh Lodge, The Thicket, Southsea, with four boarders aged 10 to 16 all listed as *"scholars"*, so perhaps he was running a mini-prep school. By 1901 he had moved to Woodend, Queen's Crescent and died there on 7 November 1901.

Sources: 16 & 39-43

REED, William

He was born in Ottery St Mary, Devon in 1847 and he graduated from St John's College, Cambridge with a BA in 1869 and a MA in 1872. He held several posts as clergyman and schoolmaster until moving to Hampshire in 1894. He was licensed as a priest in the Diocese of Winchester and at the time of his baptisms in 1895 he was living at The Hermitage, Grove Road South, Southsea, where he and his French wife were running a "Ladies School". He moved away from Southsea in 1906/7 to become rector of Clifton-Camville with Chalcote in Staffordshire and he died there on 20 January 1915.

Sources: 8, 9 & 44-45

ROMANIS, William

He was born on 30 April 1824 in London and graduated from Emmanuel College, Cambridge with a BA in 1846, coming 7th in the Classic Tripos. He was ordained as a priest in 1848 and went on to obtain his MA in 1849. He married Emma, the daughter of Lieutenant George Gill R.N., on 22 July 1847. He was latterly appointed vicar of Twyford, near Winchester in 1888 and retired to Southsea about 1895. It was during his retirement in Southsea that he deputised for Reverend York on eleven separate

occasions performing 16 baptisms in all. He died at 47, Granada Road, Southsea in November 1899 and is buried in Twyford churchyard under a splendid 'Arts & Crafts' style headstone. He wrote a number of hymns, one of which can be heard on the internet.

Sources: 8 & 46-48

RUTHERFORD, William Allen

He was born on 21 July 1830 in Dublin, Ireland, and was educated at Trinity College, Dublin and graduated with a BA in 1855 and a MA in 1858; he was also awarded a DD in 1870. He was ordained as a deacon in 1856 and a priest in 1857. He was curate at Geashill, King's County (now County Offaly), Ireland from 1854 until his enlistment as a Naval Chaplain and Instructor on 19 April 1864. His twenty-five years service saw him serve in *Barrosa* (1864-67, China), *Rodney* (1867-70, Flagship China), *Monarch* (1870-71, Channel), *Asia* (1871-73, Portsmouth), *Pallas* (1873-76, Mediterranean), *St Vincent* (1876-79, Portsmouth), *Asia* (1880-82, Portsmouth) again, *St Vincent* (1882-85, Portsmouth) again, *Asia* (1886, Portsmouth) yet again, *Excellent* (1886, Portsmouth) and finally, in October 1886 with the Royal Marine Light Infantry (Gosport). He had some exciting times during these years, including being present at the capture of the Japanese batteries in the Straights of Shimonoseki (*Barrosa*, 1864) and the occupation of Yangchow, Nankin, (*Rodney*, 1868). His spell in the Mediterranean in *Pallas* included several months patrolling off the Spanish coast in reaction to the Cantonal Revolution, part of the civil wars following the abdication of King Amadeo in February 1873. He also had his controversies. In 1882 whilst at *St Vincent* he was reported for overstaying his leave as his explanation was regarded as unsatisfactory. Admiral Ryder commented that he was *"unsatisfactory for a training ship"* but the Chaplain of the Fleet did not agree. He compounded this the following month by clashing with the captain over changes he made to his service without prior permission. Admiral Ryder wanted him superseded for this but he finished his time and in September 1885 he applied for the living of Thornyburn, but this didn't materialise and he continued his service. When he eventually retired in August 1889 he was presented to the Greenwich Hospital living of Alston with Garrigill, in Cumberland. He died in Penrith, Cumbria on 27 August 1917.

He performed just one baptism in the RMA Church and that was on 1 August 1889, between the permanent postings of Reverends Morton and Kenah. At the time he was attached to the Royal Marine Light Infantry and was presumably at Forton Barracks, Gosport, with them.

Sources: 9 & 49-56

SCOTT, Francis Montgomery

He was born in Ireland (as were his wife and children) about 1840 and was educated at Trinity College, Dublin; getting his BA in 1859 and MA in 1863. He was ordained as a deacon in 1859 and became a priest in 1861. He was curate of Ballyphilip, County Down, from 1859 to 1885 and was then appointed vicar of Poulton, Gloucestershire, where he served until 1890. He retired to Southsea just after this and was living at Craneswater Park when he deputised at the RMA Church in December 1894. He left Southsea about 1897 and died in the Farnham registration district in 1899, but his widow and family returned to Southsea and were living at 31, South Parade, in 1901.

Sources: 57-59

SHAKESPEAR, Wyndham Arthur

He was born in 1836 in Boxwell, Gloucestershire and was educated at Lytton Hall and Exeter College, Oxford, where he gained his BA in 1860 and MA in 1862. He was curate of Holy Trinity, Shoreditch, London, when he officiated at the RMA Church for the baptism of the son of his nephew, Captain Arthur Bucknall Shakespear, RMA.

Sources: 16 & 60-61

SHARP, John

There is a continuous run of 14 baptisms recorded against this name between 25 June 1876 and 30 July 1876; although only one entry has the full forename. They appear to have been added to the register by Reverend E A Williams. There are three John Sharps in Crockford's Clerical Directories for the period. First there is one who was in India from 1865, returned to Lincolnshire for the period 1870-1872, then moved back to India until 1878. The second John Sharp had been perpetual curate at Horbury, near Wakefield, Yorkshire, since 1834. The third was John Prior Sharp who had been vicar of Edenham, Lincolnshire, since 1867 and Domestic Chaplain to his benefactor Lady Willoughby de Eresby. There was also one John Sharpe active at the time who was vicar of Northleach, Gloucs. None of these candidates appear to have any connection with Portsmouth but any one of them could have been on holiday in the area at the time. However, as these baptisms are the first by a Sharp/Sharpe it is more likely that Reverend Williams recorded the name incorrectly and it was actually James Falconer Sharpe (see below) who had arrived in Southsea at this time and went on to officiate on several other occasions up until 1887.

SHARPE, James Falconer

Born in Doncaster, Yorkshire on 14 August 1815, his father was vicar of Doncaster. He was educated at Eton and then Sidney Sussex College, Cambridge where he graduated with a BA in 1840. He was ordained as a priest in 1840 and was appointed to the Calcutta Diocese in 1842, serving at various posts in Bengal until 1868. He returned to England, initially to Tranmere, but then about

1875 he moved to Waverley Road in Southsea with his wife Louisa; in the 1881 and 1891 census returns he was annotated as *"Clergyman without the cure of souls"*. He died in Waverley Road, Southsea on 24 February 1897 and is buried in Highland Road Cemetery with his wife who died in 1892. Unfortunately the grave has sunken badly and the cross has fallen (or has been laid down by the Council).
Sources: 8, 48 & 62-65

SHEPERD, Lorenzo

Born on 8 May 1842 in County Down, Ireland, he was educated at Trinity College, Dublin. He became a deacon in 1867 and was ordained as a priest by the Archbishop of Armagh on 20 September 1868. With a recommendation from the Archbishop he joined the Navy Chaplain Service on 22 March 1871. His first posting was to *Topaze* (1871-74, Detached Squadron) and then to *Aboukir* (1874-77, Jamaica). It was during this latter posting in Jamaica that he got into trouble for writing to the local newspaper about Sir William Grey. What Reverend Sheperd wrote is unknown as the Admiralty papers have not survived but Grey, who was Governor of Jamaica from 1874-1877, had been accused of corruption and misrule by the newspaper and he had responded with a libel action. Commodore Lyons reprimanded Reverend Sheperd for getting involved. His next posting was to *Crocodile* (1877-79, Portsmouth) and then to *Thetis* (1879-81, Pacific). He was soon in trouble again and in September 1881 was ordered home for *"quarrelling with other officers of ships, neglect of duty and insubordinate conduct"*. Following further complaints, on 27 January 1882 his name was ordered to be removed from the list of Navy Chaplains, but he was later allowed to *"resign at his own request"* thus avoiding this blot. In 1889 he was serving for the Society for the Propagation of the Gospel in Rapid City, Manitoba, Canada.

The four baptisms he performed on 6 August 1871 were before his first posting and a week before he had been rejected at the preliminary examination for Naval Instructor, so presumably he was in Portsmouth for this examination at the time.
Sources: 66-70

SMITH, William Edward

He was born in Portsmouth on 18 October 1833, the son of Commander Robert Smith R.N. He entered St John's College, Cambridge in 1852 and obtained his BA in 1857; he was subsequently ordained as a deacon in 1857 and a priest on 28 July 1858. He served as a curate at Burnham, Essex, and Bradwell-juxta-Mare, Essex, before joining the Navy Chaplain Service in 1858; he also qualified as a Naval Instructor. His first posting was to *Termagant* (1859-62, Pacific). In 1861 whilst the ship was at Taboga, Panama, he got into a dispute with Captain Hall over a sermon he preached on Christmas Day. After some exchange of views and an Admiralty inquiry, in April 1862 the Admiral ordered him to be placed on half pay and sent back to England on a packet ship. Four months later he was posted to *Severn* (1862, China) as a Naval Instructor and did not return to chaplain duties until June 1866 and his next posting to *Royal Oak* (Mediterranean); he moved on to *Ocean* (Mediterranean) in April 1867. He was paid-off from *Ocean* in Hong Kong in May 1870 and returned to the UK and then in January 1871 was posted to the training ship *St Vincent* (Portsmouth) and in 1872 to *Royal Adelaide* at Devonport. On 12 February 1875 he was posted to Bermuda Dockyard but within ten days this posting was cancelled and he moved to *Duke of Wellington* at Portsmouth. It was during his time in Portsmouth that he deputised for Reverend Williams. Then in September 1877 he was appointed to '*the Deal Division of Marines*' (sic) and in May 1879 he was made 'additional' to *Boadicea* for service with the Marine Battalion at Cape Town. He returned to Portsmouth with the Battalion in August 1879 together with a *"high testimony"* from Lt Col Hunt for his work with the RMLI South African Battalion. Over the next three years he served at the RM Depot, Walmer, Kent, and Chatham Dockyard before being appointed as 'additional' to *President* for service at the Admiralty as Inspector of Schools. Whilst in this post he managed to *"incur their Lordships' displeasure"* for the *"improper tone of his letters in a correspondence he had with the Admiral Superintendant of Malta"* (Admiral W Graham). He officially retired on 24 April 1888 and took the Greenwich Hospital living of Wark, where he stayed until September 1892. He then retired to Guernsey with his younger wife, where he died on 22 October 1908.

Sources: 8 & 71-74

TAYLOR, Haydon Aldersey

Born in south London, he graduated from St John's College, Oxford in 1848 gaining an MA in 1852. He was ordained as a deacon in 1849 and as a priest in 1850. After experience as a curate he became an Assistant Chaplain to the Forces (Army) at Aldershot and in the Crimea (medal). He later joined the Prison Service and served first at Portland, Dorset and then at Parkhurst, I.O.W. for many years. After retiring in 1893 he moved to Southsea, initially to Redcliffe Gardens and then to 36, South Parade, where he died in 1904 at the age of 78. He was buried in Highland Road Cemetery, Southsea on 5 December 1904.

His eight baptisms at the Crinoline Church were performed during his retirement in Southsea (1895-98).

Sources: 16, 48, 65 & 75-77

VAUGHAN, Ernest John

He was born in Darlaston, Staffordshire on 20 March 1858; his father was master at Queen Mary's School, Walsall, where Reverend Vaughan also attended. He went on to Christ's College, Cambridge where he excelled, graduating as 13th Wrangler in 1880. The following year he was ordained as a deacon and took-up the curacy of Woolvercote, Oxfordshire as well as becoming a master at St Edward's School, Oxford. Whilst there he was ordained as a priest and gained his M.A. In 1887 he moved south to become curate at St Luke's, Torquay and headmaster of St Luke's College. The following year he married Georgiana Weatherall and joined the Naval Chaplain Service, also qualifying as a Naval Instructor. He at once went to China in *Constance*, moved to *Aurora* (1889, Devonport) and then to Home waters in *Cambridge* (1889-90). He moved quickly to *Undaunted* (1890-93, Mediterannean) and three years later, after a temporary spell in the training

ship *St Vincent* (Portsmouth), he joined *Volage* (1894-98, Training Squadron). It was during his posting to *Volage* that he deputised for Reverend York. On 4 April 1898, he returned to *St Vincent* but less than a year later on 22 February 1899 he died at his home in Mortlake Terrace, Victoria Road North, Southsea, aged 41, leaving his young wife and son Reginald, aged 3. He was buried in Highland Road Cemetery, Southsea, where his grave has unfortunately suffered damage.

Sources: 8, 48, 65 & 78-79

VINER, George Barber Peregrine

Born in London about 1826, he was educated at Trinity College, Toronto, Canada, and was ordained a priest there in 1858 and spent time as a travelling missionary before becoming the incumbent of St George's, Duffin's Creek, Ontario. He moved to England in 1862 and served as a curate at Christ Church, Marylebone (1862-63) and St John, Enfield (1863-66) before being appointed vicar there (1866-75). The baptism he performed on 12 February 1893 was of his grand-daughter; the mother, Charlotte Sophia, was his daughter. At the time he was Rector of Mottingham, Kent, where he served as curate from 1876 to1881 and rector from 1881 to 1909. He retired to Lee in Kent but died in Eltham on 23 June 1919 at the age of 95.

Sources: 9 & 80-81

WALKER, Louis William Lancelot

Born on 21 January 1871 in Kingstown, County Dublin, Ireland, he was educated at Emmanuel College, Cambridge, gaining a BA in 1896 and a MA in 1907. He was ordained a priest in 1899 and served as curate at Shorwell with Mottiston, Newport, I.O.W. (1898-1901) and St James, Milton, Portsmouth (1901-4). He joined the Royal Navy as an *"acting Chaplain for temporary service"* on 1 January 1904. After five months in *Resolution* (1904, Home) and three months in *Swiftsure* (1904, Home), he was awaiting a posting to *Vulcan* (Mediterranean) when on 2 October 1904 he officiated at five baptisms in the RMA Church. Two days later he married his first wife, Barbara Jessie Cleveland at St Jude's, Southsea. She was born in Ireland but had spent most of her life in SE Hampshire with her widowed mother and siblings; firstly in Warblington and then in Salisbury Road, Southsea. Following three years in *Vulcan* (1904-07, Mediterranean) he saw service in *Achilles* (1907-08, Home), *Cressy* (1908-09, North America), *Dominion* (1909-12, Home), *Actaeon* (1912-14, Sheerness) and *Marlborough* (1914-16, 1st Battle Squadron). Perhaps luckily he was posted from *Marlborough* less than three weeks before she was involved in the Battle of Jutland. He continued his service in *Victorious* (1916-17, Channel), *Hecla* (1917, Channel), *Apollo* (1917-19, Devonport) and finally Pembroke Dockyard (1919); he retired on 26 April 1922. Following his retirement he was vicar of Purbrook, Hants, (1922-1935), rector of Parracombe, Devon (1935-1943) and finally he was appointed to the office of Salisbury Diocese (1943-1953). He retired to Parkstone, Dorset and died in the Bournemouth registration district, age 88, in 1959.

Sources: 8 & 82-86

Chapter 7 - The Fallen

The following biographies cover those comemorated on the memorial plaques that were in the old Church (see Chapter 1 – The Memorials) and those recorded to have lost their lives in WW1 and who appear in the baptism register (see Chapter 6 – Introduction for the criteria for inclusion). The dates in parentheses under the names refer to the dates that the man appears in the baptisms register.

Egypt Campaign, 1882
The campaign in Egypt between May and September 1882 was the cause of a number of Royal Marine fatal casualties that are commemorated in the memorial described in Chapter 1. Those connected to the baptism transcriptions are:

Gunner Cornelius BAKER (25 Mar 1877 and 31 Aug 1879)
His service register has not survived but we know that he was killed on 28 August 1882 whilst serving with 10th Company RMA which was part of General Graham's force at Kassassin. He suffered gunshot wound/s to the chest and lungs. Gunners Adams, Colston, Craddock, Cox, Lester and Newton were killed in the same engagement but do not appear in the baptisms register.
    Sources: 1-3

Colour Sergeant Lonsdale CLARKE (31 Dec 1882)
This baptism of his son John James must have taken place after his death although there is no mention of the father being deceased in the register. John James was born on 7 April 1882.
    Colour Sergeant Clarke's service register has not survived but from census information we can assume that he was born in Keswick, Cumberland in 1843 and he started his working life as an apprentice to a shoemaker in the village of Cleator near Whitehaven. By 1871 he had enlisted and was serving in *Caledonia* (Mediterranean) as a Gunner and in 1881 he was living with his family in Gloucester and recorded as "Sergt RMA", so he must have been on leave or possibly recruiting duties at the time.
    Sources: 2 & 4-6

World War I (1914-19)
The Register of Royal Marine Deaths 1914-19, *"With Full And Grateful Hearts"*, compiled by the Royal Marines Historical Society, lists 14 Marines that appear in the baptisms list [7]. Some of these deaths were almost certainly not combat-related and were most probably the result of natural causes.

Gunner Albert Edward BROADBENT (RMA 4663) (1 Oct 1905)
He was born on 15 July 1873 in Hackney, London, and enlisted on 15 September 1892. He completed 21 years service at the rank of Gunner. His service in *Monarch* (1899-1900) took him to South Africa where he saw plenty of action as part of a Naval Brigade; his South Africa medal carried clasps for Belmont, Lodden River, Paardeburg, Dreifontein, Johannesburg, Diamonds Hill and Belfast. In 1908 he was in the Mediterranean in *Exmouth* and was one of 3463 RN personnel who were awarded the Medaglia Commemorativa Terremoto Calabro-Siculo 1908 (The Messina Earthquake Medal) by the Italian Government for their assistance following a massive earthquake that struck Sicily and the Calabria area on 28 December 1908. He completed his 21 years on 29 August 1913, serving the last eight years as an officer's attendant, but a year later he was mobilised from the Reserve for WWI and was attached to *Cormorant* , the shore station on Ascension Island, where he died on 24 December 1915. He is buried in the New Cemetery at Georgetown on Ascension Island. In addition to the medals mentioned above he also held the Long Service and Good Conduct Medal
    Sources: 8-10

Colour Sergeant George BULLOCK (RMA 2492) (18 Apr 1895 as Corporal, 17 Jul 1898 as Sergeant, 5 Jan 1902, 3 Jan 1904 & 1 Oct 1905 as Provost Sergeant)
He died on 18 October 1914, aged 47, just five weeks after he was mobilised from the Royal Fleet Reserve and he is buried in Highland Road Cemetery, Southsea. He was born on 7 December 1866 in Cheltenham and enlisted at Hereford on 7 March 1885. During

the early part of his initial 21 years service he had survived the sinking of *Sultan* in the Mediterranean in 1889. She had accidentally grounded on rocks in the South Comino Channel between Malta and Gozo on 6 March 1889. A week later she was hit by gale force winds and slipped off the rock and sank. She was eventually recovered and returned to Portsmouth to be refitted.

He was promoted to Sergeant on 1 April 1897, Provost Sergeant on 17 October 1900 and Colour Sergeant on 22 January 1906, five months before his retirement. He was running a boarding house in Marylebone Street, Southsea when he was mobilised. He was awarded the Long Service and Good Conduct Medal.
    Sources: 9 & 11-13

Lieutenant Colonel Charles Joseph CHEETHAM (20 Jul 1890 as Major)
    He was born in Portsmouth in 1850, the son of Major Charles Cheetham, Royal Artillery. After studying at the RN College he was transferred to the RMA on 3 July

1871. He saw active service with Colonel Festing's detachment in the Ashanti War (Gold Coast, 1873) but was invalided home suffering from malaria and dysentery; he applied to return to Gold Coast but was refused. He was present at the Bombardment of Alexandria in *Sultan* (1882) as a Captain and was employed on police duty ashore. He landed again at Aboukir and was part of the force occupying the forts from 28 September to 3 November 1882 but a month later he was invalided home from Malta *"on account of debility"*. In between spells at Eastney he served on *Achilles* (Channel, 1884-85) and *Agamemnon* (Mediterranean & East Africa, 1886-89). He was promoted to Major on 21 May 1888 whilst serving in *Agamemnon*. He returned to Eastney for just over a year before being posted to Glasgow for recruiting duties (1890-93). After returning to Eastney he was granted the Brevet of Lieutenant Colonel on 21 May 1895 and retired at his own request on 30 May. He was immediately appointed Recruiting Staff Officer 1st Class at Birmingham. This appointment was renewed several times until he vacated the appointment in 1903. In March 1915 he was employed by the Army as Head Recruiting Officer of 63rd Regimental District and the following year on 9 December 1916 he died of pneumonia at Ashton-Under-Lyne at the age of 66. He is buried in Hurst Cemetery, Ashton-Under-Lyne.

He was awarded the Ashanti Medal 1873-4, Egypt Medal with Alexandria clasp, Order of the Medjidie 4th class & the Khedive's Bronze Star.

Sources: 9 & 14-15

Corporal Tom CLAYTON (RMA 3819)
(12 Apr 1896 as Bombardier & 15 Mar 1899 as Acting Bombardier)

He died on 5 August 1918 and is buried in the Royal Naval Cemetery, Haslar. He was born in Ludlow, Shropshire in 1869 and in 1901 was living with his family in Henderson Road, Eastney, and was recorded as a "Soldier RM Artillery". He had retired from the RMA by 1911 and was working as a print compositor in West Ham, so presumably he was mobilised from the Reserves in 1914 but his service register has not survived.

Sources: 3, 9, 13 & 16-19

Corporal Charles Henry DICKERSON
(RMA 7127) (25 Feb 1900 as Bombardier & 7 Feb 1904 as Corporal)

The earlier of the two records is not a baptism but his son Charles Francis Alexander being received into the Church, having been baptised privately at Turriff, Aberdeen on 25 November 1899. Corporal Dickerson's service record has not survived but he was born in Thorpe St Andrew, Norwich, Norfolk about 1869. By 1901 he was living with wife and Charles Francis in Owen Street, Portsmouth as a *"Corpl RMA"* but by

1911 he had retired and the family was living in East Cowes, Isle of Wight. Corporal Dickerson was then working as an Admiralty messenger. He was presumably mobilised from the Reserve in 1914 as he died on 13 May 1915 whilst serving in *HMS Goliath*. It was sunk by torpedoes off Cape Helles in the Dardanelles and 570 of the crew of 700 were lost. Corporal Dickerson is commemorated on the Portsmouth Naval Memorial.

Sources: 3, 9 & 20-22

Colour Sergeant George William West GIBBONS (RMA 2192) (6 Apr 1902)
He was born on 14 October 1869 in Birmingham and enlisted as a Boy Bugler at Eastney on 14 August 1884; he was 14 years and 10 months old and 4 feet 9¾ inches (1.47 m) tall. He had accumulated nearly three years sea service by the time he was promoted to Gunner on 17 September 1891. He was promoted to Bombardier on 27 September 1893 and Corporal on 1 April 1896.

He served a year in *Anson* before being promoted to Sergeant on 3 February 1898. He then served in *Royal Oak* (1898, Mediterranean) and *Phoenix* (1900-01, China) during the Boxer Rebellion but served most of his last 10 years at Eastney, being promoted to Colour Sergeant on 15 February 1907. He retired on 13 October 1908. In 1911 he was working as a postman in the Manchester area and was mobilised from the Reserve in August 1914. His service register shows no service abroad during WWI so he probably served at Eastney until his death there on 16 September 1916. He is buried in Highland Road Cemetery, Southsea. He held the China and Long Service and Good Conduct Medals.

Sources: 9, 11, 13 & 23-24

Bombardier Joseph Harry HARPER (RMA 7594) (24 Feb 1884)
The date given above is the date of his own baptism; his parents, Gunner Anthony & Annie Elizabeth Harper also baptised two other children in the RMA Church. Joseph Harry was born at Eastney on 14 January 1884 and was a *"Greenwich School Boy"* when he enlisted as a Bugler on 10 August 1898 at the age of 14. At the age of 16 he did his first sea service in *Camperdown* (1900-01, Coast Guard Lough Swilly). He was promoted to Gunner on 4 November 1901 and had further sea service in *Russell* (1903-4, Mediterranean), *Queen* (1904-06, Mediterranean), *Majestic* (1907-8, Home), *Agamemnon* (1908-10, Home) and *Leviathan* (1911, 4th Cruiser Squadron) before he was promoted to Bombardier on 1 September 1911 having already had two spells 'acting' at this rank. What should have been his final sea service was in *Monarch*

(1912-13, 2nd Battle Squadron) and he retired on 13 January 1914 having completed 12 years as an adult. A few months later on 2 August 1914 he was called up from the Reserves and on 27 July 1915 was posted to *Natal*. It was on 30 December 1915 while he was serving in *Natal* that he was killed. The armoured cruiser was at anchor in the Cromarty Firth when she was ripped apart by a series of massive internal explosions and sank with the loss of about 400 men, Bombardier Harper's body was never found. The cause has never been proven but the most likely is thought to be fires igniting the magazine although there are some that believe it was sabotage and possibly linked to the explosion that completely destroyed *Bulwark* and most of its crew in the Medway in 1914. Bombardier Harper is commemorated on the Portsmouth Naval Memorial.

Sources: 9 & 25-27

Sergeant Jonathan HEATON, MM (RMA 6269) (1 Jun 1902 as a Corporal)
He was born on 6 March 1876 in Doncaster, Yorkshire and enlisted on 15 September 1896 in Leeds. After a couple of years at Eastney he had his first sea service in *Illustrious* (1898-1900, Mediterranean) and then in *Renown* (1900, Mediterranean). After five years at Eastney, during which time he was promoted to Corporal, he went to sea again in *Duncan* (1905-08, Channel & Atlantic). He was promoted to Sergeant during his next spell at Eastney (on 13 September 1908) and spent two years in *Achilles* (1909-11, Home). He also served in *Duke of Edinburgh* (1912-13, Mediterranean) before a posting to *Invincible* on 3 August 1914. *Invincible* was involved in some serious action at the Battle of Heligoland Bight on 28 August 1914 and the Battle of the Falklands Islands on 8 December 1914 (for more information on this action see the biography of QMSI Bryan Gasson in Chapter 10). For some unrecorded reason he was demoted to Corporal and deprived of his Long Service and Good Conduct Medal during his service in *Invincible*. On return to UK he was immediately posted to *Canopus* and took part in the disastrous campaign in the Dardanelles in 1916. When he returned to Eastney he was quickly posted to the RMA Howitzer Brigade. He was promoted back to Sergeant on 15 March 1917 but on 24 September he was killed whilst in action with No 11 Battery Howitzer Brigade; he died instantly from a fragment of shell through the brain. He was buried alongside five other casualties from the same action in Gwalia Cemetery, Poperinge, West-Vlaanderen, Belgium, about 8.5 kilometres west of Ieper (Ypres).

He was posthumously awarded the Military Medal; this was gazetted on 12 December 1917. Also posthumously, on 28 July 1918, the Admiralty Board gave approval for the *"special restoration"* of his Long Service and Good Conduct Medal and a copy was passed to his widow.

Sources: 9 & 29-31

A 15-inch Howitzer in action [28]

Gunner Ernest MANN (RMA 7006) (24 Jun 1883)

This date is his own baptism; his father was Staff Sergeant Frederick Mann. He was born in Portsmouth on 15 February 1883 and was another Greenwich School Boy when he enlisted as a Boy Bugler in London on 21 September 1897 at the age of 14. He was just 4 feet 10½ inches (1.49 m) tall when he enlisted but had shot up to 5 feet 6¾ inches (1.70 m) by his 18th birthday. He was promoted to Gunner on 2 August 1901. He saw sea service in *Repulse* (1899-1901, Channel), *Resolution* (1903, Coast Guard Holyhead), *Majestic* (1903-04, Channel), *Caesar* (1904-1905, Channel), *London* (1905-1907, Mediterranean), *Duke of Edinburgh* (1908-10, Channel & Atlantic), *Vengeance* (1910, Chatham), *Neptune* (1911-13, Portsmouth), *Africa* (1913-14, Sheerness & 3rd Battle Squadron), *Commonwealth* (1914-15, 3rd Battle Squadron) and finally *Invincible*. He joined *Invincible* on 20 October 1915 but was lost when she was sunk at the Battle of Jutland on 31 May 1916.

Invincible was the flagship of the 3rd Battlecruiser Squadron under Rear Admiral the Hon Sir Horace Lambert A Hood, CB, MVO, DSO. Along with Hood's two other battlecruisers *Invincible* was engaged in a furious gun battle with three or four of Admiral Hipper's battlecruisers. The *Invincible* made a number of telling hits on the German ships from about 9000 yards (8.2 km) but suddenly the mist that was shrouding the British ships cleared to give Hipper's flagship *Lutzow* and the *Derfflinger* a clear view of the *Invincible* silhouetted against a patch of clear sky. The two German ships fired a number of rapid salvos, one of them hit and detonated *Invincible*'s midships magazines, she was rent in two by the explosion and sank in 90 seconds. Just six men, three officers and three ratings, out of 1032 survived; one of the men was Gunner Bryan Gasson, see Chapter 10 below. Gunner Mann is commemorated on the Portsmouth Naval Memorial.

Sources: 3, 9 & 32

Gunner Reuben NEWPORT (RMA 1838) (26 Sep 1898)

On the date shown above two of his sons with his first wife Louisa were baptised together. Louisa died in 1903 and he remarried in 1909. He was born on 28 October 1860 in Glastonbury, Somerset and enlisted at Taunton on his nineteenth birthday, 28 October 1879. After training at Walmer he was appointed to the RMA as a Gunner on 8 July 1880. His initial 21 years included service in *Minotaur* (1882, Mediterranean), *Neptune* (1883-85, Channel), *Pluckey* (1887, Devonport), *Porpoise* (1888-91, China) and *Repulse* (1894-97, Channel). He embarked in *Minotaur* on 4 April 1882 and was present at the bombardment of Alexandria but was discharged from Haslar Hospital on 19 December 1882 so he must have sustained some

illness or injury whilst in the Mediterranean.

He completed his 21 years in 1900 and was placed on the Reserve on 4 January 1902. He was later mobilised for WWI in August 1914 and served in *Cyclops* (1914), *Royal Arthur* (1915) and *Cyclops II* (1916, Stanger Head) all at Scapa Flow, until returning to Eastney to be demobilised on 17 August 1916 at the age of nearly 56. He died at Eastney soon after on 24 December 1916, so he didn't die in service but did die within the dates of WWI. He was buried in Highland Road Cemetery, Southsea, and the plot is marked by a Commonwealth War Graves headstone. He held the Egypt Medal, Khedive's Bronze Star and the Long Service and Good Conduct Medal.

Sources: 9, 13 & 33

Gunner John NUTTYCOMBE (RMA 5660) (24 Sep 1876)

This is the date of his own baptism; his father was Sergeant, later Colour Sergeant, Robert Nuttycombe. Gunner John was born in Milton, Portsmouth on 14 May 1876 and enlisted at Bridgewater, Somerset on 26 September 1895. His father had retired to his home village of Edington near Bridgewater and young John was working there as an agricultural labourer when he signed-on. His ship service included time in *Ramillies* (1896-98, Mediterranean), *Majestic* (1899-1900, Channel), *Hannibal* (1900-02, Channel), *Trafalgar* (1902, Portsmouth), *Royal Sovereign* (1902-04, Home), *Crescent* (1905-07, Cape of Good Hope), *Britannia* (1907-10, Channel), *Good Hope* (1911-12, Atlantic) and *Africa* (1913-16, Instructional Duties). When *Africa* came into Portsmouth for a refit in 1916 he was posted to the 3rd RM Battalion for service in Gallipoli where he was engaged in shore defences. During 1917 he was in hospital twice for *"atonic dyspepsia"* but on 19 January 1918 he was admitted to the hospital on the Island of Imbros seriously ill with dysentery and he died eleven days later. His service record gives his burial place as Kephalos, Imbros, but the Commonwealth War Graves Commission database shows he is buried at the Lancashire Landing Cemetery, near Cape Helles, so his first interment may have been temporary.

Sources: 9 & 34-35

Gunner Charles John PHILLIPS (RMA 2939) (17 Jul 1898)

He was born on 8 July 1867 in Southend, Essex and enlisted on 8 June 1886 in London. After training at Walmer he was appointed to the RMA on 13 January 1887. His initial 21 years included service in *Benbow* (1888-91, Chatham), *Alexandra* (1892-94, Coast Guard Portland) and *Penelope* (1895-97, Ascension Island). He retired on 24 June 1907 but was recalled from the Reserve in August 1914 and after the short RMA excursion to Ostend from 27 to 31 August 1914 he was posted to *Cyclops II* (Shore Batteries) at Scapa Flow. He then spent some months in *Royal Arthur*, a submarine depot ship also at Scapa Flow, before returning to *Cyclops II*. On 10 April 1917 he was sent back south arriving on 15 April. He was presumably sent direct to Haslar Hospital as he died there on 20 May 1917 from diabetes and secondary pneumonia. He was buried in Highland Road Cemetery, Southsea, and the plot is marked by a Commonwealth War Graves headstone.

Sources: 9, 13 & 36-37

Gunner William RAYSON (RMA 1929) (4 Mar 1894)
He was born on 30 October 1861 near Yeovil, Somerset and enlisted in Bristol on 30 April 1883. After initial training at Walmer he was appointed to the RMA on 8 November 1883. He served at the rank of Gunner until completion of his 21 years during which time he served in *Iron Duke* (1885-87, Channel), *Neptune* (1888-90, Coast Guard Holyhead), *Iris* (1890, Portsmouth) *Shannon* (1891-93, Coast Guard Bantry), *Victory* (1894-96, Portsmouth) and *Revenge* (1896-1899, Mediterranean). During most of 1896 *Revenge* was the flagship of a Particular Service Squadron sent to patrol off South Africa in response to the debacle of the Jameson Raid that had failed miserably to overthrow the Boer Government. His final sea service was in *Resolution* (1901-2, Coast Guard Holyhead). He retired on 29 April 1904 and was living in Portsmouth working as a jobbing gardener before he was mobilised from the Reserve in 1914. After being part of the RMA excursion to Ostend at the end of August he was posted to *Cyclops* at Scapa Flow. He died there on 7 April 1917, the cause is not recorded on his service record, and was buried in Flotta Parish Churchyard, Orkney.

Sources: 9 & 38-39

Chapter 8 - The Gallant and the Irreproachable

My explanation in Chapter 6 – Introduction about who is and who isn't covered in these biographies applies equally to this chapter.

Distinguished Service Order

The DSO was instituted by Queen Victoria on 6 September 1886. It was awarded "for distinguished services during active operations against the enemy" and, in the period we are concerned with, was awarded to officers for particularly outstanding leadership in action.

Commander William George Hastings BICKFORD, DSO (29 Oct 1872)

He was the son of Colonel William George Tomlin Bickford who was a Lieutenant RMA at the time of his son's baptism. Although he chose the Navy rather than the RMA for his career he maintained the family link by being a gunnery expert. He entered the service on 31 October 1895 and served as a Sub-Lieutenant in *Bellona* (1895-97, Channel) and as Lieutenant in *Collingwood* (1897-98, Coast Guard, Bantry), *Devastation* (1898, Devonport), *Tyne* (1898-1901, Mediterranean), *Bellona* (1901-03, Fishery Duties), *Scylla* (1904, Chatham), *Melampus* (1904-05, Kingstown), *Latona* (1905, Newfoundland), *Charybdis* (1905-06, Chatham), *Cornwall* (1907, Devonport), *Trafalgar* (1907-09, Nore, Sheerness & Chatham) and finally *Vengeance* on her becoming a Turret Drill Ship at Chatham in 1909. His assessments throughout this period could only be described as 'mixed', his navigation skills in particular coming in for criticism and he was blamed for a collision when serving as Navigator in *Charybdis*. He was granted permission to apply for the post of Captain Superintendant of the Training Ship *Arethusa* but there is no record of his getting this appointment. His posting to *Vengeance* ended on 4 May 1909 and there are no further entries on his service record until he retired at his own request on 3 September 1912 at the rank of Commander.

He was mobilized from the RN Reserve in 1914 and appointed initially to transport duties at Southampton and then to the Dover Patrol. He was soon noticed by Admiral Bacon when he was involved in the landing of a 15-inch Howitzer at Boulogne and the Admiral, impressed by his work, asked for him to be transferred to his staff. In his memoirs of the Dover Patrol Admiral Bacon says of Commander Bickford; *"The harder the work and the wetter the weather, the more thoroughly he enjoys himself; nor did he mind the poison gas or high explosive shells strewed round him by* the enemy." Later in 1917 when landing guns on the French coast he says that Commander Bickford *"would work for days and nights on end without apparently taking any rest. It was truly said of him that 'he went forty-eight hours to the gallon".* This probably refers to his work in helping to move the guns of the RMA Heavy Siege Train.

His DSO was awarded as a result of his being commended for his part in an operation against the Belgian Coast near Zeebrugge in 1915 (not to be confused with the daring but ill-fated raid on the Zeebrugge Mole in 1918). He was commended by then Vice-Admiral R H Bacon for being *"In charge of the forward observation party under the close firing of the batteries during two attacks, and largely assisted in correcting the fire of the guns."* His observation party was actually situated on a tripod platform of Bacon's design which was sitting on the sea bed within range of the shore batteries. Bickford's platform was struck below the water line and partially collapsed and *"he and two signalmen were left perched on what was left of it like soaked sparrows".* They were forgotten for nearly fourteen hours until they were picked-up by the *Viking.* The Captain of *Viking* is supposed to have asked Bickford *"Where have you been?".* Bickford's reply is not recorded! He died at Chatham on 15 October 1932 after suffering from *"Cardiac Debility and enlarged prostate".*

Sources: 1-6

Brigadier General Edmond Howard GORGES, CB, CBE, DSO, FRGS (6 Jan 1869)

Edmond was the son of Captain Richard Archibald Gorges who was lost with *HMS Captain* in September 1871 (see The Memorials in Chapter 1). He was initially schooled at St Helen's College, Southsea, then went on to the Royal Military College at Sandhurst and subsequently entered the Army on 14 September 1887. He served with the Manchester Regiment, the King's African Rifles, the Mounted Infantry, the West African Regiment and a Camel Battalion among others. He saw much active service including in the Mulaka Expedition (1898), Uganda Mutiny (1898-99), South African War (1900), Uganda again (1900) and Somaliland (1904). It was whilst he was in Uganda serving as Captain in the Turkana Punitive Expedition that he was mentioned in despatches (18 April 1902) and gazetted a Companion of the Distinguished Service Order a week later. By 1914 he was a Brevet Colonel and was Commanding Officer of the British Contingent of the Cameroon Expeditionary Force, during which period he was twice mentioned in despatches. He was made a Companion of the Bath (CB) in 1915 and an Officer of the Legion of Honour. On becoming a temporary Brigadier General he moved home to command the South Midland Brigade, Home Forces. Ultimately he was Brigade Commander of 202nd Infantry Brigade in 1918. He was made a CBE in 1919. Altogether a service record of which his father would have been very proud. He eventually retired to Petersfield, Hants, and died there on 26 October 1949.

Sources: 4, & 7-9

Brigadier Dudley Ashton Hope HIRE, DSO, MC (29 Mar 1894)
This is the date of his own baptism; he was the son of Captain Ashton Hope Hire, RMA, and the grandson of Captain Henry William Hire, RN. His father had been a Gentleman Cadet at Woolwich Academy and subsequently joined the RMA in 1883, retiring as Brevet Lieutenant Colonel in 1909. Dudley joined the Royal Artillery and distinguished himself with the Royal Garrison Artillery in WWI. See more about his WWI service under Military Cross below.

He again distinguished himself in WWII. In 1942-43 he was serving in the Royal Regiment of Artillery at the rank of Temporary Brigadier with the Heavy Anti-Aircraft Artillery of the Fortress of Malta when he was awarded the DSO. His commendation records how during the heaviest period of air attacks he was constantly present at the gun positions and his personal example on the open roof of his HQ was an encouragement to both his own Brigade and the local population. Much later following his retirement he and his wife lived in Parkstone Avenue, Southsea for some years and she died there in 1973. He died, aged 92, in Richmond upon Thames in 1986.
Sources: 10-13

Lieutenant-Colonel William Ashley NICHOLLS, DSO (20 Mar 1884)
This is the date of his own baptism; he was the son of General Sir William Charles Nicholls KCB (who was Lieutenant & Adjutant RMA at the time of this baptism) and rose to the rank of Lieutenant Colonel in the Royal Field Artillery. He was educated at the RMA School, Woolwich and Cheltenham College before joining the Royal Artillery. He served in World War I and was mentioned in despatches four times in addition to his award of the DSO that was announced in the London Gazette of 1 January 1917. He subsequently served in Iraq (1920) before retiring in 1934. He spent his later years at East Dean near Salisbury and died there on 25 June 1941.
Sources: 4, 9 & 14-16

Brigadier Arthur Talbot SHAKESPEAR, DSO, MC (28 Oct 1884)
Arthur Talbot was born on 15 September 1884, the son of Captain (later Brevet Lieutenant Colonel) Arthur Bucknell Shakespear, RMA. He was baptised by his great uncle the Reverend Wyndham Arthur Shakespear (see Chapter 8). Educated at Monmouth School and Cheltenham College he served in the Royal Engineers and on the Staff of the Army in Ireland, eventually attaining the rank of Brigadier. He was Acting Major in the Royal Engineers in France when he was gazetted for the DSO on 1 January 1918. He also served in Malta, Gibraltar, Singapore and Egypt. He retired in 1937 and was an Air Raid Precautions (ARP) Officer in Richmond, Surrey, at the outbreak of WWII but then served in Gibraltar (1940) before being posted as Commandant RE Depot (1941-42). He eventually retired to Twyford near Winchester in Hampshire and became a pillar of the local community, including being a parish councillor, a lay reader and sidesman in the local church as well as sitting on

the Parochial Church Council. He also had a great interest in the work of Oxfam. In about 1957 he moved into Winchester and he died there on 5 September 1964. He was also awarded the Military Cross (see below).

Sources: 4, 9 & 17-19

Distinguished Service Medal

The DSM was instigated on 14 October 1914 as the Royal Navy's 'other ranks' equivalent to the Distinguished Service Cross, which was restricted to naval officers and warrant officers.

Colour Sergeant Frederick George CHAPMAN, DSM (Po 27919/RMA 7919) (28 March 1900 as Drummer)

The date given above is for his own baptism as an adult, his father John Henry Chapman was recorded as a *"Pensioner Gunner RMA"* at the time. He was born on 11 December 1884 in Lower Walmer, Deal, Kent, and enlisted at Eastney on 21 January 1899. He served 7 of his initial 24 years (including just under 4 years service while under 18 that does not count towards pension) at sea including service in *Mars* (1900-02, Channel), *Duncan* (1903-05, Mediterranean), *Russell* (1906-09, Atlantic) and *Swiftsure* (1910-11, Mediterranean). In 1910 he qualified as a Physical Training Instructor and was also a Swimming Instructor. He was part of the RMA 'excursion' to Ostende from 27 to 31 August 1914 but returned to Eastney briefly before being involved in *"Operations in France with Flying Corps"* from 11 September to 17 October 1914. He then returned to Eastney before being posted to the Anti-Aircraft Brigade on 22 April 1915, returning to Eastney on 19 January 1919. His DSM was awarded for his work with the RMA AntiAircraft Brigade and was announced in the London Gazette dated 22 June 1916. He was first promoted to Colour Sergeant on 27 October 1918 whilst in France, reverted to Sergeant on 23 June 1920 and was promoted again on 12 August 1920. He completed his 21 adult years and was discharged to pension on 10 December 1923. He had been made Steward of the Sergeants Mess in 1919 and on retirement he was appointed Steward of the new NAAFI Canteen & Bar in which capacity he served for twenty-six years until 1949. He died at his home in Festing Grove, Southsea, on 29 March 1958 and was cremated at Southampton Crematorium on 3 April. In addition to the DSM he was also awarded the 1914-15 Star, British War Medal, Victory Medal, Meritorious Service Medal (see below) and the Long Service and Good Conduct Medal.

Sources: 20-24

Lieutenant William James COEN, DSM (RMA 4896) (14 Oct 1900, 17 Nov 1901 & 6 Dec 1903 all as Sergeant)

He received his medal for services with the RN Siege Guns and was gazetted on 16 March 1918. The London Gazette records that he was serving in France whereas his Officers' Service Record says Belgium.

He was born on 9 March 1875 in East Stonehouse, Plymouth and enlisted in London on 2 August 1893. His father was James John Coen, Pensioner RMLI (Plymouth 13770, 1863-1884). He gained promotions to Bombardier (10 March 1896), Corporal (1 July 1897), Sergeant (29 December 1899) and Colour Sergeant (6 December 1908) and saw sea service in *Devastation* (1895-96, Devonport), *Monarch* (1899-1900, Cape of Good Hope), *Majestic* (1902-03, Channel), *Magnificent* (1906-09, Home) and *Africa* (1912-14, Sheerness & 3rd Battle Squadron). His service on *Monarch* took him ashore in South Africa and he was involved in the actions at Paardeburg, Driefontein and Cape Colony, sustaining an injury during the latter action.

He completed his 21 years in 1914 and was immediately mobilized for WWI and continued to serve as Colour Sergeant until 26 July 1917 when he was granted a commission as Temporary Lieutenant RM. He was nominally posted to *Attentive II* on 27 July 1917 for service with the Royal Navy Siege Guns in Belgium. This posting ended on 12 August 1917 and he was then moved to the Orkney Isles to serve at the Hoxa Battery there (*Cyclops II*). On 27 March 1919 he returned to Eastney and on 1 July 1919 was placed on the retirement list. On 1 January 1920 he was appointed to the Special Reserve of Officers RM and on 8 April 1921 was *"recalled for service in emergency"* in reaction to the National Coal Strike. He served at Eastney until being demobilized on 26 May 1921. He died in the Royal Portsmouth Hospital on 22 April 1923 and is buried in Highland Road Cemetery, Southsea.

His other medals include: South Africa Medal with clasps for Paardeburg, Dreifontein and Cape Colony; Long Service and Good Conduct Medal; British War Medal and the Victory Medal.

His Colour Sergeants uniform is on display in the entrance to the Royal Marines Museum, Eastney, to the left of the main staircase.

His son, also William James (PO 214686), who was born on 27 October 1901 and baptized in the RMA Church on 17 November 1901, enlisted as a Boy Bugler in 1915 aged *"13 years, 9 months and 25 days"*; his height was 4 foot 10½ inches (1.49 metres). Within a year he was posted to the newly-built *Resolution* which was part of the 1st Battle Squadron of the Grand Fleet. He saw no direct action in the North Sea but *Resolution* was one of the fleet of British and American ships that accepted the surrender of the German High Seas Fleet off the Firth of Forth. At the age of 18 he became a Gunner RMA and went on to serve in WWII including spells in *Glasgow* (1937-40, Norway) and *Belfast* (1942-43, Arctic Convoys). He retired at the rank of Corporal in 1945. He died on 13 June 1976.

Sources: 25-32

Quartermaster Sergeant Edward Wesley WESTON, DSM (RMA 5148) (22 Jul 1904 as Bombardier)
Sergeant Weston was awarded his medal for service in *Monarch* at the Battle of Jutland (1916).

He was born on 21 May 1874 in Ashford, Kent and enlisted on 6 March 1894 in London. Over the next 24 years he served in *Edinburgh*, (1895-97, Coast Guard Queensferry), *Rodney* (1897-98, Guardship Queensferry), *Colossus* (1900-01, Guardship Holyhead), *Resolution* (1901, Channel), *Pembroke* (1904-05, Chatham), *Africa* (1906-09, Chatham & Channel), *Triumph* (1910-12, Mediterranean) and *Monarch* (1912-18, 2nd Battle Squadron). Whilst serving in *Monarch* he completed his contracted service and was nominally pensioned on 5 March 1915 but was immediately mobilized and continued to serve on the ship until July 1918, having been made Colour Sergeant on 30 November 1916. Shortly after leaving *Monarch* he was promoted to Quartermaster Sergeant at the RMA Depot, Deal, and served at this rank until his final retirement on 29 August 1919. His evocative account of the Battle of Jutland from his position on the fore top of *Monarch* is held at the RM Museum and was published in The Sheet Anchor (the journal of the Royal Marines Historical Society) in the edition of Summer 2004. He was added to the list of candidates for the Meritorious Service Medal on 11 July 1918 but was one of many who died before receiving the award. He did though receive his Long Service and Good Conduct Medal in 1909. He appears to have died in London in 1933; what must be him is recorded incorrectly in the National Probate Calendar as Edward Wellesley Weston. He was living (and presumably working) at the Royal Humane Society's Receiving House in Hyde Park and died in St George's Hospital, Hyde Park Corner on 4 May 1933.

Sources: 33-37

Military Cross

The MC was instigated on 28 December 1914 and was awarded for *".. gallantry during active operations against the enemy"*. It was awarded to commissioned officers of the rank of Captain or below and non-commissioned officers. It was the Army equivalent to the Royal Navy's Distinguished Service Cross.

Brigadier Dudley Ashton Hope HIRE, DSO, MC (29 Mar 1894)
In WWI whilst serving in the Royal Garrison Artillery he was mentioned in despatches three times; on 1 January 1916 (as Lieutenant), 18 May 1917 (as acting

Captain) and 21 May 1918 (as Captain) before being awarded the MC for his actions with the Royal Garrison Artillery 69th Siege Battery (gazetted 1 January 1919). See more about him under Distinguished Service Order above.

Sources: 38-41

Brigadier Arthur Talbot SHAKESPEAR, DSO, MC (27 Oct 1884)

He was serving with the Royal Engineers when his MC was gazetted on 1 January 1917. For more information about him see his entry under Distinguished Service Order above.

Sources: 42

Military Medal

The MM was established on 25 March 1916 but awards were backdated to 1914. It was awarded to Army personnel below commissioned rank for *"acts of gallantry and devotion to duty under fire"*, being the 'other ranks' equivalent to the Military Cross. The RMA man below was serving under Army command at the time of his act of bravery.

Sergeant Jonathan HEATON, MM (RMA 6269) (1 Jun 1902 as a Corporal)

His award was gazetted posthumously on 12 December 1917; he was killed in action on 24 September whilst serving in Belgium with the RMA Howitzer Brigade. For more information about him see his entry under WWI Fallen above.

Sources: 43-44

Distinguished Conduct Medal

The DCM was instigated on 4 December 1854 as a second level award for gallantry in the field for 'other ranks' and ranking below the Victoria Cross. It was considered in many cases to be a 'near miss' for a VC. It was initially an Army award and all the RMA NCOs listed below were fighting under Army command when their awards were made.

Lieutenant Alfred CARTER, DCM (RMA 2966) (28 Mar 1901)

This date is for his own baptism as an adult when he gave his birth date as 15 April 1868. His father is recorded as Alfred Carter and his mother as Mary Elizabeth, both deceased. The only relevant Register of Service gives a date of birth of 21 August 1867, but there are a number of other factors that match. The occupation of the father is given as butcher in the baptism register and there is an Alfred Carter, butcher, with a son Alfred aged 12, in Corsham, Wilts, in the 1881 census; the mother's name is Mary. In the service record his place of birth is given as Corsham, Wilts and occupation as butcher, so we can be certain that this is the same person. The only relevant birth registration is recorded in the April-June quarter of 1868 so presumably he had lied, or was confused, about his age at enlistment.

He enlisted on 21 July 1886 in Bristol and after initial training at Walmer he was appointed to the RMA on 17 February 1887. He served about six of his 21 years at sea including service in *Benbow* (1888-91, Chatham), *Northampton* (1892-93, Coast Guard Sheerness), *Majestic* (1997-98, Channel) and *Monarch* (1899-1900, Cape of Good Hope). He was promoted to Bombardier on 4 July 1893, Corporal on 5 November 1895, Sergeant on 13 January 1898 and Colour Sergeant on 3 September 1901. Finally, he was promoted to Quartermaster Sergeant Instructor of Gunnery on 28 January 1904 and remained at Eastney in that capacity until being discharged to pension on 20 July 1907.

His service in *Monarch* took him to South Africa where he was seconded to the Royal Horse Artillery and Royal Field Artillery during the South African War (Boer War). He received his DCM during this conflict as the result of a glowing recommendation from Lord Roberts dated 28 September 1900. His service record gives the date of his DCM award as 1 August 1902 but this is an error. He was first mentioned in a despatch issued in the London Gazette of 10 September 1901 and his DCM was then gazetted on 27 September 1901. Perhaps the date in his service record relates to when he was presented with the medal rather than the date of the award as it would normally record. After landing in South Africa on 6 February 1900 he was initially an instructor in Maxim and machine guns at Stellenbosch and later saw service with General Redfer's mounted infantry. The London Gazette of 10 September notes that he was *"attached "B" Section Pom Poms"* whereas Lord Roberts' letter refers to this unit as *"B Section Galloping Maxims"*. This unit was then re-equipped with one-pounder Maxims and he served with it in all the subsequent campaigns. His South Africa Medal has clasps for Johannesburg, Diamond Hill, Belfast, Cape Colony and Wittebergen.

In 1914 he was mobilised from the Royal Fleet Reserve as Acting Quartermaster Sergeant Instructor of Gunnery and at first remained at Eastney. Whilst there he received an accidental bullet wound fracturing his right index finger but he soon recovered and on 27 September 1915 he was promoted to Acting Brigade Sergeant Major. Less than two months later he was posted to the South African Heavy Artillery and arrived in France on 1 May 1916. He served with the 17th Corps and Canadian Corps of the 50th Heavy Artillery Group. On 18 November 1916 he was granted a commission as Temporary Lieutenant and then returned to Eastney on 1 January 1917. He was immediately posted to *Cyclops II* at Scapa Flow. He returned to Eastney on 3 September 1919 and was placed on the retired list on 4 October 1919. He was living in Brading, Isle of Wight, when he died at the Royal Isle of Wight County Hospital on 18 April 1947. See his entry under Meritorious Service Medal below.

Sources: 36 & 45-53

Company Sergeant Major Sidney Guy DACOMBE, DCM (RMA 5099)
(19 Oct 1902 as Sergeant)
He was born in Carlisle on 30 December 1874 and enlisted at Poole on 9 December 1893. His height on enlistment was 6 feet 1 & ⁷⁄₁₀ inches (1.86 metres), for that time

tall for a grown man let alone a nineteen-year old. He served less than three years in ships including service in *Benbow* (1895-96, Coast Guard Greenock) and *King Edward VII* (1908-09, Channel). He was promoted to Bombardier on 19 May 1896, Corporal on 25 August 1897 and Sergeant on 7 May 1900. On 19 September 1905 he was nominally posted to *President* but was actually engaged at the Royal Naval College, Greenwich probably as a Gymnastic Instructor. He served at Greenwich until 23 December 1907. He was well-known for his physical prowess and is recorded as being a Gymnastic Instructor from 1901-4. He was a leading RN weightlifter even giving a performance of *'heavy weightlifting'* in Eastney Barrack's Globe Theatre as part of a show in 1904. He was promoted to Colour Sergeant on 6 April 1909 but reverted to Sergeant on 1 May 1911.

World War I was declared just five months before he was due to retire after 21 years and he was soon afterwards promoted again to Colour Sergeant (20 September 1914) and posted to *Hyacinth* at Cape of Good Hope Dockyard and seconded to the South African Government for service with their Heavy Artillery in German West Africa.

He returned a year later and was then posted to France with the Royal Garrison Artillery's South Africa Contingent (East African Expeditionary Force). He was soon made acting Battery Sergeant Major (27 August 1915) of 71st Siege Battery (Transvaal). It was with this group at Ieper (Ypres) in June 1916 that he won his DCM for his actions during a Canadian-led counter-attack; the citation in the London Gazette reads: *"For conspicuous gallantry and devotion to duty. He showed great courage and determination in rescuing three wounded men in the open, under very heavy fire."* He returned to Eastney on 28 March 1918 and a few days later was promoted to Company Sergeant Major (WOII). He was finally demobilised on 28 July 1919, having served 26½ years.

Whilst CSM Dacombe had an impeccable record his RMA service wasn't without embarrassment. His physical prowess has been mentioned before and he was acknowledged as the strongest man in the Army and Navy. On 10 April 1905 a Professor Uyenishi was asked to give a demonstration of Ju-jitsu at the Royal Military College, Sandhurst. Unknown to the Professor, Dacombe was brought from Chatham to show what real strength could do against the Japanese martial art. Unannounced, he challenged the Professor who, probably suspecting something, passed the challenge on to one of his pupils who had only had five months training. The pupil threw Sergeant Dacombe several times and concluded the bout by an overhead throw and arm lock. It must have been highly embarrassing for Dacombe and there must have been a few red faces among the officers present who hatched the plan. Later in 1911 he began three and a half years as Superintendent of the Bar & Canteen at Eastney; I'm sure that no unruly elements got the better of him there.

Dacombe senior apparently died in Greenwich in 1943. Sadly his body was not returned to Highland Road Cemetery to be buried alongside his wife Louisa who had died in 1923.

The baptism quoted above was of his son John (known later as Jack – see Chapter 11) who is the young man in the photo with his parents.

Sources: 25, 31 & 54-57

Sergeant Major Charles DADD, DCM (RMA 4633) (8 Jun 1900 & 5 Apr 1903)

He was born near Chichester, Sussex, in December 1875 and enlisted at Eastney on 15 July 1892. He served just over 7 of his initial 21 years at sea including service in *Colossus* (1894-95, Coast Guard Holyhead), *Vivid* (1897-99, Devonport), *Camperdown* (1900-1902, Coast Guard Lough Swilly), *Duke of Edinburgh* (1908-09, Channel), *King Alfred* (1909-10, China) and *London* (1910-12, Atlantic). He was promoted to Bombardier on 17 March 1895, Corporal on 1 April 1897, Sergeant on 1 July 1899 and Colour Sergeant on 17 March 1908. He completed his 21 years on 14 July 1913. The following year he was mobilised at his previous rank of Colour Sergeant and after the RMA 'excursions' to Ostend and Dunkirk served with the RMA Anti-Aircraft Brigade for just over a year until returning to Eastney on 28 June 1916. On 9 September he was posted to No12 Battery RMA Howitzer Brigade and returned to France.

On 27 July 1917 he was made acting Battery Sergeant Major (WOII). He was still serving with 12 Howitzer Battery when recommended for his DCM which was first announced in the London Gazette of 1 January 1919. The citation appeared in the London Gazette of 3 September 1919 and reads;

"For gallant and distinguished conduct in the field. On many occasions he has rescued and tended wounded men under heavy fire, particularly on 27th July 1918, when he personally carried six wounded men out of a farm which was being heavily shelled, and on 2nd August 1918, when he rendered most valuable assistance under fire in digging out two civilians who had been wounded and buried under the remains of a farmhouse. For over two years he has carried out the duties of B.S.M. in a most efficient manner, and has always set a fine and inspiring example to his men under trying circumstances."

He returned to Eastney on 16 June 1919 and was demobilised on 29 July 1919 and subsequently nominated for the MSM, see below. He retired to Bexley Heath in Kent and was still living there when he died whilst working at the Vickers Engineering Works at Crayford on 17 May 1944.

Sources: 25, 36 & 58-60

A 15-inch Howitzer 'new out of the box' from the Coventry Ordnance Works. This weapon had been developed by Admiral Bacon who was the Managing Director of the COW from 1910-15. [61]

Captain Frederick JENVEY, DCM (RMA 4477) (6 May 1900 as Colour Sergeant and 12 Oct 1902 as Quartermaster Sergeant)

He was awarded the DCM for his actions at The Atbara in the Sudan on 9 April 1898 and his medal was presented by the Queen at Windsor Castle on 1 July 1899.

He was born at Hilsea, Portsmouth, on 21 November 1868 and was a Police Constable when he enlisted at Gosport on 21 October 1891. After initial training at Walmer he was posted to the RMA on 23 April 1892. He was promoted to Corporal on 19 May 1896 and weeks later on 19 June was loaned to the Egyptian Army along with nine other RMA NCOs; they were to act as gunnery commanders in the Nile gunboats. He was mentioned in dispatches on 21 October 1896 for "*Services in the Dongola Expedition*" and on 25 November 1896 was "*Specially recommended*" for his service in the same expedition. Whereas his colleagues then returned to the UK Jenvey remained and eventually joined with the second party of NCOs when they arrived in July 1897. In April 1898 he was present at the Battle of The Atbara. Although the gunboats did not take part Jenvey was selected to lead a small rocket party ashore under the command of Lieutenant (later to become First Sea Lord) Beatty RN. They were armed with one rocket tube and a supply of 24-pound rockets. After expending the rockets the party took part in the general assault and Jenvey wrote that *"we moved up to the zareba, and with a charge and a cheer were at the enemy with the bayonet."* As a result he was promoted to Colour Sergeant on 14 April 1898 "for specially good service in the field".

He returned to the RMA on 4 February 1899 and was promoted to Quartermaster Sergeant Instructor of Gunnery on 21 May 1902. He completed his 21 years and retired on 21 October 1912. He was mobilised from the Reserve in August 1914 and was at Ostend and Dunkirk before on 24 October that year he was posted to *Hyacinth* for service in South Africa, arriving at Cape Town on 19 November. He was made Acting Sergeant Major and took part in the invasion of German West Africa, where he served ashore with the Union Defence Force. He was also in command of a 6-inch quick-firing gun on an armoured train at Fishoek. He was granted a commission with this force and served as a Gunnery Instructor with the South Africa Heavy Artillery. On 1 August 1915 he returned to *Hyacinth* and was granted a temporary commission to Lieutenant RMA. He was seconded to the Royal Garrison Artillery (RGA) and was involved in the recruitment and training of the South African Contingent that was being formed for service in France. He arrived back at the RGA Depot in Bexhill with this force which was then incorporated into the RGA Siege Batteries. Lieutenant

This photo shows RMA Sergeants shortly after receiving their medals from Queen Victoria at Windsor Castle on 1 Jul 1899, but it looks as though it was taken at Eastney. The text names five RMA Sergeants as having been awarded the DCM, but as Sergeant Trowbridge was not awarded his medal until 25 Jul 1901 we must assume that it is Colour Sergeants Jenvey & Russell and Sergeants Mathieson & Lambert in this photo. The elderly man is described as "one of the oldest veteran sergeants at Eastney" and bears a likeness to Sergeant Hetheridge (see his entry and photo below) [67]

Jenvey remained as assisstant to Colonel Rose at the Brigade Depot until he returned to the RMA at Eastney on 11 June 1917. He was promoted to Temporary Captain (Instructor of Gunnery) on 23 August 1918 and served at this rank until retiring on 13 October 1919. His retirement was a short one; he was living in Wimborne Road, Southsea when he died of pneumonia less than a year later on 2 April 1920 and was buried in Highland Road Cemetery, Southsea six days later.

His other medals include: Khedive's Sudan Medal with clasps for Sudan 1897, The Atbara, Khartoum, Hafir and Gedaref; British Sudan Medal; Long Service and Good Conduct Medal; 1914 Star and the British War Medal. He would also have received the Victory Medal but he died before it was issued. The award of his DCM seems to have not been announced in the London Gazette.

Sources: 6, 32, 36 & 62-69

Lieutenant Samuel Thorburn MATHIESON, DCM (RMA 4642) (4 Apr 1897 as Corporal)

There is some confusion about his second name; his service record has it as Thomas, his Officers Service Record has it as Thorburn and the GRO Death Index has Thornburn; there is no doubt however that this is one and the same man. He was awarded his medal for his service with the Dongola Expedition in Egypt in 1896 and received the medal from the Queen at Windsor Castle on 1 July 1899. He had been formally nominated for the award on 16 May 1899, the same day as Jenvey, but neither of their awards seem to have made it into the London Gazette.

He was born in Glasgow on 13 November 1874 and enlisted there on 13 June 1892. After initial training at Walmer he was posted to the RMA at Eastney on 16 November 1892. His only 'sea service' before his secondment to the Egyptian Army in June 1896 was a year in *Victory* in Portsmouth Harbour. Whilst serving in Egypt he was mentioned in despatches *"for services in Dongola Expedition"* and was *"specially recommended"* for these same services by the Senior Naval Officer which led to the award of the DCM. He returned to the UK in November 1896 but was later selected for a second secondment when eight NCOs were sent to the Nile

An RMA Siege Gun on its way back to Dunkirk on a snowy February day in 1919 [71]

in July 1897. During his time in Egypt and Sudan he was promoted to Corporal on 20 November 1896 during his first secondment and then to Sergeant on 1 June 1898 during his second visit.

Following his return to the UK in 1899 he spent most of his remaining service at Eastney apart from just over a year in *Magnificent* (1904-06, Channel then Atlantic) and less than a year in *Niobe* (1907-08, Home). He retired on completion of 21 years on 12 June 1913 at the rank of Barrack Sergeant but was mobilised on 2 August 1914. He was made acting Sergeant Major on 10 December 1914 and apart from the RMA 'excursions' to Ostend (27 to 31 August 1914) and Dunkirk (7 to 18 October 1914) he served initially at Eastney until 28 October 1915 when he was posted to the RMA Anti-Aircraft Brigade. On 18 May 1916 he was granted a temporary commission as Lieutenant, continuing to serve with the Anti-Aircraft Brigade including in the operations on the Somme and Ancre. He returned to Eastney HQ on 29 May 1917 and was then posted to the newly formed RMA Heavy Siege Train (*Achilles II*) on 23 June 1917.

He was officially appointed Acting Captain on 18 June 1918 but General Blumberg's history of the Heavy Siege Train states that a Captain Mathieson was commanding the 9.2-inch gun at Coxyde in 1917. He reverted to Lieutenant on returning to Eastney on 15 January 1919 and was then placed on the retired list on 6 March 1919. He died on the Isle of Skye on 14 November 1952.

His other medals include: Khedive's Sudan Medal with clasps for Hafir, Sudan 1897 and Khartoum; British Sudan Medal; Long Service and Good Conduct Medal; Croix de Guerre (Belgian); 1914 Star; British War Medal and Victory Medal.

Sources: 6, 25 & 68-73

Colour Sergeant Frederick Evan SADDON, DCM (RMA 2602) (9 Feb 1902)

He was born in Portsmouth in November 1865 and enlisted at Eastney on 26 January 1886, abandoning his trade as a tailor. He served nearly four of his first twelve years at sea including service in *Neptune* (1888, Coast Guard Holyhead), *Galatea* (1889, Portsmouth) and *Magicienne* (1890-93, North America & West Indies), gaining promotions to Bombardier (11 September 1888), Corporal (11 July 1891) and Sergeant (14 September 1894). Then on 20 June 1898, he was seconded to the Egyptian Army and on 25 October promoted to Colour Sergeant His excellent service led to him being *"Noted by directions of the Lords Commissioners of the Admiralty for excellent service with the Nile Expedition, 1898"*. We know from Sergeant Trowbridge's diary that during January 1899 Saddon was serving on the gunboat Tamai; Trowbridge records *"I saw Freddie Saddon with a letter for me. I can't say how pleased I was to see him again*

The Nile Gunboat Melik. She was built by John Thornycroft at Chiswick in 1896-7, then dismantled, shipped to the Nile along with two sister ships which were then re-assembled under the guidance of Major W S Gordon RE. In addition to the 5-inch howitzer visible on the forecastle, she was armed with two 12-pounders and four Maxims. She is the only one of the Nile Gunboats to have survived and is currently awaiting restoration. [77]

with his old pleasant smile". On 18 February 1899 Colour Sergeant Saddon joined Sergeant Trowbridge in the *Melik*, taking over as 'acting captain'. Saddon appears to have continued in this role with Trowbridge as his number two until the first week of July, operating mainly between Rosaries (often referred to at the time as Rosieres) and Sennar on the Blue Nile.

They managed to hole the ship trying to get through one of the cataracts but apart from that their main problems were attacks of dysentery (Saddon) and fever, presumably malaria (Trowbridge). There is a gap in Trowbridge's diary but presumably they played a part in the decisive Battle of Omdurman (3 September 1899) but it was during the subsequent *"final pursuit of the Khalifa, Sudan, Nov 1899"* that his actions led to him being awarded the DCM. He continued to serve with the Egyptian Army until 8 October 1900 and was mentioned in despatches in January 1900 along with Colour Sergeant Seabright (see below), his entry in the London Gazette being incorrectly spelt as Seddons. He was also awarded the Queen's Sudan Medal (1900) and the Khedive's Sudan Medal (1899). On return from Egypt he remained at Eastney until he had completed his 21 years on 25 January 1907. In 1914 he was not immediately mobilised from the Reserve as he was exempted due to *"Duty at Admiralty"*. He was eventually mobilised as a Colour Sergeant on 9 February 1915 and two days later made Acting Quartermaster Sergeant until 21 January 1916 when he reverted to Colour Sergeant There is an indication on his service record that he was serving with the RMA Brigade at this time but on 20 May 1916 he was *"discharged invalided"* to Haslar Hospital but no cause was given. He died in Portsmouth on 17 July 1930, aged 64, and is buried in an unmarked grave in Highland Road Cemetery, Southsea. He 'queue-jumped' the MSM waiting list as a result of this award of the DCM (see Meritorious Service Medal below).

Sources: 31, 45 & 74-77

Colour Sergeant George Elliott SEABRIGHT, DCM* (RMA 2247) (21 Mar 1897 as Sergeant)

He was born in Southwark, London; his birth date was originally recorded as January 1866 on his service register but at some later date this has been crossed-out and replaced by 15 December 1865. He enlisted in London on 14 July 1884 and after initial training at Walmer was posted to the RMA on 18 December 1884. His sea service (just over six years) included spells in *Bellerophon* (1885-89, North America & West Indies) and *Rapid* (1892-94, Australia). He was promoted to Sergeant on joining *Rapid* on 20 December 1892 and was promoted to Colour Sergeant on secondment to the Egyptian Army on 1 July 1897, where he served until completing his 21 years in 1905. He was mentioned in despatches in Egyptian Army Order No 84 on 29 May 1898 for *"Good services during operation on the Atbara"* which led to his receiving the DCM. As the gunboats were not involved in this action he was probably serving ashore with one of the Maxim units. He was mentioned in despatches again (with Saddon, see above) in a report by Colonel Sir Reginald Wingate, Commanding Troops on the White Nile, dated 25 November 1899 and published in the London Gazette of 30 January 1900. This led to an announcement on 13 March 1900 that he had been awarded the DCM. However a further announcement on 1 May 1900 corrected this to say that he had been awarded a bar to his DCM for the *"final pursuit of the Khalifa, Sudan, Nov 1899"*. His was one of only 12 bars to the DCM awarded before World War I. Like Colour Sergeant Saddon he 'queue-jumped' the MSM waiting list as a result of this award (see Meritorious Service Medal below). He was also awarded the Khedive's Sudan Medal with clasps for Sudan 1897, Khartoum, Gedarif, Sudan 1899 & Gedid; British Sudan Medal and the Long Service and Good Conduct Medal. He was discharged to pension on 18 July 1905 and his service record shows that in 1909 he applied to become a Yeoman of the Guard but was rejected due to his height, which was 5 feet 8½ inches (1.74 metres) in 1905. He either stayed or returned to Egypt as a civil servant and in 1912 was reported as being Assistant Engineer in the Public Works Department at Malakal, Upper Nile Province. He left his wife and children (four daughters by 1911) at home, initially living with her mother and later in their own house in Fulham. He died in the Wandsworth Registration District in 1943.

Sources: 69, 75-76 & 78-83

Colour Sergeant Robert Augustus TROWBRIDGE, DCM (RMA 4599)

(12 Aug 1900 as Colour Sergeant)

He was born in Petworth, Sussex in August, 1874. His father, also Robert, was an itinerant carter whose first six children were born in different locations across southern England. His first contact with the military was in 1889 when the family were living at Beaulieu, Hants, and he travelled to Winchester to enlist as a boy soldier with the Scots Guards. He enlisted on 18 May 1889 but two days later was declared unfit for the Army due to *"Very knock knees, physical development bad"* and was discharged after 3 days for *"not being likely to become efficient"*. Quite why they took three days and generated four pages of unnecessary paperwork when he was clearly not physically suited to the Guards is a mystery.

His Royal Marine service register has not survived and so the main sources for information about his life after his army disappointment are census records and the papers and artefacts deposited in the Royal Marines Museum.

In 1891 Robert junior was living with his family who had then moved to Christchurch, Hants (now Dorset), his occupation recorded as *"employed at home"*. His Nile Campaign diary shows that he enlisted at the age of 18 on 13 June 1892, and in 1897 he was seconded to Egypt as a Corporal along with 8 other RMA NCOs including Mathieson, Saddon and Seabright. He made himself very useful on the journey out, teaching the others semaphore but he got off to a bad start in Egypt, contracting dysentery through drinking local lemonade and he had to be left behind in Cairo to recover.

He was promoted to Sergeant at some point (he had passed his Sergeants exam just before leaving the UK) before being given another promotion to Colour Sergeant for *"services rendered in the Nile Expedition"*. He learnt of this second promotion from a copy of the Hampshire Telegraph dated 22 April 1899 which he received on 29 May, but he did not receive an official notification until 5 June. He was awarded the DCM (gazetted on 30 June 1899) for his actions in the *"defeat of Ahmed Fedil's Army in the Cataract south of Roseires"* which took place on 28 December 1898. This followed his being mentioned in despatches by Lieutenant Colonel D F Lewis (London Gazette 5 May 1899) for his work with one of two

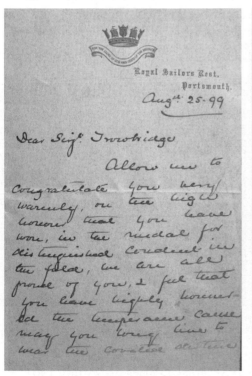
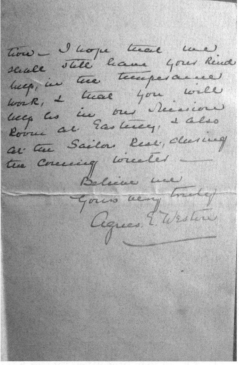

Agatha (Aggie) Weston's letter to Colour Sergeant Trowbridge, 25 August 1899 [87]

Maxim guns and for his good service and attention to the wounded. His work on the Nile gunboats had also been commended by Lieutenant (later First Sea Lord) Beatty, RN, who was a gunboat commander at the time. He is never very specific in his diary about which boat he was on other than it was initially Captain Keppell's boat (Commander C Keppell RN was the Gunboat Flotilla Commander in *Zafir*) and his diary has a gap between 14 September 1897 and 22 November 1898. The decisive Battle of Omdurman was on 3 September 1898 and so it is no surprise that he had no time for diary writing during this period. It was presumably during this period that he was promoted to Sergeant There is another gap between 2 December 1898 and 15 January 1899 which was a period of significant combat that included the action that led to the award of his DCM. In January-February 1899 he was 'acting captain' of the *Melik* for over a month until being joined aboard by Colour Sergeant Saddon who then took command. It wasn't all work on the gunboats, his diary tells of plenty of sport including the shooting of hippos, crocodiles, gazelles and even an elephant. He had many bouts of sickness (presumably malaria) whilst on the Nile and eventually in July 1899 he applied to resign and this was granted later that month after which he quickly made his way down river and home.

Trowbridge had married Edith Mary Musgrove in St Bartholomew's Church, Southsea before leaving for Egypt and on his return they were living in Tokar Street, Southsea, but in September 1904 he died at the early age of 30 leaving Edith and his only son Robert Musgrove who was just three years old. He was buried in Highland Road Cemetery, Southsea on 22 September 1904 and his grave is marked by a headstone and cross paid for by his colleagues in the Sergeant's Mess.

One interesting item held in the RM Museum is a letter from Agnes (Aggie) Weston congratulating him on the award of his DCM. This note infers that he was known personally to her and was a supporter of the temperance cause, helping at Eastney and at her Sailor's Rest in the town.

His medals – Distinguished Conduct Medal, Queen's Sudan Medal and Khedive's Sudan Medal 1896-98 with 'Sudan 1897', 'Gedaref', 'Khartoum' & 'Sudan 1899' clasps, are in the RM Museum collection. Also donated to the Museum were a number of artefacts including items belonging to a Dervish warrior at Omdurman; and his diary relating to the Sudan (1897-99).

His DCM was presented by the King at St James's Palace on 25 July 1901.

Sources: 31-32, 53, 62, 68, 74 & 84-95

Order of the British Empire (OBE)

Lieutenant Colonel William George SPARROW, OBE (RMA 2011) (2 Nov 1895 as Colour Sergeant)

This baptism of his daughter actually took place in St Saviour's Church, Victoria, British Columbia whilst he was serving in *Royal Arthur* and was added to the RMA Church register on the family's return to Eastney. Its position in the baptism register suggests that it was entered sometime in late April-early May 1896.

William George Sparrow was born in London on 2 October 1865 and enlisted at Chatham on his 18th birthday on 2 October 1883. After initial training at Walmer he was appointed to Eastney on 1 May 1884. He spent just two spells at sea; in *Bacchante* (1885-88, East Indies) and *Royal Arthur* (1893-96, Pacific). He was promoted to Sergeant on 7 June 1889 and Colour Sergeant on 10 March 1896. On 1 January 1897 he reverted to Sergeant and was then promoted again to Colour Sergeant on 12 August 1897 and then Superintendant Clerk on 19 October 1898 and Quartermaster and Honorary Lieutenant on 13 November 1901. He earned a further promotion to Honorary Captain on 13 November 1911 and at this rank he was appointed 2nd Quartermaster RMA on 22 September 1912. On promotion to Honorary Major on 24 April 1913 he became 1st Quartermaster RMA. He was promoted to Lieutenant Colonel two months before he was placed on the retirement list on 2 October 1920 on reaching the age for compulsory retirement. He was appointed to the Military Division of the Order of the British Empire in an announcement in the London Gazette of 1 January 1919. Both of his service records state that he was awarded the *"Burma Medal & Clasp"* but presumably this must mean the India General Service Medal with Burma clasp. He would have qualified for this during his service in *Bacchante*, perhaps as a member of the Naval Brigade that steamed up the Irrawaddy to eventually occupy Mandalay. He was an amateur artist – his proficiency in drawing and painting in oils is mentioned twice in his service record. He had been living in Craneswater Avenue but died in Kings Service Nursing Home, Elm Grove, Southsea on 14 July 1938 and was buried in Highland Road Cemetery, Southsea on 18 July. He is buried in a family grave with his wife Ellen, who died in 1955, and his daughter Hilda, who died in 1929. The headstone also pays remembrance to his son Captain William Gordon Morgan Sparrow of the Northamptonshire Regiment who was killed in East Africa in 1917 whilst serving with the King's African Rifles.

Lieutenant Colonel Sparrow's other medals include: Long Service and Good Conduct Medal and British War Medal

Sources: 31-32, 36, 78 & 96-97

Meritorious Service Medal

The Meritorious Service Medal (MSM) was introduced for the Army in 1845 as recognition of exemplary service by senior Non-Commissioned Officers (NCOs), meaning Sergeants and above (for example Colour Sergeants and Sergeant Majors). It was introduced by the Royal Marines in 1849 and was only to be awarded to those senior NCOs who had given long and blemish-free service; your record had to be squeaky-clean before you could even be considered. The initial regulation required that the recipient should have a *"perfectly irreproachable and meritorious character for at least 24 years, fourteen of which he shall have served as a Sergeant"*. The MSM was never awarded by the Royal Navy.

The medal came with an annuity but the problem was that initially only £250 a year was allocated to cover all the annuities. This meant that in the first year only 16 Royal Marine NCOs received the medal with an annuity ranging up to £20 a year. Later the annual annuity budget was increased and the award standardised at £10 a year but still it could not cover all those that had been selected as having the requisite standard of conduct throughout their service. It therefore became a case of 'dead man's shoes'; as recipients of the annuity died that annuity passed to the next senior on the list and so on. Some recipients did not receive their annuities until they had been retired many years and many died before their turn came. Whereas a £10 annual annuity in 1850 was not to be sniffed at, by the turn of the century it was much less significant and the award became symbolic, but none the less much prized and sought after. Altogether about 576 awards were made between 1849 and 1951. Included in this total are some medals that were awarded for gallantry or special service in action. For example, a special fund of £50 was allocated in 1905 for senior NCOs that had been awarded the Distinguished Conduct Medal; three of the initial five recipients under this scheme are included in the list below (Saddon, Seabright & Carter).

During WW1 an Immediate MSM was awarded and this is described below.

I am much indebted to John Bilcliffe for his book *"Irreproachable Character – The Award of the Royal Marine Meritorious Service Medal"* [98] for much of the information contained in this section and it should be taken as read that his work was a source for all the records listed below. Readers are recommended to refer to his book for a more detailed history of the medal. There are 32 MSM recipients represented in the Crinoline Church baptisms. They are (with the dates of their entries in the baptism register in brackets):

Colour Sergeant George BOYCE (RMA 4638) (17 Oct 1897 as Corporal and 18 Jan 1903 as Sergeant)

He was born on 25 February 1873 near Bury St Edmonds, Suffolk, and enlisted at Walmer on 25 July 1892. He served about 9 of his 21 years at sea including service in *Repulse* (1894-96, Channel), *Royal Oak* (1898-1902, Mediterranean), *Illustrious* (1904-05, Channel & Atlantic), *Natal* (1907-10, Home) and *Inflexible* (1912-13,

Mediterranean). He was promoted to Colour Sergeant whilst serving in *Natal* (1909) and completed his 21 years on 24 July 1913. He was mobilised from the Fleet Reserve in August 1914 and posted to the newly commissioned *Emperor of India* at Scapa Flow. He returned to Eastney on 14 February 1916 and was demobilised on 20 Mar 1919.

He was renowned as a gunnery marksman and is the only Royal Marine or Sailor to win the Good Shooting Medal with three clasps (that is, four times). His original medal and first clasp were won in 1904 and 1905 with a 6-inch quick fire gun whilst serving in *Illustrious*, the second clasp in 1908 whilst serving in *Natal* using a 9.2-inch Breech Loading gun and the third clasp in *Illustrious* again in 1913 firing a 12-inch Breach Loading gun. He eventually received his MSM, aged 73, on 21 October 1946. He had retired to Southbourne, West Sussex and he died in the Royal West Sussex Hospital, Chichester after a short illness on 4 September 1950.

Sources: 25 & 99-102

Colour Sergeant Albert Edward BUTLER (RMA 1353) (15 Jul 1888, 22 Nov 1891, 25 Nov 1894 & 1 Jan 1905)

He was born in Portsmouth on 13 September 1865 and enlisted on 13 September 1880 as a Boy Bugler. He served just two spells at sea, in *Achilles* (1882-84, Channel) and *Swiftsure* (1888-90, Pacific) and his remaining 24 years were served at Eastney. He remained a Bugler until 11 May 1893 when he was promoted to Bombardier; then he was made Corporal on 12 January 1894 and Sergeant Bugle Major on 16 August 1901. He retired on 20 October 1904 but was then employed at Eastney in the RN School of Music as a civilian instructor; in the 1911 census he describes himself as *"Marine Pensioner, Musician Teaching Music"*. He was mobilized in 1914 and served at Eastney as a Sergeant until being promoted to Acting Colour Sergeant on 26 September 1916. On 20
April 1918 he was posted to Chatham to serve with the Royal Marine Engineers but was hospitalised back to Haslar on 24 October 1918 with *"aortic incompetence"* and he was *'discharged invalided'* on 21 November 1918. He appears to be one of only two in this list of notables to have received the Silver War Badge and Certificate. This badge was introduced in 1916 to prove that the wearer had been honorably discharged. It had become the custom for women to present young and able-bodied men not in uniform with white feathers and this had caused some distress. The badge was introduced to overcome this and was to be worn on civilian dress only. He received his MSM and annuity on 27 November 1941, 23 years after he was discharged; he

died in Portsmouth just over a year later on 15 March 1943 and is buried in Highland Road Cemetery, Southsea. The grave is covered in a thick coat of ivy but fortunately the headstone is still uncovered, but not for very long I think.

Sources: 31-32, 53 & 103-104

Hospital Sergeant James Robert CANSDALE (RMA 667) (2 on 28 Feb 1882, 27 Apr 1884, 10 Jul 1887, 21 Apr 1889, & 29 May 1892)
He is recorded as Corporal for the first three baptism dates, then Colour Sergeant in 1887, Corporal in 1889 and Sergeant in 1892. However, his service record shows that he was a Corporal in 1887 so this must be an error in the register. He was born in December 1855 in Liverpool and enlisted there on 21 August 1875. He was appointed as a Gunner to RMA on 4 February 1876. He had just one spell at sea in *Resistance* (Coast Guard Rockferry, 1877-78). He spent the remainder of his 21 years at Eastney, being promoted to Corporal on 14 November 1879 and Hospital Sergeant on 5 August 1891. He was pensioned after completing his 21 years on 20 August 1896. He subsequently worked for the Admiralty as a *"Pensioner Writer"* and in 1911 he was doing this job at RN Hospital, Haslar. He received his MSM on 27 October 1935 and the medal is held at the RM Museum. He had been living in Jubilee Road, Waterlooville, when he died on 5 November 1938, at the age of 82.

Sources: 36, 53 & 105-108

Lieutenant Alfred CARTER, DCM (RMA 2966) (28 Mar 1901)
This date is for his own baptism as an adult. He received his medal on 17 November 1907 just four months after his retirement. He was one of the first five Sergeants to get priority due to having been awarded the Distinguished Conduct Medal; this was after an additional £50 was added to the annuity fund in 1905 (the others included Saddon and Seabright, see below). For other information on Lieutenant Carter see his entry under Distinguished Conduct Medal above. His MSM is in the RM Museum collection.

Colour Sergeant Frederick George CHAPMAN, DCM (Po 27919/RMA 7919) (28 March 1900 as Drummer)
When he was discharged to pension in 1923 the following note was added to his Register of Service; *"name noted for award of Meritorious Service Medal and Annuity in turn"*. He had to wait until 1951 before he got his medal and a further five years for the annuity. For more information on his career see his entry under Distinguished Service Medal above.

Sources: 20 & 109

Colour Sergeant Emmanuel CROOK (RMA 293) (28 Mar 1880 as Gunner, 29 Mar 1895 as Sergeant & 27 Nov 1892 as Colour Sergeant)
He was born near Tewkesbury in September 1849 and enlisted at Birmingham on 8

December 1871. After training at *Walmer* he was posted to the RMA at Eastney on 14 June 1872. His sea service accounted for about 8 of his 21 years and included service in *Achilles* (1873-5, Coast Guard Portland), *Warrior* (1875, Coast Guard Portland), *Tamar & Hecate* (1878, Particular Service), *Temeraire* (1880-84, Mediterranean), *Euryalus* (1884, to Egypt), *Hero* (1889) and *Neptune* (1890-92, Coast Guard Holyhead). He was promoted to Bombardier on 19 December 1876, Corporal on 12 December 1878, Sergeant on 17 December 1880 and Colour Sergeant on 29 December 1885. He should have retired on completion of his 21 years on 8 December 1892 but was given permission to serve until 17 December.

He took part in two campaigns in Egypt. The first was the Bombardment of Alexandria, for which he was awarded the Egypt medal with Alexandria clasp, and the second was the 1884-85 campaign where he served with the RM Battalion and earned clasps for Suakin, El-Teb and Tamaii. He was also awarded the Khedive's Bronze Star.

He received his MSM on 20 July 1920. He died in Cheltenham on 25 October 1929. Sources: 36, 105 & 110

Sergeant Major Charles DADD, DSM (RMA 4633) (8 Jun 1900 & 5 Apr 1903 both as Sergeant)

He served initially from 1892 to 1913 but was then re-engaged for the duration of WWI finally being demobilised on 29 July 1919. He was subsequently recommended for the MSM but did not receive his medal until 21 April 1941. For more information on his career see his entry under Distinguished Service Medal above.

Company Sergeant Major James DIX (Po 28397/RMA 8397) (28 Mar 1900)

This entry is of his own baptism. He was born in Haverhill, Suffolk, on 25 August 1884 and baptised nearly sixteen years later in the RMA Church on 28 March 1900 as a Bugler. His father's name is recorded as James Dix, Pensioner Colour Sergeant RMA. Dix junior enlisted in Cambridge on 21 September 1899 and saw plenty of sea service during his 21 years beginning in 1901 with a trip to Australia in *Ophir* in the company of the Duke of York and Duchess of Cornwall (the future King George V and Queen Mary) who went to Australia to open the new Federal Parliament in Melbourne. He also served time in, among others, *Duncan* (1903-5, Mediterranean), *Centurion* (1906-7, Portsmouth), *Exmouth* (1907-9, Atlantic), *Glory* (1910, The Nore), *Indomitable* (1910-14, Home & Mediterranean), *Erin* (1914-17, 2nd Battle Squadron), *Dreadnought* (1918, Flagship 4th Battle Squadron), and *Royal Sovereign* (1920, Mediterranean). This sea service saw him involved in three other notable events. First, when serving in the Mediterranean in *Exmouth*, he was one of many RN personnel who were awarded the Medaglia Commemorativa Terremoto Calabro-Siculo 1908 (The Messina Earthquake Medal) by the Italian Government for the assistance they gave following the disaster. Then whilst serving in *Erin* he saw action at the Battle of Jutland. And thirdly, when he joined *Dreadnought* in January 1918 she was part of the Atlantic Fleet but was soon sent to Constantinople (Istanbul) along with *Resolution* to rescue White Russian émigrés fleeing from the Communists. Much less exciting was a ten month period in 1919 spent recruiting in Glasgow. He was promoted to Bombardier on 14 February 1908, Corporal 13 June 1912, Sergeant on 10 October 1914, Colour Sergeant on 24 January 1919 and Company Sergeant Major on 28 December 1920. He completed his 'time' on 24 August 1923 (having 3 years 'under age' not counting towards pension) and was recommended for the MSM, he was then living in Oliver Road, Eastney. He died in SW Surrey on 5 January 1967.

Sources: 111-113

Colour Sergeant Frederick ELSTON (31 Jul 1881 as Colour Sergeant)
His service register has not survived and so we have no details of his RMA activities and only some sketchy details of his life. He was born in Leamington Spa, Warwickshire, about 1847. He had retired from the RMA by the middle of 1890 as in that year his first wife died in Swansea and in the census of the following year he is in Swansea as a widower working as a School Board Attendance Officer; sounds just the job for an ex-Colour Sergeant In the last available census (1911) he was still in the same place and job (at the age of 65) but had remarried. He received his MSM on 8 December 1916. He died on 8 July 1935 in Nantwich, Cheshire at the age of 89; he had been living latterly in Uplands, Swansea.

Sources: 36 & 114-118

Colour Sergeant William GASSON (RMA 4001) (18 Mar 1894 & 26 May 1895 as Bombardier, 7 Mar 1897 as Corporal, 24 Feb 1901 & 5 Jun 1904 as Sergeant)
The baptism on 26 May 1895 is of his son Bryan (see below). Gasson senior was born in Wilmington, Sussex, in January 1871 and enlisted at Walmer on 8 January 1890. He served in a number of ships and shore establishments including *Nelson* (1891-92, Portsmouth), *Victor Emmanuel* (1896-97, Hong Kong) and *Tamar* (1897-99, Hong Kong) but most notable was his service in *Powerful* (1899-1900, China & Cape of Good Hope). He landed in South Africa with the Naval Brigade on 20 October 1899 and was present at the actions at Belmont on 23 November 1899 and at Graspan on 25 November 1899 where he sustained a gunshot wound to his right knee, the bullet lodging in the lower end of his thigh bone. The battle at Graspan was an ill-conceived attack on well-entrenched Boer positions by infantry over flat open ground and the Royal Marines suffered 11 killed and 73 wounded, a casualty rate of 44%. He was invalided to Cape Hospital and then returned to Eastney on 2 February 1900 where he served until the completion of his service on 7 January 1911, having been promoted to Colour Sergeant on 16 January 1907. In 1914 he was mobilised from the little village of Broadhembury, near Honiton, where he was the manager of the Red Lion Inn. He served at Eastney until 26 February 1919 and then returned to his Devon idyll. In addition to his MSM, which he received on 13 May 1945, he was awarded the Queen's South Africa Medal with Belmont clasp and the Long Service and Good Conduct Medal (all are held in the Royal Marines Museum collection). He died in Devon on 9 January 1951 at the age of 80.

Sources: 53, 63 & 119-121

Quartermaster Sergeant Instructor Bryan William GASSON, BEM (Po 212610)
(26 May 1895)

Bryan Gasson was born on 26 April 1895 and baptised in the RMA Church on 26 May 1895; his father was Colour Sergeant William GASSON (see above). He was 15 years old and just 5 feet (1.52 metres) tall when he enlisted at Eastney as a bugler on 2 March 1911. He was soon posted to *Lord Nelson* and the sea air must have done him good as he had gained 8 inches (20 cm) by his eighteenth birthday and had attained the rank of Gunner. On 3 August 1914 he was posted to *Invincible* for what was the most travelled and action-packed period of his career. On 28 August *Invincible* was one of the battlecruisers under the command of Admiral Beatty at the Battle of Heligoland Bight in the North Atlantic. She returned to Devonport for repairs but these were incomplete when, on 11 November 1914, she was despatched to the South Atlantic as flagship to Admiral Sturdee in response to the sinking of much of the West Indies Squadron by Admiral Graf von Spee. The British squadron reached the Falkland Islands on 7 December 1914 just one day before Admiral Spee's squadron was spotted approaching the British supply base. The German ships were hunted down by the British Squadron and six of the eight German ships were sunk with the loss of over 1800 men. *Invincible* and her sister ship *Inflexible* accounted for two of the German ships including Admiral Spee's flagship the *Scharnhorst*, which they sank at close range after Von Spee refused to surrender. Tragically Von Spee's two sons were lost with him.

HMS Invincible then returned to home waters and later in 1916 she was part of the 3rd Battlecruiser Squadron when, on 31 May 1916, she played her part in the Battle of Jutland. Unfortunately she was sunk in an action with Admiral Hipper's *Lutzow* and the *Derflinger*. Only six men, three officers and three ratings, survived from a crew of 1032 (see Gunner Ernest Mann in The Fallen above). Bryan Gasson along with the other five survivors was lucky to be on duty in the control top at the time. After this very lucky escape he returned to Eastney where he stayed for eight years, gaining promotions to Bombardier, Corporal and then Sergeant on 14 February 1921. He went to Malta (*Egmont*) for two years before returning to Portsmouth in 1926 and subsequent promotions to Colour Sergeant on 15 January 1930 and Quartermaster Sergeant Instructor on 16 August 1932. He completed his second term of engagement (21 years from the age of 18) on 25 April 1934 and joined Malvern College as Staff Instructor in the College Combined Cadet Force. He was mobilised on 28 September 1938 but his service record appears to say that he was discharged two days later. In the New Years Honours list of January 1953 he was awarded the British Empire Medal (BEM) for his services to the College Cadet Force. He had to wait until 3 April 1974 to receive his MSM, 40 years after his retirement. His MSM, BEM, and other medals are held in the Royal Marines Museum collection. He died in South Glamorgan in 1981.

Sources: 53 & 122-124

Sergeant Instructor of Gunnery John HARDING (RMA 832) (25 Feb 1883 as Corporal)
He was born on 15 October 1856 in Cheltenham, Gloucestershire and enlisted in Liverpool on 15 February 1877. After initial training at Walmer he was posted to Eastney as a Gunner on 18 October 1877. On 4 June 1879 he went with the Royal Marine Battalion to South Africa but was back at Eastney by 23 August. He then did some sea service in *Agincourt* (Channel, 1879-1882) and after a few months at Eastney he was posted to Egypt with the Mediterranean Battalion (1882), earning an Egypt Medal with clasp for Tel el-Kebir and the Khedive's Bronze Star. After returning to Eastney he went to sea again in *Lord Warden* (1883-85, Coast Guard Queensferry,). He was promoted to Sergeant on 11 March 1886 at Eastney where he served until October 1891 except for a couple of months in *Inflexible* (1888, Portsmouth). He then embarked in *Invincible* (1891-93, Coast Guard Southampton) serving until 20 January 1893 during which period he was promoted to Colour Sergeant (on 20 December 1892). During his final years at Eastney he was promoted to Temporary Sergeant Instructor of Gunnery on 17 April 1894 before being made substantive in this rank on 17 January 1896. He retired on 14 February 1898 having completed his 21 years. He remained in Portsmouth for a few years but by 1911 he had moved to Gloucester and was working as a timber sorter. His MSM and annuity was awarded on 29 March 1927, over 29 years after he had retired. He died in Gloucester on 18 June 1937.
   Sources: 36 & 125-127

Sergeant Joseph Robert HETHERIDGE (RMA) (22 Jul 1866 as Bombardier, 7 Feb 1869 as Corporal & 7 May 1871 as Sergeant)
The baptism of his daughter, Caroline Selina, on 22 July 1866 is the very first entry in the Baptism Register, so it must have taken place in the Drill Shed rather than the Crinoline Church (see Chapter 1). His Service Register has not survived and so what we know about his life and RMA career comes from an article in the Portsmouth Evening News of 10 April 1931 (copied in the Globe & Laurel), church registers and various census returns. He was born in 1839 in Portsmouth and enlisted in 1854. He soon saw action in the Crimea serving in *Royal Albert*, which brought him the Crimea Medal with clasp for Sebastapol. For some reason although he was awarded the Turkish Medal (presumably the Turkish Crimea Medal) it was not presented to him at the time. It was not until 1910 that he received the medal at the Turkish Embassy in London from the Grand Vizier, His Highness Prince Tewik, who was the Turkish Ambassador at the time. He also served in *Warrior* and was on this ship when it escorted Princess Alexandra from Denmark to London for her marriage to Prince Edward in 1863. He was a Sergeant in 1871 and retired, having completed 24 years (with 21 'man years') in 1878. The Evening News article says that he became a nurse in the RMA Infirmary in 1881 but that year's census records him as a "Laundry Man". Either he had a job in a laundry before joining the Infirmary in the second half of the year or he started in the Infirmary laundry before becoming a nurse.

He retired a second time in 1899 and was presented with a clock as a memento of his service. He received his MSM on 24 May 1918 and died in Portsmouth on 31 March 1931 aged 92. He was buried on 4 April 1931 with his wife (who had pre-deceased him on 25 August 1900) in Highland Road Cemetery, Southsea. The grave was originally furnished with a kerbstone but this was later replaced by a cross, presumably following his burial. A tree has grown up over the grave and it is entirely covered in ivy and brambles. Removal of the vegetation is discouraged by the Council as it has been found that it is often the ivy that is holding the stones erect, but it makes a very sad sight.

Sources: 31-32 & 128-133

Colour Sergeant James INNOLES (RMA 890) (31 Aug 1879 as Gunner, 24 Apr 1881 as Bombardier, 30 Mar 1884 as Corporal & 25 Mar 1894 as Colour Sergeant) John Bilcliffe records him as Sergeant but he was a Colour Sergeant according to his Service Register. He was born in Chilton Polder near Bridgewater, Somerset, on 17 February 1856 and enlisted at Bristol on 17 August 1874. He served about 9 of his 21 years at sea including service in *Thunderer* (1877-79, Channel & Mediterranean), *Valiant* (1880-83, Coast Guard Shannon), *Briton* (1884-86, East Indies) and *Belleisle* (1892-93, Coast Guard Kingstown). Whilst serving in *Thunderer* he was lucky to be one of those only *"slightly wounded"* by the explosion of one of the guns on 2 January 1879 (see Lieut Daniel & Corporal Button in Chapter 1, The Memorials). He was awarded the Egypt medal (no clasp) and the Khedive's Bronze Star for service in Sudan (*Briton*). He was promoted to Bombardier on 30 September 1879, Corporal on 24 September 1882, Sergeant on 22 January 1884 and Colour Sergeant on 11 July 1890. He was pensioned on 19 August 1895 and moved to Bristol where he took up house painting and paper-hanging to supplement his pension. He eventually received his MSM and annuity on 30 September 1925 at the age of 69. He died in Bristol on 26 March 1934.

Sources: 125 & 134-137

Colour Sergeant Robert LAPPIN (RMA 416) (26 Dec 1880 as Sergeant & 31 Dec 1882 as Colour Sergeant)

Born October 1853 in Dromore near Magherafelt, Derry, he enlisted at Belfast on 2 October 1872. After training at Walmer he was appointed to the RMA on 8 March 1873. He spent just under three years at sea in *Newcastle* (1874-77, Detached Squadron & China) otherwise, apart from four months in the RMA Mediterranean Battallion in 1882 (Egypt Medal (no clasp) and Khedive's Bronze Star), he served the majority of his 21 years in Portsmouth, either at Eastney or in *Duke of Wellington* and *Victory*. He was promoted to Bombardier on 21 April 1875, Corporal on 6 April 1876, Sergeant on 2 January 1879 and Colour Sergeant on 25 August 1891. He retired on 2 October 1893 and at sometime moved to Fleet Street, London, where he worked for many years as a messenger with an insurance company. His MSM was announced in the London Gazette on 1 February 1921 but his service record says 7 April. He was also awarded the Long Service and Good Conduct Medal. At some point he returned to the south coast and was living in West Moors, near Wimborne, Dorset. He died in the Royal Victoria Hospital, Bournemouth on 4 April 1936.
    Sources: 36, 105 & 138-141

Colour Sergeant Allen Elliott MARDEN (31 Aug 1879 as Sergeant)

John Bilcliffe records him as Arthur E Marden but tells of confusion over his name; his Long Service and Good Conduct medal is engraved with the surname Morgan and the announcement of his MSM and annuity in General Order 32 (May 1915) gives his names as Allen Elliott Marden. His service record has not survived but Reverend Williams also recorded him as Allen Elliot Marden in the baptism entry for his daughter Ada Catherine on 31 August 1879. The census returns and birth, marriage and death registrations and his probate record all confirm this as his name. He was born in Marylebone, London, in 1841 the son of a tea dealer. He is 'missing' from the 1851, 1861 & 1871 censuses, but appears in 1881 in Deptford already retired and working as a "Shop Merchant's Clerk". He later returned to work for the Admiralty as a Writer (clerk) and appears as such in 1891 and 1901; and in 1911 he was a *"Retired Admiralty 1st Class Writer"* and living in New Cross, London. His first wife Hester Emma died in 1899 and in 1901, at the age of 60, he married Gertrude Cockerell who was just 25. By 1911 he had fathered three children whilst in his sixties. His MSM is dated 24 January 1915. He died in New Cross, South London, on 4 April 1926 at the age of 85.
    Sources: 36 & 142-149

Sergeant Charles MONK (7 Jul 1867, 7 Mar 1869, 6 Nov 1870 and 23 Feb 1873)

His Service Register does not seem to have survived but census and other searches have provided the following career information. He was born in Cardington, Bedford, in 1841 and initially enlisted with the Bedford Militia in October 1857. He joined the RMLI in 1859 and transferred to the RMA in March 1863. He served in the Second China War (Second Opium War) 1859-62 with the RMLI including all the actions against the Taipings in North

China in 1861-2 and was awarded the China Medal.

He was a Sergeant RMA by the time of the baptism of his daughter Elizabeth Martha in July 1867 and served for many years as a Sergeant Instructor of Musketry. He was discharged to pension in July 1879. On retirement he moved to Hackney and joined the Tower Hamlets Rifle Brigade (Volunteers) as a Sergeant Instructor and retired 17 years later on 30 September 1896 with the rank of Acting Sergeant Major. He then returned to his home town of Bedford. He was awarded the Long Service and Good Conduct Medal and eventually received his MSM on 20 March 1912. He died in Bedford two years later on 17 April 1914.

Sources: 150-155

Quartermaster Sergeant Herbert John NEAL (RMA 2824) (7 Aug 1904)

He was born near Swaffam, Norfolk, on 18 July 1867 and enlisted at Thetford on 18 January 1886, embarking on a lengthy career that probably has no equal. He served 7 of his initial 21 years at sea including service in *Sapphire* (1888-89, China), *Immortalité* (1890-92, Chatham) and *Ramillies* (1896-1900, Mediterranean). He was promoted to Bombardier on 22 June 1894, Corporal on 18 July 1896 and Sergeant on 14 April 1898. He passed as a Sergeant Instructor of Gunnery on 26 November 1900 and was promoted to Colour Sergeant on 1 January 1907. Seventeen days later he was discharged to pension after completing his 21 years on 17 January 1907. In 1911 he was working in Kensington, London as a chauffeur and in August 1914 he was mobilised from the Reserve for WWI at the age of 47. He was promoted to Company Sergeant Major on 2 November 1917 and demobilised on 17 March 1919, having apparently spent this war service at Eastney. Remarkably on 6 July 1940 he was mobilised again for WWII at the age of 72!

An article in the Globe & Laurel in 1942 was headed *'73 Not Out'* and stated that he was a Company Sergeant Major serving as a gunnery instructor *"somewhere on the coast"*. It reports that *"We met him on Christmas Day in the Eastney Sergeants' Mess. He stands as straight as any 'First Drill', and says he never felt fitter in his life."* A letter to the Globe & Laurel in 1956 reporting his death said that he was a Quartermaster Sergeant serving in trawlers off the East Coast as a Gunnery Instructor. The letter went on to claim that *"in 1947 he volunteered for another year at 77, which must most surely have made him the oldest serving man in any of the armed forces"*. However, he would have been 80 in 1947 so there may be an error in the year or his age. His Service Register records that when he was demobilised in 1919 it was as a result of his being *"Discharged from RNR 50 yrs of age"*, but the same document shows his birth date as 1867, so he may have 'lost' two years somewhere without anyone noticing. Whatever the truth was about his age it is still a remarkable record.

Although he was originally discharged to pension in 1907 he didn't receive his

MSM and annuity until 22 January 1946. He died in Portsmouth on 25 January 1956 and was buried on 28 January in Milton Cemetery, Portsmouth, his grave is unmarked.

Sources: 45 & 156-159

Quartermaster Sergeant Instructor Robert PRICE (RMA 1919) (15 Jul 1894 & 29 Aug 1897 as Sergeant and 3 Mar 1899 as Staff Sergeant)

Born in Liverpool on 14 December 1865 he enlisted there on 14 July 1883. After initial training at Walmer he was appointed to the RMA at Eastney on 1 May 1884. He served just under 6 years at sea, serving in *Iron Duke* (1885-87, Channel), *Northumberland* (1889-90, Channel), *Vivid*, (1891-92, Devonport), *Bellerophon* (1892-93, Pembroke & Spain) and *Alexandra* (1896-97, Coast Guard Portland). He was promoted to Bombardier on 6 January 1888, Corporal on 8 August 1890, Sergeant on 23 June 1893 and Colour Sergeant on 10 December 1897. He became 1st Sergeant Instructor of Infantry on 1 April 1898 and was promoted to Quartermaster Sergeant Instructor on 14 July 1899. He was discharged to pension on 13 December 1904 but continued his connection with the Royal Navy by working as a joiner in the Torpedo Depot in Portsmouth Dockyard. He had been a joiner before enlisting. He was awarded the Long Service and Good Conduct Medal on 22 March 1894 and eventually received his MSM and £10 annuity on 3 May 1942 at the age of 77. He died in Portsmouth on 11 June 1943 and is buried in Highland Road Cemetery, Southsea, in an unmarked grave.

Sources: 31, 103 & 160

Colour Sergeant Frank PUDDICK (RMA 1053) (25 Sep 1892 & 30 Dec 1894)

He was born in Chichester in August 1856 and was a shoemaker when he enlisted at Eastney on 13 July 1875. He served about 13 of his 21 years at sea including service in *Pelican* (1877-82, Pacific), *Iris* (1883-87, Mediterranean), *Hotspur* (1889-91, Coast Guard Harwich) and *Inflexible* (1894-96, Portsmouth). He was promoted to Bombardier on 4 June 1880, Corporal on 1 November 1882, Sergeant on 7 October 1885 and Colour Sergeant on 11 August 1892. He qualified as a Sergeant Cook at Aldershot on 1 July 1889. He served in the Egypt Campaign with the Mediterranean Battalion and was awarded the Egypt Medal, with clasps for Tel el-Kebir, Suakin 1884 and Tamaai, and the Khedive's Bronze Star. He received his Long Service and Good Conduct Medal on 13 October 1885 and retired on completion of his 21 years on 13 July 1896. He then moved to Fulford, York, to work in the Army Ordnance Depot where he was a Foreman. He was still working in York in 1911 but some time after returned to Portsmouth and was living in St Pirans Avenue, Copnor, when he died on 7 May 1927. He was buried in Milton Cemetery, Portsmouth, in an unmarked grave. His MSM and gratuity were issued on 8 October 1926 when he was aged 70 and just a year before he died.

Sources: 36, 125, 159 & 161-163

Colour Sergeant William PUTT (5 May 1869 as Sergeant and 26 Jul 1874 as Colour Sergeant)

His service register has not survived so we know nothing of his life or service other than what can be pieced together from census returns and BMD registrations. He was born about 1838 in Harberton, Devon. He enlisted in 1855 and in the 1861 census he was recorded at Eastney as a Gunner. After this he must have spent some time in Malta as one of his daughters was born there about 1871 and the family are missing from the 1871 census. His wife was alone with the children in Portsmouth in 1881 and he does not appear in a census again until 1901, when he is described as *"Master at Arms, RN Pens"*. He served in *Hecla* in the Mediterranean and must have spent some time ashore in North Africa as he was awarded the Egypt Medal with claps for 'Suakin 1884' and 'Alexandria'. He had been awarded the Long Service and Good Conduct Medal in 1875/77.

The baptism on 5 May 1869 was of his daughter Elizabeth Ann who had been born on 28 December 1861, she must have been seriously ill as the baptism was private and she died shortly afterwards, age 7. He received his MSM on 28 February 1913. He had been living in Clive Road, Fratton, Portsmouth, when he died in Milton Road on 6 February 1920. He is buried in Kinston Cemetery, Portsmouth in an unmarked grave.

Sources: 36, 62 & 164-170

Colour Sergeant Frederick Evan SADDON (RMA 2602) (9 Feb 1902)

For a summary of his career see his entry under Distinguished Conduct Medal above. As noted above he jumped the queue and received his MSM directly after he retired in January 1907 in recognition of his having been awarded the Distinguished Conduct Medal.

Colour Sergeant George Elliott SEABRIGHT (RMA 2247) (21 Mar 1897 as Sergeant)

His medal was awarded on 7 June 1906 less than a year after his discharge. Like Colour Sergeant Saddon he got priority due to having already received the Distinguished Conduct Medal. For more details about him see his entry under Distinguished Conduct Medal above.

Colour Sergeant John SEYMOUR (RMA 1970) (28 Oct 1883 as Gunner and 6 Jul 1890 as Lance Sergeant)

He was born on 7 April 1860 in Port Mulgrave, Yorkshire. He enlisted on 7 April 1881 at Wakefield and after initial training at Walmer he was posted to the RMA on 21 October 1881. He served 11 of his 21 years at sea including service in *Northumberland* (1882-84, Channel), *Sapphire* (1886-89, China), *Katoomba* (1891-94, Australia) and *Hannibal* (1898-1900, Channel). He was promoted to Bombardier on 7 October 1885, Corporal on 2 September 1887, Sergeant on 16 April 1891 and Colour Sergeant on 10 March 1896. He was pensioned on 7 April 1902 and in 1911 was living in and managing the Weslyan Victoria Soldier's Home in Highland Road, Southsea with the help of his wife. The home had been the idea of Sarah Robinson who wanted to provide the Royal Marines with an equivalent to the Royal Sailor's Rest homes created by Agatha Weston. It was opened in 1886. He was mobilised for WWI in August 1914; there is no record of him leaving Eastney and he was demobilised on 31 May 1916 at the age of 56. He had been awarded the Good Service and Good Conduct Medal on 28 August 1891 and eventually received his MSM and first £10.00 gratuity on 15 June 1938 at the age of 78. He was living at 16, Hunter Road, Southsea when he died on 22 March 1946 and he was buried in Highland Road, Cemetery, Southsea, on 25 March.

Sources: 31-32, 36, 78 & 171-172

Colour Sergeant Albert Edwin TRAYFOOT (RMA 5565) (4 Jun 1905)

John Bilcliffe lists an Albert Edward Trayfoot as a recipient of the MSM, the East & West Africa medal and the Queen's South Africa Medal. The RM Museum has index cards for both Albert Edward & Albert Edwin, although clearly the same man. No Trayfoot service register survives and I can find no trace of an Albert Edward; the only relevant Albert E Trayfoot that I can find anywhere, including in the census returns and Admiralty records is this Albert Edwin. He was a Bugle Major at this baptism of his daughter in 1905 but in the 1911 census he refers to himself as *"Sergeant Royal Marine Arty"*. Albert Edwin was born in Pimlico, London on 17 November 1873 and enlisted in the RMA on 1 April 1889. He was promoted to Bombardier on 26 October 1901, Corporal on 12 January 1904, Sergeant on 21 October 1904, Bugle Major on 1 January 1905 and Colour Sergeant on 4 June 1912.

He served in *Satellite* as a Bugler, seeing action in the Gambia (East & West Africa medal, Gambia 1894 clasp). He also served in *Monarch* during the South Africa War, still as a Bugler, and was a member of the Naval Brigade, earning the Queen's South Africa Medal with clasps for Belmont, Modder River, Paardeberg, Driefontein, Johannesburg, Diamond Hill and Belfast. He was mentioned in despatches by the Commanding Officer of the Naval Brigade on 17 October 1900.

He is listed as receiving a British War Medal (as Colour Sergeant), so he must have still been serving or had been mobilised for WWI. He was eventually awarded his MSM on 18 March 1946 and had also previously received the Long Service and Good Conduct Medal. He died in Portsmouth on 24 February 1951, aged 77 and was buried on 28 February in an unmarked grave in Milton Cemetery, Portsmouth.

Sources: 62, 159 & 173-180

Colour Sergeant William Charles WELLINGTON (RMA 201) (7 Jan 1892 as Pensioner RMA)

Although recorded in the register he may not actually have been present at the baptism of his son, also William Charles, who was being baptised as an adult, aged 21 (see below). At the time William Charles senior was a warder at the Royal Naval Prison at Lewes in Sussex. He eventually became a principal warder before retiring a second time and moving to London. He was born in Portsmouth in January 1846 and enlisted in Gosport as a Drummer boy on 14 May 1859 at the age of 13. He was posted to the RMA on 18 May 1859 and was promoted to Gunner on 5 September 1866, Bombardier on 4 July 1868, Corporal on 29 January 1870, Sergeant on 12 June 1872 and Colour Sergeant on 5 January 1877. He served about 9 years at sea including service in *Wivern* (1868, Particular Service), *Clio* (1870-74, Australia) and *Monarch* (1882-84, Mediterranean). However, his most notable sea trip was in *Discovery* as part of the RN Arctic Expedition (see George Porter in Chapter 1 and The Arctic Expedition of 1875-76, in Chapter 9) for which he was awarded the Arctic Medal 1875-76. In 1882 he was '*recommended for advancement*' for his actions in the bombardment and subsequent occupation of Alexandria. He was serving in *Monarch* at the time and his service record sheet says that he was awarded the "*Egypt Clasp*", but presumably this means the Alexandria clasp to the Egypt Medal; he also received the Khedive's Bronze Star. He retired to pension on 15 January 1885 and subsequently joined the RN Prison Service becoming Chief Warder at the RN Prison in Lewes, Sussex. He received his MSM on 22 December 1917 at the age of 71 and died in Leigh-on-Sea, Essex on 16 August 1930, aged 83.

Sources: 36, 105 & 181-184

Captain William Charles WELLINGTON (RMA 3663) (7 Jan 1892)

William Charles junior, followed his father into the RMA, enlisting at Eastney on 19 February 1889. After training at Walmer he was posted to Eastney on 27 June 1889. He was promoted to Bombardier on 11 September 1891, Corporal on 19 June 1894, Sergeant on 20 October 1896, Colour Sergeant on 17 October 1902, Quartermaster Sergeant on 12 June 1907 and Sergeant Major on 6 October 1909. He served less than five years at sea including service in *Invincible* (1890-91, Coast Guard Southampton), *Thunderer* (1896, Guardship Pembroke Dock), *Hood* (1898-1900, Mediterranean) and *Devastation* (1900-02, Guardship Gibraltar). Shortly after the outbreak of WWI, having already served for 25 years, he was commissioned from the ranks to Lieutenant (20 September 1914). On 18 April 1916 he was posted to the Somme area of France with the RMA Howitzer Brigade but on 25 November he was sent to hospital suffering from "*Pleuresy & dilated heart*" and was returned to Eastney by the Red Cross on a hospital ship, arriving at Eastney on 29 November 1916. After a recovery period he went on to serve two years (1917-19) at the Cromarty Garrison, first as Temporary Captain and then as full Captain from 3 April 1918. He was placed on the retired list on 1 April 1920 and was living in Velmore Road, Chandler's Ford, when he died on 21 February 1938.

Sources: 36 & 185-187

Sergeant Isaac Albert WHEATON (RMA 2102) (1 Mar 1896, 30 Jul 1899, 3 Jun 1900 & 4 Jan 1903)

In the first baptism entry he is erroneously listed as 'Albert Isaac' but the other three entries have his first names in the correct order. He was born in Aylesbeare, near Exeter, Devon on 5 April 1864 and enlisted at Exeter on 5 May 1882. His initial months at Walmer were rated *"Exemplary"* and he was posted to the RMA on 7 December 1883. He served about 9 years at sea including service in *Agincourt* (1886-87, Channel), *Boadicea* (1891-94, East Indies), *Alexandra* (1895-96, Coast Guard Portland), *Howe* (1898-1901, Coast Guard Queenstown) and *Empress of India* (1901-02, Queenstown). As a Gunner he served with the RM Battalion in Egypt from February 1884 to July 1885, earning the Egypt Medal with Suakin 1885 clasp and the Khedive's Bronze Star. He was promoted to Bombardier on 31 December 1888, Corporal on 8 October 1891 and Sergeant on 9 January 1895. He completed his 21 years on 4 May 1903 and subsequently joined the Prison Service in Maidstone but was later mobilised from the Reserve in August 1914. He was in Ostend for the five-day RMA 'excursion' at the end of August 1914 but otherwise served at Eastney until being invalided out on 23 March 1918. As a result, like Colour Sergeant Butler (above), he was issued with the Silver War Badge and Certificate. He had been awarded the Long Service and Good Conduct medal in 1892 and eventually received his MSM on 11 December 1935. He died in Portsmouth on 4 February 1942 at the age of 77 and was buried in Highland Road Cemetery, Southsea.

Sources: 31-32, 78 & 188

Barrack Sergeant John WILTON (RMA 1213) (24 Feb 1884 & 27 Mar 1887)

He was born in Spittal, Peterborough on 18 September 1860 and enlisted in Portsmouth as a bugler on 18 May 1875 at the age of 14. He became Gunner shortly after his eighteenth birthday. He served just over 4 years at sea including service in *Defence* (1880, Coast Guard Rockferry), *Monarch* (1885-86, Channel) and *Raleigh* (1891-94, Cape of Good Hope & West Coast Africa). He was promoted to Bombardier on 8 September 1880, Corporal on 3 August 1883, Sergeant on 1 July 1886 and Colour Sergeant on 14 August 1894. Whilst serving in *Raleigh* he saw action ashore as part of the Gambia Expedition; this earned him the East & West Africa medal with the Gambia 1894 clasp. He was ashore during February and March 1894 and was *"specially recommended for services"*. Following this action he was invalided

John Wilton's swimming certificate, 1875, signed by Lieutenant Robilliard [189] (see Chapter 1 – The Memorials)

to Cape Hospital suffering from the after effects of malaria.

In July 1887 he qualified as a Sergeant Instructor in Musketry with knowledge of the Nordenfelt and Gardner machine guns. He was promoted to Barrack Sergeant on 13 April 1897, completing his 21 adult years on 13 November 1899.

He moved to east London after retiring and was working as a *"Builder's Timekeeper"* in 1901 but by 1911 he was living in High Road, Chiswick and was the Verger of the local church. He was mobilised from the Reserve in 1914 but less than a year later was *'discharged invalided'* from Haslar Hospital with *"defective vision"*. Oddly he is recorded in the British War Medal Roll as being a Private.

His papers in the RM Museum and his entry in the National Probate Calendar indicate that he was living in Hartlebury, near Stourport, Worcestershire, from about 1915. He received a letter formally thanking him for his assistance by the West Worcestershire Parliamentary Recruiting Committee in December 1915 and in February 1917 he applied to serve as a National Service Volunteer from an address in Hartlebury, signing as John T Wilton. This application was declined on the basis that there were other men available who were *"engaged in work of less essential importance"*. Quite what important work he was engaged in is not recorded but perhaps he was again helping with recruitment.

He eventually received his MSM and annuity on 18 July 1930 at the age of 70 and died in Hartlebury three years later on 27 March 1933. From the GRO Indexes it would appear that his first wife Laura died in 1912 and he married a Margaret Alice Symonds the following year. The National Probate Calendar records that probate was granted to his widow Margaret Alice Wilton. This death and the subsequent probate are recorded as John Thomas Wilton and he appears to have been registered as John T Wilton at birth and appears as John T in the 1861 census. His register of service states that his first marriage took place on 9 July 1881, but this marriage to Laura Elizabeth Emery was not registered until the July-September quarter of 1882.

His MSM together with his East & West Africa Medal with 'Gambia' clasp and Long Service and Good Conduct Medal are in the RM Museum collection.

Sources: 36, 53, 125 & 189-198

Colour Sergeant Daniel YARDY (RMA 571) (8 Nov 1885 as Sergeant)
He was born in Whittlesea, near Peterborough, Cambridge in May 1855 and enlisted

at Lincoln on 14 November 1873. He initially joined the RMLI but five months later on 11 April 1874 he was posted to the RMA. He served about 6 years at sea including service in *Sultan* (1875-6, Channel), *Hector* (1876, Coast Guard Southampton) and *Alexandra* (1877-83, Mediterranean). He was promoted to Bombardier on 19 May 1876 and Corporal on 3 January 1878. On 1 March 1881 whilst serving in *Alexandra* he was promoted to Sergeant, just a year before the Bombardment of Alexandria and he qualified for the Egypt Medal and Alexandria clasp and the Khedive's Bronze Star. He returned to Eastney on 12 February 1883 and was promoted to Colour Sergeant on 16 April 1886 but was reduced to Sergeant on 2 September 1887 having been appointed to "*Canteen Duties*". He was restored to Colour Sergeant on 21 May 1890 and served at that rank until the completion of his service on 15 November 1894. Following his retirement he moved back to Cambridgeshire and in 1901 was a Licensed Victualler and Butcher in the village of Benwick. By 1911 he had moved the six miles back to his birth village of Whittlesea (now known as Whittlesey). He had received the Long Service and Good Conduct Medal on 6 September 1884 and he eventually received his MSM and gratuity on 1 May 1922 at the age of 67. He died at his home in Station Road, Whittlesey on 22 January 1946, aged 90.

Sources: 36, 105 & 199-200

Immediate Meritorious Service Medal

This award was quite different from the 'normal' MSMs listed above as its issue was not necessarily reliant on the recipient having an immaculate conduct record. These medals were issued during WWI for gallant and meritorious conduct but not in the face of the enemy, and were available for all ranks. Later, in 1928, this award was absorbed into the British Empire Medal. Although the medals were issued immediately there was still a waiting list for the annuity as will be seen in the records below.

Quartermaster Sergeant William John SAUNDERS (RMA 4145) (25 Mar 1877)

This is the date of his own baptism, his father was Gunner John Saunders. He was born on 14 August 1876 in Portsmouth and enlisted as a Boy Bugler at Eastney on 6 March 1891. He went to sea as a Boy Bugler in *Royal Sovereign* (1892-94, Channel) and was promoted to Gunner on 16 October 1894 shortly after returning to Eastney and then earned further promotions to Bombardier on 11 May 1905, Corporal on 24 November 1907 and Sergeant on 9 October 1911. During this period his sea time included service in *Hood* (1896-1900, Mediterranean), *Irresistible* (1902-1904, Mediterranean), *Powerful* (1905-07, Australia), *Superb* (1909-11, Home), *Invincible* (1911-13, Portsmouth & Mediterranean) and *Prince George* (1914-16, Channel & Dardanelles/Gallipoli). Whilst in *Prince George* he completed his 21 adult years on 13 August 1915 and was immediately mobilised. On 1 February 1917 he was posted to the RMA Siege Gun Team (*Attentive II*). He was promoted to Acting Quartermaster Sergeant (WOII) on 18 December 1917 and served at this rank until his demobilisation on 2 August 1919, having returned to Eastney on 1 April 1919. He was awarded an Immediate MSM *"For Miscellaneous Services"* whilst he was serving with the Siege Gun Team; the award was gazetted on 15 February 1919. Although he got his medal in 1919 he still had to wait twenty-seven years for the annuity which was not paid until 12 May 1946.

His service record and his death announcement in the Globe & Laurel state that he died on 30 July 1961 and there is a death registered in North Bucks in the July-September period of the right age that must be him. For some reason his service record states that he was not Discharged Dead (DD) until 4 September 1961.

Sources: 63 & 201-203

Colour Sergeant Thomas Edward STEVENS (RMA 3165) (23 Jun 1895 as Lance Sergeant & 11 Jan 1903 as Sergeant)

He was born in Amersham, Bucks, on 13 January 1867 and enlisted in London on 13 December 1886. After initial training at Walmer he was posted to the RMA on 14 July 1887. He served just over 6 of his initial 21 years at sea including service in *Wildfire* (1889, Sheerness), *Anson* (1892-3, Channel), *Empress of India* (1893-5, Channel), *Monarch* (1897-1900, Cape of Good Hope), *Resolution* (1902-3, Coast Guard Holyhead) and *Pembroke* (1903-4, Chatham). He was promoted to Bombardier on 16 August 1889, Corporal on 15 July 1892, Sergeant on 10 September 1895 and Colour Sergeant on 9 August 1904 and was pensioned on completion of 21 years on 12 December 1907. He was mobilised from the Reserve in 1914 and, apart from the RMA visit to Ostend at the end of August, served nearly all his war service in or near Scapa Flow, Orkney, first in *Royal Arthur* and then at the Holm Battery (*Cyclops II*); he was demobilised on 1 April 1919. His Immediate MSM was gazetted on 12 July 1919 but he did not receive the annuity until 6 February 1936. He moved to Fulham after retirement and in 1911 had a very appropriate job for a retired Colour Sergeant – as a *"Timekeeper"* in a motor garage. He was living in Sandilands Road, Fulham when he died in the Princess Beatrice Hospital, Earls Court on 11 January 1944. He also held the Long Service & Good Conduct Medal and the WWI 'trio'.

Sources: 36, 185 & 204-205

Chapter 9 - The Lucky, the Unlucky and the Musical

It was not surprising to find that some of the fathers and sons recorded in the baptisms were involved in some of the major naval incidents and disasters of the second half of the nineteenth century.

HMS Captain

The loss of *HMS Captain* on its trial voyage is described in Chapter 1. In addition to Captain Gorges there were three RMA marines that appear in the Baptism Register on board for that fatal voyage. Unfortunately none of their Service Registers appear to have survived, they were:

Gunner Benjamin PORTER (1 Mar 1868 & 4 Dec 1870)

The first baptism is of his daughter Kate Amelia. The second date is for the baptism of a son, born just three weeks after his death on 1 October 1870, and named Benjamin William Captain Porter. His wife Ann re-married and moved to Rochford, Essex, and young Benjamin went into the Navy. In 1901 he was serving in *Prosperine* as a Stoker and by 1911 was a Petty Officer Stoker in *Crescent* on China Station.

    Sources: 1-4

Bombardier David HUGHES (6 Sep 1868)

This baptism is for his only child, a daughter named Elizabeth after his wife. Elizabeth junior went on to become a schoolmistress. He was a Gunner at the time of this baptism.

    Sources: 1 & 5-6

Corporal George William MORSE (7 May 1871)

This baptism is of his only child, Annie Georgie Ellen, who was born six months after the disaster on 17 March 1871. Young Annie married a policeman, Constable George Epps, in 1894 but her mother, who never re-married, was recorded in the 1901 census as living on a *"Pension Patriotic Fund"*, presumably meaning the Royal Patriotic Fund that had been set-up during the Crimean War to provide assistance to the widows, orphans and other dependents of members of the armed forces. There is no mention of this pension in 1911 when she was living alone in Canal Walk, Portsmouth.

    Sources: 1 & 7-11

HMS Victoria

The memorial recording the RMA men lost on *HMS Victoria* is detailed in Chapter 1. None of these men appear in the baptisms list but there were twelve RMA survivors of the incident of whom the following four appear in the baptism records.

Colour Sergeant Alfred BUNN (RMA 655) (4 Oct 1896)

He was only posted to *Victoria* on 2 March 1893 but was one of the lucky ones when she sank on 22 June. He was born near Weymouth in February 1857 and enlisted at Portsmouth on 22 November 1875. He saw plenty of sea service including in *Raleigh* (1877-79, Mediterranean), *Thunderer* (1879-81, Mediterranean), *Imperieuse* (1888-90, China) and *Victoria* (1893, Mediterranean). He was part of the RM Battalion in Egypt (May 1884-July 1885) and was awarded the Egypt Medal with Suakin 1985 clasp and the Khedive's Bronze Star. He was promoted to Bombardier on 14 September 1878, Corporal on 6 April 1880 and Sergeant on 10 August 1882. He was initially promoted to Colour Sergeant on 10 July 1885, reverted to Sergeant on 14 June 1889 (*Imperieuse*) and was then promoted again on 1 May 1895. Whatever it was that caused his demotion it also entailed the loss of his Good Conduct Medal that had been awarded on 30 January 1886. He completed his 21 years on 23 November 1896 and was placed on the Reserve. He worked as a labourer in the RN Ordnance Depot before he died, age 46, on 10 June 1903 and was buried in Kingston Cemetery, Portsmouth in an unmarked grave.

Sources: 12-15

Gunner Edwin BLACKMAN (RMA 626) (1 Apr 1896)

He was born in Portsmouth in March 1857 and began his working life as a shoemaker before enlisting on 30 September 1875, aged 18. He served as a Gunner throughout his service and although the assessments of his character were excellent in the first eighteen months they fell back to mostly 'Good' and 'Fair' with just a few 'Very Goods' for the rest of his time. This is supported by the entries on his record showing that in the course of his career he spent a total of 73 days in the cells and 63 days in prison. His main sea service was in *Agincourt* (1877-79 & 1880-82, Channel), *Conquest* (1885-89, Pacific) and *Camperdown* (1890-92, Channel). He served in the RM Battalion in Egypt (1884) but his service there was cut short by his being invalided home via the hospital at Suez. He was awarded the Egypt Medal and the Khedive's Bronze Star. He was posted to *Victoria* on the same day as Colour Sergeant Bunn (2 March 1893) and he had previously served on *Camperdown*, the ship that collided with the *Victoria*. He completed his 21 years on 15 February 1897 and was placed on the Reserve but was discharged on 11 April 1903. He died in Southampton Registration District on 29 December 1923.

Sources: 12, 14 & 16

Captain Horace CULLIMORE (RMA 2772) (2 Sep 1900 as a Sergeant)
He was born in Bristol on 11 November 1868 and enlisted there on 11 January 1886. After initial training at Walmer he was appointed to the RMA on 23 September 1886. He served 11 years as a Gunner and then over the next 10 years was promoted to Bombardier on 1 October 1897, Corporal on 14 July 1898, Sergeant on 1 April 1900 and finally Colour Sergeant on 21 May 1902. His sea service included time in *Dreadnought* (1887-90, Mediterranean), *Camperdown* (1890, Channel), *Victoria* (1890-93, Mediterranean), *Sans Pareil* (1893-94, Mediterranean), *Ramillies* (1894-96, Mediterranean) and *Monarch* (1899-1900, Guardship Cape of Good Hope). He had been serving in *Victoria* for two and a half years when she sank and like Gunner Blackman he had also served briefly in *Camperdown* prior to their collision. In 1900 he landed on active service in South Africa as an instructor in Maxim and machine guns at Stellenbosch but afterwards served some time at the front, earning the South Africa Medal with clasps for Paarderburg, Dreifontein and Cape Colony.

On 4 June 1902 just a few weeks after being promoted to Colour Sergeant he was posted to the staff of His Highness the Sultan of Johore (Malaya). He was granted the local rank of Lieutenant in the Johore Forces and served there until his discharge on 20 November 1907. However, he remained in the Johore Forces after his discharge from the RMA and attained the rank of Captain. He was Adjutant and second in command at Tanglin when he was killed during the mutiny on 15 February 1915 and subsequently buried in the Kranji War Cemetery, Singapore, now marked by a Commonwealth War Graves Commission headstone. The mutiny involved about half of the 850 Indian sepoys of the 5th Native Light Infantry who had heard rumours that they were to be sent to Europe or Turkey to fight against other Muslims. When they were ordered to Hong Kong they reacted, killing 47 British soldiers and local civilians before the mutiny was quelled and the last mutineers captured on 20 February.

Memorial plaque to Captain H Cullimore in St Andrew's Cathedral, Singapore [21]

A memorial plaque to Captain Cullimore is in St Andrew's Cathedral, Singapore; the inscription reads:
"In Memory of Captain & 2nd in Command
Horace Cullimore
Staff – Johore Military Forces
Late Royal Marine Artillery
Born 11 November 1869
Killed at Tanglin 15 Feby 1915
Erected by the Sergeants Mess RM Artillery" [21]

This birth date of 1869 contradicts the date of 1868 on his service record. His birth was registered in the April-June quarter of 1869, a bit late for November 1868 but too early for a birth in November 1869, so presumably 1868 is correct.

His wife Clara had gone to be with him in Singapore leaving their son Gordon Horace at Manor House Boarding School in Havant. After Horace senior's death Clara and six-year old son Richard Cecil (presumably born in Singapore) returned to the UK, initially to Exeter Road, Southsea.

Sources: 14 & 17-24

Gunner George PERKINS (26 Jan 1902 as Gunner & 17 Jun 1903 as Late Gunner) Unfortunately his service register has not survived and so we know little about his life and career. He was born in Bermondsey, south London about 1869 and may be the George Perkins, RMA 3141, whose Long Service and Good Conduct Medal is in the RM Museum collection although I have been unable to make a positive connection. We know that he served in the Mediterranean in *Victoria* and was previously serving in *Northampton* which was at Sheerness at the time of the 1891 census although he was listed among those "*not on board*" on the night of the census.

George was called to testify at the Court Martial following the loss of the *Victoria* and was asked "*Which hatch did you close on the day of the collision?*"; he replied " *The foremost hatch of the capstan engine flat, leading from the paints stores*". To "*Which side, starboard or port?*" he answered "*Starboard*". Then lastly he was asked "*Did you see the port hatch at the same time?*" to which he replied "*No*".

He married Rosina Mary Kenting (born in Plymouth) in 1899 and these two baptisms were of their only two children as Gunner Perkins died in late 1902 at the age of just 32 and is buried in an unmarked grave in Highland Road Cemetery, Southsea. In 1909 Rosina married Reinhold Dumke, another RMA Gunner.

Sources: 14 & 25-31

HMS Vanguard

The loss of *HMS Vanguard* in 1875 was an operational catastrophe every bit as bad as the loss of *Victoria* eighteen years later but because there was no loss of life, apart from the captain's pet dog, it is not so well-known. *Vanguard* was part of the 1st Reserve Squadron under the command of Vice-Admiral Sir Walter Tarleton, which also included the *Warrior* (flagship), *Hector* and *Iron Duke*. The squadron was on a summer cruise around Ireland and had just left Kingstown (Dun Laoghaire) bound for Queenstown (Cobh) when it was enveloped in thick fog. Even though the weather prevented the ships from signalling to one another they were steaming at twice the recommended speed for the conditions. To compound the situation the fog horn in *Iron Duke* was broken. Captain Hawkins of the *Vanguard*, who had just gone below for a much needed rest, was roused by his second in command and they were discussing what the appropriate steam-whistle signal should be when a sailing ship was spotted ahead. Hawkins decided to reduce speed and swing slightly to port to miss the sailing vessel but within moments *Vanguard* was rammed from behind by *Iron Duke* which was still steaming at the original speed. Both ships lowered their boats and all the Vanguard's crew were saved but she sank in about an hour. There were 27 RMA men on board *Vanguard*; 1 Lieutenant, 1 Sergeant, 2 Corporal/Bombardiers and 23 Gunners [32].

The following have connections to the baptisms register, but unfortunately in only one case has a service record survived.

Colour Sergeant George BURGESS (30 Dec 1877)

He was a Sergeant at the time and was transferred to *Iron Duke* following the collision. He was born in South Molton, Devon about 1843, the son of a farm labourer. He appears in the 1881 census at Walmer as a Colour Sergeant but by 1891 he has retired and is living in Wandsworth and working as a messenger. Ten years on and he is still working as a messenger at the Board of Trade. George's wife Mary was living in Battersea as a widow in 1911 and it appears that George died there in the summer of 1903. I cannot be positively sure but it would appear that it is probably his Ashanti Medal and Long Service and Good Conduct Medal that are in the RM Museum's reserve collection.

Sources: 31-37

Gunner Reuben FIDLER (25 Feb 1877, 27 Oct 1878 & 31 Oct 1880)

He was transferred to *Iron Duke* following the collision. He was born in Witney, Oxfordshire about 1843 the son of a blanket weaver. He had enlisted by 1861 (RM Barracks, Woolwich) and married by 1881 (Eastney Barracks). By 1891 he had retired and was working as a watchman in Mill Bridge, Liversedge, West Yorkshire. He died in Yorkshire on 15 January 1922 at the age of 79.

Sources: 17, 32 & 38-44

Company Sergeant Major Thomas KNIGHT (26 Mar 1882)

He was transferred to *Iron Duke* following the collision.

CSM Knight is the only one of these survivors for who we have a service record. He was born in Slinfold, near Horsham, Sussex in 1855 and enlisted at Portsmouth on 6 December 1873. He appears to have initially joined the RMLI but on 11 April 1874 was appointed to the RMA. *Vanguard* was his very first ship and he had joined her on 1 May 1875. He also served at sea in *Pert* (North America & West Indies, 1877-1879) and *Audacious* (Flagship, China, 1882-1886). He was promoted to Bombardier on 1 November 1875, Corporal on 6 February 1877, Sergeant on 11 October 1879, Colour Sergeant on 14 April 1885 and Quartermaster Sergeant on 29 January 1891. He completed his 21 years on 16 April 1894 and joined the 2nd Hants Artillery Volunteers. In the 1901 census he is recorded as *"Col Sergt Major R G Artillery"* but by 1911 he had retired to his home village of Slinfold and was working as an Assistant Overseer and Rate Collector for the Parish Council and Guardians of the Poor. On 7 October 1914 he travelled to London to re-enlist in the Royal Garrison Artillery (RGA) at the age of 58 for one year's service as a *"special reservist"*. His surviving service papers indicate that he was Acting Company Sergeant Major of 10th Company RGA which on-line sources record as being at Queenstown (Cobh). He didn't serve the full term of the war as he was discharged on medical grounds on 24 May 1918 due to a *"Diseased Floating Kidney aggravated by Service"*. He probably died in Brighton in 1930.

Sources: 12, 17, 32 & 45-49

Gunner George H SMITH, alias Henry GARRETT (14 Oct 1870)

He was transferred to *Iron Duke* following the collision.

The entry in the register records the baptism of Frederick George Garrett the son of Gunner Henry and Eliza Garrett. Young Frederick survived just a few months before he died in the last quarter of 1870 thus depriving me of the only known birth date on which to base my searches. Without any other information and with no service record I have been unable to find any more about George Smith/Henry Garrett with any degree of certainty.

Sources: 32, & 50-51

Gunner William VENNER (27 Feb 1876 & 1 October 1876)

He was transferred to the frigate *Achilles* at the time of rescue and was sent to *"Haughbauline Hospital to do duty as a servant"*.

The first baptism is of his son, William George Hastings, who had been born on 1 Oct 1874, thus clarifying the closeness of the two baptisms.

William senior was born near Tiverton, Devon in 1842. Evidence from the 1861 census suggests that he might have initially enlisted in the RMLI as there is a William Venner of the right age listed as one of the crew of *St George* in Royal Harbour, Jamaica. However, by 1871 he is a RMA Gunner at Eastney Barracks. He was still a Gunner in 1881 but by 1891 he had retired back to Tiverton and was working as a labourer. He died in Tiverton in 1910.

Sources: 32 & 52-57

HMS Pearl Naval Brigade

The exploits of the Naval Brigade that landed from the *Pearl* in response to the Indian Mutiny are described in the biography of Reverend Williams in Chapter 5. There were also a sergeant, a corporal and ten gunners from the RMA contingent sent ashore. Only one of these is represented in the baptisms list.

Gunner William OBORN (7 July 1867)

His career is something of a mystery as his service register has not survived. He is recorded as a Gunner at the time of his involvement with the *Pearl's* naval brigade but Reverend Beale failed to enter his rank in the baptism register in 1867 even though he did so for two other baptisms on the same day. Census records indicate that he was born in Fonthill, Wiltshire about 1828 but he was presumably abroad in 1851 and 1861 as he does not appear in those censuses. He married Caroline Mabbett on 25 July 1866 in All Saints, Portsea but by 1871 he had retired and was back in Wiltshire, living in Mere, as a *'Sergeant Rifle Volunteers'*. In 1881 he was *'Sergeant Major of Volunteers, Greenwich Pensioner'* but by 1891, when he was 63, he was in Warminster as a *'Provisions Dealer'*. In the meantime his first wife had died in early 1877, leaving him with 5 children and he married Sarah Talbot in 1878, this marriage producing two daughters. He died in Warminster (recorded as Oborne) in late 1894. According to my interpretation of the records this baptism of Charles William Oborn was probably the last to be performed in the Drill Shed before the move to the Crinoline Church.

Sources: 58-65

The Arctic Expedition of 1875-76

There were eight RMA marines involved in this expedition, all earning the Arctic Medal 1875-6. The outline story including the demise of Gunner George Porter has been told in Chapter 1 - The Memorials. Of the other seven RMA participants three appear in the baptisms, they are:

Colour Sergeant Wilson Mowbray DOBING (RMA 7061) (25 May 1873 & 25 Nov 1877)

Sergeant Dobing is another whose service register has not survived. From census records we know that he was born in Selby, Yorkshire in about 1847. In 1871 he was a Gunner in *Beacon* on the South East Coast of America. Like George Porter he too suffered badly from scurvy in the Arctic but lived to tell the tale. He was part of a sledging party exploring the North Greenland coast under the command of Lieutenant Beaumont. Beaumont describes how Dobing and Able Seaman Peter Craig *"dragged themselves along, their breath failing entirely at every ten yards – this appears to be the most marked feature of the advanced stage of the disease."* A day later both Dobing and Craig had to be carried in order for the group to make any progress at all. Fortunately, two days later, they met-up with a rescue party and although Able Seaman Charles Paul died on the way back, both Dobing and Craig eventually recovered. His performance during the expedition may have had a beneficial effect on his career as by 1881 he was at Eastney as a Sergeant and had been promoted again to Colour Sergeant by the time he retired.

By 1891 he had moved back to Hunslet in his native county of Yorkshire with his second wife; he was a gatekeeper in a foundry at first and then a commercial clerk. He died there on 17 May 1922, aged 73. He was sent his Arctic Medal in May 1877 but for some reason had a duplicate issued in March 1883.

Sources: 17 & 66-75

Corporal Thomas OAKLEY (RMA 135) (1 Sep 1872)

He was born in the hamlet of Foy, near Ross, Herefordshire, in May 1847 and enlisted at Gloucester on 20 June 1865. A month later he was allocated to the RMA, serving at Eastney until January 1868. He went on to serve just under 12 of his 21 years at sea including service in *Hercules* (1868-70, Portsmouth), *Penelope* (1872-74, Coast Guard Harwich), *Albatross* (1880-83, China) and the Torpedo Training ship *Vernon* (1883-86, Portsmouth) in addition to his 20 month trip to the Arctic in *Alert*. His service register records that he was '*absent from 'Alert' on Arctic Sledging Service 36 days*'. Captain Nares rated his conduct as '*Exemplary*' and he was promoted to Bombardier midway through the expedition. He may have gained a promotion through his exploits but he did lose something as well, his right great toe was amputated due to frostbite on 17 September 1876. On 8 December 1876, shortly after returning to Eastney, he was promoted to Corporal and served at this rank until his discharge on 21 June 1886. He was awarded his Long Service and Good Conduct Medal on 17 February 1877 and his Arctic Medal on 29 May 1877. After retirement he moved back very close to his birthplace in Herefordshire, initially to Yatton and then to Brampton Abbots, latterly working as a road contractor for the District Council. He died there in 1919, aged 72.

Sources: 12, 66 & 76-79

Sergeant William Charles WELLINGTON (senior) (RMA 201) (7 Jan 1892)

This date is for the adult baptism of his son, also William Charles. Wellington senior's career is outlined in his entry under Meritorious Service Medal in Chapter 8. He was a Sergeant when he volunteered for the Arctic Expedition and served under Captain Henry Stephenson in *Discovery*. He is recorded as being one of those afflicted with scurvy when exploring away from the ship with one of *Discovery's* sledge parties, but he clearly made a good recovery, going on to complete his 21 adult years in January 1885.

Source: 66

The Musical

It seems a great shame not to have a representative of the Band Service in these biographies so I am disregarding my rule of including only the fallen, irreproachable or gallant for just this one entry.

Drum Major John 'Jack' DACOMBE (19 Oct 1902)

Jack Dacombe was the son of Sergeant (later Barrack Sergeant Major) Sidney Guy Dacombe (see Distinguished Conduct Medal in Chapter 8). He enlisted in the RM Band Service as a trombonist and cellist in 1916 having previously joined the RM Association Cadet Band at the age of eight as a drum

Jack Dacombe (second from left) in his athletic days [83]

and fife player. He was appointed Drum Major of the Portsmouth Division in 1929 and served at this rank until his retirement in 1941. He then joined the BBC for another 23 years of music-making before returning to the School of Music at Deal in 1964 as Professor of Trombone until finally retiring in 1976. As well as his musical achievements he was also a top athlete as the photo from the RM Museum archives shows. He obviously maintained his fitness as in 1976 the Principal Director of Music queried why he wanted to retire when *he could still run up three flights of stairs to his classroom*.

He died on 1 October 1993 in Kent, aged 90.

Sources: 80-83

The Others

My opening comments in Chapter 9 tried to make my excuses to all those excellent marines of all ranks who gave great service to Corps and Country but, as I explained there, I had to draw a line somewhere. That doesn't mean that I do not have guilty feelings about those omitted. The range of stories I have discovered are only the tip of the iceberg of the vast repository of tales of gallantry and derring-do, sad and amusing, that must be hidden behind the names in the baptisms register. The un-named marine Bugler who whilst serving in *Glasgow* during the Battle of the Falkland Islands (1914) *got a fragment of shell in the centre of his cap badge which shaved the hair of his head and came out of the top of his cap without injuring him at all*[84] is just one example – Bless Them All.

Part Three

The Baptisms List

These baptisms have been transcribed from the original register held by The National Archives at ADM 6/437.

As I explained in Chapter 1 the precise dates of the first and last baptisms in the Crinoline Church are unknown. For the sake of tidiness these transcriptions cover the period from the start of the register (21 July 1866) to the end of 1905 even though it is known that the earliest and latest of these baptisms did not take place in the old church. There are in all 2340 baptisms recorded in this period. Three of the baptisms took place in Victoria, British Columbia; one in St Mary's, Portsea; one seems to be a record of a birth registration (see the biography of T W Anderson in Chapter 8) and at least eighty were performed in the barracks or nearby accommodation, presumably where the infant and/or mother were ailing. Twenty five baptisms were of adults and not all the infant baptisms were children of RMA personnel. Of the non-RMA fathers, 3 were RMLI, 13 were Royal Navy, 20 were Coastguards and 6 were Army. A further thirty-two of the fathers were civilians, and these include 6 labourers, 2 butchers, 2 painters, 2 masons and one each of the following: accountant, blacksmith, carpenter, coachman, confectioner, engine driver, engineer, grocer, iron moulder, joiner, licensed victualler, policeman, porter, railway policeman, solicitor's clerk, stationer, wheelwright and lastly but definitely not least, a gentleman. Some of these may have been employed at the barracks but three of them are annotated "by permission" indicating that they probably lived locally and had some association or affection for the old church.

It is not uncommon to find two or more children from the same family being baptised at the same time and this is to be expected in a military church where the fathers are often away from home for long periods. There are two instances of six children being baptised together; on 27 January 1876 Colour Sergeant Harris's six were all under 12 and on 27 March 1881 Corporal Cheeseman's six were all under 10. The winners numerically though were the Jacksons, Sergeant George & Emily Jackson had seven children baptised by Chaplain Cawston on 6 June 1869, the ages ranging from 6 months to 12 years. The Stoakes family however may have set some kind of a record as when their five children were baptised by Chaplain Morton on 30 March 1887, the youngest was 8 and the oldest 20! Richard Stoakes was a civilian and was recorded as a master builder in the census of 1881 and a builder's clerk in 1891, so he was probably working in the barracks at the time.

Being a family historian I am fascinated by surnames and it was not only Captain Gorges name that I struggled with whilst transcribing the records. The Genealogist website has a search engine which counts and maps surnames for the seven censuses from 1841 to 1901. Using this facility and allowing for variations in spelling I identified nine surnames in the baptism register which average 10 or less entries in the seven available census returns for England and Wales. In order of rarity they are: Baysting, Artifold, Treend, Gorges, Innoles, Fruton, Tarryer, Trayfoot and Setch.

The list of baptisms is a faithful copy of what is in the register, warts and all. However, in the interests of clarity, uniformity and consistency the ranks in the rank column have been written in full using the same spelling for each rank throughout. Additional information added to the register by the Chaplain, a child's age for instance or a civilian address when the baptism took place away from the Church, has been shown in the "Notes to the baptisms" list that follows the baptisms and the numbers in the Note column in the baptism list reference to them.

One more word of warning - the transcriptions are in the order that they were added to the register and there are subsequently a number out of chronological sequence because the entries were not made at the time of the baptism.

The Note references follow the baptisms list.

Born	Baptised	Child	Parents	Surname	Rank	Note
	22 Jul 1866	Caroline Selina	Joseph & Caroline	Hetheridge	Bombardier RMA	
	22 Jul 1866	Edwin Percy	John Varville & Sarah Jane	Scott	Sergeant RMA	
	7 Oct 1866	Emily Anne	Jacob & Emily	Dowdeswell	Sergeant RMA	
	7 Oct 1866	Elizabeth Frances	Jacob & Emily	Dowdeswell	Sergeant RMA	
	7 Oct 1866	Kate Elizabeth	William & Eliza Mary Ann	Carthy	Gunner RMA	
	4 Nov 1866	Ernest William	William & Ann	Dore	Pensioner RMA	
	4 Nov 1866	Henry William	Joseph & Sarah	Bailey	Sergeant RMA	
	4 Nov 1866	Willie John	Joseph & Sarah	Bailey	Sergeant RMA	
	4 Nov 1866	Anne Frances	John & Mary Ann	Smith	Sergeant RMA	
	2 Dec 1866	Robert Albert Harry	Robert & Jane	Lucas	Gunner RMA	
	6 Jan 1867	Alice Catherine	Benjamin & Leonora	Harding	Sergeant RMA	
	6 Jan 1867	Frederick William	Benjamin & Leonora	Harding	Sergeant RMA	
	6 Jan 1867	Edward Alfred	Benjamin & Leonora	Harding	Sergeant RMA	
	6 Jan 1867	Kate	Benjamin & Leonora	Harding	Sergeant RMA	
	6 Jan 1867	James	James & Sarah Jane	Lindsay	Gunner RMA	
	7 Apr 1867	George Alfred	William & Mary Jane	Head	RMA	
	7 Apr 1867	Alice Mary	Jacob & Emily	Dowdeswell	Sergeant RMA	
	7 Apr 1867	James Alfred	James & Rosanna	Simpson	Bandsman RMA	
	7 Apr 1867	Rose	James & Rosanna	Simpson	Bandsman RMA	
	2 Jun 1867	George William	William & Sarah	Sale	Bombardier RMA	
	2 Jun 1867	Jane Amelia	Charles & Sarah	Davey	Sergeant RMA	
	2 Jun 1867	Louisa Matilda	James & Emma	Brockwell	Gunner RMA	
	2 Jun 1867	George	William & Caroline	Rivett	Gunner RMA	
	7 Jul 1867	Henrietta	Stephen & Emma	Edwards	Gunner RMA	
	7 Jul 1867	Elizabeth Martha	Charles & Elizabeth Jane	Monk	Sergeant RMA	
	7 Jul 1867	Charles William	William & Caroline	Oborn	blank	
	4 Aug 1867	Donald Mundy	Eli & Mary Ann	Fookes	blank	
	4 Aug 1867	Arthur David	David & Jane	Hayward	blank	
	4 Aug 1867	Mary	William & Rosina	Day	blank	
	1 Sep 1867	Edward Joseph	Joseph & Mary	Brown	Bombardier RMA	
	1 Sep 1867	Eliza* Constance Kate	William Percival & Elizabeth	Austin	Sergeant RMA	1

	1 Sep 1867	Edith Louisa	James & Rosanna	**Simpson**	Bandsman RMA	
	6 Oct 1867	Charles	Thomas & Mary Ann	**Pitt**	Gunner RMA	
	6 Oct 1867	Grace Isabella Ann	George & Charlotte Elizabeth	**Addicott**	Gunner RMA	
	6 Oct 1867	Martha Elizabeth	Samuel & Emily	**Carnell**	Gunner RMA	
	6 Oct 1867	Jane Hannah	James & Ellen	**Carruthers**	Sergeant RMA	2
	20 Oct 1867	Maria Catherine Penrice	Edward Congreve Langley & Julia	**Durnford**	Staff Captain RMA	3
	3 Nov 1867	John William	William & Jane	**Howell**	Sergeant RMA	
	3 Nov 1867	William Edward	John & Kath	**Care**	Gunner RMA	
	3 Nov 1867	Alfred	George & Esther	**Fox**	Gunner RMA	
	3 Nov 1867	Francis Charles	Thomas & Emma	**Stallard**	Gunner RMA	
	1 Dec 1867	Ellen Jane	Stephen & Jane	**Matthews**	Gunner RMA	
	1 Dec 1867	William George	George & Emma Ellen	**Quayle**	Gunner RMA	
	5 Jan 1868	Emily Anne	Richard James & Elizabeth Sarah	**Ball**	Sergeant RMA	
	5 Jan 1868	Mary	Christopher & Eliza	**Sproates**	Bombardier RMA	
	5 Jan 1868	Edith Jane	Robert & Jane	**Lucas**	Gunner RMA	
	16 Aug 1867	Thomas Vicars	Robert & Eliza Jane	**Blakey**	Quarter Master Sergeant RMA	4
	2 Feb 1868	William Logan	William James & Mary Jane Richardson	**Auketh**	Gunner RMA	
	2 Feb 1868	Lucy Elizabeth	George & Jane Anne	**Haskell**	Gunner RMA	
	2 Feb 1868	Anne Eliza	William & Martha	**Eason**	Gunner RMA	
	2 Feb 1868	George William (Cystn)	William & Jane	**Dosset**	Labourer	5
	2 Feb 1868	Selina Rose	Stephen & Eliza	**Borer**	Sergeant RMA	
	2 Feb 1868	Minnie	Samuel & Margaret	**Duesbury**	Sergeant RMA	
	2 Feb 1868	Clara	Charles & Fanny	**Finney**	Bandsman RMA	
	2 Feb 1868	Alice Matilda	Jonas & Matilda	**Bicheno**	Gunner RMA	
	1 Mar 1868	John Samuel	John & Fanny	**Bragg**	Gunner RMA	6
	1 Mar 1868	John Thomas	Joseph & Ellen	**Capper**	Gunner RMA	
	1 Mar 1868	Elizabeth	Joseph & Harriet	**Welsh**	Gunner RMA	6
	1 Mar 1868	Henry George	Joseph & Harriet	**Welsh**	Gunner RMA	7
	1 Mar 1868	Elizabeth Ann	James & Mary Ann	**Sprague**	Gunner RMA	8
	1 Mar 1868	Emily	James & Mary Ann	**Sprague**	Gunner RMA	6
	1 Mar 1868	William Henry	James & Mary Ann	**Sprague**	Gunner RMA	9
	1 Mar 1868	Louisa Jane	James & Mary Ann	**Sprague**	Gunner RMA	
	1 Mar 1868	William John	Charles Briggs & Eliza	**Perry**	Bandsman RMA	
	1 Mar 1868	Kate Amelia	Benjamin & Ann	**Porter**	Gunner RMA	
	1 Apr 1868	Ellen	James & Mary Ann Elizabeth	**Clark**	Gunner RMA	10
	5 Apr 1868	Francis Edward	George & Sophia	**Walters**	Gunner RMA	
	5 Apr 1868	John	George & Sophia	**Walters**	Gunner RMA	8
	5 Apr 1868	Eleanor Flora	William & Ellen Mary	**Golding**	Gunner RMA	
	5 Apr 1868	Loveday	James & Sarah Ann	**Cotterell**	Gunner RMA	
	5 Apr 1868	Margaret Sophia	John & Rachel	**Dorey**	Gunner RMA	
	5 Apr 1868	Sophia	George & Sophia	**Cox**	Gunner RMA	
	5 Apr 1868	Albert Edward	Philip & Fanny	**Sibley**	Corporal RMA	
	5 Apr 1868	Sarah	William & Ann	**May**	Gunner RMA	
	5 Apr 1868	William	William & Maria	**Bramble**	Bombardier RMA	
	5 Apr 1868	Annie	James & Eliza	**Evans**	Gunner RA	
	12 Apr 1868	Alice	James & Ann	**Johns**	Pensioner RMA	11
27 Dec 1866	3 May 1868	Thomas Herod	Frederick & Ann	**Pitchforth**	Gunner RMA	12
29 Mar 1868	3 May 1868	John Henry	John & Sarah	**Jackson**	Bombardier RMA	

	7 Jun 1868	Arthur	John & Sarah	Scott	Sergeant RMA	
	7 Jun 1868	George Herbert	William & Jane	Hitchman	Gunner RMA	
	7 Jun 1868	Elizabeth Annie	William & Emily	Johnston	Gunner RMA	
	7 Jun 1868	Mary Elizabeth	Christopher & Mary	Traves	Gunner RMA	13
	7 Jun 1868	Alice Clare	Frances & Eliza	Cheshire	Gunner RMA	
	5 Jul 1868	James Edward	James & Elizabeth	Fitch	Gunner RMA	
	5 Jul 1868	Annie Elizabeth	Richard & Elizabeth Ann	Cole	Sergeant RMA	
31 May 1868	2 Aug 1868	John Archer	John & Emma	Willey	Gunner RMA	
	2 Aug 1868	Charles James	Charles & Susan	Perry	Sergeant RMA	
20 May 1868	2 Aug 1868	James Herbert	Henry & Emily Jane	Wallace	Gunner RMA	
18 Jul 1868	2 Aug 1868	Elizabeth	John & Elizabeth	Flower	Gunner RMA	
27 Aug 1867	2 Aug 1868	Joseph	Joseph & Sarah Ann	Jeanes	Gunner RMA	
29 Aug 1859	6 Sep 1868	James William	William Edward & Anna Maria	Elton	Sergeant RMA	
30 Jun 1861	6 Sep 1868	Jane Ann	William Edward & Anna Maria	Elton	Sergeant RMA	
9 Sep 1865	6 Sep 1868	Jessie Maria	William Edward & Anna Maria	Elton	Sergeant RMA	
29 May 1868	6 Sep 1868	Adeline Lutchie	John & Eliza	Brown	BombardierRMA	
4 Aug 1868	6 Sep 1868	Louisa	Samuel & Charlotte	Nowell	Sergeant RMA	
17 Jul 1868	6 Sep 1868	Francis William	William & Emma	Jones	Gunner RMA	
7 Jul 1868	6 Sep 1868	Isabella Martha Mary	John & Isabella	Rowlatt	Sergeant RMA	
6 Aug 1868	6 Sep 1868	John	John & Mary Ann	Smith	Sergeant RMA	
4 Apr 1868	6 Sep 1868	Thomas	William & Jane	Williams	Gunner RMA	
9 May 1868	6 Sep 1868	Frederick George	Peter & Ellen	Hutley	Gunner RMA	
10 Apr 1868	6 Sep 1868	Elizabeth	David & Elizabeth	Hughes	Gunner RMA	
6 Aug 1868	6 Sep 1868	William Henry Robert	Henry & Frances	Brooks	Gunner RMA	
4 Jul 1868	6 Sep 1868	Catherine Esther	John & Esther	Rines	Bombardier RMA	
25 Mar 1868	6 Sep 1868	Daniel Abraham Robert Thomas	Daniel & Mary Ann	Artifold	Gunner RMA	
	31 Aug 1868	Lilian Rose	David & Jane	Hayward	Gunner RMA	14
28 Oct 1866	4 Oct 1868	Alice Louisa	William & Anna Marie	Elton	Sergeant RMA	
13 Sep 1868	4 Oct 1868	George	George & Mary Ann	Freckelton	Gunner RMA	
5 Apr 1868	4 Oct 1868	Annie Louisa	Richard Urban & Sarah Anna	Nicholls	Sergeant RMA	
31 Jul 1868	4 Oct 1868	Sarah Susannah	William Blanchard & Annie	Lovell	Gunner RMA	
19 Aug 1867	4 Oct 1868	Charles Samuel	Robert & Jane	Lucas	Gunner RMA	
7 Jul 1868	4 Oct 1868	Henry Isaac	Henry & Annie	Reynolds	Gunner RMA	
	1 Oct 1868	Charles Edward	Charles & Jane	Challen	Gunner RMA	15
	23 Oct 1868	Allan Cameron	Robert Ballard & Christina	Gardner	Brevet Major RMA	16
	1 Nov 1868	Henry Arthur	William & Elizabeth	Strong	Sergeant RMA	
	1 Nov 1868	James Francis	James & Sarah	Bunce	Bugler RMA	
	6 Dec 1868	Eleanor Edith Ann	Joseph Richard & Rebecca	Nicholas	Gunner RMA	
	6 Dec 1868	John Edward	William & Maria	Heathfield	Gunner RMA	
	6 Dec 1868	Henry John	John & Elizabeth	Hyde	Gunner RMA	
	6 Dec 1868	Harry Gwy(am)	Henry & Eliza Ann	Parker	Corporal RMA	
11 Oct 1868	3 Jan 1869	Harry	Emannuel Lewis & Elizabeth	Potter	Sergeant RMA	
25 Jun 1867	3 Jan 1869	Sarah Ellen	Edward & Sarah	Sheridan	Gunner RMA	
23 Nov 1868	6 Jan 1869	Edmond Howard	Richard Archibald & Louisa Martha	Gorges	Captain RMA	
	31 Jan 1869	Sarah Jane	Thomas & Mary	Barnard	blank	17
	7 Feb 1869	Alice	Thomas & Mary	Barnard	blank	17
8 Apr 1867	7 Feb 1869	James William	James & Catherine	Gibbs	Sergeant RMA	
17 Jan 1869	7 Feb 1869	Mary Georgina	Thomas & Martha	Powell	Corporal RMA	

3 Dec 1868	7 Feb 1869	Emily Elizabeth	Richard & Mary Baker	**Meredith**	Bandsman RMA	
13 Dec 1868	7 Feb 1869	Laura Kate	William Benjamin & Annie Elizabeth	**Bryan**	Gunner RMA	
17 Sep 1862	7 Feb 1869	Georgina Ann	George & Ann	**Young**	Bombardier RMA	
13 Aug 1864	7 Feb 1869	Elizabeth Mary Angelina	George & Ann	**Young**	Bombardier RMA	
9 Nov 1868	7 Feb 1869	Alfred Edward	Alfred & Ann	**Sawyer**	Gunner RMA	
18 Jan 1869	7 Feb 1869	William George	Joseph & Caroline	**Hetheridge**	Corporal RMA	
9 Sep 1862	7 Feb 1869	Richard John	Richard & Catherine Louisa	**Tiner**	Gunner RMA	
6 Dec 1866	7 Feb 1869	George Albert	Richard & Catherine Louisa	**Tiner**	Gunner RMA	
26 Dec 1868	7 Feb 1869	Kate Louisa	Richard & Catherine Louisa	**Tiner**	Gunner RMA	
	7 Feb 1869	Mary Alice	George Deen & Annie	**Birch**	Sergeant RMA	
	28 Feb 1869	Emily	William John & Emma	**Avenell**	Labourer	17
26 Nov 1868	7 Mar 1869	Charles Joseph	Charles & Elizabeth Ann	**Monk**	Sergeant RMA	
12 Feb 1869	7 Mar 1869	Agnes Mary	Jesse & Mary	**Sollors**	Corporal RMA	
30 Nov 1868	4 Apr 1869	Fanny Richards	John & Caroline	**Richards**	Bombardier RMA	
7 Jan 1869	4 Apr 1869	Elizabeth Ann	Henry & Bessie	**Dobson**	Gunner RMA	
20 Jan 1869	4 Apr 1869	Minnie Jane	Samuel & Sarah	**Ross**	Bugler RMA	
20 Jan 1869	4 Apr 1869	Katie Louisa	Samuel & Sarah	**Ross**	Bugler RMA	
30 Jan 1869	4 Apr 1869	William Alderman	Thomas & Ellen	**Howard**	Gunner RMA	
13 Apr 1869	2 May 1869	Richard William	Samuel & Emily	**Carnell**	Gunner RMA	
21 Nov 1868	2 May 1869	Charles Frederick	George Frederick & Elizabeth Ann	**Showell**	Bombardier RMA	
31 Dec 1866	2 May 1869	Georgina Elizabeth	George Frederick & Elizabeth Ann	**Showell**	Bombardier RMA	
13 Jan 1859	2 May 1869	Sarah Ann	George & Caroline	**Hobbs**	Gunner RMA	
31 Mar 1861	2 May 1869	Harriett	George & Caroline	**Hobbs**	Gunner RMA	
20 Mar 1869	2 May 1869	William Joseph	William & Sarah	**Sale**	Bombardier RMA	
3 Mar 1869	2 May 1869	Charles	Charles & Betsey	**Lilly**	Corporal RMA	
7 Feb 1869	2 May 1869	Elizabeth Ellen	John & Ann	**Jackson**	Gunner RMA	
28 Dec 1861	5 May 1869	Elizabeth Ann	William & Maria	**Putt**	Sergeant RMA	12
12 Apr 1869	9 May 1869	Nesta Frances Dora	Owen Thomas & Celia	**Jones**	Lieutenant RMA	
8 May 1869	6 Jun 1869	Arthur Henry	Thomas & Rebecca	**Lawrence**	Sergeant RMA	
1 Feb 1869	6 Jun 1869	Edward Ernest	John & Sarah	**Targett**	Sergeant RMA	
5 Apr 1869	6 Jun 1869	Frederick Hyde	John & Louisa	**Lewis**	Corporal RMA	
31 Jan 1869	6 Jun 1869	Elizabeth	Christopher & Eliza	**Sproates**	Gunner RMA	
6 Aug 1857	6 Jun 1869	George	George & Ellen	**Jackson**	Sergeant RMA	
26 Dec 1858	6 Jun 1869	Emily Florence	George & Ellen	**Jackson**	Sergeant RMA	
15 Sep 1860	6 Jun 1869	William Henry	George & Ellen	**Jackson**	Sergeant RMA	
3 Sep 1862	6 Jun 1869	Elizabeth Ellen	George & Ellen	**Jackson**	Sergeant RMA	
24 Feb 1865	6 Jun 1869	Hannah Maria	George & Ellen	**Jackson**	Sergeant RMA	
1 Feb 1867	6 Jun 1869	Hester Emma	George & Ellen	**Jackson**	Sergeant RMA	
4 Jan 1869	6 Jun 1869	Alice Maud	George & Ellen	**Jackson**	Sergeant RMA	
20 Apr 1869	6 Jun 1869	Walter Thorne	Francis & Margaret	**Staples**	Corporal RMA	
12 Feb 1869	6 Jun 1869	Lily Alma	Richard & Fanny	**Ox**	Corporal RMA	
15 Apr 1869	6 Jun 1869	Sarah Jane	Philip & Maria	**Clift**	Gunner RMA	
17 May 1869	6 Jun 1869	Edwin Burgess	Edwin & Caroline	**Budd**	Corporal RMA	
12 Apr 1869	6 Jun 1869	King George	John & Elizabeth	**Fitt**	Bombardier RMA	
10 May 1869	4 Jul 1869	William Henry	William & Rosina	**Day**	Gunner RMA	
13 May 1869	4 Jul 1869	George Francis	George & Fanny Georgina	**Avery**	Sergeant RMA	
16 Sep 1864	4 Jul 1869	Frances Augusta	Daniel & Sarah	**Neale**	Sergeant RMA	
25 Apr 1867	4 Jul 1869	Alice Maud Mary	Daniel & Sarah	**Neale**	Sergeant RMA	
9 Jan 1858	4 Jul 1869	Elizabeth	Samuel & Elizabeth	**Porter**	Dockyard Labourer	18

13 Jun 1855	4 Jul 1869	Richard John	Daniel & Mary Ann Macey	Thurston	Confectioner	18
18 Feb 1858	4 Jul 1869	William Robert	Daniel & Mary Ann Macey	Thurston	Confectioner	18
26 Jun 1869	1 Aug 1869	Joseph Charles	John & Emma	Hazlehurst	Bombardier RMA	
8 May 1869	1 Aug 1869	Mary Ann Emily	John & Ruth	Care	Gunner RMA	
28 Feb 1869	1 Aug 1869	Flora Ellen	Robert & Elizabeth	Fraser	Gunner RMA	
8 Jun 1869	1 Aug 1869	William	Christopher & Mary	Traves	Gunner RMA	
2 Aug 1869	7 Aug 1869	Ada Isabel Ena	Edward Henderson & Elizabeth Mary	Starr	Captain RMA	12
9 Jun 1869	5 Sep 1869	John Frederick	Daniel & Mary Ann	Artifold	Gunner RMA	
7 Jun 1865	5 Sep 1869	Rebecca Ann	John & Catherine	Hooper	Gunner RMA	
7 Nov 1868	5 Sep 1869	John Samuel	John & Catherine	Hooper	Gunner RMA	
2 Jul 1869	5 Sep 1869	William Francis	William & Emily Sophia	Stallworthy	Gunner RMA	
2 Jun 1869	5 Sep 1869	Annie	Joseph & Mary Grace	Blackwell	Gunner RMA	
27 Aug 1869	3 Oct 1869	Thomas John	James & Catherine	Gibbs	Sergeant RMA	
14 Jul 1869	3 Oct 1869	Edith Annie	Richard & Ellen	Osborn	Sergeant RMA	
15 Sep 1869	3 Oct 1869	Rosina Matilda	James & Mary Ann	Sprague	Pensioner RMA	
20 Aug 1864	3 Oct 1869	John	James & Ann	Anderson	Gunner RMA	
9 Oct 1866	3 Oct 1869	Ann Christina	James & Ann	Anderson	Gunner RMA	
29 Aug 1869	3 Oct 1869	Frances Ann	William & Harriet	Beney	Corporal RMA	
4 Aug 1869	3 Oct 1869	Robert James Murray	George Murray & Mary Ann	Dighton	Bombardier RMA	
13 Sep 1869	5 Oct 1869	Maria Ann	Charles William & Maria	Cailes	Sergeant RMA	2
27 Oct 1867	7 Nov 1869	William John	William & Martha	McManus	Sergeant RMA	
30 Sep 1869	7 Nov 1869	Charles George	William & Martha	McManus	Sergeant RMA	
19 Apr 1868	7 Nov 1869	Ellen Blanche	James & Annie	Bright	Sergeant RMA	
2 Sep 1869	7 Nov 1869	James Harry	James & Annie	Bright	Sergeant RMA	
24 Sep 1869	7 Nov 1869	William Thomas	Frederick & Susan	Jenkins	Bombardier RMA	
25 Sep 1869	7 Nov 1869	Richard Henry	James & Mary Maria	Diment	Gunner RMA	
6 Jun 1869	7 Nov 1869	John Hezekiah	John & Mary Jane	Coombes	Gunner RMA	
24 Aug 1869	7 Nov 1869	George Thomas	Thomas & Ann	Collier	Gunner RMA	
23 Feb 1869	7 Nov 1869	Catherine Jane	Thomas & Catherine	Cox	Gunner RMA	
17 Sep 1869	7 Nov 1869	Walter George	Thomas & Mary Jane	Boswell	Gunner RMA	
21 Aug 1858	7 Nov 1869	Ellen	Samuel & Susan	Musgrove	Pensioner Gunner RMA	
14 Nov 1862	7 Nov 1869	Rosalina	Samuel & Susan	Musgrove	Pensioner Gunner RMA	
28 May 1864	7 Nov 1869	Samuel Francis	Samuel & Susan	Musgrove	Pensioner Gunner RMA	
12 Feb 1866	7 Nov 1869	Susan Jane	Samuel & Susan	Musgrove	Pensioner Gunner RMA	
13 Jul 1868	7 Nov 1869	Eliza	Samuel & Susan	Musgrove	Pensioner Gunner RMA	
13 Nov 1869	5 Dec 1869	George Hutchings	Thomas & Jane	Foster	Pensioner RMA	
9 Nov 1869	5 Dec 1869	Frederick James	William & Amy	Cann	Corporal RMA	
3 Jun 1869	5 Dec 1869	Thomas John	William James & Mary Jane	Aukett	Gunner RMA	
17 Sep 1869	5 Dec 1869	Lily Maria Emma	William & Ellen Margaret	Golding	Gunner RMA	
25 Sep 1869	5 Dec 1869	Elizabeth Ellen	Frederick & Ellen	Wilton	Acting Sergeant RMA	
26 Sep 1869	5 Dec 1869	Beatrice	James William & Rose Anna	Simpson	Bombardier RMA	
15 Nov 1869	2 Jan 1870	William James	William & Eliza Mary Ann	Carthy	Corporal RMA	
2 Nov 1869	2 Jan 1870	Alice Margaret	Samuel & Margaret	Duesbury	Sergeant RMA	
18 Sep 1869	2 Jan 1870	John Benjamin	John & Isabella	Rowlatt	Sergeant RMA	
4 Dec 1869	2 Jan 1870	Eliza	James & Sarah Ann	Cotterell	Sergeant RMA	
3 Dec 1869	2 Jan 1870	Ellen Rosina	Robert & Jane	Lucas	Gunner RMA	
2 Oct 1869	2 Jan 1870	Harriet Jane	Charles & Sarah	Frampton	Gunner RMA	

	9 Jan 1870	Francis James Cunynghawe	George & Augusta Z T C	Robertson	Assistant Surgeon RMA	19
4 Jul 1855	6 Feb 1870	James	James & Ann	Kirby	Gunner RMA	
6 Jul 1864	6 Feb 1870	Willie	James & Ann	Kirby	Gunner RMA	
22 Nov 1869	6 Feb 1870	Mary Ann	James & Ann	Kirby	Gunner RMA	
29 Oct 1869	6 Feb 1870	James William	William James & Mary Ann	Lyons	Acting Bombardier RMA	
28 Oct 1856	6 Feb 1870	James Thomas	Thomas & Mary	Foster	Late Gunner RMA	
27 Jan 1868	6 Feb 1870	John Henry Shepherd	Thomas & Jane	Foster	Late Gunner RMA	
2 Dec 1869	6 Feb 1870	Charles Henry	John & Eliza	Fisher	Gunner RMA	
14 Dec 1869	6 Feb 1870	Thomas James	Absalom & Mary	Berry	Gunner RMA	
18 Nov 1869	6 Feb 1870	Clara Louisa	John Tom & Louisa Mary	Smith	Sergeant RMA	
25 Dec 1869	6 Feb 1870	George Henry Robert	George & Charlotte	Addicott	Gunner RMA	
17 Jan 1870	6 Mar 1870	Hannorah Elizabeth	Richard & Catherine Louisa	Tiner	Gunner RMA	
29 Dec 1869	6 Mar 1870	Arthur William St John	Charles & Susan	Perry	Sergeant RMA	
14 Feb 1870	9 Mar 1870	Bessie Kate	Richard James & Elizabeth Sarah	Ball	Sergeant RMA	
31 Dec 1869	25 Mar 1870	Charles Walter Joseph	Charles & Ann	Richards	Gunner RMA	
25 Mar 1870	25 Mar 1870	Charles	John & Sarah	Jackson	Sergeant RMA	
25 Mar 1870	25 Mar 1870	Florence	John & Sarah	Jackson	Sergeant RMA	
12 Nov 1868	28 Mar 1870	Maude Olive	Amos & Maria	Snooks	Gunner RMA	
3 Feb 1870	3 Apr 1870	Sarah Jane	George & Ellen	Quayle	Gunner RMA	
11 Feb 1870	3 Apr 1870	Harry Herbert Hans	Henry & Sarah Ann	Woodward	Schoolmaster RMA	
1 Feb 1870	3 Apr 1870	Helen	John Varvill & Sarah Jane	Scott	Sergeant RMA	
11 Jan 1870	3 Apr 1870	Charles Henry	William & Maria	Heathfield	Gunner RMA	
26 Sep 1869	3 Apr 1870	Violet Louisa	William & Ann	Lovell	Gunner RMA	
14 Jan 1870	3 Apr 1870	Ginevra	Edward & Mary Ann Harvey	King	Late Sergeant RMA	
23 Feb 1870	1 May 1870	Caroline Lucy	James Huntsman & Elizabeth Henrietta	Fitch	Gunner RMA	
6 Oct 1869	1 May 1870	George John Morgan	John Morgan & Sarah	Kite	Gunner RMA	
13 Apr 1870	1 May 1870	James John	James & Susanna	Taylor	Gunner RMA	
7 Mar 1870	1 May 1870	Thomas Henry	Thomas & Elizabeth Jane	Cousins	Sergeant RMA	
5 Feb 1870	1 May 1870	Eva Ann	George & Sarah Jane	Walker	Sergeant RMA	
24 Feb 1870	9 May 1870	James Campbell	Robert Ballard & Christina	Gardener	Brevet Major RMA	20
16 May 1870	24 May 1870	Edith Dora	Owen Thomas & Celia	Jones	Captain RMA	20
15 Mar 1870	5 Jun 1870	Alice	John & Alice	Shuffell	Sergeant & Bugle Major RMA	
27 Jul 1869	5 Jun 1870	Daniel	Daniel & Julia	Hanson	Gunner RMA	
29 Aug 1868	5 Jun 1870	Kate Maria Beutley	William & Ann Elizabeth Beutley	Woodfield	Gunner RMA	
17 Feb 1870	5 Jun 1870	Ann Elizabeth Beutley	William & Ann Elizabeth Beutley	Woodfield	Gunner RMA	
10 Feb 1870	5 Jun 1870	Catherine Sarah	George & Catherine	Smart	Gunner RMA	
24 Apr 1870	5 Jun 1870	Martha Ann Cyster	William & Martha	Eason	Gunner RMA	
12 Mar 1870	5 Jun 1870	William Henry Abbott	William & Sarah Jane	Abbott	Bandsman RMA	
19 Mar 1870	23 Jun 1870	Anne Esther	Thomas & Esther	Barringer	Sergeant RMA	
2 Jun 1870	26 Jun 1870	George William	Richard Turberville & Catherine Georgiana	Ansell	Captain RMA	21
3 Feb 1867	3 Jul 1870	Martha Mary	Edmund William & Martha	Micklewright	Sergeant RMA	
27 Aug 1868	3 Jul 1870	Edmund William	Edmund William & Martha	Micklewright	Sergeant RMA	
2 Feb 1870	3 Jul 1870	Walter	Edmund William & Martha	Micklewright	Sergeant RMA	

8 Jun 1870	3 Jul 1870	James	John & Caroline	**Richards**	Bombardier RMA	
23 Mar 1870	3 Jul 1870	Florence Eliza	David & Jane	**Hayward**	Gunner RMA	
1 Mar 1870	3 Jul 1870	Elizabeth	James & Emily	**Walker**	Gunner RMA	
26 Mar 1869	3 Jul 1870	Margaret Alice	Edward & Sarah	**Sheridan**	Gunner RMA	
6 May 1870	3 Jul 1870	Edith Ann	Thomas & Elizabeth Ann	**Allen**	Gunner RMA	
8 Mar 1869	3 Jul 1870	Amelia	Frederick & Ellen	**Ford**	Bombardier RMA	
23 Aug 1865	3 Jul 1870	Robert William Benjamin	Robert & Emma	**Simms**	Gunner RMA	
13 Feb 1867	3 Jul 1870	Alfred Richard John	Robert & Emma	**Simms**	Gunner RMA	
2 Mar 1870	3 Jul 1870	Ellen Louisa Alice	Robert & Emma	**Simms**	Gunner RMA	
7 May 1870	3 Jul 1870	Charles George Richard	Henry & Henrietta	**Reynolds**	Gunner RMA	
14 Jul 1870	28 Jul 1870	John Hewitson Marshall	John & Jane Elizabeth	**Brown**	Sergeant RMA	
2 Jul 1870	7 Aug 1870	Elizabeth Ann	John & Elizabeth	**Hyde**	Gunner RMA	
11 Jun 1870	7 Aug 1870	Ellen Mary	George & Sophia	**Cox**	Bombardier RMA	
25 Jun 1870	7 Aug 1870	Mary Jane	David & Emma Eliza	**McKay**	Gunner RMA	
3 May 1870	7 Aug 1870	Abraham John	Abraham & Georgina	**Sharp**	Bombardier RMA	
17 Jul 1870	7 Aug 1870	Una Maria	John & Sarah Ann	**Hutchings**	Gunner RMA	
5 Jun 1870	7 Aug 1870	Samuel	John & Elizabeth	**Fitt**	Bombardier RMA	
17 Jun 1870	26 Aug 1870	Henry Lancelot	Henry Way & Catherine Susan Deane	**Mawbey**	Lieutenant Colonel RMA	
14 May 1870	4 Sep 1870	Leonora Kate	Daniel & Sarah	**Neale**	Sergeant RMA	
8 Jul 1870	4 Sep 1870	Emma Jane	John & Emma	**Willey**	Gunner RMA	
25 Jun 1870	4 Sep 1870	Arthur Alfred James	John & Sarah	**Target**	Sergeant RMA	
1 Aug 1870	4 Sep 1870	Frederick George	Thomas & Mary Ann	**Pitt**	Gunner RMA	
29 May 1870	4 Sep 1870	William Joseph	James & Mary Ann	**Willis**	Gunner RMA	
28 Jan 1869	4 Sep 1870	Emma Jemima	James & Mary Ann	**Willis**	Gunner RMA	
14 Aug 1870	4 Sep 1870	Margaret Ann	Robert & Elizabeth	**Fraser**	Gunner RMA	
11 Aug 1870	4 Sep 1870	Willie Edward	Edward & Sarah	**Sheridan**	Gunner RMA	
24 Jul 1870	4 Sep 1870	Ada Georgina	George & Fanny Georgina	**Avery**	Sergeant RMA	
24 Aug 1870	12 Sep 1870	William Thomas	Samuel & Isabella	**Cook**	Gunner RMA	22
23 Aug 1870	2 Oct 1870	Elizabeth Ann	William & Annie	**Richards**	Corporal RMA	
22 Aug 1870	2 Oct 1870	George Charles	William & Emma	**Jones**	Gunner RMA	
10 Aug 1870	9 Oct 1870	Gertrude May	William & Charlotte	**Dearing**	Late Sergeant RMA	
18 Aug 1870	14 Oct 1870	Frederick George	Henry George & Eliza	**Garrett**	Gunner RMA	
9 Oct 1870	24 Oct 1870	George Kynaston	Edward Henderson & Elizabeth Mary	**Starr**	Captain RMA	
12 Oct 1870	6 Nov 1870	William Edward	William Benjamin & Ann Elizabeth	**Bryan**	Gunner RMA	
29 Jul 1870	6 Nov 1870	George Drowley	Charles & Elizabeth Jane	**Monk**	Sergeant RMA	
25 Aug 1870	6 Nov 1870	Annie Kate	Edmund & Caroline	**Budd**	Corporal RMA	
27 Aug 1870	6 Nov 1870	Ellen Charlotte	Charles William & Maria	**Cailes**	Sergeant RMA	
18 Sep 1870	6 Nov 1870	Albert Alonzo	Albert & Caroline	**Helyar**	Gunner RMA	
28 Jul 1870	6 Nov 1870	Mary	Richard & Mary	**Meredith**	Bandsman RMA	
3 Sep 1870	6 Nov 1870	Thomas George	Joseph & Jane	**Austin**	Gunner RMA	
3 Sep 1870	6 Nov 1870	Alfred	Emanuel Lewis & Elizabeth	**Potter**	Sergeant RMA	
5 Nov 1870	4 Dec 1870	William Henry	William & Margaret	**Jones**	Gunner RMA	
5 Aug 1870	4 Dec 1870	Alice	William & Ellen	**Wolridge**	Gunner RMA	
27 Oct 1870	4 Dec 1870	John	John & Jane	**Dawson**	Sergeant RMA	
1 Oct 1870	4 Dec 1870	Benjamin William Captain	Benjamin & Ann	**Porter**	Gunner RMA	
13 Nov 1870	4 Dec 1870	Alfred Alonzo	Stephen & Eliza	**Borer**	Sergeant RMA (Pensioner)	

31 Aug 1870	4 Dec 1870	Emily Esther	Charles Edward & Emily	Briggs	Bandsman RMA	
11 Oct 1870	4 Dec 1870	Victor Gottfried	Frederick & Martha	Kreyer	Bandsman RMA	
5 Nov 1870	4 Dec 1870	William Richard	William & Margaret	Pike	Gunner RMA	
11 Nov 1870	4 Dec 1870	Elizabeth	Charles & Betsey	Lilley	Sergeant RMA	
3 Sep 1870	1 Jan 1871	Ellen Jane	James & Sarah	Bunce	Bugler RMA	
21 Aug 1870	1 Jan 1871	William Joseph	Joseph & Mary Ann	Wade	Gunner RMA	
22 Nov 1870	1 Jan 1871	John Joseph Thomas	William & Harriet	Foden	Sergeant RMA	
1 Dec 1870	1 Jan 1871	William David	William & Lily	Webster	Sergeant RMA	
20 Sep 1870	1 Jan 1871	Amy Laura	William & Elizabeth	Strong	Late Sergeant RMA	
25 Nov 1870	1 Jan 1871	Arthur Charles	Alfred & Anna	Freeman	Late Sergeant RMA	
29 Nov 1870	5 Feb 1871	John Thomas	Thomas & Mary	Searle	Gunner RMA	
15 Jan 1871	5 Feb 1871	Henry	Samuel & Emily	Carnell	Gunner RMA	
9 Dec 1870	5 Feb 1871	John George Bailey	Thomas & Anna Maria	Weston	Corporal RMA	
29 Nov 1870	5 Feb 1871	John William	John & Emma	Hay	Gunner RMA	
6 Nov 1870	19 Mar 1871	William Edward	John & Mary Alice	Reynolds	Gunner RMA	
3 Jan 1871	19 Mar 1871	Adeline Emmeline Emma	James & Emma Sophia	Woodger	Bandsman RMA	
12 Jan 1871	22 Mar 1871	George Edward William	Charles & Ann	Richards	Gunner RMA	
14 Feb 1871	2 Apr 1871	Lucy Helen	George & Annie	Birch	Sergeant RMA	
23 Jan 1871	2 Apr 1871	Beatrice Elizabeth	Stephen & Jane	Matthews	Gunner RMA	
2 Feb 1867	2 Apr 1871	Ellen Mary	Peter & Mary Ann	Jordan	Bombardier RMA	
27 Oct 1869	2 Apr 1871	Emma Kate	Peter & Mary Ann	Jordan	Bombardier RMA	
7 Jan 1871	2 Apr 1871	Ellen	George & Mary Ann	Tucker	Gunner RMA	
20 Aug 1869	2 Apr 1871	Ann	George & Jane Anna	Haskell	Gunner RMA	
26 Feb 1871	2 Apr 1871	Alice	George & Jane Anna	Haskell	Gunner RMA	
3 Nov 1870	2 Apr 1871	Alice Maude Mary	Samuel & Sarah Mary	Ross	Bugler RMA	
3 Nov 1870	2 Apr 1871	Emily Elizabeth Pardue	Samuel & Sarah Mary	Ross	Bugler RMA	
27 Mar 1871	14 Apr 1871	Alice Louisa	George & Mary Jane	Miller	Gunner RMA	23
30 Mar 1871	7 May 1871	Selina Caroline	Joseph & Caroline	Hetheridge	Sergeant RMA	
20 Mar 1871	7 May 1871	Charles Henry	Charles & Elizabeth Jane	Oakley	Corporal RMA	
25 Mar 1871	7 May 1871	Alice Mary	Richard & Fanny	Ox	Corporal RMA	
23 Dec 1870	7 May 1871	Frederick John	Samuel & Sarah	Denning	Gunner RMA	
17 Mar 1871	7 May 1871	Edith Douglas	Thomas Douglas & Penelope	Askew	School Master RMA	
17 Mar 1871	7 May 1871	Annie Georgie Ellen	George William & Annie Louisa	Morse	Late Corporal RMA	
15 Apr 1871	4 Jun 1871	Adeline	Abraham & Ann	Jarvis	Gunner RMA	
14 Apr 1871	4 Jun 1871	Frederick Charles	James & Emma	Mortlock	Corporal RMA	
12 Apr 1871	2 Jul 1871	Frances Mary	Richard & Catherine Louisa	Tiner	Gunner RMA	
22 May 1871	2 Jul 1871	Harry	Thomas & Selina	Young	Gunner RMA	
26 May 1871	5 Jul 1871	Maggie Burnett	Richard & Emma Mary	Strawbridge	Sergeant RMA	20
6 Apr 1871	26 Jul 1871	Launcelot Charles	Edmund Henry & Frances Emily Cadogan	Cox	Captain RMA	
26 Jul 1871	19 Aug 1871	Violet Mary	Edward & Anna Mary Campbell	McArthur	Captain RMA	
	6 Aug 1871	Patience Ruth	Robert & Elizabeth	Haskett	Sergeant RMA	24
	6 Aug 1871	Alice Maud	Christopher & Elizabeth	Gibbs	Sergeant RMA	24
	6 Aug 1871	Elizabeth Ann	James & Caroline	Court	Gunner RMA	24
	6 Aug 1871	Annie	Thomas & Ann	Baker	Gunner RMA	24
	3 Sep 1871	Mary Maud Margaret	Francis & Margaret	Staples	Corporal RMA	
	3 Sep 1871	William Edward	Daniel & Julia	Hawson	Gunner RMA	

	3 Sep 1871	Maria Annie Laurie	James & Martha	Green	Gunner RMA	
	3 Sep 1871	William Henry	Thomas & Mary Jane	Boswell	Gunner RMA	
	3 Sep 1871	Harriet Louisa	Henry & Frances	Brooks	Gunner RMA	
	3 Sep 1871	Edith Sarah	Frederick & Ellen	Wilton	Sergeant RMA	
	3 Sep 1871	Eliza Minnie	James & Annie	Knight	Colour Sergeant RMA	
	24 Sep 1871	Harry Edward	Richard & Ellen	Osborn	Sergeant RMA	
	24 Sep 1871	Ellen Amy	William & Amy	Cann	Corporal RMA	
	24 Sep 1871	Mary Hayles	John & Isabella	Rowlatt	Sergeant RMA	
	9 Oct 1871	Sarah Jane	William & Sarah	Sale	Bombardier RMA	25
	29 Oct 1871	Catherine Louisa	Sampson & Mary	Miles	Bombardier RMA	
	29 Oct 1871	Edith Henrietta	John & Emma	Hazelhurst	Corporal RMA	
	29 Oct 1871	John Thomas	William & Rosina	Day	Gunner RMA	
	29 Oct 1871	Elizabeth	Joseph & Mary Grace	Blackwell	Gunner RMA	
	26 Nov 1871	Arthur Ernest	Henry & Eliza Anne	Parker	Sergeant RMA	
	26 Nov 1871	Charles	Henry Mark & Grace	Pawson	Gunner RMA	
	26 Nov 1871	William Frederick Charles	William Frederick Charles & Ellen	Stubbs	Gunner RMA	
	26 Nov 1871	Catherine Jane	William & Mary Jane	Aukett	Gunner RMA	
	31 Dec 1871	Elizabeth Frances Annie	John Banks & Annie	Williams	Sergeant RMA	
	31 Dec 1871	Fritz Ernest	Frederick & Martha	Kreyer	Band Corporal RMA	
	31 Dec 1871	Thomas	Thomas & Elizabeth	Tunnicliffe	Gunner RMA	
	31 Dec 1871	Henry Thomas	Henry & Emma	James	Sergeant RMA	
21 Mar 1869	31 Dec 1871	Adelaide Amelia	Henry & Emma	James	Sergeant RMA	
	28 Jan 1872	Caroline	John & Caroline	Richards	Bombardier RMA	
	28 Jan 1872	James Henry	Charles & Sarah	Frampton	Gunner RMA	
	28 Jan 1872	Henry Lionel	Henry & Mary Anne	Street	Gunner RMA	
	28 Jan 1872	William John	Thomas & Elizabeth Jane	Cousins	Colour Sergeant RMA	
	28 Jan 1872	Albert Fowler	Charles & Susan	Perry	Colour Sergeant RMA	
	28 Jan 1872	Harry Charles Guy	Henry & Louisa	Peters	Gunner RMA	
	28 Jan 1872	John Albert	Charles & Mary	Warren	Bombardier RMA	
	28 Jan 1872	Frederick William	Thomas & Sarah	Buick	Gunner RMA	
	16 Feb 1872	Richard Thomas	Richard & Emma	Lecassale	Civilian	26
	25 Feb 1872	Adeline May	Richard Urbane & Sarah Anne	Nicholas	Sergeant RMA	
	25 Feb 1872	James	James & Sarah Anne	Cotterill	Gunner RMA	
	25 Feb 1872	George	George & Mary	Pugh	Gunner RMA	
	18 Mar 1872	Lavinia	John & Elizabeth	Saunders	Gunner RMA	12
	31 Mar 1872	James William	William & Jane	Williams	Gunner RMA	
	28 Apr 1872	Louisa Rose	Edmund & Louisa	Budd	Corporal RMA	
	28 Apr 1872	Samuel	Absalom & Mary	Berry	Gunner RMA	
	23 May 1872	Ann	John & Sarah Anne	Rider	Gunner RMA	12
	25 May 1872	Gertrude	George & Sarah Jane	Walker	Sergeant RMA	
	26 May 1872	Louisa Alice	Frederick & Elizabeth	Mann	Sergeant RMA	
						27
	30 Jun 1872	Charles Percy	Henry & Sarah Anne	Woodward	School Master	
	30 Jun 1872	Annie	Joseph & Ellen	Capper	Gunner RMA	
	30 Jun 1872	Clara May	Joseph & Ellen	Capper	Gunner RMA	
	30 Jun 1872	Charles William	John & Sarah	Loveridge	Bombardier RMA	
	30 Jun 1872	Henry John	John & Sarah	Loveridge	Bombardier RMA	

	30 Jun 1872	Albert Geary	George & Patty	Holbrey	Corporal RMA	
	30 Jun 1872	Thomas James	Thomas & Emily	Middleton	Gunner RMA	
	30 Jun 1872	Emily Elizabeth	Thomas & Emily	Middleton	Gunner RMA	
	28 Jul 1872	Sarah Alice	William & Sarah	Bennett	Bandsman RMA	
	28 Jul 1872	Luther James Evan	James & Gemma Sophia	Woodger	Bandsman RMA	
	28 Jul 1872	Wilmot Mary Elizabeth	William & Margaret	Pike	Gunner RMA	
	28 Jul 1872	Annie Maud	Richard & Anna Maria	Matthews	Gunner RMA	
	28 Jul 1872	George Aaron	James & Mary Ann	Lyons	Bombardier RMA	
	28 Jul 1872	Ernest	John & Isabella	Snook	Sergeant RMA	
	28 Jul 1872	Anne	George & Maryanne	Freckelton	Gunner RMA	12
	14 Aug 1872	Robert	Robert Ballard & Christina	Gardner	Major RMA	
	25 Aug 1872	Charles	Charles Edward & Emily	Briggs	Bandsman RMA	
	25 Aug 1872	William Henry	John & Philadelphia	Hammond	Corporal RMA	
	25 Aug 1872	Louisa Ellen	John & Emma	Willey	Gunner RMA	
	25 Aug 1872	Charles John	Thomas & Susannah	Bolton	Gunner RMA	
	25 Aug 1872	Harry	Thomas & Susannah	Bolton	Gunner RMA	
	1 Sep 1872	Alice Jesse Keziah	Thomas & Keziah	Oakley	Gunner RMA	
	8 Sep 1872	Bertie	Samuel & Margaret	Duesbury	Gunner RMA	12
	23 Sep 1872	George Kirkpatrick	Richard Turberville & Catherine Georgina	Ansell	Captain RMA	
	29 Sep 1872	Martha Annie	Thomas & Esther	Barringer	Sergeant RMA	
	29 Sep 1872	Louisa Kate	James & Rosanna	Simpson	Bandsman RMA	
	29 Sep 1872	George Cornelius	Cornelius & Emma	Woodman	Gunner RMA	
	29 Sep 1872	Robert George William	Robert & Mary Elizabeth	Rann	Gunner RMA	
	29 Sep 1872	James Harvey Frederick	Robert & Mary Elizabeth	Rann	Gunner RMA	
	29 Sep 1872	Alice	Joseph & Ellen	Saley	Gunner RMA	28
	29 Sep 1872	Emily Violet (Arms)	George & Elizabeth	Bell	Gunner RMA	
	7 Oct 1872	Gertrude Georgiana	Enbule Dayshe & Mary Elizabeth Dorothea	Thelwall	Captain RMA	
22 Sep 1872	19 Oct 1872	Hugh Vibart	Edward & Anna Mary Campbell	McArthur	Captain RMA	
	27 Oct 1872	Mary Anne	Thomas & Harriet	Evans	Gunner RMA	
	27 Oct 1872	Alfred	John & Sarah	Jackson	Sergeant RMA	
	27 Oct 1872	George Frederick William	James & Sarah	Bunce	Bugler RMA	
	27 Oct 1872	Elizabeth Anne	William Blanchard & Anne	Lovell	Gunner RMA	
	27 Oct 1872	Charles Henry	Joseph & Jane	Austin	Gunner RMA	
	29 Oct 1872	William George Hastings	William George Tomlin & Mary Elizabeth	Bickford	Lieutenant RMA	
	24 Nov 1872	Elizabeth Jane	Joseph & Maryanne	Wade	Gunner RMA	
	24 Nov 1872	George Henry	John & Ruth	Case	Gunner RMA	
	24 Nov 1872	Eliza	Obadiah & Sarah Jane	Higby	Bombardier RMA	
	24 Nov 1872	William Potter	John & Emma	Hazelhurst	Corporal RMA	
	29 Dec 1872	Henry Hunt	Henry Thomas & Elizabeth Jago	Page	Chaplain's Orderly RMA	
	29 Dec 1872	Francis Charles	Francis & Margaret	Staples	Corporal RMA	
	29 Dec 1872	Clara Maud	Thomas & Elizabeth	Martin	Corporal RMA	
	29 Dec 1872	Effie Sidonia	John & Sophia	Gilbert	Corporal RMA	
	26 Jan 1873	Henry Douglas	James & Susanna	Taylor	Gunner RMA	
	26 Jan 1873	Rose Elizabeth	John & Jane Elizabeth	Brown	Sergeant RMA	
	26 Jan 1873	Frederick William	Henry & Jane	Weeks	Gunner RMA	

24 Dec 1864	26 Jan 1873	Lucretia	Walter Far & Mary Jane	**Savage**	Gunner RMA	
25 Feb 1865	26 Jan 1873	Rose	Walter Far & Mary Jane	**Savage**	Gunner RMA	
30 Jun 1861	26 Jan 1873	Walter	Edward & Harriet	**Paradise**	Gunner RMA	
	26 Jan 1873	Jesse Isabella	Thomas & Selina	**Young**	Gunner RMA	
	29 Jan 1873	James	William & Mary	**Boyd**	Gunner RMA	12
2 Aug 1841	2 Feb 1873	Harriet	Samuel & Eliza	**Bennett**	Cloth Worker	29
	23 Feb 1873	Ernest Douglas	Thomas Douglas & Penelope	**Askew**	School Master RMA	
	23 Feb 1873	Herbert Edward	Charles & Elizabeth Jane	**Monk**	Sergeant RMA	
	23 Feb 1873	Henry Herbert	Stephen Edward & Emma	**Edwards**	Gunner RMA	
	23 Feb 1873	James Arthur	William & Sarah	**Sale**	Bombardier RMA	
	23 Feb 1873	Catherine	George & Fanny Georgina	**Avery**	Sergeant RMA	
	23 Feb 1873	James Richard	Francis & Eliza	**Cheshire**	Gunner RMA	
	23 Feb 1873	Elizabeth Emily	Job & Ellen	**Green**	Gunner RMA	
	3 Mar 1873	John Henry	Frederick & Sarah Jane	**Nicholls**	Sergeant RMA	12
	30 Mar 1873	Robert George	Robert & Elizabeth	**Haskett**	Sergeant RMA	
	30 Mar 1873	Mary Alice	John Banks & Annie	**Williams**	Sergeant RMA	
	30 Mar 1873	Emma Jane	William & Martha	**Eason**	Gunner RMA	
	22 Apr 1873	Mary Anne	James & Sarah	**Morris**	Gunner RMA	12
	27 Apr 1873	William	Emanuel Lewis & Elizabeth	**Potter**	Staff Sergeant RMA	
	27 Apr 1873	William Richard	Richard & May	**Meredith**	Bandsman RMA	
	27 Apr 1873	Eliza Margaret	Charles William & Maria	**Cailes**	Sergeant RMA	
	27 Apr 1873	George	Samuel & Emily	**Carnell**	Gunner RMA	
	27 Apr 1873	Alfred Tom	George & Maryanne	**Tucker**	Gunner RMA	
	27 Apr 1873	George	George & Jane Anne	**Haskell**	Gunner RMA	
	27 Apr 1873	Anne Elizabeth	Thomas & Sarah	**Buick**	Gunner RMA	
26 Mar 1872	13 Jun 1872	Laura Mary Grace Katherine	Henry Way & Katherine Susan Deane	**Mawbey**	Lieutenant Colonel RMA	30
	25 May 1873	Mary Anna	Wilson Mowbray & Diana	**Dobing**	Gunner RMA	
	25 May 1873	Elizabeth Frances	Daniel & Julia	**Anson**	Gunner RMA	
	25 May 1873	Francis William	Francis & Rose Julia	**Best**	Gunner RMA	
	29 Jun 1873	Sarah Elizabeth	Thomas & Mary Jane	**Boswell**	Gunner RMA	
	29 Jun 1873	Frederick Walter Lloyd	Edmond & Caroline Louise	**Budd**	Corporal RMA	
	27 Jul 1873	Alfred Charles	David & Charlotte	**Barnes**	Bandsman RMA	
	27 Jul 1873	Ethel Annie	George & Jemima	**Birch**	Sergeant RMA	
	27 Jul 1873	Frederick William	Sampson & Mary	**Miles**	Sergeant RMA	31
	27 Jul 1873	Richard Reuben	Richard & Elizabeth	**Hartnell**	Gunner RMA	
	27 Jul 1873	Alice Jane	John & Elizabeth	**Williams**	Gunner RMA	
	27 Jul 1873	Rosina	John & Elizabeth	**Saunders**	Gunner RMA	
	13 Aug 1873	Joseph	John Morgan & Sarah	**Kite**	Gunner RMA	12
	31 Aug 1873	Alfred Herman	Frederick & Martha	**Kreyer**	Band Corporal RMA	
	31 Aug 1873	John Albert	John & Martha Ann	**Owen**	Sergeant RMA	
	31 Aug 1873	Horace	William & Jane	**Howell**	Sergeant RMA	
	31 Aug 1873	Frederick Charles Henry	Frederick & Elizabeth	**Mann**	Sergeant RMA	
	31 Aug 1873	Tom Albert	James & Elizabeth	**Fitch**	Bombardier RMA	
	28 Sep 1873	Walter William	John & Isabella	**Rowlatt**	Sergeant RMA	
	28 Sep 1873	William Henry	William Brougham & Sarah	**Robinson**	Gunner RMA	
	28 Sep 1873	Joseph Bradshaw	William Brougham & Sarah	**Robinson**	Gunner RMA	
	26 Oct 1873	Sidney John George	William & Margaret	**Pike**	Gunner RMA	
	26 Oct 1873	Elizabeth Gertrude	James & Annie	**Knight**	Colour Sergeant RMA	

	Date	Name	Parents	Surname	Rank	
	9 Nov 1873	Maryanne	Eli & Maryanne	Fookes	Sergeant RMA	12
	30 Nov 1873	Frederick	Thomas & Rosina	Tunnicliffe	Gunner RMA	
	30 Nov 1873	Kate	Frederick & Ellen	Wilton	Band Sergeant RMA	
	30 Nov 1873	Benjamin Mark	Benjamin & Martha	Henly	Sergeant RMA	
	28 Dec 1873	Frederick Charles	Samuel & Maryanne	Down	Gunner RMA	
	28 Dec 1873	Rosina	James & Sarah	Cottrell	Gunner RMA	
	25 Jan 1874	Rose	William & Sarah Jane	Bennett	Bandsman RMA	
	25 Jan 1874	George Edward	George Edward & Elizabeth Anne	Harris	Bandsman RMA	
	25 Jan 1874	Rosina	William & Rosina	Day	Gunner RMA	
	25 Jan 1874	Edith Adrianna	George & Annie	Laker	Acting Bombardier RMA	
	22 Feb 1874	George Frederick Augustus	Francis & Margaret	Staples	Sergeant RMA	
	22 Feb 1874	Edward	Charles & Susan	Perry	Sergeant RMA	
	22 Feb 1874	Henrietta Mary	Charles & Henrietta	Avery	Gunner RMA	
	22 Feb 1874	Kate Ethel	Henry & Eliza	Parker	Sergeant RMA	
	22 Feb 1874	Clara Lavinia	Richard & Catherine	Tiner	Gunner RMA	
	28 Mar 1874	William Campbell	Robert Ballard & Christina	Gardner	Sergeant Major RMA	
	28 Mar 1874	Walter Wilson	Jonathon Barnard & Maryanne	Wiltshire	Sergeant RMA	
	29 Mar 1874	Alfred Freckelton	George & Maryanne	Freckelton	Gunner RMA	
	29 Mar 1874	George William	George & Mary	Miller	Sergeant RMA	32
	29 Mar 1874	Arthur Ernest	George & Mary	Miller	Sergeant RMA	
	29 Mar 1874	Robert	James & Susanna	Taylor	Gunner RMA	
	30 Mar 1874	William Charles Alfred	Robert Charles & Anne Elizabeth	Cooper	Gunner RMA	12
	26 Apr 1874	Frederick John	Henry & Sarah Anne	Woodward	School Master	
	26 Apr 1874	Bertie	Samuel & Margaret	Dewsbury	Gunner RMA	
	26 Apr 1874	Mary Anne	Samuel & Margaret	Dewsbury	Gunner RMA	
	13 May 1874	Charles Francis	William George Tomlin & Mary Elizabeth	Bickford	Captain RMA	
	22 May 1874	Grace Alice	William & Anne	Sidebottom	Sergeant RMA	33
	22 May 1874	Martha Anne	William & Anne	Sidebottom	Sergeant RMA	34
	22 May 1874	Jane Elizabeth	William & Anne	Sidebottom	Sergeant RMA	35
	22 May 1874	Amber Lilian	William & Anne	Sidebottom	Sergeant RMA	36
	22 May 1874	Frances Laura	William & Anne	Sidebottom	Sergeant RMA	37
	31 May 1874	Alphanzo	James & Caroline	Scott	Gunner RMA	
	31 May 1874	Lonsdale William	Lonsdale & Eliza	Clark	Gunner RMA	
	12 Jun 1874	May	William Davis & Alida Sarah	Welch	Captain RMA	
	28 Jun 1874	Letty Lavinia	William & Jane	Howell	Sergeant RMA	
	28 Jun 1874	Adelaide	William & Jane	Howell	Sergeant RMA	38
	28 Jun 1874	William Walter	William & Maryanne	Eden	Colour Sergeant RMA	
	28 Jun 1874	Frederick	Frederick & Susan	Jenkins	Corporal RMA	
	28 Jun 1874	Jemima Elizabeth	William Scotney & Elizabeth	Thorpe	Gunner RMA	
	28 Jun 1874	Lillie Benson	William Blanchard & Anne	Lovell	Gunner RMA	
	28 Jun 1874	George Thomas	Thomas & Maryanne	Bishop	Gunner RMA	
	26 Jul 1874	Florence Maude	William & Maria	Putt	Colour Sergeant RMA	
	26 Jul 1874	Walter	William & Sarah	Sale	Bombardier RMA	
	12 Aug 1874	Cecil Mary Harriette	Richard Turberville & Katherine Georgiana	Ansell	Brevet Major RMA	

	16 Aug 1874	Florence Annie	Albert & Patience	Allen	Gunner RMA	12
	30 Aug 1874	Maud Mary	Henry & Maryanne	Street	Gunner RMA	
	30 Aug 1874	Ellen	John & Caroline	Richards	Bombardier RMA	
	30 Aug 1874	Emily Sophia	Thomas & Esther	Barringer	Sergeant RMA	
	30 Aug 1874	Stephen Edward	John & Cordelia	Smith	Gunner RMA	
	30 Aug 1874	Walter Charles	Job & Ellen	Green	Gunner RMA	
	27 Sep 1874	Louisa	Stephen & Jane	Matthews	Gunner RMA	
	27 Sep 1874	Ellen Lydia	William & Maria	Heathfield	Gunner RMA	
	27 Sep 1874	Edwina Elizabeth	James & Emma	Mortlock	Corporal RMA	
	25 Oct 1874	James Richard	Richard & Fanny	Ox	Corporal RMA	
	25 Oct 1874	Agnes Esther	John & Emma	Hazlehurst	Corporal RMA	
	25 Oct 1874	Jessie	John & Ellen Maria	Jackson	Sergeant RMA	
	25 Oct 1874	Alice Caroline	William Benjamin & Ann Elizabeth	Bryan	Gunner RMA	
	29 Nov 1874	Edith Florence	John & Sarah	Loveridge	Sergeant RMA	
	27 Dec 1874	Mary Jane Ellen Stacy	Thomas & Mary Jane	Lane	Gunner RMA	
	27 Dec 1874	Leonard Alexander	Lion & Millicent	Kite	Gunner RMA	
	27 Dec 1874	Helena Louisa	Cornelious & Mary Anne	Woodman	Gunner RMA	
	27 Dec 1874	Alfred John	Joseph & Mary Anne	Wade	Gunner RMA	
	27 Dec 1874	Frederick William	David & Charlotte	Barnes	Musician RMA	
	27 Dec 1874	William Frederick	John & Martha Anne	Owen	Colour Sergeant RMA	
	27 Dec 1874	William	John & Elizabeth	Flower	Gunner RMA	
	27 Dec 1874	Martha Ellen	William James & Mary Jane	Aukett	Gunner RMA	
	12 Feb 1875	Harry	John & Anne	Mannings	Gunner RMA	12
	14 Feb 1875	Annie Hester	Thomas & Annie	Sandwell	Sergeant RMA	
	14 Feb 1875	Sidney Albert	John Banks & Annie	Williams	Sergeant RMA	
	14 Feb 1875	Millicent	Frederick John & Henrietta Anne	McRill	Gunner RMA	
	22 Feb 1875	Catherine	Henry Way & Katherine Susana Deane	Mawbey	Lieutenant Colonel RMA	12
	28 Feb 1875	Hetty Annie	James & Sarah	Bunce	Bugler RMA	
	28 Mar 1875	Mabel Dorothy	Thomas Douglas & Penelope	Askew	Schoolmaster RMA	
	28 Mar 1875	Maryanne	Frank & Fanny	Jacobs	Bandsman RMA	
	28 Mar 1875	Ellen Joanna	George & Catherine	Smart	Sergeant RMA	
	28 Mar 1875	Louisa Sarah	Charles William & Maria	Cailes	Sergeant RMA	
	28 Mar 1875	Agnes Margaret	William & Margaret	Pike	Gunner RMA	
	28 Mar 1875	Ellen Minnie	Edmond & Caroline	Budd	Sergeant RMA	
	28 Mar 1875	Agnes Lucy	William & Emily Jane	Vines	Gunner RMA	
	28 Mar 1875	Edward Elam	Joseph & Sarah Anne	Jeanes	Gunner RMA	
	28 Mar 1875	George William	Joseph & Sarah Anne	Jeanes	Gunner RMA	
	29 Mar 1875	Adair Colpoys	Colpoys Pashyns & Lucy Anne Maria	Heaslop	Captain RMA	
	10 Apr 1875	Elizabeth Mary	Harvey & Elizabeth Martha	Horner	Corporal RMA	12
16 Mar 1875	25 Apr 1875	Alice Elizabeth	William & Martha	Eason	Gunner RMA	
11 Mar 1875	25 Apr 1875	Amelia Hawes	Charles & Mary	Davis	Gunner RMA	
25 Jan 1875	25 Apr 1875	Clara	Joseph & Fanny	Bennett	Gunner RMA	
17 Nov 1874	25 Apr 1875	Ann	John & Frances	Harding	Gunner RMA	
4 Feb 1867	25 Apr 1875	Charles	John & Frances	Harding	Gunner RMA	
20 Mar 1875	30 May 1875	Alfred Norman	Alfred & Maria	Rimmington	Gunner RMA	
22 Nov 1874	30 May 1875	Henry Edward	Henry & Mary Ann	Taylor	Gunner RMA	
5 Feb 1875	30 May 1875	Harry Lahan	Joseph & Rebecca	Hart	Gunner RMA	

29 Mar 1875	30 May 1875	Sophia Mary	George & Rose	**More**	Bombardier RMA	
20 Apr 1875	30 May 1875	Edwin Oscar	Edwin & Eliza	**Pritchard**	Bombardier RMA	
6 Apr 1875	30 May 1875	Alfred George Ernest	George John & Fanny	**Darby**	Bombardier RMA	
	7 Jun 1875	Rosanna Mary	James & Mary Ann Elizabeth	**Clark**	Gunner RMA	12
3 Nov 1874	27 Jun 1875	Caroline Mary	John & Emma	**Willey**	Gunner RMA	
22 Mar 1875	27 Jun 1875	Frederick John	Thomas & Elizabeth Rachel	**Hobson**	Gunner RMA	
23 Mar 1875	27 Jun 1875	Joseph John	Obadiah & Sarah Jane	**Higby**	Corporal RMA	
	25 Jul 1875	Bertram	Frederick & Elizabeth	**Mann**	Sergeant RMA	
	25 Jul 1875	Leopold Frederick	William & Martha	**McManus**	Sergeant RMA	
	25 Jul 1875	Henry James	William & Martha	**McManus**	Sergeant RMA	
	25 Jul 1875	Ann Amelia	Thomas & Catherine	**Shore**	Gunner RMA	
	25 Jul 1875	Florence Louise	Thomas & Elizabeth	**Martin**	Corporal RMA	
	25 Jul 1875	William Charles	George & Patty	**Holbry**	Sergeant RMA	
	25 Jul 1875	Charles Stewart	Thomas & Sarah	**Buick**	Gunner RMA	
	29 Aug 1875	Harry George	Thomas & Emma	**Middleton**	Gunner RMA	
	29 Aug 1875	Louisa Mary	James Frederick & Annie	**Willcox**	Corporal RMA	
	29 Aug 1875	William Henry	William & Eliza	**Harley**	Gunner RMA	
	29 Aug 1875	Frederick George	William & Eliza	**Harley**	Gunner RMA	
	29 Aug 1875	Herbert Baldock	Thomas & Sarah Jane	**Ellis**	Gunner RMA	
	29 Aug 1875	James Edward	William & Elizabeth	**White**	Sergeant RMA	
	29 Aug 1875	William Henry	William & Elizabeth	**White**	Sergeant RMA	
	29 Aug 1875	Florence Jane	Samuel & Mary Ann	**Setch**	Gunner RMA	
	29 Aug 1875	William John Aspinall	William & Elizabeth	**Ford**	Seaman RN	
	29 Aug 1875	George Edward	William & Elizabeth	**Ford**	Seaman RN	
	29 Aug 1875	Margaret	John & Ellen	**Doody**	Gunner RMA	
	29 Aug 1875	Ellen	John & Ellen	**Doody**	Gunner RMA	
	29 Aug 1875	Caroline	John & Ellen	**Doody**	Gunner RMA	
15 Aug 1875	26 Sep 1875	Alfred	William & Jane	**Williams**	Bombardier RMA	
30 Jun 1875	26 Sep 1875	Louisa Harriet	John & Matilda	**Herring**	Gunner RMA	
6 Apr 1870	26 Sep 1875	Elizabeth Mary	Eli & Mary Ann	**Fookes**	Sergeant RMA	
30 Mar 1872	26 Sep 1875	Louisa	Eli & Mary Ann	**Fookes**	Sergeant RMA	
21 Dec 1874	26 Sep 1875	Alice Annie	Eli & Mary Ann	**Fookes**	Sergeant RMA	
13 Jun 1875	26 Sep 1875	Ann Elizabeth	Gabriel & Dinah	**Mundy**	blank	
27 Jun 1875	26 Sep 1875	William James	William & Harriet	**Flower**	Gunner RMA	
11 Jun 1875	31 Oct 1875	Fanny Rose	Emanuel Lewis & Elizabeth	**Potter**	Sergeant RMA	
8 Aug 1875	31 Oct 1875	William	Joseph & Elizabeth	**Clapp**	Corporal RMA	
6 Jul 1874	31 Oct 1875	Louisa Jane	George William & Sarah	**Briggs**	Drummer RMA	
9 Jul 1875	31 Oct 1875	Frederica Helena	Frederick & Martha	**Kreyer**	Band Sergeant RMA	
24 Jul 1875	28 Nov 1875	Harvey Charles	John Charles & Susanna Charlotte	**Meader**	Sergeant RMA	
20 Oct 1875	28 Nov 1875	William Henry	Thomas & Mary Ann	**Bishop**	Gunner RMA	
27 Nov 1875	28 Nov 1875	Julia Fanny	Algernon & Fanny Mary	**Gardener**	Gunner RMA	12
13 Nov 1875	26 Dec 1875	Elizabeth Jane	Richard & Elizabeth	**Hartnell**	Bombardier RMA	
17 Nov 1875	26 Dec 1875	Bessie	George & Elizabeth	**Dixon**	Corporal RMA	
20 Nov 1875	26 Dec 1875	George Thomas	Thomas & Mary	**Corbett**	Gunner RMA	
8 Sep 1875	26 Dec 1875	Ellen Louisa	Jabez & Ellen Fanny	**Ault**	Sergeant RMA	
28 Oct 1875	26 Dec 1875	Alice Maud	George & Fanny	**Avery**	Sergeant RMA	
17 Sep 1875	26 Dec 1875	Mabel Caroline	John & Isabella	**Rowlatt**	Staff Sergeant RMA	
22 Nov 1875	30 Dec 1875	Nora Eleanor Louise	William George Tomlin & Mary Elizabeth	**Bickford**	Captain RMA	39

31 Jan 1875	27 Jan 1876	Frederick William	William & Eliza	Dennison	Gunner RMA	12
4 Jun 1864	30 Jan 1876	Ellen Maria	William & Ellen Maria	Harris	Colour Sergeant RMA	
18 Aug 1867	30 Jan 1876	Charles William	William & Ellen Maria	Harris	Colour Sergeant RMA	
30 May 1869	30 Jan 1876	Emily	William & Ellen Maria	Harris	Colour Sergeant RMA	
23 Apr 1871	30 Jan 1876	Mary Ann	William & Ellen Maria	Harris	Colour Sergeant RMA	
12 Apr 1873	30 Jan 1876	James	William & Ellen Maria	Harris	Colour Sergeant RMA	
26 Dec 1875	30 Jan 1876	Caroline Selina	William & Ellen Maria	Harris	Colour Sergeant RMA	
7 Jan 1876	30 Jan 1876	Arthur Percy	Charles & Elizabeth Jane	Oakley	Bugle Major RMA	
5 Jul 1873	30 Jan 1876	Mary Ellen	Abraham & Ann	Jarvis	Gunner RMA	
8 Oct 1875	30 Jan 1876	George	Abraham & Ann	Jarvis	Gunner RMA	
5 Nov 1875	30 Jan 1876	Stella	John & Harriet E	Westaway	School Master RMA	
25 Oct 1875	30 Jan 1876	Jessie Deem	George Deem & Annie	Birch	Civilian	
3 Oct 1875	30 Jan 1876	Sarah Ann Harriet	James & Sarah	Mitchell	Coast Guard	
30 Dec 1875	3 Feb 1876	Sibyl Violet	Owen Thomas & Celia	Jones	Captain RMA	39
30 Sep 1875	27 Feb 1876	Laura Mary	John & Cordelia	Smith	Gunner RMA	
25 Jan 1876	27 Feb 1876	Samuel	Samuel & Margaret	Duesbury	Gunner RMA	
5 Jan 1875	27 Feb 1876	Sarah Jane	Gilbert & Jane	Gardener	Gunner RMA	
28 Jan 1876	27 Feb 1876	Alice Rose	Samuel & Emily	Carnell	Gunner RMA	
1 Oct 1874	27 Feb 1876	William George	William & Fanny	Venner	Gunner RMA	
15 Dec 1874	26 Mar 1876	Harriet Edith	William & Harriet	Hooper	Gunner RMA	
5 Jan 1876	26 Mar 1876	John Thomas	Hugh & Ellen	Roach	Corporal RMA	
20 Feb 1876	26 Mar 1876	Harry	Edward & Maria	Usmar	Bandsman RMA	
1 Aug 1873	30 Apr 1876	Florence Louisa	John & Fanny	Bragg	Gunner RMA	
21 Apr 1872	30 Apr 1876	George Henry	Henry & F. J.	Harries	Gunner RMA	
22 Dec 1875	30 Apr 1876	Alfred James	James & Elizabeth	Court	Gunner RMA	
	30 Apr 1876	blank	William	Day	Gunner RMA	40
17 Apr 1876	20 May 1876	Rosa	Samuel Hamilton Bunce & Rhoda Ann	Northcote	Captain RMA	
28 Mar 1863	28 May 1876	Annie	Josiah & Annie	Ansell	Gunner RMA	
10 Aug 1870	28 May 1876	Lucy Ellen	Josiah & Annie	Ansell	Gunner RMA	
13 Nov 1873	28 May 1876	Jane	Josiah & Annie	Ansell	Gunner RMA	
13 Feb 1876	28 May 1876	Josiah	Josiah & Annie	Ansell	Gunner RMA	
13 Mar 1876	28 May 1876	Louisa	Thomas & Rosina Elizabeth	Tunnicliff	Gunner RMA	
19 Apr 1876	28 May 1876	John	John & Mary Ann	Clements	Corporal RMA	
13 May 1876	28 May 1876	William Ernest	Thomas & Emily	Middleton	Gunner RMA	
27 Dec 1864	28 May 1876	Jessie	John & Selina	Matthews	Bandsman RMA	
17 Oct 1867	28 May 1876	Beatrice	John & Selina	Matthews	Bandsman RMA	
9 Dec 1875	28 May 1876	Florence	John & Selina	Matthews	Bandsman RMA	
5 Mar 1871	28 May 1876	Arthur William	George & Sarah Jane	Harwood	Gunner RMA	
29 Sep 1873	28 May 1876	Albert	George & Sarah Jane	Harwood	Gunner RMA	
22 Feb 1876	28 May 1876	Charles John	George & Sarah Jane	Harwood	Gunner RMA	
9 Apr 1875	28 May 1876	Elizabeth Charlotte	Robert & Elizabeth H.	Haskett	Quarter Master Sergeant RMA	
20 Mar 1875	28 May 1876	William Nelson	Frederick John & Henrietta Anne	McRill	Bombardier RMA	
31 Jan 1876	25 Jun 1876	Ellen Eva	Henry & Ellen Jane	Fox	Gunner RMA	
22 Dec 1875	25 Jun 1876	Frances Lillian	George & Elizabeth Ann	Bell	Sergeant RMA	

25 Dec 1875	25 Jun 1876	Arthur Edmund	William & Sarah Jane	Bennett	RMA	
2 Dec 1875	25 Jun 1876	Arthur Henry	George Henry & Lucy	Budden	Sergeant RMA	
14 Oct 1872	25 Jun 1876	Walter Charles	Robert & Emma	Simms	Gunner RMA	
28 May 1876	25 Jun 1876	Florence Annie Edith	Robert & Emma	Simms	Gunner RMA	
26 Feb 1876	25 Jun 1876	Lilian	Frederick & Elizabeth	Mann	Sergeant RMA	
4 May 1876	25 Jun 1876	Margaret	James & Eliza	Cheshire	Gunner RMA	
11 Jun 1876	30 Jul 1876	Maria Isabel	Henry & Eliza Ann	Parker	Sergeant RMA	
29 May 1876	30 Jul 1876	Louisa	James & Sarah Ann	Cotterill	Gunner RMA	
25 Jun 1876	30 Jul 1876	Harriet	Frederick & M A	Draper	Gunner 10th Company	
5 May 1872	30 Jul 1876	Elizabeth Ruth	Joseph & Elizabeth	Johns	Gunner RMA	
10 Jun 1876	30 Jul 1876	Josephine	Joseph & Elizabeth	Johns	Gunner RMA	
1 Jun 1876	30 Jul 1876	Florence Helena	Lion & Millicent	Kite	Gunner RMA	
24 Jan 1876	14 Aug 1876	Thomas Henry	John & Martha Ann	Owen	Colour Sergeant RMA	12
9 Jul 1876	27 Aug 1876	Maude Elizabeth	John & Eliza	Brown	blank	
13 May 1876	27 Aug 1876	Arthur Walter	John & Sarah	Loveridge	Sergeant RMA	
24 May 1876	27 Aug 1876	Charlotte Jessy	Philip & Jane	Crumpton	Gunner RMA	
22 Jun 1876	27 Aug 1876	Violet Mary	Samuel & Mary Ann	Setch	Gunner RMA	
3 Aug 1876	27 Aug 1876	Priscilla Maude	Thomas & Emma Jane	Newman	Coast Guard RN	
8 Jun 1876	29 Aug 1876	Elizabeth Lucy	Richard Turberville & Katherine Georgiana	Ansell	Lieutenant Colonel RMA	
9 Aug 1876	24 Sep 1876	James Edwin	Joseph & Anna Maria	Masters	Gunner RMA	
16 Jun 1875	24 Sep 1876	Nelly Jane	Edward & Mary Anne	Burt	Pensioner	
14 May 1876	24 Sep 1876	John	Robert & Mary Jane	Nuttycombe	Sergeant RMA	
16 Jul 1876	24 Sep 1876	Beatrice Emily	Anthony & Annie Elizabeth	Harper	Gunner RMA	
19 Aug 1876	24 Sep 1876	Edith Miriam	John & Emma	Willey	Gunner RMA	
30 Sep 1876	1 Oct 1876	Francis	William & Frances	Venner	Gunner RMA	12
31 Jul 1876	29 Oct 1876	Frederick Charles	William & Eliza Mary Ann	Carthy	Corporal RMA	
25 Aug 1876	29 Oct 1876	Bessie	William & Eliza	Webster	Sergeant RMA	
27 Sep 1876	29 Oct 1876	Amelia Ann	Charles & Sarah Elizabeth	Wallbridge	Gunner RMA	
9 Aug 1876	29 Oct 1876	William James	Robert & Jane	Hawkins	Gunner RMA	
3 Sep 1876	29 Oct 1876	Edith Sarah	George & Sarah	Griffin	Gunner RMA	
13 Aug 1876	29 Oct 1876	William Jeremiah	John William & Sarah	Dixon	Gunner RMA	
20 Sep 1876	29 Oct 1876	Elizabeth Millicent	George & Ann	Laker	Gunner RMA	
8 Oct 1876	29 Oct 1876	Adelaide Louisa	William & Harriet	Hooper	Gunner RMA	
3 Jul 1876	29 Oct 1876	Cecelia Alice	William John & Ellen	Swain	Drummer RMA	
18 Feb 1860	5 Nov 1876	James George	blank	Willis	Gunner RMA	17
30 Oct 1876	26 Nov 1876	Alice Mary	John & Ellen	Doody	Gunner RMA	
5 Jun 1876	26 Nov 1876	Florence Frances	Henry & Mary Ann	Taylor	Gunner RMA	
7 Sep 1876	26 Nov 1876	Sarah Matilda	William James & Mary Jane	Aukett	Gunner RMA	
14 Sep 1876	26 Nov 1876	Herbert Watson	George Murray & Mary Ann	Dighton	Staff Sergeant	
21 Dec 1875	26 Nov 1876	Ada Ellen	William Blanchard & Ann	Lovell	Gunner RMA	41
12 Aug 1876	26 Nov 1876	Rosina Kate	John & Jane	Matthews	Gunner RMA	
8 Oct 1876	26 Nov 1876	Georgina	Charles & Georgina	Marriott	Gunner RMA	
5 Nov 1876	31 Dec 1876	Thomas Enos	Thomas & Mary Jane	Channon	Gunner RMA	
19 Oct 1876	28 Jan 1877	John Stephen	Elias & Emma	Bushnell	Gunner RMA	
1 Oct 1873	28 Jan 1877	Frank Samuel	Samuel & Mary	Lewis	Gunner RMA	
16 Nov 1876	28 Jan 1877	Benjamin	Samuel & Mary	Lewis	Gunner RMA	
15 Dec 1876	28 Jan 1877	Margaret Jane	Henry & Sarah Ann	Woodward	School Master RMA	
31 Dec 1876	28 Jan 1877	Fanny Bessy	William P & Elizabeth	Austin	Gunner RMA	
2 Jan 1877	21 Feb 1877	Ernest Drummond	Edmund Henry & Frances Emily Cadogan	Cox	Lieutenant Colonel RMA	

8 Jan 1877	25 Feb 1877	Mary Louisa	John & Ellen	**Ford**	Gunner RMA	
29 Nov 1876	25 Feb 1877	Alice	John & Eliza	**Jacobs**	Sergeant RMA	
25 Nov 1876	25 Feb 1877	Mary	Frederick & Emma	**Cridland**	Gunner RMA	
12 Jan 1877	25 Feb 1877	Mary Louise Cunningham	Charles & Mary	**Davis**	Gunner RMA	
6 Oct 1875	25 Feb 1877	Frederick Ewen	Martin Parkinson & Louisa Jane	**Whitwell**	Bandsman RMA	
1 Jan 1877	25 Feb 1877	Louisa Maude	Martin Parkinson & Louisa Jane	**Whitwell**	Bandsman RMA	
13 Dec 1876	25 Feb 1877	Sarah Jane	John & Elizabeth	**Flowers**	Gunner RMA	
9 Jan 1877	25 Feb 1877	William Henry	Reuben & Emily	**Fidler**	Gunner RMA	
3 Jan 1874	25 Mar 1877	Charles William	William Henry & Hannah Elizabeth	**Frost**	blank	
2 Jan 1877	25 Mar 1877	Emma Jane	James & Fanny	**Talbot**	Gunner RMA	
15 Mar 1877	25 Mar 1877	John Allen	Thomas & Mary	**Corbett**	Gunner RMA	
14 Aug 1876	25 Mar 1877	William John	John & Elizabeth	**Saunders**	Gunner RMA	
20 Dec 1876	25 Mar 1877	Walter Sidney	Jabez & Ellen Fanny	**Ault**	Sergeant RMA	
30 Jan 1877	25 Mar 1877	Florence Kate Louise	Cornelius & Mary	**Baker**	Gunner RMA	
24 Jan 1877	25 Mar 1877	Charles Edgar	Charles & Pamela	**Turner**	Gunner RMA	
19 Nov 1876	25 Mar 1877	Walter Albert	George & Lydia	**Keys**	Gunner RMA	
2 Nov 1876	25 Mar 1877	Frederick Henry	Frederick & Martha Kingswood	**Kreyer**	Band Sergeant RMA	
14 Feb 1877	27 Mar 1877	Eli Valentine	Eli & Mary Ann	**Fookes**	Sergeant RMA	12
25 Feb 1877	29 Apr 1877	Arthur Edwin Clement	Arthur & Sarah	**Farr**	Sergeant RMA	42
24 Feb 1877	29 Apr 1877	Kate Ann	Richard & Mary	**Meredith**	blank	42
26 Feb 1877	29 Apr 1877	John Henry	John Thomas & Elizabeth	**Oldham**	Gunner RMA	42
9 Jan 1877	29 Apr 1877	Fitzjames	James & blank	**Page**	Corporal RMA	42
6 Feb 1877	29 Apr 1877	Annie Louise	N. S. & Annie	**Williams**	Sergeant RMA	42
10 Nov 1875	29 Apr 1877	James Alfred	James & Caroline	**Scott**	Gunner RMA	42
27 Oct 1842	6 May 1877	Emma	Edmond & Alice Ann	**Prince**	blank	43
10 Mar 1846	6 May 1877	Charles	John & Sarah	**Garton**	blank	44
8 May 1877	27 May 1877	William Francis	Henry & Mary	**Street**	Gunner RMA	
11 Jul 1867	27 May 1877	Martha Ann	Samuel & Elizabeth	**Perrin**	Gunner RMA	
14 Mar 1877	27 May 1877	Adeline	Samuel & Elizabeth	**Perrin**	Gunner RMA	
14 Mar 1877	24 Jun 1877	John	Robert & Emily	**Bunyan**	Sergeant RMA	
21 Mar 1877	24 Jun 1877	Herbert Henry	William & Mary Ann	**Eden**	Colour Sergeant RMA	
24 Feb 1877	24 Jun 1877	Ellen Louisa	John & Cordelia	**Smith**	blank	
15 Oct 1876	24 Jun 1877	Elizabeth Sarah	Samuel & Elizabeth Philadelphia	**Kent**	Gunner RMA	45
23 May 1877	26 Jun 1877	Hamilton Bunce	Samuel Hamilton Bunce & Rhoda Ann	**Northcote**	Captain RMA	
13 May 1877	7 Jul 1877	Janie Alexandra	William Davis & Alida Sarah	**Welch**	Captain RMA	39
24 May 1877	29 Jul 1877	Mary Blanche	Richard & Mary Jane	**Lucas**	Gunner RMA	
11 Apr 1877	29 Jul 1877	Maud Margaret	J. B. & Elizabeth	**Wiltshire**	Sergeant RMA	
12 Jul 1877	29 Jul 1877	Gertrude May	John & Frances Susannah	**Jesse**	blank	46
5 Jul 1877	3 Aug 1877	Albinia Gertrude	Thomas & Isabella Mary	**Cowry**	Surgeon RMA	
9 Jul 1877	17 Aug 1877	Florence Kathleen	William George Tomlin & Mary Elizabeth	**Bickford**	Captain RMA	
5 Jul 1877	26 Aug 1877	Agnes Alma Jane	James & Mary Ann	**Willis**	Gunner RMA	
29 Jul 1877	26 Aug 1877	Caroline Ethel	Thomas & Mary Ann	**Bishop**	Gunner RMA	
13 May 1876	26 Aug 1877	Edward Henry	Edward C & Caroline Harriet	**Foster**	Gunner RMA	
3 Jul 1877	26 Aug 1877	Edith Isabel	Charles Thomas & Alice	**Moore**	Sergeant RMA	

7 Jul 1877	26 Aug 1877	Frank	Frank & Eliza	**Cheshire**	Gunner RMA	
30 Aug 1872	26 Aug 1877	John William	John & Mary Jane	**Richards**	Gunner RMA	39
23 May 1877	26 Aug 1877	Louisa Annie Eliza	John & Mary Jane	**Richards**	Gunner RMA	39
11 Jun 1877	30 Sep 1877	Grace	Edward & Mary Ann	**Burt**	Gunner RMA	
31 Jul 1877	30 Sep 1877	Emily Sophia	James & Sophia	**Weeks**	Master Gunner Royal Artillery	
16 Sep 1877	30 Sep 1877	Thomas John	Thomas & Harriet	**Pearce**	Gunner RMA	
	30 Sep 1877	Lily Beatrice	Joseph & Mary	**Brown**	Sergeant RMA	
2 Jul 1877	30 Sep 1877	Mary Amelia	Charles William & Maria	**Cailes**	Sergeant RMA	
2 Jul 1877	29 Oct 1877	Minnie	Samuel & Elizabeth	**Townsend**	Colour Sergeant RMA	
12 May 1877	29 Oct 1877	Eliza Mary Ann Amelia	William & Eliza	**Ford**	Carpenter's Mate HMS Minotaur	
25 Jun 1877	29 Oct 1877	Edward George	G. H. & Lucy	**Budden**	Sergeant RMA	
22 May 1877	29 Oct 1877	George Henry	George Henry & Anne	**Raynard**	Seaman RN	
16 Mar 1877	29 Oct 1877	Harry Walter	Frederick & Frances	**Callaway**	Sergeant RMA	
19 Sep 1877	29 Oct 1877	Lily Ellen	William & Martha	**Eason**	Acting Bombardier RMA	
10 Sep 1877	29 Oct 1877	Bertha Elizabeth	William & Elizabeth	**White**	Colour Sergeant RMA	
31 Aug 1877	29 Oct 1877	Walter Ernest	Charles & Susan	**Perry**	Quarter Master Sergeant	
2 Sep 1877	29 Oct 1877	James	William & Ellen	**Baldwin**	Gunner RMA	
24 Jul 1877	29 Oct 1877	Frederick William Charles	William & Ann	**Lovell**	Gunner RMA	
23 Mar 1877	25 Nov 1877	Alice Elizabeth	Charles E & Emily	**Briggs**	Bandsman RMA	47
	25 Nov 1877	Emily	Henry & Minnie	**Gillett**	Gunner RMA	
12 Oct 1877	25 Nov 1877	Henry Ira	Charles H & Ellen Emma	**Morris**	Colour Sergeant RMA	
11 Aug 1877	25 Nov 1877	Emily	Wilson Mowbray & Diana	**Dobing**	Bombardier RMA	
30 May 1870	25 Nov 1877	Annie	George & Fanny	**Cheeseman**	Gunner RMA	
8 Jul 1872	25 Nov 1877	Bessie	George & Fanny	**Cheeseman**	Gunner RMA	
23 Nov 1877	30 Dec 1877	Alfred Henry	Benjamin & Mary	**Ingham**	Corporal RMA	
3 Dec 1877	30 Dec 1877	Fanny	George & Fanny	**Cheeseman**	Gunner RMA	
31 Oct 1877	30 Dec 1877	Annie Isabel	John & Ellen	**Muir**	Sergeant Major RMA	
26 Nov 1877	30 Dec 1877	George Frederick	George & Mary	**Burgess**	Sergeant RMA	
11 Mar 1877	30 Dec 1877	Ernest John	David & Charlotte	**Barnes**	Bandsman RMA	
24 Dec 1876	30 Dec 1877	W. P.	W. P. & Clara	**Sims**	11th Regt	
7 Oct 1877	21 Jan 1878	James William Charles	James & Mary Ann	**Saunders**	Gunner RMA	12
5 Jan 1878	28 Jan 1878	Lily Rosetta	Lion & Millicent	**Kite**	Gunner RMA	48
2 Sep 1874	27 Jan 1878	Susan Sawyer	Joseph & Susan Ann	**Bell**	Gunner RMA	
13 Jan 1876	27 Jan 1878	Lily Sarah Ann	James & Emma Sophia	**Woodger**	Bombardier RMA	
4 Nov 1877	27 Jan 1878	Florence Maria	Charles & Maria	**Long**	Gunner RMA	
27 Sep 1870	27 Jan 1878	Solomon	Simon & Elizabeth	**Haynes**	Pensioner RMA	
16 Nov 1877	27 Jan 1878	Jessica Elizabeth Mary Maud	Amos & Mary Ann	**Haynes**	Bugler RMA	
6 Dec 1877	27 Jan 1878	Frederick John	Thomas & Mary Jane	**Channon**	Gunner RMA	
26 Nov 1877	17 Feb 1878	Ada	Walter & Jane	**Dicker**	Sergeant RMA	
23 Jan 1878	24 Feb 1878	Elizabeth Sarah Louisa	George & Sarah	**Denley**	Corporal RMA	
20 Jan 1878	24 Feb 1878	Harry	William Hill & Fanny	**Pinney**	Bombardier RMA	
21 Mar 1875	31 Mar 1878	Ellen Sarah Letty	Solomon & Elizabeth	**Case**	Gunner RMA	
3 Feb 1877	31 Mar 1878	Elizabeth Louisa	Solomon & Elizabeth	**Case**	Gunner RMA	

12 Jan 1878	31 Mar 1878	Susan Jane	William & Harriet	Flower	Gunner RMA	
18 Feb 1874	31 Mar 1878	Albert Edward	Henry & Jane	Weeks	Gunner RMA	
22 Feb 1878	28 Apr 1878	George Bernard	Bernard & Elizabeth	Morey	Sergeant RMA	
5 Apr 1878	28 Apr 1878	Florence Annie	George & Anne	Laker	Gunner RMA	
21 Mar 1878	28 Apr 1878	Nellie Melita	Eli & Mary	Fookes	Sergeant RMA	
28 Apr 1875	28 Apr 1878	Ada Isabella	John & Isabella	Snook	Colour Sergeant RMA	
5 Aug 1877	28 Apr 1878	Mabel Annie Pescott	Henry & Rosina	Wright	Gunner RMA	
1 Feb 1878	26 May 1878	William Ralph	John & Emma	Willey	Gunner RMA	
12 Jan 1878	26 May 1878	Maurice Victor	Alfred & Maria Jane	Rimmington	Gunner RMA	
31 Mar 1878	26 May 1878	Ada Rosetta	Frederick John & Henrietta Ann	McRill	Corporal RMA	
25 Mar 1878	26 May 1878	John	John & Ellen	Doody	Gunner RMA	
23 May 1878	27 Jun 1878	John Henry Charles	Charles & Charlotte	Gosling	Corporal RMA	
5 Jun 1878	30 Jun 1878	Josephine Lillian	Henry & Minnie	Gillett	Gunner RMA	
22 Jun 1874	30 Jun 1878	Thomas	Thomas & Annie	Musgrove	Gunner RMA	
22 Sep 1876	30 Jun 1878	William James	Thomas & Annie	Musgrove	Gunner RMA	
16 Apr 1878	30 Jun 1878	Edith Mary	Thomas & Annie	Musgrove	Gunner RMA	
15 May 1878	30 Jun 1878	William	Solomon & Hannah Elizabeth	Hayles	Gunner RMA	
2 May 1878	30 Jun 1878	Ellen Elizabeth	James & Ellen Jane	Barron	Colour Sergeant RMA	
18 Mar 1878	30 Jun 1878	Kate Elizabeth	George E & Elizabeth A	Harris	RMA	
19 May 1878	30 Jun 1878	Willie Gwynn	John Henry & Eliza Ann	Bowles	Sergeant RMA	
2 Jul 1878	4 Jul 1878	William Arthur	Walter Arthur & Sarah Elizabeth	Parker	Gunner RMA	12
26 Jan 1878	7 Jul 1878	Frederick	Charles Edward & Emily	Briggs	Musician RMA	12
30 Jun 1878	13 Jul 1878	Louisa	Joseph & Fanny	Bennett	Gunner RMA	12
10 May 1878	15 Jul 1878	Edith Mary	Henry & Rebecca	Gouge	Gunner RMA	49
8 Apr 1878	21 Jul 1878	Albert Victor	Peter & Elizabeth	Meaker	Ship's Corporal RN	
4 May 1878	28 Jul 1878	Charles William	Charles & Mary	Rule	Gunner RMA	
11 May 1878	28 Jul 1878	Edward James Rhodes	James & Lenness	Jones	Corporal RMA	
13 Jun 1878	28 Jul 1878	John Francis	George & Jemima Annie	Birch	Late Sergeant RMA	
23 May 1878	28 Jul 1878	Nathaniel James	Nathaniel & Rebecca	Worsey	Gunner RMA	
9 Apr 1878	28 Jul 1878	Fred	Edward & Maria	Usmar	Musician RMA	
30 Jun 1878	28 Jul 1878	Florence Mabel	James & Elizabeth	Court	Gunner RMA	
23 Sep 1877	25 Aug 1878	Henry Joseph	H & E	Napping	blank	39
25 Aug 1873	25 Aug 1878	Gertrude Anne	William & Eliza Mary Anne	Carthy	Corporal RMA	
3 Jul 1878	25 Aug 1878	Elizabeth Mary Ann	Samuel & Elizabeth Jane	James	Corporal RMA	
20 Jul 1878	25 Aug 1878	William Henry	George & Jane Anna	Haskill	blank	
12 Sep 1876	25 Aug 1878	William Alfred	Henry & Emma H	James	Colour Sergeant RMA	
13 Jul 1878	22 Aug 1878	Charles William	Charles & Elizabeth	Garton	Gunner RMA	50
3 Jun 1878	29 Sep 1878	Ernest William	John & Eliza	Brown	Sergeant RMA	
10 Apr 1878	29 Sep 1878	John Dennis	Dennis & Elizabeth	O'Connell	blank	
10 Aug 1878	29 Sep 1878	William	Richard & Elizabeth	Boxall	blank	
22 Jul 1878	29 Sep 1878	William Henry	Henry & Mary	Oram	blank	
7 Jul 1878	29 Sep 1878	William	Frederick & Emma	Cridland	Gunner RMA	
13 Jun 1878	29 Sep 1878	Richard Heaton	Edward Charles & Caroline Harriett	Foster	Gunner RMA	
5 Sep 1878	27 Oct 1878	Ellen	John & Ellen	Ford	Gunner RMA	
24 Sep 1878	27 Oct 1878	Reuben Daniel	Reuben & Emily	Fidler	Gunner RMA	

6 May 1878	27 Oct 1878	William Archibald	James & Emma Sophia	**Woodger**	Bandsman RMA	
18 Jul 1878	30 Nov 1878	Edmond Rudolph	Frederick & Martha	**Kreyer**	Band Sergeant RMA	
3 Oct 1878	12 Dec 1878	Kate Edith	William Davis & Alida Sarah	**Welch**	Captain RMA	
7 Nov 1878	29 Dec 1878	Alice Maude Mary	Thomas & Josephine Eliza	**Cooksley**	Sergeant RMA	
6 Nov 1878	29 Dec 1878	Arthur George	George & Lydia	**Keys**	Gunner RMA	
11 Nov 1878	29 Dec 1878	William Thomas	William & Sarah	**Hawkins**	Gunner RMA	
20 Sep 1878	26 Jan 1879	Walter John	John & Cordelia	**Smith**	Pensioner RMA	
12 Oct 1878	23 Feb 1879	Jessie Georgina	Richard Thomas & Mary Jane	**Lucas**	Gunner RMA	
31 Dec 1878	23 Feb 1879	Albert William	James & Ellen	**Lockyer**	Gunner RMA	
30 Dec 1878	23 Feb 1879	Benjamin James	Robert & Emily	**Bunyan**	Sergeant RMA	
1 Feb 1879	23 Feb 1879	Robert James	Robert & Mary	**Lappin**	blank	
9 Nov 1878	23 Feb 1879	Elizabeth Annie	William & Emma	**Jones**	Gunner RMA	
23 Jan 1879	10 Mar 1879	Philip Gresley	Edmond Henry & Frances Emily Cadogan	**Cox**	Lieutenant Colonel RMA	
28 Sep 1878	30 Mar 1879	Mary Eliza Letitia	Murray & Mary	**Dighton**	Sergeant RMA	
11 Feb 1879	30 Mar 1879	Edwin Charly	Edward & Elizabeth	**Cannon**	blank	
30 Jan 1879	30 Mar 1879	William Morgan	David & Maria	**Easton**	Coast Guard	
1 Feb 1879	30 Mar 1879	Peter Edgar	David & Maria	**Easton**	Coast Guard	
11 Jan 1879	30 Mar 1879	Alice Gertrude	Daniel & Arnenell	**Hambrooke**	blank	51
24 Jan 1879	30 Mar 1879	George William Augustus	Adam & Emma	**Brown**	RMA	
1 Dec 1878	27 Apr 1879	John Thomas	James & Mary Ann	**Willis**	Gunner RMA	
21 Mar 1879	27 Apr 1879	Alice Maud	Thomas & Harriett	**Pearce**	Gunner RMA	
4 Feb 1879	27 Apr 1879	George James	Solomon & Elizabeth	**Case**	Gunner RMA	
11 Dec 1878	27 Apr 1879	Elizabeth Margaret	Henry & Mary Jane Kate	**Malyan**	Sergeant RMA	
16 Jul 1870	27 Apr 1879	Walter Egbert	George & Emily	**Gregg**	Sergeant RMA	
17 Jan 1872	27 Apr 1879	Emily Laura	George & Emily	**Gregg**	Sergeant RMA	
3 Sep 1874	27 Apr 1879	Alice Carlisle	George & Emily	**Gregg**	Sergeant RMA	
20 Aug 1878	27 Apr 1879	Sydney Beauchamp	George & Emily	**Gregg**	Sergeant RMA	
22 Feb 1870	25 May 1879	Margaret Mary	James & Margaret Mary	**Tallyn**	blank	
6 Apr 1879	25 May 1879	Florence Isabel	Benjamin & Mary	**Ingham**	Sergeant RMA	
6 Apr 1879	25 May 1879	Gertrude Blanche	Charles & Mary Howes	**Davis**	blank	
3 Apr 1879	25 May 1879	Lily	John & Mary Ann	**Griffiths**	blank	
5 Apr 1879	25 May 1879	Margaret Rosina	Albert & Isabella	**Parker**	blank	
13 Apr 1879	25 May 1879	Catherine Susannah	Charles & Georgina Eliza	**Marriott**	Gunner RMA	
16 Mar 1879	25 May 1879	John Samuel	Abel & Eliza	**Lenny**	Gunner RMA	
16 Sep 1870	25 May 1879	Joseph	Joseph & Ellen	**Wylie**	Gunner RMA	
25 Apr 1879	25 May 1879	Rosina	Joseph & Ellen	**Wylie**	Gunner RMA	
27 Apr 1879	29 Jun 1879	William George	John Thomas & Elizabeth	**Oldham**	Corporal RMA	
20 May 1877	27 Jul 1879	Henry Edward George	Henry George & Amelia Maria	**Graham**	RMA	
26 Jun 1879	27 Jul 1879	Frederick Richard	Thomas & Annie	**Wheeler**	RMA	
7 Jul 1879	27 Jul 1879	Kate	Henry & Mary Ann	**Street**	Gunner RMA	
18 Jul 1879	31 Aug 1879	Ada Catherine	Allen Elliott & Hester Emma	**Marden**	Sergeant RMA	
19 Apr 1879	31 Aug 1879	Annie Kate	Charles & Sarah E	**Wallbridge**	Gunner RMA	
5 May 1879	31 Aug 1879	Cornelius William George Perry	Cornelius & Mary	**Baker**	Gunner RMA	
19 Apr 1879	31 Aug 1879	Ellen	Thomas & Ellen	**Baldwin**	Gunner RMA	
14 Mar 1878	31 Aug 1879	Esmeralda	John Morgan & Sarah	**Kite**	Gunner RMA	
22 Jul 1879	31 Aug 1879	Bertha Novena Agnes	R & Emma	**Simms**	Gunner RMA	52
23 Oct 1878	31 Aug 1879	Francis James	James & Fanny	**Talbot**	Gunner RMA	
26 Apr 1873	31 Aug 1879	blank	Daniel & Sarah Ann	**Baggs**	RMA	53

24 May 1879	31 Aug 1879	Lillian Alice	James & Alice	**Innoles**	Gunner RMA	
12 Jun 1879	31 Aug 1879	Florence Elizabeth Jane	Henry & Jane	**Weeks**	RMA	
15 Apr 1879	31 Aug 1879	blank	James &	**Hunt**	Gunner RMA	54
30 May 1879	31 Aug 1879	Ellen Tryphena	William & Tryphena	**Strong**	Gunner RMA	
13 Jun 1879	31 Aug 1879	Richard Arthur	Charles & Charlotte	**Gosling**	Sergeant RMA	
13 Jun 1879	31 Aug 1879	John Richard Henry	John & Bessy	**Maynard**	blank	
28 Aug 1879	29 Aug 1879	Thomas	Charles James & Susan	**Perry**	Late Sergeant RMA	20
25 Apr 1879	31 Aug 1879	William Ellis	Frederick & Ellen	**Mattex**	RMA	
15 Aug 1879	31 Aug 1879	James	James & Frances	**Hunt**	Gunner RMA	
26 Apr 1878	31 Aug 1879	Sarah Ann	Daniel & Sarah Ann	**Baggs**	Sergeant RMA	
22 Jul 1879	31 Aug 1879	Bertha Novenia Agnes	Robert & Emma	**Simms**	Gunner RMA	
5 Jul 1879	28 Sep 1879	Florence Louisa	Albert & Emma	**Hayes**	Corporal RMA	
7 Jul 1879	28 Sep 1879	Alice Anne	Anthony & Annie Elizabeth	**Harper**	Gunner RMA	
27 Jul 1879	28 Sep 1879	Kate Eveline	Charles Richard & Maria	**Marlow**	Master Gunner RMA	
23 Aug 1879	26 Oct 1879	George	Joseph & Fanny	**Bennett**	RMA	
24 Jul 1879	26 Oct 1879	Walter Arthur	Bernard & Elizabeth	**Morey**	Sergeant RMA	
4 Oct 1879	26 Oct 1879	Amelia Elizabeth	John & Harriett Eliza	**Finley**	Gunner RMA	
17 May 1879	26 Oct 1879	FitzWilliam	John & Eliza	**Jacob**	Sergeant RMA	
6 Oct 1879	29 Oct 1879	Robert John	Benjamin Arthur & Gertrude Elizabeth	**Milne**	Captain RMA	12
25 Feb 1879	30 Nov 1879	Edith	John & Jane	**Matthews**	Gunner RMA	
9 Sep 1879	30 Nov 1879	Kate	George & Elizabeth	**Dixon**	Sergeant RMA	
3 Nov 1879	30 Nov 1879	Richard George	Joseph & Susan	**Bell**	Gunner RMA	
12 Nov 1879	28 Dec 1879	Mary Ann Harriett	Richard & Eliza	**Goodall**	Bombardier RMA	
18 Nov 1879	25 Jan 1880	James George	James & Mary Jane	**Fee**	Musician RMA	
1 Dec 1879	25 Jan 1880	Edith Louisa	William Albert & Julia Mary	**Shergold**	RMA	
1 Jan 1880	25 Jan 1880	William Henry	Alexander & Rosetta Sabina	**Barker**	Sergeant RMA	
16 Dec 1879	29 Feb 1880	Charles Herbert	Edward C & Caroline H	**Foster**	RMA	
4 Dec 1879	29 Feb 1880	Bessie	John & Emma	**Willey**	Gunner RMA	
16 Feb 1873	29 Feb 1880	Harry Alfred William	Harry & Jane	**Johns**	Gunner RMA	
31 Mar 1875	29 Feb 1880	Frank Edward	Harry & Jane	**Johns**	Gunner RMA	
11 Oct 1879	29 Feb 1880	Emma	W & Jane	**Dicker**	Sergeant RMA	
30 Nov 1879	29 Feb 1880	Mary Susannah	Henry & Emma Harriett	**James**	Colour Sergeant RMA	
15 Oct 1879	29 Feb 1880	Alice Jane	Richard & Jane	**Bailey**	Gunner RMA	55
9 Feb 1880	29 Feb 1880	Jessie Louisa	James & Louisa	**Aslin**	Gunner RMA	
22 Jan 1880	29 Feb 1880	Alice Maud	William & Martha	**Hamley**	Gunner RMA	
28 Dec 1875	28 Mar 1880	George Allan	Joseph & M A	**Wade**	Gunner RMA	
13 Jan 1880	28 Mar 1880	Alice Mary	Joseph & M A	**Wade**	Gunner RMA	
28 Jun 1879	28 Mar 1880	Thomas	James & Ann	**Musgrove**	Gunner RMA	
1 Dec 1879	28 Mar 1880	William Henry	Emanuel & Annie	**Crook**	Gunner RMA	
24 Dec 1879	28 Mar 1880	Mary Alice	David & Sarah Ellen	**Ivy**	Gunner RMA	
2 Feb 1880	28 Mar 1880	Bertha Victoria	George & Sarah	**Denley**	Corporal RMA	
1 Mar 1880	28 Mar 1880	Florence	Charles E & Emily	**Briggs**	RMA	
15 Nov 1879	28 Mar 1880	Alice Maud Mary	John & Louisa Matilda	**Attridge**	Corporal RMA	
1 Dec 1879	28 Mar 1880	Edith Hannah Maria	Henry & Hannah	**Bareham**	RMA	
8 Oct 1879	28 Mar 1880	Edith Emily	Walter Arthur & Sarah Elizabeth	**Parker**	Gunner RMA	
2 Jul 1878	28 Mar 1880	William Arthur	Walter Arthur & Sarah Elizabeth	**Parker**	Gunner RMA	56

7 Feb 1880	25 Apr 1880	Ellen Maria	John & Ellen	**Muir**	RMA	
10 Jan 1880	25 Apr 1880	Nora Isabella	F J & H A	**McRill**	Corporal RMA	
21 Feb 1880	25 Apr 1880	Frederick James	James & Ellen Jane	**Barron**	RMA	
17 Mar 1880	25 Apr 1880	Edith Rose	blank	**blank**	blank	57
10 Apr 1880	25 Apr 1880	Kate Joclyn	Richard Joclyn & Kate	**Pincombe**	RMA	
14 Sep 1879	25 Apr 1880	William Robert Evelyn	Robert Henry & Fanny	**Nunn**	RMA	
26 May 1880	30 May 1880	Louisa Elizabeth	George & Louisa	**Parkhouse**	RMA	
21 Mar 1873	30 May 1880	Christopher	Christopher & Emma	**Treaves**	RMA	
8 May 1875	30 May 1880	Alice	Christopher & Emma	**Treaves**	RMA	
24 Apr 1880	16 Jun 1880	Harry Holdsworth	Elizabeth & Henry	**Kelly**	Staff Captain RMA	
3 Apr 1880	27 Jun 1880	Joseph Henry	John & Cordelia	**Smith**	Pensioner RMA	
5 May 1880	27 Jun 1880	Alfred William	Harry & Minnie	**Gellett**	Corporal RMA	
9 May 1880	27 Jun 1880	George Henry	Henry & Sophia	**Tagget**	Gunner RMA	
29 May 1880	8 Jul 1880	Rowland Hall	William George Tomlin & Mary Elizabeth	**Bickford**	Captain RMA	
1 Jun 1880	25 Jul 1880	William John	John Bennett & Maria	**Adams**	Acting Corporal RMA	
30 May 1880	25 Jul 1880	Henry George Michael	John & blank	**Ford**	Gunner RMA	
4 Jun 1880	25 Jul 1880	George Frederick	John & blank	**Snook**	Colourr Sergeant RMA	
4 May 1880	25 Jul 1880	Florence May	George & Lydia	**Keys**	Gunner RMA	
4 Jun 1880	26 Jul 1880	Lucy Marion Freda	William Davis & Alida Sarah	**Welch**	Major RMA	
8 Apr 1880	29 Aug 1880	Alice Rose	George William & Sarah	**Briggs**	Bugler RMA	
12 Jun 1880	29 Aug 1880	Bertie	Edward & Maria	**Usmar**	Musician RMA	
10 Jul 1880	29 Aug 1880	Ellen Ada	Herbert & Mary	**Green**	Gunner RMA	
30 Jun 1880	29 Aug 1880	Ellen Elizabeth	George & Annie	**Rogers**	Bombardier RMA	58
18 Aug 1880	26 Sep 1880	Louisa Ann	Thomas & Mary	**Corbett**	Gunner RMA	
28 Oct 1879	26 Sep 1880	Philip Cecil John	John & Harriet Elizabeth	**Westaway**	School Master RMA	
27 Jun 1880	31 Oct 1880	John	James & Mary	**Denholm**	Gunner RMA	
10 Jun 1880	31 Oct 1880	George James	James & Emily	**Burbidge**	Gunner RMA	
15 Sep 1880	31 Oct 1880	Mary Ann	John & blank	**Flower**	RMA	
26 Sep 1880	31 Oct 1880	Emily Blanche	Reuben & blank	**Fidler**	RMA	
28 Aug 1880	28 Nov 1880	Eva Catherine May	George & Selina	**Wilson**	Gunner RMA	
30 Oct 1880	28 Nov 1880	Christopher Bertie	Richard & Elizabeth	**Hartnell**	Sergeant RMA	
14 Oct 1880	23 Nov 1880	Elizabeth Jane	William & Elizabeth	**Campbell**	Drum Major RMA	12
31 Jul 1878	26 Dec 1880	James Brougham	William B & Sarah	**Robinson**	Gunner RMA	
21 Nov 1880	26 Dec 1880	Sarah Ellen	William B & Sarah	**Robinson**	Gunner RMA	59
21 Nov 1880	26 Dec 1880	Harry	William B & Sarah	**Robinson**	Gunner RMA	60
9 Nov 1880	26 Dec 1880	Alfred	Solomon & Hannah Elizabeth	**Hayles**	Coast Guardsman	
5 Nov 1880	26 Dec 1880	Harry Guy	Edward & Maria Louisa	**Lodge**	Sergeant RMA	
19 Nov 1880	26 Dec 1880	Percy Harold	Robert & Mary	**Lappin**	Sergeant RMA	
10 Nov 1880	? Jan 1881	Albert Henry John	Henry & Mary Jane	**Malyan**	Sergeant RMA	
11 Dec 1880	? Jan 1881	Eliza Emily	Robert & Emily	**Bunyan**	Sergeant RMA	
9 Oct 1880	? Jan 1881	Mabel Vilato	John & Eliza	**Brown**	Sergeant RMA	
28 Dec 1880	1 Feb 1881	Charles Douglas Owst	Arthur B & Edith A	**Shakespear**	Captain RMA	
31 Dec 1874	27 Feb 1881	Ellen Augusta Corith	John & Ada	**Haines**	Gunner RMA	
11 Jan 1881	27 Feb 1881	Frederick John	John & Ada	**Haines**	Gunner RMA	
18 Dec 1880	27 Feb 1881	William James	Charles & Sarah	**Wallbridge**	Gunner RMA	
23 Dec 1880	27 Feb 1881	Clara Ada Gerthrude	Robert & Emma	**Sims**	Gunner RMA	

25 Oct 1880	27 Feb 1881	Annie	Solomon & Elizabeth	Case	Gunner RMA	
26 Nov 1880	27 Feb 1881	Thomas Robert Ruben	George & Mary Ann	Greenway	Bombardier RMA	
26 May 1876	27 Feb 1881	Eliza Jane	Alexander & Rosetta Sabina	Barber	Sergeant RMA	
6 Apr 1881	27 Feb 1881	Frederick James	Alexander & Rosetta Sabina	Barber	Sergeant RMA	
10 Nov 1880	27 Mar 1881	Thomas Herbert	Thomas & Sarah Jane	Ellis	RMA	
31 Jan 1881	27 Mar 1881	James Henry	Henry & Elizabeth	Massam	RMA	
3 Feb 1881	27 Mar 1881	Annie Eliza	Thomas & Annie	Musgrove	Labourer	
31 Jan 1881	27 Mar 1881	Mable Ellen Bowen	Joseph & Ellen	Maddock	Gunner RMA	
5 Mar 1881	27 Mar 1881	William Edward	John Thomas & Elizabeth	Oldham	Corporal RMA	
15 Jul 1872	27 Mar 1881	Clara Louisa	Stephen & Clara Elizabeth	Cheeseman	Corporal RMA	
25 Sep 1873	27 Mar 1881	Stephen Harry	Stephen & Clara Elizabeth	Cheeseman	Corporal RMA	
1 Apr 1875	27 Mar 1881	Eleanor Kate	Stephen & Clara Elizabeth	Cheeseman	Corporal RMA	
5 Mar 1877	27 Mar 1881	Edwin George	Stephen & Clara Elizabeth	Cheeseman	Corporal RMA	
6 Sep 1878	27 Mar 1881	Earnest Augustus	Stephen & Clara Elizabeth	Cheeseman	Corporal RMA	
20 Jan 1881	27 Mar 1881	Alfred Herbert	Stephen & Clara Elizabeth	Cheeseman	Corporal RMA	
23 Jan 1881	24 Apr 1881	Georgina Lelian	Charles William & Maria	Cailes	Staff Sergeant RMA	
18 Nov 1880	24 Apr 1881	William George	William & Mary	Goodman	Musician RMA	
20 Jan 1881	24 Apr 1881	Emmeline Kate	James & Alice	Innoles	Bombardier RMA	
24 Jan 1881	2 May 1881	Charles Fraser	William Hogarth & Charlotte	Adam	Fleet Surgeon	58
25 May 1881	26 May 1881	William George Alfred John	William George & Emily Alice	Bowden	Gunner RMA	
12 May 1881	29 May 1881	Ethel May	John & Annie	Thornton	Corporal RMA	
10 Apr 1881	29 May 1881	Alice Elizabeth	John & Elizabeth	Holloway	Musician RMA	
11 Dec 1880	29 May 1881	William Henry George	George & Elizabeth Ann	Bell	Pensioner RMA	
28 Feb 1881	26 Jun 1881	Walter Herbert	Walter Arthur & Sarah Elizabeth	Parker	Gunner RMA	
29 Apr 1881	31 Jul 1881	Kate Elizabeth	William & Rosina	Day	Pensioner RMA	
19 May 1881	31 Jul 1881	Frederick John	Frederick & Elizabeth	Elston	Colour Sergeant RMA	
4 May 1881	31 Jul 1881	Frederick George	James & Sarah	Dyer	Gunner RMA	
6 Nov 1880	31 Jul 1881	Thomas	Thomas & Mary Ann	Kilshaw	Bombadier RMA	
3 Jul 1881	28 Aug 1881	Benjamin Northcote	Benjamin & Mary	Ingham	Sergeant RMA	
19 Jun 1881	25 Sep 1881	William	William & Ellen	Baldwin	Gunner RMA	
26 Jul 1881	25 Sep 1881	Elizabeth Jane	Stephen & Elizabeth Jane	Fox	Gunner RMA	
3 Aug 1881	25 Sep 1881	Florence Elizabeth Ann	John & Elizabeth Ann	Armstrong	Gunner RMA	
11 Jun 1881	25 Sep 1881	James Walter	George William & Sarah	Briggs	Bugler RMA	
9 Jan 1881	30 Oct 1881	John Thomas Prout	John & Eliza	Jacob	blank	
24 Jan 1881	30 Oct 1881	Alice	John & Clara Ann	Collins	Staff Sergeant RMA	
11 Aug 1877	30 Oct 1881	Ivy	Frederick & Elizabeth	Mann	Staff Sergeant RMA	
3 Aug 1879	30 Oct 1881	Frederick	Frederick & Elizabeth	Mann	Staff Sergeant RMA	
19 Aug 1881	30 Oct 1881	Ada	Frederick & Elizabeth	Mann	Staff Sergeant RMA	
14 Aug 1881	30 Oct 1881	Fanny	Joseph & Fanny	Bennett	Gunner 5th Co	
23 Jun 1881	30 Oct 1881	Henry Samuel	James & Mary Jane	Fee	Musician RMA	
5 Sep 1881	30 Oct 1881	George Thomas	George & Alice Matilda	Woodhouse	Corporal RMA	
14 Oct 1878	30 Oct 1881	Herbert Thomas	James & Ann	Harris	Gunner RMA	
20 Jul 1881	30 Oct 1881	Sarah Annie	John & Ann	Walker	Gunner RMA	

1 Aug 1881	30 Oct 1881	James Richard	James & Charlotte	**Andrews**	Corporal RMA	
8 Oct 1881	30 Oct 1881	Harriett Caroline	William & Harriett	**Flower**	Gunner RMA	
2 Mar 1874	27 Nov 1881	Harry Charles	James & Emma	**Woodger**	Late Musician 'B' RMA	
20 Aug 1881	27 Nov 1881	Florence Ethel	Thomas & Margaret Jane	**Goodman**	Sergeant RMA	
15 Oct 1881	27 Nov 1881	Florence Jessie	John & Ellen	**Minor**	blank	
21 Aug 1881	27 Nov 1881	Lenness Boys	James & Lenness Boys	**Jones**	Corporal RMA	
1 Dec 1881	25 Dec 1881	Thomas Arthur	Edward Charles & Caroline	**Foster**	blank	
27 Sep 1881	25 Dec 1881	Thomas William	John & Harriett Eliza	**Finley**	Bombardier RMA	
	13 Jun 1872	Laura Mary Grace Katherine	Henry Way & Katherine Susan Deane	**Mawbey**	Colonel RMA	61
9 Jan 1882	16 Jan 1882	Charles	Charles & Emilie	**Purt**	Gunner RMA	62
7 Mar 1881	29 Jan 1882	Arthur James	John William & Sarah	**Dixon**	Gunner RMA	
15 Oct 1881	29 Jan 1882	Horace Charles	Charles John & Hannah	**Dyer**	Bombardier RMA	
3 Nov 1881	29 Jan 1882	William Henry	William & Mary Jane	**James**	Gunner RMA	
29 Dec 1881	29 Jan 1882	Mary Elizabeth	Thomas & Mary Jane	**Kilshaw**	Bombardier RMA	
21 Nov 1881	29 Jan 1882	Ellen Louisa	Robert & Mary Jane	**Nuttycombe**	Colour Sergeant RMA	
18 Aug 1877	31 Jan 1882	Joseph William	Joseph & Elizabeth Ann	**Parish**	Sergeant RMA	
19 Jan 1882	26 Feb 1882	Francis Charles	Francis & Eliza	**Teagle**	Gunner RMA	
26 Dec 1881	26 Feb 1882	Mabel Gertrude	John Bennett & Maria	**Adams**	Corporal RMA	
5 Nov 1881	26 Feb 1882	Margaret Lilly	James & Louisa Jane	**Kent**	Musician RMA	
9 Oct 1881	26 Feb 1882	Harry Richard	Richard & Mary Jane	**Lucas**	Gunner RMA	
8 Jun 1881	26 Feb 1882	Charles Herbert	Thomas & Josephine Eliza	**Cooksley**	Colour Sergeant RMA	
26 Feb 1880	26 Feb 1882	Edwin James	James Robert & Louisa Emma	**Cansdale**	Corporal RMA	
22 Dec 1881	26 Feb 1882	Herbert William	James Robert & Louisa Emma	**Cansdale**	Corporal RMA	
4 Feb 1882	26 Mar 1882	William Henry	William & Mary Anne	**Sinclair**	Bugler RMA	
4 Jan 1882	26 Mar 1882	William George	William & Clara	**Hill**	Corporal RMA	
1 Mar 1882	26 Mar 1882	Henrietta	Charles Henry & Eliza Mary Grace	**Bell**	Coast Guardsman	
24 Jan 1882	26 Mar 1882	Wilfred Henry	Thomas & Charlotte	**Knight**	Sergeant RMA	
10 Sep 1881	26 Mar 1882	Katherine Maud	John & Sarah Anne	**Lee**	Private 41st Regt	
10 Feb 1882	26 Mar 1882	Ada	Thomas & Eliza	**Brown**	Colour Sergeant RMA	
3 Sep 1881	23 Mar 1882	Nellie Elizabeth	Walter & Jane	**Luckey**	Gunner RMA	63
24 Feb 1881	7 Apr 1882	Annie Griffiths	Robert Morgan & Emma	**Farlam**	Sergeant RMA	64
26 Mar 1882	25 Apr 1882	Violet Blanche	Arthur & Edith	**Shakespear**	Captain RMA	
13 Nov 1881	30 Apr 1882	Ellen Dinah	James & Frances	**Hunt**	Gunner RMA	
20 Jan 1882	30 Apr 1882	John George	George & Mary Jane	**Pearson**	Gunner RMA	
29 Sep 1881	28 May 1882	Arthur	John & Ellen	**Doody**	Gunner RMA	
26 Apr 1882	28 May 1882	Florence Mabel	William & Elizabeth	**Vivian**	Musician RMA	
13 Feb 1882	28 May 1882	Mabel Josephine	Joseph & Jane	**Radford**	Musician RMA	
21 Mar 1882	28 May 1882	Henry Charles	Henry & Susan	**Goddard**	Gunner RMA	
19 Mar 1882	28 May 1882	Emily Mary	Charles & Georgina Eliza	**Marriott**	Gunner RMA	
6 Sep 1881	28 May 1882	John Edward	John & Charlotte Anne	**Luff**	Bombardier RMA	
15 Apr 1882	28 May 1882	William Edward	Thomas & Mary	**Corbett**	Gunner RMA	
19 Apr 1882	28 May 1882	William David	James & Mercy Ann	**Duffett**	Gunner RMA	
6 May 1882	25 Jun 1882	Sarah Mabel	Arthur & Maria	**Rodman**	Gunner RMA	
16 Mar 1882	25 Jun 1882	Jim Bicknall	James & Fanny	**Talbott**	Gunner RMA	
10 May 1882	25 Jun 1882	Harry	John & Emma Jane	**Holton**	Gunner RMA	
23 Jun 1881	25 Jun 1882	Kate Eleanor	Robert & Martha Alice	**James**	Corporal RMA	

23 May 1882	27 Jul 1882	Eveline Christie	James Felix & Emily	Campbell	Clerk (Solicitor's)	65
20 Apr 1882	30 Jul 1882	Frederick Edward	James & Mary Jane	Clifton	Gunner RMA	
12 Jun 1880	30 Jul 1882	William George	Samuel & Mary Ann	Williams	Gunner RMA	
25 Jun 1882	30 Jul 1882	Annie Jane Beatrice	Samuel & Mary Ann	Williams	Gunner RMA	
19 May 1882	27 Aug 1882	Annie Maud Mary May	Richard & Elizabeth	Hartnell	Sergeant RMA	
7 Jun 1882	27 Aug 1882	Mabel Gertrude Clare	James McDonald & Maria	Hull	Gunner RMA	
19 May 1882	1 Oct 1882	Minnie Louise	John & Louise	Attridge	Pensioner Corporal RMA	
17 Aug 1882	29 Oct 1882	Daisy Helen	Zechariah & Mary	Baxter	Corporal RMA	
25 Sep 1882	29 Oct 1882	Elizabeth Emma	Thomas & Rosina Elizabeth	Tunnecliff	Gunner RMA	
3 Sep 1882	29 Oct 1882	Ethel Kate	Frederick & Matilda	Priday	Musician RMA	
2 Sep 1882	29 Oct 1882	Bessie Annie Maud	Christopher & Hannah Jane	Thacker	Sergeant RMA	
2 Sep 1882	29 Oct 1882	Bertha Ann	William & Ellen	Harrison	Gunner RMA	
16 Aug 1882	29 Oct 1882	Arthur	Charles Edward & Emily	Briggs	Sergeant RMA	
14 Aug 1882	29 Oct 1882	Edna Mary	John & Harriett	Westaway	School Master RMA	
12 Sep 1882	26 Nov 1882	Ernest James	George Henry & Lucy	Budden	Sergeant RMA	
11 Aug 1882	26 Nov 1882	Walter John	William & Fanny Matilda	Eaton	Gunner RMA	
17 Sep 1882	26 Nov 1882	Walter Thomas	Walter & Henrietta	Ross	Civilian	
25 Nov 1882	31 Dec 1882	John William	Matthew & Mary Ann	Ellis	Musician	
7 Apr 1882	31 Dec 1882	John James	Lonsdale & Eliza	Clarke	Colour Sergeant RMA	
19 Nov 1882	31 Dec 1882	Walter	Walter & Elizabeth	Ware	Pensioner RMA	
19 Nov 1882	31 Dec 1882	William	Walter & Elizabeth	Ware	Pensioner RMA	
10 Nov 1882	31 Dec 1882	Frederick Cyril	Thomas & Alice	Moore	Colour Sergeant RMA	
10 Nov 1882	31 Dec 1882	Herbert Edwin	Robert & Mary	Lappin	Colour Sergeant RMA	
9 Nov 1882	31 Dec 1882	Amy Elizabeth	Henry & Emma Harriett	James	Colour Sergeant RMA	
23 Oct 1882	31 Dec 1882	Hugh Charles George	William George & Emily Alice	Bowden	Gunner RMA	66
21 Jan 1883	22 Jan 1883	Emily	James & Emily	Wilson	Gunner RMA	12
15 Nov 1882	28 Jan 1883	Ellen Mary	Jonathan & Elizabeth	Wiltshire	Quarter Master Sergeant RMA	
19 Oct 1882	28 Jan 1883	Walter	John & Isabella	Snook	Colour Sergeant RMA	
21 Nov 1882	28 Jan 1883	Sidney Ernest Hugh	John & Ellen	Ford	Gunner RMA	
13 Oct 1882	28 Jan 1883	Emily Ethel	Edward & Emily Selina	Loscombe	Musician RMA	
28 Nov 1882	28 Jan 1883	Ellen	Thomas & Annie	Musgrove	Pensioner Gunner RMA	
16 Oct 1882	25 Feb 1883	Ellen Florence	John & Elizabeth	Harding	Corporal RMA	
5 Oct 1882	25 Mar 1883	Mary Lucy	George & Mary	Hother	Corporal RMA	
21 Jan 1883	25 Mar 1883	Ellen Maud	George & Elizabeth	Dixon	Colour Sergeant RMA	
23 Jan 1883	10 Apr 1883	Alfred Davis	William Davis & Alida Sarah	Welch	Major RMA	
18 Feb 1883	29 Apr 1883	Katie Bessie	John & Annie	Thornton	Sergeant RMA	
26 Sep 1882	29 Apr 1883	Emma	John & Elizabeth	Flowers	Pensioner Gunner RMA	
2 Dec 1882	2 May 1883	George	Henry & Jane	Purnell	Corporal	12
1 Apr 1883	27 May 1883	Cecilia Mary Alice	William James & Alice	Cox	Bombardier RMA	
18 Jan 1883	27 May 1883	Frederick	George & Mary Jane	Pearson	Gunner RMA	
2 Mar 1883	27 May 1883	Lily Edith	John Morgan & Sarah	Kite	Pensioner RMA	

21 Mar 1883	27 May 1883	Edith	Bernard & Elizabeth	**Morley**	Sergeant RMA	
24 Mar 1883	27 May 1883	Adeline Matilda	Robert & Mary	**Jones**	Gunner RMA	
10 Jan 1883	27 May 1883	Florence Gertrude	John & Harriet Eliza	**Finley**	Corporal RMA	
28 Mar 1883	24 Jun 1883	Edith Mary Rose	Henry & Kate	**Malyan**	Sergeant RMA	
16 May 1883	24 Jun 1883	Herbert	Charles & Charlotte	**Gosling**	Sergeant RMA	
16 Feb 1883	24 Jun 1883	Ernest	Frederick & Elizabeth	**Mann**	Staff Sergeant RMA	
24 Nov 1882	24 Jun 1883	Henry Joseph	Joseph & Ellen	**Maddock**	Gunner RMA	
6 Jun 1883	29 Jul 1883	Edith Eliza	John & Mary Ann	**Griffiths**	Gunner RMA	
17 Jun 1883	29 Jul 1883	Agnes Kate	William & Julia	**Shergold**	Gunner RMA	
10 Jun 1883	29 Jul 1883	Edith Mary	William & Mary Ann	**Sinclair**	Bugler RMA	
4 Jun 1883	29 Jul 1883	Ellen Sarah	William & Sarah	**Hawkins**	Gunner RMA	
30 Jun 1883	26 Aug 1883	Arthur Robert	Robert George & Emma	**Farlam**	Staff Sergeant RMA	
2 Sep 1881	26 Aug 1883	Emma Jane	Rowland & Eliza	**Herring**	Musician RMA	
2 Jun 1883	26 Aug 1883	Ellen Anne	Rowland & Eliza	**Herring**	Musician RMA	
1 Sep 1881	26 Aug 1883	Charles Augustus Thomas	Charles & Alice	**Hughes**	Musician RMA	
25 Jun 1883	26 Aug 1883	Sidney Francis	Charles & Alice	**Hughes**	Musician RMA	
5 Jun 1883	26 Aug 1883	Anne Margery	James & Jane	**Fee**	Musician RMA	
24 May 1883	26 Aug 1883	Harry Victor	Walter & Sarah Elizabeth	**Parker**	Gunner RMA	
12 Aug 1883	30 Sep 1883	James Robert Theophilus	James & Laura	**Jackson**	Gunner RMA	
30 Jun 1883	30 Sep 1883	Lily	Robert & Sarah	**Tuckey**	Gunner RMA	
11 Aug 1883	30 Sep 1883	Edward Alford	Edward & Elizabeth	**Doust**	Sergeant RMA	
18 Sep 1882	30 Sep 1883	Mabel Nina Madeline	George Archibald & Selina Catherine	**Wilson**	Bombardier RMA	
22 Sep 1883	28 Oct 1883	Lucy Ellen	James Robert & Annie	**Savage**	Gunner RMA	
17 Jul 1883	28 Oct 1883	Alfred Frank	Henry & Jane	**Weeks**	Pensioner RMA	
19 Aug 1883	28 Oct 1883	Frank	Solomon & Hannah	**Hayles**	Coast Guard	
30 Aug 1883	28 Oct 1883	Eveline Alice	Harry & Phyllis	**Preen**	Gunner RMA	
24 Jun 1883	28 Oct 1883	Laura Frances	John & Frances Clara	**Seymour**	Gunner RMA	
15 Jul 1883	30 Sep 1883	Sidney Charles Hutchings	William Thomas & Thirza	**Mead**	Borough Asylum Engineer Milton	67
21 Jul 1881	25 Nov 1883	Annie Eliza	John & Eliza	**Outram**	Gunner RMA	
31 Jan 1883	25 Nov 1883	Edith Elizabeth	John & Eliza	**Outram**	Gunner RMA	
10 Oct 1883	25 Nov 1883	Francis Olive Laird	Edward Henry & Margaret Marge Gordon	**Moore**	Major RMA	
4 Aug 1883	30 Dec 1883	Esther Louisa	Charles & Eliza	**Hewitt**	Corporal RMA	
25 Oct 1883	30 Dec 1883	William John	William & Johanna	**Fleetwood**	Corporal RMA	
10 Sep 1883	30 Dec 1883	Clara	William & Clara	**Hill**	Corporal RMA	
19 Sep 1883	30 Dec 1883	William Thomas	Thomas & Elizabeth	**Jackson**	Gunner RMA	
16 Dec 1883	5 Jan 1884	Winifred Elizabeth Gertrude Lee	William Lee & Obhamia Helena	**Skinner**	Bombardier RMA	68
	28 Jan 1884	Stephen	Walter & Jane	**Luckey**	Gunner RMA	69
17 Dec 1883	27 Jan 1884	Frederick Reuben	Christopher & Hannah Jane	**Thacker**	Sergeant RMA	
1 Jan 1884	27 Jan 1884	Ethel Kate	Richard & Elizabeth	**Hartnell**	Sergeant RMA	
20 Oct 1882	2 Feb 1884	Egbert George	Sidney & Gertrude Susan	**Davis**	Corporal RMA	12
15 Dec 1883	24 Feb 1884	Ethel	John & Betsey	**Maynard**	Sergeant RMA	
10 Dec 1883	24 Feb 1884	Annie Eliza	Walter George & Ruth	**Smith**	Pensioner RMA	
14 Jan 1884	24 Feb 1884	Joseph Harry	Anthony & Annie	**Harper**	Pensioner RMA	
19 Jan 1884	24 Feb 1884	Ellen Laura	John & Laura Elizabeth	**Wilton**	Corporal RMA	
2 Feb 1879	24 Feb 1884	Ada Mary	Jabez & Ellen Fanny	**Ault**	Staff Sergeant RMA	

2 Jun 1881	24 Feb 1884	Jabez	Jabez & Ellen Fanny	Ault	Staff Sergeant RMA
1 Aug 1883	24 Feb 1884	Nelly	Jabez & Ellen Fanny	Ault	Staff Sergeant RMA
13 Dec 1883	24 Feb 1884	Mabel Lydia	John & Lydia	McGee	Gunner RMA
14 Dec 1883	20 Mar 1884	William Ashley	William Charles & Ellen	Nicholls	Lieutenant & Adjutant RMA
6 Jan 1884	30 Mar 1884	Maud	Frank Alfred & Mary Ann	Rawlings	Bombardier RMA
17 Dec 1883	30 Mar 1884	Edith Maud Louise	Benjamin & Orpah Amelia	Ware	Gunner RMA
5 Feb 1884	30 Mar 1884	Albert	Charles Edward & Emily	Briggs	Pensioner RMA
5 Nov 1883	30 Mar 1884	Marian Annie	James & Alice	Innoles	Corporal RMA
21 Jan 1884	30 Mar 1884	Mabel Jessie Mary	Edward & Emily	Luscombe	Musician RMA
16 Mar 1884	27 Apr 1884	William Thomas	Thomas & Margaret Jane	Goodman	Sergeant RMA
29 Feb 1884	27 Apr 1884	Miriam Emily Ellen	James & Louisa	Cansdale	Corporal RMA
4 Apr 1884	25 May 1884	Amy Mary	George & Charlotte	Green	Corporal RMA
15 Mar 1884	25 May 1884	William Francis Henry	William & Bertha Kate	Carey	Sergeant RMA
3 Feb 1884	25 May 1884	Beatrice Hannah	Charles John & Hannah	Dyer	Corporal RMA
2 Mar 1884	25 May 1884	Bessie Maud	Thomas & Emily Selina	Fruton	Gunner RMA
23 Feb 1884	25 May 1884	Rosey Henrietta	Henry & Rose	Livingstone	Gunner RMA
16 Feb 1884	25 May 1884	Alice May	John & Charlotte Annie	Love	Gunner RMA
24 Apr 1884	25 May 1884	Eva Mary Ellen	George & Sarah Jane	King	Engineer Eastney Pumping Station
7 May 1884	18 Jun 1884	Charles Curle James	Thomas & Isabel Maria	Matthews	Gunner RMA
15 May 1884	29 Jun 1884	Alice	John & Elizabeth	Flowers	Pensioner RMA
29 Aug 1883	29 Jun 1884	William George	Alfred & Maria Jane	Davey	Gunner RMA
18 Jun 1884	27 Jul 1884	James Louis Phillip	James & Louise	Kent	Musician RMA
10 Mar 1884	27 Jul 1884	George William	Henry Charles & Matilda Ellen	Lees	Gunner RMA
22 Feb 1884	27 Jul 1884	Annie Isabella	James & Jane	Serare	Porter
4 Jun 1884	27 Jul 1884	Annie	William & Ellen	Baldwin	Gunner RMA
9 Aug 1884	31 Aug 1884	Thomas	Rowland & Eliza	Herring	Musician RMA
17 Sep 1880	31 Aug 1884	Catherine	Thomas & Eliza	Cope	Gunner RMA
13 Mar 1882	31 Aug 1884	Isabel	Thomas & Eliza	Cope	Gunner RMA
8 Aug 1884	31 Aug 1884	Matilda	Thomas & Eliza	Cope	Gunner RMA
22 Jun 1884	31 Aug 1884	William	George & Mary Jane	Pearson	Gunner RMA
3 Jul 1884	31 Aug 1884	Rosina	Charles Henry & Eliza Mary	Bell	Seaman Retired (Coast Guard)
8 Jul 1884	31 Aug 1884	Charles John	James & Elizabeth	Court	Gunner RMA
9 Jun 1884	31 Aug 1884	Ethel Rose	Stephen & Clara Elizabeth	Cheeseman	Corporal RMA
24 Jun 1884	31 Aug 1884	Elizabeth Margaret	John & Elizabeth Ann	Hill	Gunner RMA
17 Jul 1884	5 Sep 1884	Freeman Charles Nepean	Charles Louis Nepean & Fanny Jessie	Bishop	Lieutenant RMA
21 Jul 1884	28 Sep 1884	James	Edward & Elizabeth	Cannon	Gunner RMA
3 Jul 1884	28 Sep 1884	Susan Holland	Edward & Elizabeth	Cannon	Gunner RMA
10 Aug 1884	28 Sep 1884	Herbert Henry	William & Ann	Williams	Gunner RMA
19 Sep 1881	28 Sep 1884	Edward Thomas	Albert & Isabel	Parker	Gunner RMA
30 Jul 1884	28 Sep 1884	Albert William	Albert & Isabel	Parker	Gunner RMA
6 Sep 1884	26 Oct 1884	David	David & Armnell	Hembroke	Coast Guard
17 Sep 1884	26 Oct 1884	Minnie Hester	Jonathan Barnet & Elizabeth	Wiltshire	Quarter Master Sergeant RMA
31 May 1882	26 Oct 1884	Albert Edward	John & Sarah Maria	Jerrard	Gunner RMA
29 Jun 1884	26 Oct 1884	George Fox	William & Fanny	Eaton	Gunner RMA

15 Sep 1884	27 Oct 1884	Arthur Talbot	Arthur Bucknall & Edith Annie	Shakespear	Captain RMA	
25 Sep 1884	26 Oct 1884	William	John & Eliza	Outram	Gunner RMA	70
14 Sep 1884	26 Oct 1884	William	Frederick & Elizabeth	Mann	Staff Sergeant RMA	70
19 Dec 1873	27 Nov 1884	John William	John & Sarah Maria	Jerrard	Gunner RMA	
21 Oct 1876	27 Nov 1884	Francis Henry	John & Sarah Maria	Jerrard	Gunner RMA	
10 Dec 1879	27 Nov 1884	Charles	John & Sarah Maria	Jerrard	Gunner RMA	
20 Sep 1884	30 Nov 1884	John Henry	John Henry & Elizabeth	Dry	Gunner RMA	
24 Oct 1884	30 Nov 1884	William James	Foulds & Harriet Elizabeth	Berry	Colour Sergeant RMA	
10 Nov 1884	30 Nov 1884	Beatrice	John & Mary Ann	Griffiths	Corporal RMA	
28 Oct 1884	30 Nov 1884	Edith	John & Emma Jane Martha	Holton	Gunner RMA	
24 Sep 1884	30 Nov 1884	Louisa Mary	Zechariah & Mary	Baxter	Corporal RMA	
10 Jan 1878	28 Dec 1884	Philip Charles	Philip & Martha Maria	Jacomb	Corporal RMA	
19 Oct 1884	28 Dec 1884	Josiah Ernest	Philip & Martha Maria	Jacomb	Corporal RMA	
11 Oct 1884	28 Dec 1884	Florence Beatrice	Henry & Amelia	Graham	Bugler RMA	
22 Nov 1884	25 Jan 1885	George Percival	Charles Thomas & Alice Frances	Moore	Colour Sergeant RMA	
5 Dec 1882	25 Jan 1885	William John	William & Esther	Webber	Gunner RMA	
19 Oct 1884	25 Jan 1885	Amelia Esther	William & Esther	Webber	Gunner RMA	
10 Nov 1884	25 Jan 1885	Alice Maud Mary	Frederick William & Harriet	Butler	Musician RMA	
12 Dec 1884	25 Jan 1885	Frederick Ernest	William Ernest & Georgina	Andrews	Gunner RMA	
5 Oct 1884	25 Jan 1885	Margaret Mary	Henry & Victoria	Jackson	Gunner RMA	
11 Dec 1884	22 Feb 1885	Harry	Bernard & Elizabeth	Morey	Sergeant RMA	
4 Oct 1884	22 Feb 1885	William Victor	William & Rhoda Charlotte	Hounsell	Corporal RMA	
12 Jan 1885	22 Feb 1885	Lily	William & Clara	Hill	Sergeant RMA	
11 Nov 1884	22 Feb 1885	Henry	Thomas & Annie Eliza	Musgrove	Labourer	
21 Dec 1884	22 Feb 1885	Amy Eliza Jane	William George & Emma Eliza	Bowden	Gunner RMA	
20 Dec 1884	22 Feb 1885	Alice Maud	Thomas & Sarah	Lowe	Gunner RMA	
9 Dec 1883	7 Mar 1885	Willie	Joseph & Ellen Jane	Henderson	Sergeant RMA	12
26 Feb 1885	26 Mar 1885	George Hastings	George Farquharson & Annie Sarah	Pengelly	Major RMA	
8 Feb 1885	29 Mar 1885	Evelyn Grace	John & Annie	Thornton	Sergeant RMA	
5 Feb 1885	29 Mar 1885	Emily	Emanuel & Annie	Crook	Sergeant RMA	
5 Feb 1885	26 Apr 1885	Annie Lilian	Thomas & Sarah	Chaplin	Bombardier RMA	
9 Apr 1885	17 May 1885	Margaret	William & Annie	McTurk	Gunner RMA	
2 Mar 1885	31 May 1885	Ellen Frances Mary	Francis & Harriet	Hanaghan	Gunner Coast Brigade RA	
17 Jan 1885	31 May 1885	Nina Kate	Henry & Mary Fanny Jane	Malyan	Sergeant RMA	
24 Feb 1880	31 May 1885	Ernest Charles	Richard & Elizabeth	Hartwell	Pensioner Sergeant RMA	
12 Apr 1885	31 May 1885	Richard Bertie	William & Mary Ann	Sinclair	Pensioner Bugler RMA	
3 Mar 1880	31 May 1885	Annie Eliza	John & Eliza Victoria	Andrews	Gunner RMA	
26 Feb 1885	31 May 1885	Albert Henry	William James & Alice	Cox	Bombardier RMA	
10 Apr 1885	31 May 1885	Henry	Laban & Annie	Mattock	Gunner RMA	
9 May 1885	12 Jul 1885	Annie Edith	Joseph & Ellen	Maddock	Pensioner RMA	
31 May 1885	18 Jul 1885	Zoe Jessie Nepeane	Charles Louis Nepeane & Fanny Jessie	Bishop	Lieutenant RMA	
21 Jun 1885	19 Jul 1885	Alice Georgina Lilian	John & Alice Louisa	Glover	Corporal RMA	
8 Jun 1885	26 Jul 1885	Agnes Henrietta	David & Fanny	Brown	Gunner RMA	
5 Jul 1885	26 Jul 1885	Violet Ethel	Charles & Eliza	Hewitt	Corporal RMA	

1 Jun 1885	26 Jul 1885	Leonard William	Leonard William & Elizabeth	**Short**	Bombardier RMA
10 Jun 1885	9 Aug 1885	Maud	Frank Alfred & Mary Ann	**Rawlings**	Corporal RMA
1 Jul 1885	16 Aug 1885	Lucy Annie	Robert & Elizabeth Ann	**Kemp**	Gunner RMA
19 Jun 1885	23 Aug 1885	Alice Florence	Alfred & Alice Annie	**Cliffe**	Sergeant RMA
15 Jul 1885	23 Aug 1885	Mabel Maud	John & Harriet Eliza	**Finley**	Corporal RMA
28 Apr 1885	30 Aug 1885	Claire Broughton	John & Harriet Elizabeth	**Westaway**	School Master RMA
20 Mar 1875	30 Aug 1885	Edmund Egerton	Robert George & Mary Ann	**Broughton**	Pensioner RMA
24 Jun 1885	30 Aug 1885	Sydney Margaret	Robert George & Emma	**Farlam**	Barrack Sergeant RMA
13 Jul 1885	30 Aug 1885	Ethel May	John Bennett & Maria	**Adams**	Sergeant RMA
20 Jun 1885	30 Aug 1885	Frank	William & Sarah	**Hawkins**	Gunner RMA
23 Aug 1885	13 Sep 1885	Laura Ellen	George & Sarah Mary	**Packe**	Gunner RMA
27 Aug 1885	20 Sep 1885	Jessie Lily	William & Ann Elizabeth	**Pryer**	Sergeant RMA
3 Aug 1885	27 Sep 1885	Solomon	Solomon & Hannah Elizabeth	**Hayles**	Coast Guard
13 Sep 1885	1 Nov 1885	Martha Ann	William & Sarah Jane	**Cove**	Gunner RMA
10 Sep 1885	8 Nov 1885	William	Daniel & Ellen Maria	**Yardy**	Sergeant RMA
22 Jun 1878	15 Nov 1885	William Albert	Walter George & Ruth	**Smith**	Pensioner RMA
4 Oct 1885	15 Nov 1885	Mabel Mary	John & Louisa	**Williams**	Bombardier RMA
1 Jul 1879	22 Nov 1885	Maud Edith	Robert & Mary Ann Elizabeth	**Cope**	Corporal RMA
3 Dec 1880	22 Nov 1885	Edith Mary	Robert & Mary Ann Elizabeth	**Cope**	Corporal RMA
23 Sep 1885	22 Nov 1885	Harry	Charles & Charlotte	**Gosling**	Sergeant RMA
23 Sep 1885	22 Nov 1885	Elizabeth	Charles & Charlotte	**Gosling**	Sergeant RMA
14 Aug 1874	29 Nov 1885	George	Walter George & Ruth	**Smith**	Pensioner RMA
25 Sep 1885	29 Nov 1885	Rosina	Henry William & Sarah Susannah	**Hawkes**	Gunner RMA
5 Sep 1885	29 Nov 1885	Florence	Robert & Sarah	**Tuckey**	Gunner RMA
22 Oct 1885	1 Dec 1885	Marjorie Henry Gordon	John Frederick & Frances Mary	**Crease**	Colonel RMA
6 Oct 1885	6 Dec 1885	Valetta Florence Mary	George & Mary Jane	**Marshall**	Corporal RMA
21 Oct 1885	27 Dec 1885	Frederick James	George John & Emily	**Welch**	Bugler RMA
9 Oct 1885	27 Dec 1885	William Campbell	William Robert & Elizabeth	**Sutton**	Bugler RMA
10 Nov 1885	31 Jan 1886	Edward Charles	William & Esther	**Webber**	Gunner RMA
7 Jan 1886	7 Feb 1886	Arthur James	William & Ann	**Williams**	Gunner RMA
27 May 1880	7 Feb 1886	William	Nathaniel & Rebecca	**Worsey**	Gunner RMA
16 Sep 1883	7 Feb 1886	Margaret Rebecca	Nathaniel & Rebecca	**Worsey**	Gunner RMA
16 Nov 1885	7 Feb 1886	Ethel	Nathaniel & Rebecca	**Worsey**	Gunner RMA
11 Feb 1879	21 Feb 1886	Caroline Martha	Robert James & Mary Louisa	**Heath**	Blacksmith RM
18 Feb 1886	13 Jun 1886	Arthur Percy	Walter Arthur & Sarah Elizabeth	**Parker**	Gunner RMA
1 May 1886	20 Jun 1886	Alfred Thomas Evan	Alfred & Jane Caroline	**Beavan**	Gunner RMA
6 Jun 1886	27 Jun 1886	Florence Blanch	Ebenezer & Eliza Kate	**Mattock**	Gunner RMA
28 Mar 1886	27 Jun 1886	Thomas William	Thomas & Sarah	**White**	Bombardier RMA
8 May 1886	13 Jul 1886	May Elizabeth	Frederick William & Harriet	**Butler**	Bugler RMA
12 May 1885	13 Jul 1886	Minnie Flora	Frederick & Emma	**Jones**	Sergeant RMA
13 Jun 1886	1 Aug 1886	Lillian Louise	William Henry & Elizabeth	**Newman**	blank
31 May 1886	1 Aug 1886	William Thomas	Thomas Merritt & Elizabeth	**Addy**	Sergeant RMA
21 Jun 1886	22 Aug 1886	Harold	Henry Francis & Marianna Helen	**Millett**	Sergeant RMA
28 Oct 1885	5 Sep 1886	Sarah Emily	John & Sarah	**Clark**	Sergeant RMA

25 Aug 1886	12 Sep 1886	Thomas James	Thomas & Eliza Ann	**Cope**	Gunner RMA	
26 Mar 1886	19 Sep 1886	Eliza Jane	Charles & Sarah	**Waters**	Gunner RMA	
31 Jul 1886	26 Sep 1886	Nora	Laban & Amy	**Mattock**	Gunner RMA	
17 Jul 1886	3 Oct 1886	Robert William Robertson	Robert Robertson & Anne Amy	**Jardine**	Corporal RMA	12
11 Oct 1882	10 Oct 1886	Sarah Elizabeth	Joseph & Susan Ann	**Bell**	Gunner RMA	
9 Apr 1884	10 Oct 1886	Joseph William	Joseph & Susan Ann	**Bell**	Gunner RMA	
24 May 1886	10 Oct 1886	Ellen Mary Sturgess	Joseph & Susan Ann	**Bell**	Gunner RMA	
14 Aug 1886	31 Oct 1886	Alfred Charles Tobias	Alfred George & Mary Caroline	**Fox**	Gunner RMA	12
1 Oct 1886	14 Nov 1886	Nora Margaret	John & Louisa	**Williams**	Corporal RMA	
5 Sep 1886	21 Nov 1886	Charles Henry	Charles Henry & Eliza Mary Grace	**Bell**	Coast Guard	
28 Sep 1886	21 Nov 1886	Mabel Annie	Frederick & Mary	**Baxter**	Sergeant RMA	
25 Feb 1883	12 Dec 1886	Emily Louisa Deborah	Thomas & Isabel Maria	**Matthews**	Bombardier RMA	
2 May 1886	12 Dec 1886	Gertrude Mabel Grace	Thomas & Isabel Maria	**Matthews**	Bombardier RMA	71
28 Nov 1885	26 Dec 1886	Jack	John & Anne	**Thornton**	Sergeant RMA	
5 Mar 1882	9 Jan 1887	George Herbert	George & Hannah	**Staiyer**	Gunner RMA	
1 Aug 1886	9 Jan 1887	James Walter	James & Anne	**Savage**	Gunner RMA	
27 Jan 1887	20 Feb 1887	William Henry Edwin	George & Sarah	**Pack**	Gunner RMA	
18 Dec 1886	27 Feb 1887	Edith Emily	Isaac & Emma	**Anderson**	Bombardier Coast Brigade RA	
8 Feb 1887	20 Mar 1887	Annie Clara	William & Ann	**Williams**	Gunner RMA	
6 Feb 1887	27 Mar 1887	John Benjamin	John & Laura	**Wilton**	Sergeant RMA	
6 Feb 1867	30 Mar 1887	Eva Mary Wellstead	Richard & Mary Elizabeth	**Stoakes**	blank	
26 Jun 1868	30 Mar 1887	Mary Grace Wellstead	Richard & Mary Elizabeth	**Stoakes**	blank	
13 Aug 1872	30 Mar 1887	Elizabeth Emma Wellstead	Richard & Mary Elizabeth	**Stoakes**	blank	
25 Feb 1875	30 Mar 1887	Nelly Emily Wellstead	Richard & Mary Elizabeth	**Stoakes**	blank	
9 Jun 1878	30 Mar 1887	Alfred Wellstead	Richard & Mary Elizabeth	**Stoakes**	blank	
12 Mar 1887	24 Apr 1887	Jessie Beatrice	James & Jessie Ann	**Roxburgh**	Sergeant RMA	
8 Feb 1887	24 Apr 1887	Harry James	Henry & Mary Jane Kate	**Malyan**	Sergeant RMA	
20 Mar 1887	24 Apr 1887	Maria Jane	Walter & Jane	**Dicker**	Sergeant RMA	
2 Mar 1887	24 Apr 1887	Ruth Marion	Albert & Rebecca Jane	**Baker**	Sergeant RMA	
27 Mar 1887	1 May 1887	Annie Margaret	Edward Siddell & Lucy Olive	**Walker**	Master Gunner Gunner Coast Brigade RA	
3 May 1887	29 May 1887	Ethel Mary	Christopher & Hannah Jane	**Thacker**	Colour Sergeant RMA	
9 May 1887	29 May 1887	Edward William	William James & Edith Mary	**Handley**	Musician RMA	
3 May 1887	29 May 1887	Lilly Maud	William & Mary	**Sinclair**	Pensioner Bugler RMA	
4 May 1887	7 Jun 1887	Claudia Mary	Francis Harwood & Harriett Elizabeth	**Poore**	Lieutenant Colonel RMA	
11 Feb 1887	12 Jun 1887	Caroline Hariett	Edward Charles & Caroline Harriett	**Foster**	Gunner RMA	
4 Apr 1887	26 Jun 1887	Ernest William James	William George Thomas & Emily Georgina	**Young**	Bombardier RMA	
5 Apr 1887	26 Jun 1887	George Thomas	George & Mary Annie	**Greenway**	Corporal RMA	
12 May 1887	10 Jul 1887	Henry	James Robert & Louisa	**Cansdale**	Acting Sergeant RMA	

10 Jun 1887	24 Jul 1887	Albert Edward	John & Elizabeth	Flowers	Pensioner	
7 May ????	14 Aug 1887	John Oscar	Joseph & Sarah	Osborne	Tradesman	72
7 May 1887	25 Sep 1887	Annie Emily	Bernard & Elizabeth	Morey	Sergeant RMA	
14 Jul 1887	25 Sep 1887	Frederick John	William & Sarah	Hawkins	Gunner RMA	
23 Jul 1887	25 Sep 1887	Walter Victor Charles	Walter & Mary Ann	Wagstaff	Colour Sergeant RMA	
30 Aug 1887	2 Oct 1887	William	John & Elizabeth Ann	Hill	Gunner RMA	
13 Sep 1887	16 Oct 1887	Joseph Henry	Benjamin & Harriet	Stockley	Gunner RMA	
15 Jun 1887	23 Oct 1887	Albert Stanley	Jasper & Alice Maud	Thompson	Bombardier RMA	
20 Jan 1880	30 Oct 1887	Mary Ann Florence	James & Emma Charlotte	Andrews	Pensioner	
15 Oct 1887	23 Oct 1887	Annie	John & Annie	Hitherly	Gunner	12
13 Sep 1887	6 Nov 1887	Albert Selwood	Thomas & Elizabeth	Jackson	Corporal RMA	
22 Oct 1887	13 Nov 1887	Annie	Thomas Joseph & Catherine	Kerwin	Bombardier RMA	
24 Aug 1887	13 Nov 1887	William George Henry	Alfred George & Mary Caroline	Fox	Gunner RMA	
19 Dec 1886	20 Nov 1887	George	John & Elizabeth	Outram	Gunner RMA	
6 Jul 1887	4 Dec 1887	Horace David	David & Charlotte	Barnes	Musician RMA	
9 Nov 1887	1 Jan 1888	Emily Gertrude	Henry & Emily	Mapp	Sergeant RMA	
30 Nov 1887	1 Jan 1888	William	John & Sarah	Clarke	Sergeant RMA	
25 Jan 1887	29 Jan 1888	Albert Charles Henry	Charles & Eliza	Hewitt	Sergeant RMA	
1 Dec 1887	5 Feb 1888	Kathleen Mary	Thomas & Mary	Reynolds	Sergeant RMA	
17 Sep 1887	4 Mar 1888	Ellen Matilda	Walter & Matilda	Luckey	Gunner RMA	
27 Apr 1886	1 Apr 1888	Rhoda Beatrice	William & Rhoda Charlotte	Hounsell	Corporal RMA	
21 Nov 1887	1 Apr 1888	Olive Blanche	William & Rhoda Charlotte	Hounsell	Corporal RMA	
1 Mar 1888	1 Apr 1888	Ellen Grace	Thomas & Ellen	Handley	Corporal RMA	
6 Mar 1888	8 Apr 1888	Elizabeth Annie	Thomas Merritt & Elizabeth	Addy	Sergeant RMA	
13 Feb 1888	20 May 1888	Hilda Millicent	Frederick William & Harriet	Butler	Musician RMA	
20 Apr 1888	27 May 1888	Arthur Lee	William & Elinor	Skinner	Corporal RMA	
8 May 1888	8 Jul 1888	Elizabeth May	William & Esther	Webber	Gunner RMA	
1 Oct 1887	8 Jul 1888	Priscilla Lavinia	John & Emma Jane	Holton	Gunner RMA	
15 Apr 1888	15 Jul 1888	Albert Edward	Albert Edward & Alice	Butler	Bugler RMA	
18 Feb 1888	15 Jul 1888	Annie Beatrice	William Thomas & Elizabeth Maria	Willisford	Gunner RMA	
28 May 1888	5 Aug 1888	Arthur	Arthur & Margaret Ann	Glass	Gunner RMA	
1 Aug 1888	27 Aug 1888	Harriet Elizabeth	Francis Harwood & Harriett Elizabeth	Poore	Lieutenant Colonel RMA	
20 Jun 1888	2 Sep 1888	Alice Rosina	William George Thomas & Emily	Young	Corporal RMA	
29 Mar 1885	2 Sep 1888	Ernest William Robert	Robert & Sarah	Young	Accountant	
10 Sep 1888	18 Oct 1888	Kate Ethel	George Edward & Mary Ann	Pyne	Sergeant RMA	2
2 Oct 1888	25 Nov 1888	Edith Nellie	John & Annie	Thornton	Sergeant RMA	
1 Oct 1888	25 Nov 1888	Edith	William & Fannie Matilda	Eaton	Sergeant RMA	
20 Nov 1888	16 Dec 1888	Alfred John Algernon	Charles & Eliza	Hewett	Sergeant RMA	
24 Nov 1888	23 Dec 1888	Albert James	Albert & Rebecca Jane	Baker	Sergeant RMA	
28 Sep 1888	3 Feb 1889	Ellen Susan	Henry & Mary Jane Kate	Malyan	Sergeant RMA	
19 Nov 1888	17 Feb 1889	Arthur Henry	Frank & Eliza	Northrop	Corporal RMA	
10 Sep 1888	24 Feb 1889	Gertrude Alice Mabel	John & Alice	Squire	Sergeant RMA	
17 Feb 1889	21 Apr 1889	Ruth	James Robert & Louisa	Cansdale	Corporal RMA	
12 Apr 1889	21 Apr 1889	Nelson Cecil	James Evelyn & Mary Jane	Beagley	Sergeant RMA	2
12 Apr 1889	21 Apr 1889	Hilda Cecily	James Evelyn & Mary Jane	Beagley	Sergeant RMA	2
15 Jun 1889	7 Jul 1889	Elizabeth Dinah	Thomas & Eliza Ann	Cope	Gunner RMA	
7 May 1889	13 Jul 1889	Thomas	George Henry & Agnes	Turner	Sergeant RMA	2

20 Jun 1889	28 Jul 1889	Leonard David	William & Sarah	**Hawkins**	Gunner RMA	
17 Mar 1889	1 Aug 1889	William George	William & Jane	**Barrett**	Bombardier RMA	2
3 Sep 1889	29 Sep 1889	William John	Benjamin & Harriet	**Stockley**	Gunner RMA	
14 Aug 1889	6 Oct 1889	Charles Edward Ernest	Thomas Richard & Rosina	**Budd**	Corporal RMA	
7 Oct 1889	6 Nov 1889	Winifred Emily	William George Thomas & Emily Georgina	**Young**	Corporal RMA	
1 Jan 1877	10 Nov 1889	Louisa Maud	Martin Parkinson & Louisa Jane	**Whitwell**	Musician RMA	
9 Nov 1878	10 Nov 1889	George Edward	Martin Parkinson & Louisa Jane	**Whitwell**	Musician RMA	
15 May 1880	10 Nov 1889	Lilian	Martin Parkinson & Louisa Jane	**Whitwell**	Musician RMA	
1 Sep 1889	10 Nov 1889	Charles Henry	Alexander & Ellen	**Lane**	Bombardier RMA	
24 Oct 1889	15 Nov 1889	William	James & Frances	**Hunt**	Gunner RMA	
14 Nov 1889	4 Dec 1889	Beatrice Alice	Charles & Emily	**Jeggo**	Gunner RMA	
29 Oct 1889	8 Dec 1889	William John	Henry William & Elizabeth	**Taplin**	Sergeant RMA	
5 Nov 1889	15 Dec 1889	Ada Elizabeth	Webster & Emma	**Smithson**	Gunner RMA	
26 Jul 1882	20 Dec 1889	John Arthur Gee	Amos & Mary Ann	**Haynes**	Bugler RMA	
16 Dec 1885	20 Dec 1889	Simeon Harry	Amos & Mary Ann	**Haynes**	Bugler RMA	
26 Jul 1882	20 Dec 1889	Ivy Ada Ellen	Amos & Mary Ann	**Haynes**	Bugler RMA	
1 Mar 1887	22 Dec 1889	Emily Eliza Victoria	Henry & Amelia Maria	**Graham**	Bugler RMA	
23 Nov 1889	22 Dec 1889	Esther Betsey	Thomas Arthur & Esther Charlotte	**Evans**	Corporal RMA	
28 Aug 1889	22 Dec 1889	Lily Frances	Alfred James & Amy	**Bushell**	Musician RMA	
12 Dec 1889	19 Jan 1890	George Edward	Frederick William & Jessie	**Burnham**	Musician RMA	12
13 Aug 1888	16 Feb 1890	Daisy Maud	Alfred & Harriet	**Blandford**	Gunner RMA	
23 Dec 1889	16 Feb 1890	Morden Herbert Sydney	Henry & Mary Jane Kate	**Malyan**	Sergeant RMA	
6 Feb 1890	9 Mar 1890	Charles Edward	Charles & Hannah	**Heath**	Corporal RMA	
26 Nov 1889	16 Mar 1890	Francis	William & Jane	**Gunnell**	Gunner RMA	
16 Dec 1889	16 Mar 1890	William Alexander	William David & Emily Ann	**Esau**	Gunner RMA	
16 Feb 1890	4 May 1890	Marian Amy Dorothea	Edward Liddell & Lucy Olive	**Walker**	Master Gunner RA	
30 Mar 1890	25 May 1890	Frank	John & Louisa	**Williams**	Sergeant RMA	
20 May 1890	6 Jul 1890	Lydia May	John & Frances Clara	**Seymour**	Lance Sergeant RMA	
18 May 1889	17 Jul 1890	Albert Thomas	William & Rhoda	**Hounsell**	Corporal RMA	
25 Apr 1890	20 Jul 1890	Dorothy Winifred	Charles Joseph & Constance Annie Grace	**Cheetham**	Major RMA	
14 May 1890	29 Jul 1890	Hubert Leonard Thurston	Robert & Martha Alice	**James**	Sergeant RMA	
1 Mar 1890	4 Aug 1890	Henry William	Henry & Elizabeth	**Goodchild**	Gunner RMA	
13 Jul 1890	23 Aug 1890	Eric Louis Nepean	Charles Louis Nepean & Fanny Jessie	**Bishop**	Captain RMA	
6 Jul 1890	31 Aug 1890	Geoffrey	Edward Stanley & Amy Bloomfield	**Combe**	Captain Connaught Rangers	
13 Aug 1890	12 Sep 1890	William	William & Maud	**Travis**	Corporal RMA	
31 Aug 1890	19 Sep 1890	Frederick	Albert & Harriet	**Lamb**	Corporal RMA	
14 Aug 1890	16 Oct 1890	Daisy Amelia	Alfred George & Mary Caroline	**Fox**	Gunner RMA	
20 Sep 1890	26 Oct 1890	Agnes Annie	William & Fanny Matilda	**Atkinson**	Gunner RMA	
28 Sep 1890	2 Nov 1890	Lilian Annie	William & Fanny Matilda	**Eaton**	Gunner RMA	
9 Oct 1890	2 Nov 1890	Esther Davis	George Henry & Agnes	**Turner**	Sergeant RMA	

30 Sep 1890	2 Nov 1890	Elizabeth Constance Gough	Maurice & Fanny	Smith	Gunner RMA	
15 Sep 1890	9 Nov 1890	Charles Herbert	Thomas & Mary	Corbett	Gunner RMA	
7 Oct 1890	16 Nov 1890	Willie Reginald Norman	Henry Walter & Annie	Haynes	Gunner RMA	
8 Nov 1890	22 Dec 1890	Kathleen Violet	William & Susan Jane	Ayling	Sergeant RMA	
25 Dec 1890	11 Jan 1891	Mary Ellen	Robert Ward & Harriet Elizabeth	Emmerson	Corporal RMA	
9 Dec 1890	8 Feb 1891	Robert James	John & Ellen	Reynolds	Gunner RMA	
20 Jan 1891	8 Feb 1891	George William	George & Charlotte	Gordon	Gunner RMA	
23 Dec 1890	15 Feb 1891	Daisy Ellen Gertrude	Henry Robert & Emily	Carter	Gunner RMA	
29 Nov 1890	22 Feb 1891	Alice Hilda	Frank & Eliza	Northrop	Corporal RMA	
30 Dec 1890	26 Feb 1891	Percy Edward Durant	David James & Rosa	Waldron	Gunner RMA	73
26 Jan 1891	29 Mar 1891	Frederick Henry	William Henry & Elizabeth	Taplin	Sergeant RMA	
22 Feb 1891	12 Apr 1891	Arthur Edward	Thomas & Sarah Jane	Ellis	Sergeant RMA	
6 Mar 1891	26 Apr 1891	Gwendolen May	Stephen Henry & Sarah Edith	Welsh	Bugler RMA	
4 Apr 1891	3 May 1891	Annie Beatrice	Henry Stephen & Jane	England	Gunner RMA	
17 May 1891	31 May 1891	Mildred	Rowland & Miriam Eliza	Herring	Musician RMA	
29 May 1891	14 Jun 1891	Ethel Harewood	Arthur Francis & Kate Lavinia	Fenn	Gunner RMA	
10 Jun 1891	2 Jul 1891	William George	John & Caroline	Jones	Drum Major RMA	74
9 Jan 1891	26 Jul 1891	John	William & Rhoda Charlotte	Hounsell	Corporal RMA	
23 Apr 1891	9 Aug 1891	Douglas	Frederick William & Jessie	Burnham	Musician RMA	
27 Jul 1891	10 Sep 1891	Francis Hugh	John & Elizabeth Ann	Hill	Gunner RMA	
29 Aug 1891	9 Oct 1891	Ethel May	David & Fanny	Brown	Gunner RMA	75
22 Sep 1891	18 Oct 1891	Arthur Edward	Edward & Agnes	Taber	Late Gunner RMA	
6 Oct 1891	25 Oct 1891	Beatrice Victoria	William Henry & Victoria	Robinson	Corporal RMA	
23 Sep 1891	1 Nov 1891	Gertrude Florence	James & Harriet	Thomas	Gunner RMA	
29 Sep 1891	1 Nov 1891	Mary Jane	Edward Donald & Mary Ann	Fry	Bombardier RMA	
31 Aug 1891	22 Nov 1891	Frederick John Livingstone	Albert Edward & Alice	Butler	Bugler RMA	
15 Sep 1890	20 Dec 1891	Florence Beatrice	Alfred & Emily	Hall	Gunner RMA	
19 Oct 1891	20 Dec 1891	Ethel Daisy	Alfred & Emily	Hall	Gunner RMA	
16 Dec 1891	20 Dec 1891	Leonard Thalet	Robert & Louisa Emily	Williamson	Gunner RMA	76
8 May 1872	14 Jan 1892	George	Charles	Barker	blank	17
25 Jul 1870	17 Jan 1892	William Charles	William Charles & Maria Louisa	Wellington	Pensioner RMA	17
7 Nov 1891	17 Jan 1892	Albert George	Benjamin & Harriet	Stockley	Bombardier RMA	
13 Dec 1891	17 Jan 1892	Arthur John	William John & Mary Ann	Lee	Gunner RMA	
6 Dec 1891	4 Feb 1892	Jane Emily	William & Jane Maria	Gunnell	Gunner RMA	
14 Feb 1892	17 Feb 1892	Violet Lee	William Lee & Helena	Skinner	Sergeant RMA	77
1 Mar 1892	18 Mar 1892	Eva May Victoria	Henry Robert & Emily	Carter	Gunner RMA	65
7 Jan 1892	20 Mar 1892	Christopher George	William & Bessie Margaret	Matthews	Gunner RMA	
23 Dec 1891	20 Mar 1892	Violet Rose May	John James & Elizabeth	Harding	Sergeant RMA	
2 Mar 1886	27 Mar 1892	Robert George Ford	Robert & Nellie	Wadford	Civilian (Stationer)	
6 Mar 1892	27 Mar 1892	William Albert	Thomas Henry & Sarah Ann	Jones	Gunner RMA	
6 Mar 1892	3 Apr 1892	Eva May	Andrew & Alice	Thomson	Sergeant Major RA	
12 Apr 1892	1 May 1892	George	George & Kate Eliza	McCloghrie	Staff Sergeant RMA	
31 Mar 1892	3 May 1892	Beatrice May	Thomas & Margaret Ann	Hanley	Sergeant RMA	
26 Apr 1892	29 May 1892	Bertha Ellen	Albert & Elizabeth	Davies	Gunner RMA	
18 Mar 1892	29 May 1892	Arthur	James Robert & Louisa Emma	Cansdale	Sergeant RMA	

11 Apr 1892	29 May 1892	Amelia	Robert & Amelia Delphine	**Duncan**	Gunner RMA	
10 May 1892	11 Jun 1892	Ada Esther Louisa	James & Elizabeth Mary	**Hall**	Sergeant RMA	
4 Jun 1892	26 Jun 1892	Gertrude Ethel	Robert Ward & Harriet Elizabeth	**Emmerson**	Corporal RMA	
8 Jul 1892	24 Jul 1892	Olive	William & Fanny Matilda	**Eaton**	Gunner RMA	
14 Jul 1892	31 Jul 1892	George Edward	John & Charlotte	**Whelan**	Gunner RMA	
23 Jul 1892	14 Aug 1892	Laura Constance	Felix & Fanny	**Gower**	Pensioner RMA	
9 Apr 1892	20 Aug 1892	William Henry	George Henry & Elizabeth	**Wolfe**	Bombardier RMA	78
8 Aug 1892	26 Aug 1892	Gwendolen	William & Susan Jane	**Ayling**	Sergeant RMA	
22 Jun 1892	28 Aug 1892	William Sydney	William George Thomas & Emily Georgina	**Young**	Sergeant RMA	
22 Jun 1892	28 Aug 1892	John Raggett	Charles William & Ann	**Wilkins**	Gunner RMA	
20 Aug 1892	25 Sep 1892	Daisy Caroline	Frank & Frances	**Puddick**	Colour Sergeant RMA	
24 Sep 1892	6 Oct 1892	Charles	Charles & Lily	**Clarke**	Sergeant RMA	79
9 Jan 1891	9 Oct 1892	Elizabeth	William & Esther	**Webber**	Gunner RMA	
27 Sep 1892	23 Oct 1892	Agnes Beveridge	George Henry & Agnes Beveridge	**Turner**	Provost Sergeant RMA	
11 Sep 1892	23 Oct 1892	Mary Ewing	Alexander & Ellen	**Wallace**	Gunner RMA	
29 Aug 1892	13 Nov 1892	Alice Mary	Richard Samuel & Catherine Sarah Elizabeth	**Spanton**	Gunner RMA	
26 Sep 1892	20 Nov 1892	Arthur Ernest	William & Joanna	**Fleetwood**	Sergeant RMA	
12 Jul 1889	27 Nov 1892	Margaret	Emanuel & Annie	**Crook**	Colour Sergeant RMA	
29 Jul 1889	11 Dec 1892	Margaret Jane Shaw	Thomas & Margaret	**Parkins**	Gunner RMA	
24 Apr 1891	11 Dec 1892	Thomas Alexander	Thomas & Margaret	**Parkins**	Gunner RMA	
1 Nov 1892	11 Dec 1892	Alice Esther	Thomas & Margaret	**Parkins**	Gunner RMA	
14 Nov 1892	22 Jan 1893	Ivy Maud Beatrice	George & Bertha	**Clapp**	Corporal RMA	
24 Dec 1892	29 Jan 1893	Richard George Nicholson	Albert & Rebecca	**Baker**	Sergeant Instructor RMA	
23 Dec 1892	12 Feb 1893	Keith Morehead Gunning	Gunning Morehead & Charlotte Sophia	**Campbell**	Captain & Adjutant RMA	
5 Jan 1893	12 Feb 1893	Bernard Harold	Robert & Louisa	**Williamson**	Gunner RMA	
14 Feb 1893	5 Mar 1893	Frederick James	Frederick & Sarah	**Andrews**	Gunner RA	
1 Feb 1893	5 Mar 1893	Harry Wilfred	Harry & Ellen	**Howard**	Gunner RMA	
6 Feb 1893	12 Mar 1893	Arthur Walter Nelson	Henry & Ellen Stanley	**Saunders**	Gunner RMA	
9 Feb 1893	17 Mar 1893	Harry	Albert & Harriet	**Lamb**	Sergeant RMA	
12 Jan 1893	26 Mar 1893	Edward Leonard	Charles Frederick & Elizabeth	**Taylor**	Gunner RA	
27 Jan 1893	26 Mar 1893	Leonard Thomas Alexander	Albert Hodges & Ada	**Gillett**	Sergeant RMA	
14 Jan 1893	9 Apr 1893	Ada Florence	Martin & Ada Alice	**Duncuff**	Sergeant RMA	
2 Feb 1893	16 Apr 1893	Roy Sargent	Stephen Henry & Sarah Edith	**Welsh**	Bugler RMA	
28 Feb 1893	23 Apr 1893	Margaret Amy Elizabeth	Hamilton & Emma	**Capper**	Staff Sergeant RMA	
20 Mar 1893	27 Apr 1893	William Henry	Frances William & Rose	**Alexander**	Gunner RMA	80
13 Apr 1893	30 Apr 1893	Rowland	Rowland & Miriam Eliza	**Herring**	Pensioner (Late Musician) RMA	
19 Apr 1893	31 May 1893	Harold Richard	William & Rhoda	**Hounsell**	Corporal RMA	
1 Jun 1893	25 Jun 1893	Raymond John	Robert & Elizabeth	**Barr**	Pensioner (Late Sergeant) RMA	
25 Mar 1886	29 Jun 1893	Edith Marian	William Henry & Marian	**White**	Musician RMA	
6 Mar 1888	29 Jun 1893	Julia Mary	William Henry & Marian	**White**	Musician RMA	
23 Oct 1889	29 Jun 1893	Daisy Lavinia	William Henry & Marian	**White**	Musician RMA	

27 Jul 1891	29 Jun 1893	William Henry	William Henry & Marian	White	Musician RMA	
21 May 1893	29 Jun 1893	Harold Adolphus	William Henry & Marian	White	Musician RMA	
7 Jun 1893	9 Jul 1893	Beatrice Alice	Walter & Emma	Whiting	Corporal RMA	
15 May 1893	11 Jul 1893	May Louisa Mary	Frederick John & Sarah Anne	Binns	Musician RMA	
10 Jul 1892	14 Jul 1893	George	Albert & Esther Hetty	Clouter	Gunner RMA	81
9 Jun 1893	16 Jul 1893	Lilian Jane	James & Jessie	Roxburgh	Sergeant RMA	
4 Jul 1893	23 Jul 1893	Albert Henry	William Henry & Victoria	Robinson	Corporal RMA	
6 Jul 1893	30 Jul 1893	William George	George & Annie Elizabeth	Plant	Bombardier RA	
16 Jul 1893	3 Aug 1893	Florence May	John & Alice May	Wilmer	Gunner RMA	
1 Aug 1893	3 Aug 1893	Dorothy	David & Fanny	Brown	Gunner RMA	82
21 Jul 1893	6 Aug 1893	Archibald Frederick Eli	Frederick & Ellen	Willingale	Corporal RMA	
20 Jul 1893	13 Aug 1893	William Alfred	Thomas & Sarah Jane	Ellis	Sergeant RMA	
4 Jul 1893	27 Aug 1893	Agnes Elizabeth	Frederick & Mary Elizabeth	Peck	Engine Room Artificer RN	
23 Jul 1893	28 Aug 1893	Alfred	Albert & Esther Hetty	Clouter	Gunner RMA	81
9 Aug 1893	3 Sep 1893	Albert Henry	William John & Mary Ann	Lee	Gunner RMA	
22 Jul 1893	17 Sep 1893	Raymond	Frank & Eliza	Northropp	Sergeant RMA	
4 Mar 1874	5 Nov 1893	William Henry	John & Lucy	Bishop	Civilian (Iron Moulder)	17
15 Oct 1893	5 Nov 1893	Thomas James	Thomas Richard & Rosina	Budd	Sergeant RMA	
23 Sep 1893	5 Nov 1893	Harriet Elizabeth	Robert Ward & Harriet Elizabeth	Emmerson	Sergeant RMA	
14 Nov 1893	17 Dec 1893	Mabel	Alexander & Ellen	Wallace	Gunner RMA	
15 Sep 1893	21 Dec 1893	William Edmund	Joseph Charles & Alice Amelia	Mingay	Sergeant RMA	
2 Dec 1893	21 Dec 1893	John Frederick	John & Matilda	Rolt	Gunner RMA	
31 Oct 1893	28 Dec 1893	Basil Graham Burnett	Burnett Greive & Eleanor	Hall	Lieutenant Colonel RMA	
29 Dec 1893	4 Feb 1894	Robert Charles	John & Elizabeth Ann	Hill	Gunner RMA	
1 Jan 1894	9 Feb 1894	Ethel	John & Mary Lucy	Harrison	Corporal RMA	83
6 Feb 1894	18 Feb 1894	Winifred Bertha	Francis & Matilda Elizabeth	Collins	Corporal Dorset Regiment	
13 Sep 1891	21 Feb 1894	Gladys Isabelle	Walter Henry Backhouse & Elizabeth Martha	Hawkins	Corporal RMA	84
29 Dec 1893	4 Mar 1894	William Arthur	William & Agnes	Rayson	Gunner RMA	
7 Feb 1894	4 Mar 1894	Edward Alexander	William David & Emily Ann	Esau	Gunner RMA	
19 Jun 1886	11 Mar 1894	Trevorlyn Montague	Walter Henry Backhouse & Elizabeth Martha	Hawkins	Corporal RMA	
17 Apr 1888	11 Mar 1894	Hilda Mary	Walter Henry Backhouse & Elizabeth Martha	Hawkins	Corporal RMA	
9 Jan 1894	18 Mar 1894	Gilbert George	William & Florence	Gasson	Bombardier RMA	
24 Jan 1894	18 Mar 1894	Robert	Robert & Amelia	Duncan	Gunner RMA	
20 Sep 1893	18 Mar 1894	Lucy	John & Sarah	Pratt	Gunner RMA	
18 Feb 1894	25 Mar 1894	William Frank	James & Alice	Innoles	Colour Sergeant RMA	
11 Feb 1894	25 Mar 1894	Marion Jeanette	Frederick & Elizabeth	Ward	Gunner RMA	
3 Mar 1894	25 Mar 1894	Mabel Elizabeth	John & Mary Jane	Wood	Colour Sergeant RMA	
18 Feb 1894	29 Mar 1894	Dudley Ashton Hope	Ashton Hope & Minnie Mary	Hire	Captain RMA	
25 Dec 1893	1 Apr 1894	Ernest George	Benjamin & Harriet	Stockley	Corporal RMA	
11 Mar 1894	8 Apr 1894	Henry Frank	William & Sarah Jane	Willmott	Colour Sergeant RMA	
11 Nov 1889	12 Apr 1894	John Mansell	Henry & Louisa	Peters	Pensioner RMA	
22 Mar 1894	12 Apr 1894	Lily Caroline	Henry & Louisa	Peters	Pensioner RMA	

24 Nov 1893	25 Apr 1894	Trevor Walter Leslie	William Henry & Mary Jane	Jones	Colour Sergeant RMA	85
3 Mar 1894	6 May 1894	John David	John & Jane Amelia	Francis	Sergeant RMA	
12 Apr 1894	13 May 1894	Vivian	Henry & Sarah Jane	Harnett	Schoolmaster RM	
22 Sep 1882	20 May 1894	Henry William	Henry James & Elizabeth	Ride	Sergeant RMA	
13 Feb 1894	20 May 1894	Percy Leonard	Henry James & Elizabeth	Ride	Sergeant RMA	
6 Feb 1894	3 Jun 1894	Louisa Mercy	William & Louisa	Humphreys	Civilian	
26 Apr 1894	3 Jun 1894	Albert Edward	William & Joanna	Fleetwood	Sergeant RMA	
2 May 1891	4 Jul 1894	Mabel Ethel	Amos & Mary	Haynes	Pensioner RMA	
11 May 1893	4 Jul 1894	Hazel Violet	Amos & Mary	Haynes	Pensioner RMA	
31 Dec 1893	4 Jul 1894	Alan Edward	Edward & Catherine Jane	Sigrist	Corporal RMA	
10 Mar 1894	4 Jul 1894	Frederick Albert	Alexander & Ellen	Lane	Lance Sergeant RMA	
4 Jun 1894	15 Jul 1894	Louisa Winifred	Robert & Clara	Price	Sergeant RMA	
23 Apr 1894	29 Jul 1894	Maggie Elizabeth	John & Elizabeth	Robertson	Sergeant RMA	
24 Jun 1894	2 Aug 1894	Audrey Edoline	Arthur Bucknell & Amy Edoline	Shakespear	Major & Brevet Lieutenant Colonel RMA	
4 Jul 1894	5 Aug 1894	Ethel May	Arthur & Bertha	Chatfield	Bombardier RMA	
31 Jul 1894	19 Aug 1894	Henry William	Thomas & Eliza Ann	Cope	Gunner RMA	
25 Aug 1894	16 Sep 1894	Ernest James	William Dexter & Annie Maria	Clements	Corporal RMA	
25 May 1894	16 Sep 1894	William Hamilton	Hamilton & Emma	Capper	Staff Sergeant RMA	
20 Aug 1894	23 Sep 1894	Agnes Kathleen	Arthur George & Emily Evangeline	Guard	Sergeant RMA	
23 Sep 1894	21 Oct 1894	Charles William	William & Annie	Limb	Gunner RMA	
19 Oct 1894	4 Nov 1894	Nellie	Charles James & Elizabeth	Perry	Bombardier RMA	
5 Oct 1894	4 Nov 1894	Walter	William & Georgina	Moseley	Gunner RMA	
28 Sep 1894	11 Nov 1894	Frederick James	James & Minnie	Clements	Sergeant RMA	
26 Oct 1894	21 Nov 1894	Margery Fanny	Thomas Edward & Caroline Fanny	Richards	Sergeant RMA	
9 Sep 1894	25 Nov 1894	Elsie Jane	Albert Edward & Alice	Butler	Corporal RMA	
3 Nov 1894	25 Nov 1894	Ernest William	Charles William & Jane Annie	Wilkins	Gunner RMA	
4 Nov 1894	2 Dec 1894	James Alexander	William George Thomas & Emily Georgina	Young	Sergeant RMA	
12 Nov 1894	2 Dec 1894	William Ewart	Thomas & Margaret Gillespie	Parkins	Gunner RMA	
23 Sep 1894	9 Dec 1894	Arthur William	William & Alice	Thompson	Sergeant RMA	
26 Nov 1894	16 Dec 1894	Albert William Ernest	Frederick & Ellen	Willingdale	Corporal RMA	
23 Nov 1894	16 Dec 1894	James Frederick	James & Rose	Cake	Gunner RMA	
9 Nov 1894	16 Dec 1894	Albert John	Albert & Elizabeth	Davies	Gunner RMA	
20 Jun 1894	16 Dec 1894	Lilian Olive	Albert & Elizabeth	Davies	Gunner RMA	
24 Oct 1894	30 Dec 1894	Violet Kathleen	Frank & Frances	Puddick	Colour Sergeant RMA	
25 Sep 1891	8 Jan 1895	Joseph Meilor	David & Hannah Elizabeth	Wynne	Staff Sergeant RMA	86
3 Sep 1893	23 Jan 1895	Kathleen Rebecca Ellen	John & Kathleen	Roberts	Gunner RMA	87
23 Dec 1894	27 Jan 1895	Edward Charles Augustus	Henry William Charles Augustus & Amelia Parrick	Wheeler	Petty Office 1st Class RN	
12 Dec 1894	3 Feb 1895	Malcolm Joseph	John & Kathleen	Roberts	Gunner RMA	
14 Dec 1894	3 Feb 1895	Alec Ernest	Francis William & Rose	Alexander	Gunner RMA	
18 Jan 1895	10 Mar 1895	Samuel Thomas	John & Annie	Bentley	Gunner RMA	

31 Jan 1895	3 Mar 1895	William Arthur	William & Fanny Matilda	Eaton	Pensioner Gunner RMA	
	24 Mar 1895	John Henry	William & Sarah	Barrett	Corporal RMA	
8 Mar 1895	15 Apr 1895	Henry	William & Alice Maud	Travis	Bombardier RMA	
31 Oct 1894	15 Apr 1895	Albert George	George & Bertha	Clapp	Sergeant RMA	
24 Oct 1894	16 Apr 1895	Marie Rose	Edward & Caroline	Finn	Corporal RMA	
23 Mar 1895	16 Apr 1895	Albert Thomas	Samuel Longley & Emilie	Spittles	Gunner RMA	
20 Mar 1895	18 Apr 1895	George James	George & Alice	Bullock	Corporal RMA	
28 Feb 1895	21 Apr 1895	William Douglas	William Edward & Eliza Ann	King	Sergeant RMA	
9 Mar 1895	28 Apr 1895	George Reuben Henry	Walter George & Elizabeth Mitchell	Beautyman	Corporal RMA	
18 Apr 1895	5 May 1895	Violet Mary	Ernest & Ellen	Young	Gunner RMA	
13 Apr 1895	26 May 1895	Edith Melita	Augustus & Mary	Kimber	Gunner RMA	
26 Apr 1895	26 May 1895	Bryan William	William & Florence Ellen Mary	Gasson	Bombardier RMA	
7 Dec 1894	2 Jun 1895	Nellie Edith	Harry & Emma Margaret	Willimott	Bombardier RMA	
5 Aug 1890	2 Jun 1895	Phoebe Victoria	William Thomas & Elizabeth Maria	Willisford	Gunner RMA	
16 Feb 1895	9 Jun 1895	William James	William & Frances Ellen	Hazlehurst	Gunner RMA	
24 May 1895	9 Jun 1895	Emeline Victoria Violet	John & Mary Jane	Wood	Colour Sergeant RMA	
15 Jun 1895	16 Jun 1895	William Mark	William & Sarah	Rogerson	Corporal RMA	88
	23 Jun 1895	Agnes May	Thomas Edward & Margaret Mary	Stevens	Lance Sergeant RMA	
	30 Jun 1895	Mabel Jane	Harry & Ellen	Howard	Gunner RMA	
	30 Jun 1895	Henry Alexander	Alexander & Ellen	Wallace	Gunner RMA	
	30 Jun 1895	Kathleen Jessie	Arthur Joseph & Jessie Elizabeth	Lunn	Corporal RMA	
	30 Jun 1895	Evelyn Nina	Thomas & Nina Maud	Holding	Sergeant RMA	
	7 Jul 1895	Norman Arthur	William Henry & Victoria	Robinson	Corporal RMA	
	14 Jul 1895	Dorothy Beatrice	William & Minnie Maud	Lee	Gunner RMA	
26 Jun 1895	21 Jul 1895	Joseph Rawlings	Thomas & Sarah Jane	Ellis	Sergeant RMA	
13 Aug 1895	1 Sep 1895	Annie Ethel	Alfred & Jane Ada	Warwick	Gunner RMA	
2 Aug 1894	3 Sep 1895	Dorothy	Thomas & Elizabeth Jane	Reed	Gunner RMA	89
30 Jul 1895	8 Sep 1895	Alice Ethel	Alfred & Harriet	Shopland	Bombardier RMA	
22 Jul 1895	8 Sep 1895	Charlotte Ellen	James Henry & Emily	Manton	Corporal RMA	
19 Aug 1895	8 Sep 1895	George Emanuel	John James & Elizabeth	Harding	Sergeant RMA	
9 Aug 1895	9 Sep 1895	Agnes Emma	Humphrey & Mary Elizabeth	Glover	Corporal RMA	90
1 Aug 1895	22 Sep 1895	John Gordon	Albert & Rebecca	Baker	Staff Sergeant RMA	
29 Aug 1895	22 Sep 1895	Alice Maud	Septimus & Eliza	Collier	Sergeant RMA	
25 Apr 1895	25 Sep 1895	Harold Arthur	Arthur & Caroline	Hill	Quartermaster Sergeant RMA	
25 May 1895	29 Sep 1895	Frederick	William & Rhoda Charlotte	Hounsell	Corporal RMA	
14 Sep 1895	29 Sep 1895	Florence Gertrude	Albert George & Mary Ann	Pain	blank	
14 Sep 1895	29 Sep 1895	William John	William & Ellen	Simister	blank	
21 Aug 1895	29 Sep 1895	Harry Frederick Rayner	Thomas & Elizabeth Maria	Willisford	Gunner RMA	
7 Oct 1893	29 Sep 1895	Norman Thomas	Thomas & Elizabeth Maria	Willisford	Gunner RMA	
9 Feb 1895	16 Oct 1895	George Albert Edward	George Albert Edward & Eleanor Matilda	Bedford	Gunner RMA	91
8 Sep 1895	27 Oct 1895	Lily Johana	John & Mary Jane	Flower	Sergeant RMA	
19 Sep 1895	10 Nov 1895	Annie Barbara	Edward & Lizzie	Dewhurst	Gunner RMA	
3 Oct 1895	17 Nov 1895	Arthur Douglas	Thomas & Alice Beatrice	Layzell	Gunner RMA	

23 Sep 1895	17 Nov 1895	Evelyn Sybil	Albert John & Mary Jane	Kirby	Decorator	
1 Nov 1895	17 Nov 1895	Arthur Henry	Arthur John & Louisa	Rush	Gunner RMA	
11 Oct 1895	17 Nov 1895	Maurice Tom	Thomas Edward & Caroline Fanny	Richards	Sergeant RMA	
7 Oct 1895	17 Nov 1895	Edmund Ferguson	blank	Gale	Gunner RMA	
1 Apr 1895	17 Nov 1895	Jane Gladys	George & Charlotte	Gordon	Gunner RMA	
3 Oct 1895	1 Dec 1895	William Arthur	Charles & Roseanna Eliza	Bent	Bombardier RMA	
12 Nov 1895	8 Dec 1895	Charles Victor	William John & Mary Ann	Lee	Gunner RMA	
15 Nov 1895	8 Dec 1895	George	Isaac & Mary Ann	Chubb	Gunner RMA	
24 Nov 1895	16 Dec 1895	Ethel Florence	David & Amelia	Butler	Gunner RMA	92
26 Nov 1895	22 Dec 1895	Adelaide Elizabeth	William Walter & May	Mitchell	Gunner RMA	
6 Dec 1895	22 Dec 1895	Florence Fanny	Charles & Mary	Houghton	Gunner RMA	
23 Nov 1895	29 Dec 1895	Charles	Robert & Amelia	Duncan	Gunner RMA	
19 Dec 1895	1 Jan 1896	Louis William	Louis & Elizabeth	Milner	Gunner RMA	
4 Nov 1895	5 Jan 1896	Hilda Rosa	Thomas & Elizabeth Jane	Read	Gunner RMA	
8 Aug 1895	12 Jan 1896	Edith Beatrice	Henry & Elizabeth Jane	Preston	Sergeant RMA	
9 Dec 1895	12 Jan 1896	Frederick Ernest Stanley	Charles & Clara	Curtis	Gunner RMA	
16 Dec 1895	12 Jan 1896	Ellen Florence	Edward & Alice Ruth	Young	Sergeant RMA	
27 Dec 1895	19 Jan 1896	William Henry	Francis & Elizabeth Emily	Kwasniewski	Gunner RMA	
29 Dec 1895	19 Jan 1896	Gladys Adelaide	John Ernest & Adelaide Ophelia	Austin	Private RMLI	
22 Dec 1895	26 Jan 1896	Elsie Lilian	Thomas William & Annie	Chambers	Corporal RMA	
	26 Jan 1896	Evelyn Emily	Charles & Emily Elizabeth	Dyer	Sergeant RMA	
1 Dec 1895	2 Feb 1896	Claude Frederick James	Frederick John & Sarah Ann	Binns	Musician RMA	
11 Feb 1892	19 Feb 1896	Albert Norman	Alfred & Elizabeth	Sugar	Gunner RMA	
17 Jan 1896	1 Mar 1896	Edward Charles	Benjamin & Harriet	Stockley	Corporal RMA	
23 Jan 1896	1 Mar 1896	Arthur Harold	Albert Isaac & Sarah Ann	Wheaton	Sergeant RMA	
24 Jan 1896	1 Mar 1896	William Frederick	William & Emma Jane	Overbury	Gunner RMA	
17 Jan 1896	1 Mar 1896	Edith Emmeline	Charles & Mary Ann	Smith	Gunner RMA	
17 Jan 1896	8 Mar 1896	Hilda Olive Spencer	Robert & Mary Ann	Butfield	Sergeant RMA	
9 Jan 1896	15 Mar 1896	Kathleen	Edward & Catherine Jane	Sigrist	Sergeant RMA	
7 Nov 1895	15 Mar 1896	Robert Henry	Robert & Sarah	Collier	Gunner RMA	
14 Jul 1892	29 Mar 1896	George William	George James & Sophia Amelia	Styles	Bombardier RMA	
10 Feb 1896	1 Apr 1896	Florence Jane	Edwin & Elizabeth Jane	Blackman	Gunner RMA	
12 Mar 1896	6 Apr 1896	Kathleen Marie	William Arthur & Emily	Osborne	Gunner RMA	
19 Feb 1896	12 Apr 1896	Dorothy Beatrice	Tom & Annie	Clayton	Bombardier RMA	
24 Mar 1896	21 Apr 1896	Edward Terence	Edward & Caroline Sarah	Finn	Corporal RMA	
21 Feb 1887	25 Apr 1896	William Ernest	William Henry & Mary Jane	Jones	Staff Sergeant RMA	93
7 Sep 1895	3 Oct 1895	Winifred Elizabeth	Thomas & Eveline Alice	Fuller	Gunner RMA	90
20 Sep 1895	2 Nov 1895	Hilda Ellen	William George & Ellen Mildred	Sparrow	Colour Sergeant RMA	90
23 Apr 1896	17 May 1896	Ada Lizzie Annie	Frederick Charles George & Emily	Salmon	Sergeant RMA	
24 Mar 1896		Elsie Grace	Albert Abraham & Isabella	Holden	Gunner RMA	94
14 May 1896	14 Jun 1896	William John	George Frederick William & Louisa	Gould	Corporal RMA	
20 Jul 1895	14 Jun 1896	Florence Louisa	Joseph & Louisa	Baits	Gunner RMA	
29 May 1896	21 Jun 1896	Herbert John	Arthur & Bertha	Chatfield	Corporal RMA	
30 May 1896	28 Jun 1896	Mary Lydia	George & Mary Lydia	Hughes	Gunner RMA	
21 Dec 1893	12 Jul 1896	Florence Mabel	Frederick John & Anna	Wright	Gunner RMA	

22 Jun 1896	12 Jul 1896	Annie Esther	Frederick John & Anna	**Wright**	Gunner RMA	
30 May 1896	29 Jul 1896	Claude Richard	Solomon & Sarah	**Ford**	Gunner RMA	95
7 May 1896	31 Jul 1896	Dorothy	Albert & Ellen	**Smith**	Sergeant RMA	
20 Mar 1896	11 Sep 1896	Robert James	William Thomas & Annie	**Joyce**	Gunner RMA	96
11 Aug 1896	13 Sep 1896	Daisy Hilda	Walter William & Kate Harriet	**Sharpe**	Gunner RMA	97
11 Jul 1896	13 Sep 1896	Frederick John	Francis William & Rose	**Alexander**	Gunner RMA	
16 Aug 1896	13 Sep 1896	William Walter Charles	Walter & Georgina	**Roberts**	Gunner RMA	
24 May 1896	13 Sep 1896	Arthur Albert	Walter & Eliza	**Brockliss**	Staff Sergeant	
10 Oct 1893	20 Sep 1896	Rosalie Ethel	Frederick James & Rose	**Sessions**	Pensioner RMA	
1 Jun 1895	20 Sep 1896	Alice Lilian	Frederick James & Rose	**Sessions**	Pensioner RMA	
10 Aug 1894	2 Oct 1896	Robert Edward	Alfred & Elizabeth	**Sugar**	Pensioner RMA	
26 Aug 1896	4 Oct 1896	Alfred Henry	Alfred & Isabella	**Bunn**	Colour Sergeant	
3 Sep 1896	4 Oct 1896	William John	James Biggs & Jane	**Hobbs**	Pensioner RMA	
1 Sep 1888	11 Oct 1896	Winifred Ethel	William Henry & Mary Jane	**Jones**	Staff Sergeant RMA	
5 Oct 1891	11 Oct 1896	Ivy Emeline	William Henry & Mary Jane	**Jones**	Staff Sergeant RMA	
27 Jul 1896	11 Oct 1896	Winifred Annie	Charles William & Jane Ann	**Wilkins**	Gunner RMA	
19 Aug 1896	18 Oct 1896	Horace Edward	William Edward & Eliza	**King**	Sergeant RMA	
26 Sep 1895	25 Oct 1896	Kathleen Agnes Mary	Patrick Thomas & Mary Ella	**Carrol**	Gunner RMA	
13 Apr 1895	25 Oct 1896	Edith Kathleen	James Henry & Amy Jane	**Cripps**	Gunner RMA	
4 Nov 1896	22 Nov 1896	Annie Aitken	Thomas & Margaret	**Parkin**	Gunner RMA	
29 Oct 1896	22 Nov 1896	Rose	William & Fanny Matilda	**Eaton**	Pensioner RMA	
31 Oct 1896	29 Nov 1896	Samuel William Edward	Edward & Elizabeth	**Dewhurst**	Corporal RMA	
22 Sep 1895	29 Nov 1896	Cecilia Elizabeth	William Robert & Cecilia Harriett	**Pruden**	Sergeant RMA	
5 Oct 1896	29 Nov 1896	Gladys	John & Louisa	**Williams**	Colour Sergeant RMA	
17 May 1896	29 Nov 1896	Ethel Francis	Thomas & Lizzie	**Williams**	Pensioner RMA	
17 Oct 1896	6 Dec 1896	Stella	Charles & Emily	**Raper**	Gunner RMA	
3 Nov 1896	13 Dec 1896	Gladys Florence Lobelia	Henry William Charles Augustus & Amelia Parrick	**Wheeler**	Petty Officer 1st class RN	
23 Nov 1896	13 Dec 1896	Arthur Robert	William & Laura	**Asher**	Musician RMA	
19 Nov 1896	13 Dec 1896	Gordon Cecil	Robert & Louisa	**Williamson**	Gunner RMA	
25 Nov 1896	13 Dec 1896	Charles James	Henry & Alice	**Keen**	Gunner RMA	
19 Nov 1896	31 Dec 1896	Dorothy Louise	William Charles & Ellen	**Nicholls**	Major RMA	
	3 Jan 1897	Grace Adelaide	Stephen Henry & Sarah Edith	**Welsh**	Bugler RMA	
8 Dec 1896	3 Jan 1897	Adelaide Nellie	Isaac & Sarah	**Lawrence**	Sergeant RMA	
8 Jun 1895	3 Jan 1897	Alfred James Henry	James Alfred & Edith Ellen	**Banting**	Blacksmith	
11 Nov 1896	24 Jan 1897	Harold William Joseph	Alfred William & Georgina	**Tildesley**	Bombardier RMA	
27 Jan 1897	28 Jan 1897	Arthur John	John & Sarah Elizabeth	**Brindley**	Musician RMA	98
22 Jul 1896	31 Jan 1897	William Ian	William & Florence Charlotte Emily	**Fraser**	Corporal RMA	
26 Jan 1897	3 Feb 1897	Elsie Sarah	John & Sarah Elizabeth	**Barrett**	Corporal RMA	99
15 Jan 1897	7 Feb 1897	Florence Mary	William & Sarah	**Rogerson**	Corporal RMA	
18 Jan 1897	21 Feb 1897	George Edward	William Joseph George & Mary Annie	**Young**	Sergeant RMA	
27 Jan 1897	7 Mar 1897	Charles David	Charles William & Bessie	**Reynolds**	Bombardier RMA	
12 Feb 1897	7 Mar 1897	John Roff George	John Roff & Agnes	**Roberts**	Gunner RMA	
3 Jan 1897	7 Mar 1897	Elizabeth	Alexander & Ellen	**Lane**	Sergeant RMA	

10 Feb 1897	7 Mar 1897	Harry	Robert & Amelia	Duncan	Gunner RMA	
27 Dec 1896	7 Mar 1897	Eva Florence Janetta	William & Florence	Gasson	Corporal RMA	
1 Jan 1897	21 Mar 1897	Dora Louise	David & Fanny Louise	Brown	Pensioner RMA	
6 Mar 1897	21 Mar 1897	Dora Esther	George Elliott & Dora	Seabright	Sergeant RMA	
11 Oct 1871	27 Mar 1897	Annie	William & Esther	Porter	Musician RMA	17
6 Mar 1897	28 Mar 1897	Dorothy Elizabeth	James & Rose	Cake	Gunner RMA	
8 Oct 1896	4 Apr 1897	Frank Samuel	Samuel & Jessie	Mathieson	Corporal RMA	
24 Mar 1897	11 Apr 1897	Walter Henry	John & Alice	Wilmer	Gunner RMA	
12 Mar 1897	11 Apr 1897	Evelyn Elizabeth	Joseph & Eileen	Lawrence	Corporal RMA	
18 Sep 1896	2 May 1897	Francis William	James & Emma	Squire	Staff Sergeant RMA	
5 Oct 1896	2 May 1897	Florence Mary	William Alfred & Mary Ann	Thorp	Lance Sergeant RMA	
26 May 1897	13 Jun 1897	Edith Ellen	Albert George & Mary Ann	Pair	Corporal RMA	
10 Jun 1897	4 Jul 1897	Albert Victor	Thomas & Sarah Jane	Ellis	Sergeant RMA	
3 Dec 1888	11 Jul 1897	Ernest Albert	Thomas & Priscilla	Clarke	Gunner RMA	
2 Jan 1890	11 Jul 1897	Charles Victor	Thomas & Priscilla	Clarke	Gunner RMA	
14 May 1897	11 Jul 1897	Eva May	Thomas & Priscilla	Clarke	Gunner RMA	100
21 Jan 1897	11 Jul 1897	William Thomas	Thomas & Priscilla	Clarke	Gunner RMA	
20 Jul 1897	20 Jul 1897	Albert	Albert Henry & Esther Ellie	Clouter	Gunner RMA	93
14 Oct 1897	25 Jul 1897	Doris Vaughan	Richard & Nellie	Burke	Musician RMA	101
11 Jul 1897	1 Aug 1897	Edith Grace	Charles & Mary	Houghton	Bombardier RMA	
28 Jun 1897	4 Aug 1897	Arthur	Henry & Sarah Jane	Harnett	Head School Master RMA	
8 Jul 1897	11 Aug 1897	William Percival	William & Ada Sarah	Boughtflower	Bombardier RMA	102
25 Jul 1897	15 Aug 1897	Hilda Annie	William & Minnie Maud	Lee	Pensioner RMA	
4 Jul 1897	22 Aug 1897	Grace Lilian	Albert Herbert & Eleanor Maud	Pearson	Musician RMA	
4 Aug 1897	19 Sep 1897	Albert Edward George	William & Emma Jane	Overbury	Gunner RMA	
8 Sep 1895	19 Sep 1897	Cecil Thomas	George William & Sarah Louisa	Bannister	Gunner RMA	
8 Jun 1897	26 Sep 1897	May Victoria Florence	George & Bertha	Clapp	Sergeant RMA	
11 Sep 1897	26 Sep 1897	Flora Edith May	Alfred George & Mary Caroline	Fox	Gunner RMA	
25 Sep 1897	27 Sep 1897	Kathleen Nellie	Alexander & Ellen	Wallace	Gunner RMA	101
6 Sep 1897	3 Oct 1897	Charles Frederick	Alfred Francis & Ada	Carne	Gunner RMA	
10 Aug 1897	17 Oct 1897	Violet Elsie	Edward Thomas & Harriet Jane	Rixon	Labourer	
22 Sep 1897	17 Oct 1897	Lilian Eliza	George & Eliza Annie	Boyce	Corporal RMA	
28 Jul 1897	29 Aug 1897	Edith Mary Alexandra	Robert & Clara	Price	Sergeant RMA	103
4 Sep 1897	24 Oct 1897	Gladys Emma	Henry & Elizabeth	Stephens	Bombardier RMA	
9 Oct 1897	31 Oct 1897	Sydney Edward John	Sydney Richard & Edith	Stephens	Corporal RMA	
20 Mar 1897	7 Nov 1897	Lily Gladys	George Henry & Linda	Care	Gunner RMA	
25 Aug 1897	7 Nov 1897	Dora May	Thomas Edward & Caroline Fanny	Richards	Sergeant RMA	
19 Sep 1897	7 Nov 1897	Dorothy Ellen	Edward Thomas & Amy Lydia	Heaver	Gunner RMA	
18 Oct 1897	7 Nov 1897	William James	Ernest & Ellen	Young	Gunner RMA	
20 Oct 1897	7 Nov 1897	Ruth Mary	Samuel Longley & Emily	Spittles	Bombardier RMA	
2 Nov 1897	21 Nov 1897	Florence Rose	Isaac & Mary Ann	Chubb	Gunner RMA	
27 Oct 1897	21 Nov 1897	Emily	William George & Jessie	Triance	Corporal RMA	
26 Oct 1897	21 Nov 1897	Charles Flowerdew	Charles William & Clara May	Dowell	Bombardier RMA	

17 Oct 1897	21 Nov 1897	Emily Louisa	George Frederick William & Louisa	**Gould**	Corporal RMA	
	21 Nov 1897	Nora Rene	Thomas & Alice	**Layzell**	Gunner RMA	
4 Nov 1897	5 Dec 1897	Gwendoline Charlotte	William John & Eliza	**Sills**	Corporal RMA	
17 Jul 1897	12 Dec 1897	Joseph Fred	Charles Frederick George & Emily	**Salmon**	Sergeant RMA	93
2 Nov 1897	2 Jan 1898	Barbara Urseley	John & Kate	**Roberts**	Gunner RMA	104
3 Jun 1888	27 Jan 1898	Harold Lorenzo	William & Annie	**Fleetwood**	Late Sergeant RMA	
7 Jul 1889	27 Jan 1898	Esther Lilian	William & Annie	**Fleetwood**	Late Sergeant RMA	
3 Jan 1898	30 Jan 1898	Grace Kathleen	Frederick John & Georgina Grace	**Chivers**	Corporal RMA	
16 Jan 1898	16 Jan 1898	Violet Winifred	William & Ellen	**Simister**	Pensioner	105
31 Jan 1898	27 Feb 1898	Herbert Baldwin	Percy Mortimer & Kathleen Mary	**Gross**	Gunner RMA	
6 Jan 1898	20 Mar 1898	Richard	Charles & Clara	**Curtis**	Gunner RMA	
18 Aug 1897	20 Mar 1898	Alice Marian	William Thomas & Elizabeth Maria	**Willisford**	Bombardier RMA	
28 Jan 1898	3 Apr 1898	Florence Gertrude	Francis William & Rose	**Alexander**	Gunner RMA	
23 Mar 1898	17 Apr 1898	Elsie Frances	David & Amelia Elizabeth	**Butler**	Gunner RMA	
10 Dec 1897	17 Apr 1898	Henry Martin	Frederick John & Sarah Ann	**Binns**	Musician RMA	
15 Mar 1898	8 May 1898	Lilian	John & Beatrice	**Williams**	Sergeant RMA	
6 Apr 1898	8 May 1898	Jack	Alfred & Susannah	**Dalton**	Sergeant RMA	
5 Jan 1898	15 May 1898	Nellie Dorothy Catherine	George Frederick & Eleanor Fanny	**Huddle**	Sergeant RMA	
10 Apr 1898	15 May 1898	Hubert Mervyn Benham	Horace Fewster & Rosetta Mary	**Wilson**	Gunner RMA	
9 Apr 1898	15 May 1898	Edith Amy	Benjamin & Priscilla	**Bridgewater**	Gunner RMA	
27 Mar 1898	15 May 1898	Clara	Alma Victor & Margaret	**Jones**	Lance Corporal RMLI	
29 Apr 1898	22 May 1898	Marjorie	Edward & Catherine	**Sigrist**	Sergeant RMA	
20 May 1898	5 Jun 1898	May Gladstone	Thomas & Margaret	**Parkins**	Gunner RMA	
10 Jul 1893	19 Jun 1898	Nellie	George & Ellen	**Langley**	Sergeant RMA	
19 Apr 1895	19 Jun 1898	Amy Edith	George & Ellen	**Langley**	Sergeant RMA	
26 Sep 1897	19 Jun 1898	Ethel May	George & Ellen	**Langley**	Sergeant RMA	
27 May 1898	30 Jun 1898	Atbara Constance Winifred	Arthur & Caroline	**Hill**	2nd Lieutenant RMA	
22 Apr 1898	2 Jul 1898	John Mackenzie Bax	John Robert Henry & Margaret Emily	**Homfray**	Captain RMA	
16 Jun 1898	3 Jul 1898	Elsie Ada Louise	William & Ada Sarah	**Boughtflower**	Corporal RMA	
22 Jun 1898	17 Jul 1898	Evelyn Helen	George & Alice	**Bullock**	Sergeant RMA	
30 Jun 1898	17 Jul 1898	Ivy Dorothy	William John & Mary Ann	**Lee**	Gunner RMA	
15 Feb 1898	17 Jul 1898	Annie Rosina	Charles John & Emma Elizabeth	**Phillips**	Gunner RMA	
22 Jun 1898	17 Jul 1898	Ernest William	Ernest & Minnie	**Jackson**	Gunner RMA	
14 Aug 1898	30 Aug 1898	Flora Alice	Joseph Samuel & Ada Emily	**Stanton**	Sergeant RMA	93
22 Jul 1898	25 Aug 1898	Dorothy	Francis Arthur & Sarah	**Butt**	Gunner RMA	103
15 Apr 1897	4 Sep 1898	Rowland Arthur	William Arthur & Emily	**Osborne**	Gunner RMA	
30 Jul 1898	4 Sep 1898	Beatrice Louisa	William Arthur & Emily	**Osborne**	Gunner RMA	
28 May 1898	4 Sep 1898	Violet Winifred	Peter & Marian	**Richardson**	Gunner RMA	
27 May 1896	4 Sep 1898	George	George & Ellen	**Langley**	Sergeant RMA	
17 Aug 1898	4 Sep 1898	Emma Louisa	Henry & Ellen Louisa	**Barker**	Gunner RMA	
18 Apr 1898	4 Sep 1898	Cecil Vaughan	Richard & Nellie	**Burke**	Musician RMA	

20 Aug 1898	4 Sep 1898	Beatrice May	Robert & Louisa	**Williamson**	Gunner RMA	
24 Aug 1898	11 Sep 1898	Gladys	Henry William & Laura	**Lodder**	Sergeant RMA	
3 Sep 1898	26 Sep 1898	Winifred Charlotte Darham	Stephen George & Winifred Lilian	**Rodway**	Corporal RMA	
12 Apr 1897	26 Sep 1898	George Albert Edward	George Albert Edward & Helena Matilda	**Bedford**	Gunner RMA	
14 May 1897	26 Sep 1898	Emma Jane Elizabeth	Alfred Arthur & Charlotte Harriet	**Cole**	Gunner RMA	
19 Aug 1898	26 Sep 1898	William Edward	William Edward & Mary	**Sames**	Gunner RMA	
3 Sep 1894	26 Sep 1898	Stephen Reuben George	Reuben & Louisa	**Newport**	Gunner RMA	
9 Apr 1896	26 Sep 1898	Harold William James	Reuben & Louisa	**Newport**	Gunner RMA	
28 Aug 1898	26 Sep 1898	Frederick Charles	Frederick John & Hannah	**Wright**	Gunner RMA	
12 Sep 1898	16 Oct 1898	Charles George Cecil	Charles Samuel & Mary Emily	**Kelsey**	Corporal RMA	
5 Apr 1893	6 Nov 1898	Edward	Edward & Ada	**Button**	Gunner RMA	
29 Apr 1898	6 Nov 1898	Joseph	Edward & Ada	**Button**	Gunner RMA	
8 Oct 1898	6 Nov 1898	John George	George John & Isabella	**Tarryer**	Corporal RMA	
12 Oct 1898	13 Nov 1898	William Sydney John	Sydney Richard & Edith	**Stephens**	Corporal RMA	
16 Oct 1898	13 Nov 1898	Christopher Henry	John & Matilda	**Rolt**	Gunner RMA	
4 Jun 1898	20 Nov 1898	Frederick George	Arthur William & Nellie	**Height**	Sergeant RMA	
8 Sep 1898	20 Nov 1898	Thomas John	Charles & Jane	**Smith**	Gunner RMA	
13 Nov 1898	27 Nov 1898	Samuel	John & Lily	**Doidge**	Acting Bombardier RMA	
2 Dec 1898	23 Dec 1898	Charles Ernest	Alfred & Jane Ada	**Warwick**	Gunner RMA	
21 Nov 1898	23 Dec 1898	blank	William & Mary	**Hutchings**	Corporal RMA	
7 Dec 1898	23 Dec 1898	Edward	George Henry & Clara Annie	**Dossett**	Gunner RMA	106
4 Nov 1898	8 Jan 1899	Anthony	David & Nellie Elizabeth	**Ferguson**	Gunner RMA	107
14 Dec 1898	8 Jan 1899	Albert Wesley	Augustus Wesley & Mary	**Kimber**	Acting Bombardier RMA	107
26 Nov 1898	6 Jan 1899	Sydney	William John & Mary Ann	**Marshall**	Colour Sergeant RMA	108
3 Dec 1898	6 Jan 1899	Cecil Stanley	William Edward & Eliza	**King**	Sergeant RMA	108
25 Nov 1897	6 Jan 1899	Ada Dorothy	Henry & Elizabeth Jane	**Preston**	Sergeant RMA	108
3 Jan 1899	29 Jan 1899	Ernest Frank	James & Rose	**Cake**	Gunner RMA	
2 Jan 1899	29 Jan 1899	Ralph Arthur	Henry Edward & Lydia	**Fitzgerald**	Sergeant RMA	
11 Jan 1899	5 Feb 1899	Leonard Alexander	George James & Sophie Amelia	**Styles**	Corporal RMA	
12 Sep 1898	12 Feb 1899	William Colin	William Robert & Cecilia Elizabeth	**Pruden**	Sergeant RMA	
4 Jan 1899	15 Feb 1899	Michael	Edward Henry Fitzharding & Gertrude	**Heaton-Ellis**	Lieutenant RN	
4 Feb 1899	19 Feb 1899	Edward George	Charles & Emily	**Raper**	Gunner RMA	
3 Mar 1899	3 Mar 1899	David	Robert & Clara	**Price**	Staff Sergeant RMA	109
2 Jan 1899	5 Mar 1899	Lily Ella	James Charles & Lily Alma	**Carter**	Gunner RMA	
4 Feb 1899	10 Mar 1899	George Frederick	Thomas & Sarah Jane	**Ellis**	Clerk Late Colour Sergeant RMA	
7 Jan 1899	12 Mar 1899	Helena Alice Kate	Alfred James & Charlotte	**Clifton**	Gunner RMA	
23 Feb 1899	12 Mar 1899	Albert Henry	Albert John & Amelia	**Burridge**	Private RMLI	
27 Feb 1899	15 Mar 1899	Norah Ethel	Tom & Annie	**Clayton**	Acting Bombardier RMA	
26 Feb 1899	17 Mar 1899	Elsie	Oscar & Rose	**Norris**	Colour Sergeant RMA	

17 Feb 1899	19 Mar 1899	Albert William	Thomas Arthur & Esther Charlotte	Evans	Gunnery Instructor Sergeant RMA	
7 Jan 1899	26 Mar 1899	George Arthur Jeffery	George Henry & Adelaide Jeffery	Messenbird	Lance Sergeant RMA	
13 Jan 1899	26 Mar 1899	Minnie Agnes	John & Annie	Bentley	Gunner RMA	110
13 Jan 1899	26 Mar 1899	Dorothea	John & Annie	Bentley	Gunner RMA	110
28 Mar 1899	14 Apr 1899	Violet Annie	Selgar Bartlett & Annie Edith Jane	Richards	Joiner	
18 Mar 1899	16 Apr 1899	Barbara Edith	Herbert & Julia Maxwell	Kidd	Gunner RMA	
27 Mar 1899	23 Apr 1899	William Reginald	William Henry & Lizzie Isabel	Walker	Sergeant RMA	
9 Mar 1899	30 Apr 1899	Patricia Hamilton	Aubrey Hamilton & Louisa Elinor	Cox	Captain RMA	
27 Jul 1897	11 May 1899	Victor James	Charles & Rosanna Eliza	Bent	Acting Bombardier RMA	
5 Feb 1899	11 May 1899	Eleanor Florence	Charles & Rosanna Eliza	Bent	Acting Bombardier RMA	
24 Apr 1899	21 May 1899	Giffer Lucy	Albert James & Louisa Laura	Guyton	Sergeant RMA	
27 Apr 1899	28 May 1899	Alice	Thomas & Mary	Hayes	Gunner RMA	
24 Mar 1899	4 Jun 1899	Frederick Arthur	George Frederick William & Louisa	Gould	Sergeant RMA	
1 May 1899	4 Jun 1899	Dorothy Ellen	David & Amelia Elizabeth	Butler	Gunner RMA	
27 Apr 1899	11 Jun 1899	William Alfred	William Anthony & Bessie	Harper	Sergeant RMA	
6 May 1899	11 Jun 1899	George	George Thomas & Jane	Merrick	Corporal RMA	
28 Apr 1899	16 Jun 1899	Dorothea	John & Kate	Ryder	Corporal RMA	
16 May 1899	18 Jun 1899	Frederick	Frederick John & Georgina Grace	Chivers	Sergeant RMA	
14 Mar 1899	23 Jun 1899	Elsie Ellen	John & Mary Lucy	Harrison	Colour Sergeant RMA	
4 Jun 1899	23 Jun 1899	Winifred Ellen	Albert Job & Louisa	Chatfield	Sergeant RMA	
5 Mar 1897	30 Jun 1899	Kathleen Annie	Thomas & Elizabeth Jane	Read	Gunner RMA	
7 Apr 1899	30 Jun 1899	Daisy	Thomas & Elizabeth Jane	Read	Gunner RMA	
27 May 1899	30 Jun 1899	Lillian Maud May	Robert & Emma Eliza	Spencer	Bombardier RMA	
30 Jun 1899	25 Jul 1899	Florence Kathleen	Charles & Mary Ann	Smith	Gunner RMA	
6 Mar 1899	30 Jul 1899	Hector Herbert	Isaac Albert & Sarah Ann	Wheaton	Sergeant RMA	111
28 Jun 1899	30 Jul 1899	Robert William	William George & Jessie	Triance	Lance Sergeant RMA	
13 Jul 1899	30 Jul 1899	Gladys Esther	Thomas & Helena Ann	Spain	Corporal RMA	
5 Jul 1899	31 Jul 1899	George Edward	George Henry & Emma Jane	Browning	Sergeant RMA	112
5 Jul 1899	31 Jul 1899	William James	George Henry & Emma Jane	Browning	Sergeant RMA	112
4 May 1899	6 Aug 1899	Winifred May	John & Lucy	Gilliam	Armourer Sergeant RMA	
21 Jul 1899	14 Aug 1899	Walter Charles	Frank Felix & Alice	Crowe	Gunner RMA	109
23 Jul 1899	13 Aug 1899	Richard Phillip Caleb	Richard & Minnie	Newman	Bombardier RMA	
17 Jul 1899	11 Aug 1899	Edward Jack Henry	Frederick Joshua & Helen	Roe	Petty Officer 1st Class RN	
26 Jun 1899	10 Sep 1899	Walter	Walter & Emma	Whiting	Sergeant RMA	
14 Aug 1899	10 Sep 1899	Florence Hetty	Ernest & Ellen	Young	Gunner RMA	
20 Aug 1899	10 Sep 1899	Dorothy Elizabeth Ruth	Charles Arthur & Naomi Ruth	Jones	Corporal RMA	
31 Aug 1899	24 Sep 1899	Ada Margaret Charlotte	Ernest John & Ada Margaret	Barnes	Lance Sergeant RMA	
14 Jun 1899	24 Sep 1899	Hilda Eleanor Elizabeth	Walter William & Alice Annie	Golding	Corporal RMA	
18 Aug 1899	24 Sep 1899	Elsie Leila Gertrude	Edward Augustus & Gertrude Ellen	Wheeley	Bombardier RMA	

19 Sep 1899	6 Oct 1899	Alexander Alfred William	Alexander & Annie Louise	Johnston	Corporal RMA	
3 Jul 1899	8 Oct 1899	Charles Edmund	Percy Edmund & Edith	Maitland	Staff Surgeon RN	
11 Sep 1899	8 Oct 1899	Nellie Cecilia	Richard & Nellie	Burke	Musician RMA	
21 Aug 1899	8 Oct 1899	Ethel Nellie	Maurice & Kate Louisa	De Cort	Gunner RMA	
19 Aug 1899	15 Oct 1899	Leonard John	Leonard James & Emma Louisa	Saunders	Gunner RMA	
4 Oct 1897	26 Oct 1899	Walter Henry	Alfred Stewart & Frances Elizabeth	Dutton	Corporal RMA	
5 Oct 1899	26 Oct 1899	Stewart Harold	Alfred Stewart & Frances Elizabeth	Dutton	Corporal RMA	
30 Sep 1899	27 Oct 1899	Winifred Caroline	Thomas Edward & Caroline Fanny	Richards	Sergeant Instructor RMA	
30 Sep 1899	31 Oct 1899	Henry William	Henry & Alice Jane	Nash	Gunner RMA	
9 Oct 1899	12 Nov 1899	Walford Charles	Walford & Agnes Bertha	Howell	Sergeant RMA	
14 Oct 1899	12 Nov 1899	Kathleen Frances	Thomas Peter & Jessie	Hanlon	Sergeant RMA	
4 Nov 1899	17 Nov 1899	Elsie May	William & Margaret	Williams	Acting Bombardier RMA	
3 Oct 1899	19 Nov 1899	John Maurice Ross	John James & Mildred	Mathews	Grocer East Meon	
7 Oct 1899	19 Nov 1899	Alan Ernest	Albert & Rebecca	Baker	Sergeant Major RMA	
	1899	Cecil	blank	Lavender	Blank	113
2 Nov 1899	3 Dec 1899	Arthur Frederick	Charles & Margaret	Roberts	Sergeant RMA	
5 Nov 1899	3 Dec 1899	Mortimer Guy	Percy Mortimer & Kathleen Mary	Gross	Gunner RMA	
14 Nov 1899	10 Dec 1899	Edith Mary	John & Mary	Brackstone	Gunner RMA	
	29 Dec 1899	Ellen	blank	Ruff	Blank	114
1 Dec 1899	7 Jan 1900	Norah Ethel	Robert & Sarah Jane	Speight	Colour Sergeant RMA	
23 Dec 1899	12 Jan 1900	Arthur Richard	William & Georgina Harriet	Moseley	Gunner RMA	
21 Dec 1899	25 Jan 1900	Ellen	Thomas & Margaret	Parkins	Bombardier RMA	
24 Dec 1899	28 Jan 1900	Arthur Noel	Arthur & Evangeline	Spencer	Musician RMA	
5 Dec 1899	19 Jan 1900	Beatrice Emily	William Charles & Emily	Wall	Sergeant RMA	103
28 Dec 1899	2 Feb 1900	Ellen Olive	Thomas & Ellen	Seddon	Gunner RA Fort Cumberland	
13 Jan 1900	2 Feb 1900	Edward William	Edward William & Caroline Ann	Prior	Quarter Master Sergeant RMA	
5 Jan 1900	4 Feb 1900	Charles Henry	Henry & Caroline	Collett	Corporal RMA	
1 Jan 1900	22 Feb 1900	James John	Christopher & Clara	Weatherley	Colour Sergeant RMA	
6 Jan 1900	22 Feb 1900	Edith Ada	Harry & Ellen	Howard	Pensioner RMA	
3 Nov 1899	25 Feb 1900	Charles Francis Alexander	Charles Henry & Mary Martha	Dickerson	Bombardier RMA	115
31 Jan 1900	25 Feb 1900	Edward George	Edward & Arabella	Mayne	Lance Corporal 2 Batt Devon Regt	
26 Jan 1900	25 Feb 1900	Bertha Grace	George Thomas & Frances Laura	Manly	Sergeant RMA	
3 Feb 1900	4 Mar 1900	Queenie Olive	Thomas Henry & Sarah Ann	Jones	Gunner RMA	
7-Feb 1900	18 Mar 1900	Oliver William	William & Mary	Hutchings	Corporal RMA	
29 Dec 1899	21 Mar 1900	William John	Wallis & Emily	Kennington	Gunner RMA	
11 Dec 1884	28 Mar 1900	Frederick George (Drummer)	John Henry & Mary Ann	Chapman	Gunner Pensioner RMA	17
25 Aug 1884	28 Mar 1900	James (Drummer)	James & Elizabeth	Dix	Colour Sergeant Pensioner RMA	17
	1 Apr 1900	Ruth Violet	blank	Joyce	Gunner RMA	109
22 Dec 1899	1 Apr 1900	Roderick Duncan	Thomas & Alice Beatrice	Layzell	Gunner RMA	

16 Feb 1900	1 Apr 1900	Stuart	Frederick & Martha Catherine	Goyns	Trumpeter RHA	
22 Feb 1900	1 Apr 1900	Walter Redvers	Walter & Harriet	Chatfield	Bombardier RMA	
26 Feb 1900	1 Apr 1900	Ida Gwendoline	Robert & Louisa	Williamson	Gunner RMA	
20 Jan 1900	8 Apr 1900	Euphemia Jessie	Walter George & Elizabeth	Beautyman	Sergeant RMA	
13 Mar 1900	11 Apr 1900	Jeannette Winifred Elsie	George & Annie	Thorne	Bombardier RMA	
10 Jan 1900	22 Apr 1900	Emma Cordelia Elizabeth	Arthur William & Emma Harriet Marian	Baysting	Corporal RMA	
18 Jan 1900	27 Apr 1900	John William	John & Mary Jane	Flower	Drum Major RMA	
23 Dec 1900	29 Apr 1900	Dorothy Annie	Louis & Elizabeth Annie	Milner	Acting Bombardier RMA	116
25 Feb 1900	29 Apr 1900	Frank Olive	Albert & Annie	Day	Sergeant RMA	
21 Feb 1900	6 May 1900	Millicent Mary	Edward Charles Grills & Charlotte Agnes	Brock	Sergeant RMA	
19 Apr 1900	6 May 1900	Fanny May	Frederick & Fanny Maria	Jenvey	Colour Sergeant RMA	
29 Nov 1900	6 May 1900	Ethel	John & Maria	Ellingham	Sergeant RMA	116
6 Mar 1900	6 May 1900	Kathleen Blanche	Arthur Henry & Edith	Wallis	Gunner RMA	
20 Apr 1900	13 May 1900	Josephine Wynbery	Joseph & Isabella	Craig	Private, Army Medical Corps	
29 Apr 1900	20 May 1900	Henry James	Joseph & Louisa	Bates	Gunner RMA	
4 May 1900	27 May 1900	John Alfred	John & Clara Elizabeth	Pitcher	Gunner RMA	
14 Mar 1900	3 Jun 1900	Linda Ruth	George Henry & Linda	Care	Bombardier RMA	
16 Mar 1900	3 Jun 1900	George Alfred Charles	George Henry & Edith Gertrude	Pickering	Bombardier RMA	
29 Mar 1900	3 Jun 1900	Gladys Elaine	Henry & Elizabeth Jane	Preston	Sergeant RMA	
2 Apr 1900	3 Jun 1900	Wilfred Walter	Isaac Albert & Sarah Anne	Wheaton	Sergeant RMA	
22 Mar 1900	8 Jun 1900	Clarence Leslie	Charles & Emily	Dadd	Sergeant RMA	
3 May 1900	17 Jun 1900	Arthur Stanley	George Edward & Alice Ellen	Turner	Sergeant RMA	
19 May 1900	17 Jun 1900	Ethel Mary	John & Ethel	Crockett	Musician RMA	
1 Jun 1900	24 Jun 1900	Edward Francis	Alfred Francis & Ada	Carne	Railway Policeman Late RA	
19 Mar 1900	1 Jul 1900	Albert Edward	Albert Edward & Jane Bessford	Cartwright	Labourer formerly Bombardier RMA	
6 Jun 1900	1 Jul 1900	Ivy Isabel	Charles & Ellen	Atkinson	Gunner RMA	
5 Apr 1900	1 Jul 1900	Elsie Amy	Joseph & Emma	Lindsay	Corporal RMA	
23 May 1900	1 Jul 1900	May Florence	Charles & Elizabeth	Pitt	Colour Sergeant RMA	
20 Jun 1900	15 Jul 1900	Winifred May	Harry Llewellyn & Lavinia	Freeman	Commissioned Boatman RN	
4 Jul 1900	20 Jul 1900	Edith Gertrude	Alfred & Jane Ada	Warwick	Gunner RMA	
12 Jun 1900	22 Jul 1900	Frederick Charles	Thomas & Nina Maud	Holding	Band Sergeant RMA	
2 Jul 1900	22 Jul 1900	Flora Ada Emma	Joseph Samuel & Ada Emily	Stanton	Sergeant RMA	
15 Jul 1900	3 Aug 1900	Charles Herbert	Henry (deceased) & Annie	Hay	Gunner RMA	
9 Jul 1900	4 Aug 1900	Stephen Leslie	Benjamin & Caroline	Green	Band Master RMA	109
16 Jul 1900	12 Aug 1900	Victor Charles Anthony	William Anthony & Bessie	Harper	Sergeant RMA	
17 Jul 1900	12 Aug 1900	Robert Musgrove	Robert Augustus & Edith Mary	Trowbridge	Colour Sergeant RMA	
18 Jul 1900	12 Aug 1900	Terence Stephen Ludlow	Thomas & Emily Margaret	Tunnicliff	Sergeant RMA	
9 Dec 1899	26 Aug 1900	Victor Alfred	Alfred Herbert & Eleanor Maud	Pearson	Musician RMA	109

21 Jun 1900	2 Sep 1900	Edith Emily	Tom & Emily	**England**	Corporal RMA	
18 Jul 1900	2 Sep 1900	Gordon Horace	Horace & Clara Anna	**Cullimore**	Sergeant RMA	
18 Nov 1899	3 Sep 1900	Blanche Olive	John Joseph & Beatrice	**Jeram**	ERA RN	109
11 Aug 1900	9 Sep 1900	Richard	Robert & Amelia	**Duncan**	Gunner RMA	
11 Jul 1900	11 Sep 1900	John William	George & Helena	**Bedford**	Gunner RMA	109
30 Jun 1900	16 Sep 1900	Florence Edna Gladys	John & Bessie	**Bragg**	Gunner RMA	
28 Aug 1900	16 Sep 1900	Edith Louisa Whomes	Albert Job & Louisa	**Chatfield**	Sergeant RMA	
20 May 1900	23 Sep 1900	Harry	Harry Amos & Annie	**Lawrence**	Acting Bombardier RMA	
16 Aug 1900	23 Sep 1900	Robert George	Robert & Emma Eliza	**Spencer**	Corporal RMA	
22 Mar 1900	30 Sep 1900	Clarence Leslie	John & Ada	**Bradley**	Butcher (Nottingham)	
3 Oct 1900	5 Oct 1900	John	John Walter & Helen	**Field**	Gunner RMA	109
14 Sep 1900	7 Oct 1900	Matilda Jane	John & Matilda	**Rolt**	Gunner RMA	
24 May 1900	14 Oct 1900	Lionel Roberts	Charles & Rosanna Eliza	**Bent**	Acting Bombardier RMA	
6 Jul 1900	14 Oct 1900	Dorothy Elizabeth Rickaby	William James & Elizabeth Rickaby	**Coen**	Sergeant RMA	
26 Jul 1900	14 Oct 1900	Dorothy Fanny	James & Fanny	**Atkins**	Corporal RMA	
25 Aug 1900	14 Oct 1900	Alfred Ernest Edmund Archibald	Alfred William & Elizabeth	**Chinn**	Painter	
9 Sep 1900	14 Oct 1900	Beatrice May	Francis William & Mabel	**Baker**	Gunner RMA	
24 Sep 1900	19 Oct 1900	Frederick Francis Thomas	Frank & Emily	**Chell**	Sergeant RMA	
26 Dec 1888	25 Oct 1900	Percy	William & Louisa	**Hopkins**	Stonemason	17
16 Sep 1900	26 Oct 1900	Dora Lucy	Benjamin & Harriet	**Stockley**	Pensioner RMA	
6 Nov 1894	28 Oct 1900	Herbert Victor	Frederick Adolphus Rosenheim & Harriet	**Roper**	Pensioner RN	
14 Apr 1897	28 Oct 1900	Diamond Jubilee May	Frederick Adolphus Rosenheim & Harriet	**Roper**	Pensioner RN	
28 Aug 1900	28 Oct 1900	Florence Fanny	Robert Shrimpton & Florence Louise	**Baxter**	Corporal RMA	
23 Oct 1900	11 Nov 1900	Dorothy Maud	Richard & Clara Maud	**Parker**	Gunner RMA	
25 Oct 1900	25 Nov 1900	Madeleine Maud	Thomas & Mary Ann	**Jefferies**	Bombardier RMA	
28 Oct 1900	25 Nov 1900	Rhoda	Thomas & Mary	**Hayes**	Gunner RMA	
13 Oct 1900	29 Nov 1900	James George William	John & Sarah	**Reoch**	Gunner RMA	
May 1898	29 Nov 1900	Nellie Beatrice Myrtle	Harry Herbert & Ellen	**Bury**	Gunner RMA	117
30 Oct 1900	2 Dec 1900	Florence Charlotte Edith	Sydney Richard & Edith	**Stephens**	Sergeant RMA	
13 Nov 1900	2 Dec 1900	Ellen Margaret Kathleen	Frederick Joshua & Helen	**Roe**	Petty Officer 1st Class RN	
20 Sep 1900	7 Dec 1900	Gilbert Geoffrey	Albert Edward & Alice Louisa	**Griffin**	Sergeant RMA	
6 Nov 1900	14 Dec 1900	Christopher Herbert	William & Sarah	**Rogerson**	Sergeant RMA	
5 Dec 1900	23 Dec 1900	George Samuel	Albert & Amelia	**Burridge**	Private RMLI	
22 Sep 1900	20 Jan 1901	John Roberts	William Henry & Lizzie	**Walker**	Sergeant RMA	
25 Dec 1900	20 Jan 1901	Dorothea Emily	John & Jane	**Roberts**	Sergeant RMA	
21 Dec 1900	20 Jan 1901	Sybil Tabitha	James & Mary Ann	**Jeffery**	Sergeant RMA	
8 Jan 1901	27 Jan 1901	Percival Henry	Charles Ernest & Elizabeth Ellen	**Jory**	Commissioned Boatman Coast Guard	
17 Nov 1900	3 Feb 1901	Hilda Annie	Frederick George & Sarah Anne	**Goater**	Corporal RMA	

	10 Feb 1901	Mary	blank	Joyce	Gunner RMA	109
28 Jan 1901	17 Feb 1901	Ernest Victor	Edwin George Thomas & Kathleen	Tims	Sergeant RMA	
21 Jan 1901	24 Feb 1901	May Victoria	William & Florence Ellen Mary	Gasson	Sergeant RMA	
19 Jan 1901	24 Feb 1901	William Edward James	William Charles & Emily	Wall	Sergeant RMA	
29 Jan 1901	24 Feb 1901	Henry William Cecil	Henry William & Laura	Lodder	Corporal RMA	
30 Jun 1864	28 Feb 1901	Margaret	Thomas & Jane	Muirhead	Civilian (Mason)	
1 Sep 1900	3 Mar 1901	Maud Jane	Arthur Albert & Maud Caroline	Mastin	Colour Sergeant RMA	
4 Mar 1889	3 Mar 1901	Ada Jessie	Edgar Stibbard & Mary Ann	Lines	Wheelwright	
5 Apr 1864	7 Mar 1901	Emily Keziah	Thomas & Emily	Davies	Shipright Portsmouth Dockyard	118
29 Jan 1901	10 Mar 1901	Ethel Lilian	John & Lucy Mary	Gilliam	Armourer Sergeant RMA	
17 Jan 1901	17 Mar 1901	Kenneth Edward	Albert & Sarah Jane	Gibson	Colour Sergeant RMA	
7 Feb 1901	17 Mar 1901	Harold Stuart Patrick	Albert Edward & Elizabeth Ann	Stevens	Corporal RMA	
15 Apr 1868	28 Mar 1901	Alfred	Alfred & Mary Elizabeth	Carter	Butcher	119
20 Dec 1900	14 Apr 1901	Bessie	Charles Frederick George & Emily	Salmon	Sergeant RMA	
21 Feb 1901	14 Apr 1901	Charles Arthur Claud	Charles Arthur & Naomi Ruth Louisa Jane	Jones	Corporal RMA	
12 Feb 1901	14 Apr 1901	William Alfred Frederick	Walter William & Alice Annie	Golding	Corporal RMA	
3 Apr 1901	17 Apr 1901	Eva May	William & Ada Sarah	Boughtflower	Sergeant RMA	109
22 Mar 1901	21 Apr 1901	Norah Eileen Jessie	Thomas Peter & Jessie	Hanlon	Sergeant RMA	
23 Apr 1901	9 May 1901	Walter Harry	Richard & Minnie James	Newman	Bombardier RMA	
16 Mar 1901	19 May 1901	Frank	George & Ellen	Langley	Sergeant RMA	
29 Apr 1901	19 May 1901	Winifred Ada	Percy Mortimer & Kathleen Mary	Gross	Gunner RMA	
4 May 1901	21 May 1901	Alice Caroline	Henry & Alice Jane	Nash	Gunner RMA	
3 May 1901	24 May 1901	Elsie May	William & Susan Jane	Ayling	Corporal RMA	
25 Mar 1901	24 May 1901	Hollis	Edwin & Maria	Stevens	Gunner RMA	
13 Mar 1901	31 May 1901	Beatrice Rosina May	Arthur Edwin Charles & Ellen Elizabeth	Gosling	Gunner RMA	
19 May 1901	9 Jun 1901	Violet Gladys	Robert & Mary Ann	Butfield	Colour Sergeant RMA	
23 May 1901	9 Jun 1901	Dorothy Hilda	Alfred Henry & Ada Jane	Walker	Musician RMA	
26 Feb 1901	16 Jun 1901	Eva May	Ernest & Rose	Perring	Sergeant RMA	
16 Mar 1901	16 Jun 1901	Ivy Alice	John & Alice	Wilmer	Gunner RMA	
27 May 1901	23 Jun 1901	Walter Edward	George Thomas & Jane	Merrick	Sergeant RMA	
23 Apr 1901	30 Jun 1901	Elsie Isabel	John William & Fanny	Flynn	Corporal RMA	
3 Jun 1901	7 Jul 1901	Crispin	Walter & Emma	Whiting	Sergeant RMA	
1 Jun 1900	9 Jul 1901	Ida Florence	William & Florence Charlotte Emily	Fraser	Sergeant RMA	
31 May 1901	14 Jul 1901	Arthur Charles Drowley	Arthur Stephen & Rose Caroline	Edwards	Corporal RMA	
2 Jul 1901	21 Jul 1901	Richard James	Richard Daniel & Annie Maud	Juffs	Sergeant RMA	
29 May 1870	26 Jul 1901	Richard Daniel	James & Louisa	Juffs	Horse Foreman	17
26 Jun 1901	28 Jul 1901	Barbara Elizabeth	Louis & Elizabeth Annie	Milner	Acting Bombardier RMA	

27 Jun 1901	3 Aug 1901	Lilias Frances Effreta	William & Frances Maria	**Campbell**	Colonel RMA	
24 Jun 1901	11 Aug 1901	Norrie Sidney	Joseph & Rosina	**Ethridge**	Corporal RMA	
4 Jul 1901	11 Aug 1901	Charles Henry	George Henry & Edith Gertrude	**Pickering**	Corporal RMA	
6 Jul 1901	18 Aug 1901	William Henry	William & Annie	**Priddy**	Lance Sergeant RMA	
1 Aug 1901	25 Aug 1901	Julia May Kathleen	Thomas & Harriet	**Hoare**	Acting Bombardier RMA	
28 May 1901	1 Sep 1901	John Granville	John & Alice	**Kershaw**	Gunner RMA	
19 Aug 1901	8 Sep 1901	Dorothea	Albert Job & Louisa	**Chatfield**	Sergeant RMA	
15 Aug 1901	8 Sep 1901	Edith Dorothea	Frederick John & Hannah	**Wright**	Bombardier RMA	
31 Aug 1901	15 Sep 1901	Gwladys Mary	Walter & Helen Maud	**Dibble**	Gunner RMA	
28 Aug 1901	20 Sep 1901	Elsie Eliza	Henry & Mary Elizabeth	**Pocock**	Gunner RMA	
2 Sep 1901	22 Sep 1901	Archibald Isaac	Archibald & Ada Louisa	**Goodwin**	Gunner RMA	
8 Sep 1901	22 Sep 1901	Susie Alice	John & Susan Ann	**Collier**	Bombardier RMA	
24 Jul 1901	6 Oct 1901	Frederick Arthur Leslie	William Thomas & Mary Ann	**Weston**	Colour Sergeant RMA	
4 Jul 1901	6 Oct 1901	Thomas	Thomas & Charlotte	**Cathie**	Corporal RMA	
6 Sep 1901	6 Oct 1901	James William John	James Henry & Agnes Lucy	**Millis**	Bombardier RMA	
8 Sep 1901	6 Oct 1901	William Basil	William Benjamin & Ada	**Cooper**	Gunner RMA	
4 Oct 1901	19 Oct 1901	Herbert George	Frank & Annie	**Hendley**	Gunner RMA	109
18 Sep 1901	27 Oct 1901	Ruby Gertrude	David & Amelia Elizabeth	**Butler**	Gunner RMA	
17 Jul 1901	27 Oct 1901	Daisy Munday	William & Jane Mary	**Tate**	Gentleman	
11 Sep 1901	27 Oct 1901	Robert George	Ernest & Mary Elizabeth	**Spink**	Quarter Master Sergeant RMA	
21 Sep 1901	27 Oct 1901	Violet Maud	Joseph & Louisa	**Tallent**	Gunner RMA	
11 Jan 1897	27 Oct 1901	Frederick George Lionel	James Alfred & Blanche Rose	**Simpson**	Late Bugle Major RMA	
29 Sep 1901	27 Oct 1901	Dorothy	Charles & Lily	**Clarke**	Colour Sergeant RMA	
29 Sep 1901	27 Oct 1901	Lettia	Charles & Lily	**Clarke**	Colour Sergeant RMA	
8 Oct 1901	3 Nov 1901	Reginald Charles	Richard Charles & Annie Beatrice	**Leonard**	Gunner RMA	
30 Sep 1901	3 Nov 1901	Charles Arthur	Roland Stephen & Emily	**Pottinger**	Lance Sergeant RMA	
17 May 1901	3 Nov 1901	Robert Stewart	William Griffiths & Winifred Maud	**Partridge**	Gunner RMA	
23 Dec 1892	3 Nov 1901	Eva Lily	Michael & Eva Emily	**Martin**	Gunner RA	
	8 Nov 1901	Arthur	blank	**Porter**	Gunner RMA	109
30 Oct 1901	17 Nov 1901	Herbert Macdonald	Albert George & Mary Ann	**Pain**	Sergeant RMA	
27 Oct 1901	17 Nov 1901	William James	William James & Elizabeth Rickaby	**Coen**	Sergeant RMA	
4 Oct 1901	24 Nov 1901	Frederick Alan	Frank & Annie	**Symons**	Gunner RMA	
6 Jul 1901	24 Nov 1901	Flora Ethel	Frederick & Amelia	**Gold**	Ships Corporal RN	
15 Oct 1901	1 Dec 1901	Louisa Elizabeth	Ernest Albert & Louisa	**Kelsey**	Sergeant RMA	
10 Oct 1901	1 Dec 1901	Richard William	Richard William & Annie Elizabeth	**Harriman**	Acting Bombardier RMA	
22 Nov 1901	15 Dec 1901	Lilian Annie	Henry & Caroline	**Collett**	Corporal RMA	
24 Nov 1901	15 Dec 1901	Albert Edward	Harry & Annie	**Lawrence**	Acting Bombardier RMA	
8 Nov 1901	15 Dec 1901	Arthur	John & Mary Jane	**Brackstole**	Gunner RMA	
15 Sep 1901	15 Dec 1901	Edwin Walter Samuel	Edwin Holloway & Edith Emily	**Roost**	Lance Sergeant RMA	
28 Oct 1901	15 Dec 1901	Eileen Mildred	Alfred Charles & Angelina Elizabeth	**Barnes**	Musician RMA	

1 Nov 1901	22 Dec 1901	Dorothy Gladys Ophir	William John & Eliza	Sills	Gunner RMA	
28 Nov 1901	22 Dec 1901	Sidney James	William & Margaret	Williams	Acting Bombardier RMA	
9 Dec 1901	5 Jan 1902	Frederick Charles	George & Alice	Bullock	Provost Sergeant RMA	
1 Jan 1902	26 Jan 1902	George	George & Rosina Mary	Perkins	Gunner RMA	
9 Dec 1901	9 Feb 1902	Cyril Edgar	Thomas & Rosina Ada	Hall	Acting Bombardier RMA	
25 Dec 1901	9 Feb 1902	Daisy Amy Christine	Frederick Evan & Daisy Amy Charlotte	Saddon	Colour Sergeant RMA	
11 Jan 1902	2 Mar 1902	Lilian Emma	John Albert Edward & Mary Ann	Norris	Bombardier RMA	
12 Feb 1902	2 Mar 1902	Martha Grace Maud	Herbert Walter & Frances Mary Ann	Thompson	Gunner RMA	
8 Dec 1901	21 Mar 1902	Albert Edward	Richard & Maud	Parker	Gunner RMA	
17 Feb 1902	22 Mar 1902	Edith Daphne	Edward & Edith Constance	McCarthy	Captain RMA	
10 Mar 1902	6 Apr 1902	Cecil Bryan	George William West & Alice Caroline	Gibbons	Sergeant RMA	
4 Mar 1902	6 Apr 1902	Edward Harold	Charles Arthur & Naomi Ruth Louisa Jane	Jones	Corporal RMA	
4 Mar 1902	11 Apr 1902	Lelsie Thomas Ludlow	Thomas & Emily Margaret	Tunnicliff	Sergeant RMA	
24 Jan 1902	13 Apr 1902	Ewart Percy	Thomas & Alice	Layzell	Gunner RMA	
24 Mar 1902	29 Apr 1902	Winifred Beatrice	Alfred & Beatrice	Goad	Gunner RMA	
29 Jan 1902	4 Feb 1902	Annie Joan	George & Elizabeth Anna	Wilgaus	Gunner RMA	120
8 Mar 1902	16 May 1902	George Leslie	George Stacey & Ellen	Barton	Corporal RMA	
9 Mar 1902	16 May 1902	James Leslie	James & Fanny	Atkins	Corporal RMA	
5 May 1902	25 May 1902	Arthur Ernest	Ernest & Ellen	Saunders	Colour Sergeant RMA	
1 Apr 1902	1 Jun 1902	James Sydney	Jonathan & Jane	Heaton	Corporal RMA	
30 Apr 1902	8 Jun 1902	Dora	Robert Ward & Harriet Elizabeth	Emmerson	Barrack Sergeant RMA	
18 May 1902	22 Jun 1902	George Arthur	William Arthur & Amy Rosina	Hill	Gunner RMA	
2 May 1902	29 Jun 1902	McKenzie Turpie	George & Elizabeth	Beautyman	Sergeant RMA	
21 Jun 1902	13 Jul 1902	Albert Edward Arthur	Joseph Arthur & Agnes Amelia	Wainwright	Gunner RMA	
25 Jun 1902	13 Jul 1902	Dorothy Helena	Thomas & Mary	Hayes	Gunner RMA	
4 Jul 1902	20 Jul 1902	Doris Frances	Albert Edward & Elizabeth Ann	Stevens	Lance Sergeant RMA	
15 Jul 1902	3 Aug 1902	William Frederick	William Richard & Lizzie Amelia	Lavender	Acting Bombardier RMA	
28 Apr 1902	17 Aug 1902	Lelsie Robert	Robert Gray & Amy Evelyn	Boyd	Colour Sergeant RMA	
5 May 1899	24 Aug 1902	Ethel May	Moses & Jane	Crompton	Orderly Netley Hospital (Civilian)	
3 Aug 1902	24 Aug 1902	Alexander Joseph	Moses & Jane	Crompton	Orderly Netley Hospital (Civilian)	
4 May 1902	24 Aug 1902	Elizabeth Florence	John & Ethel	Crockett	Musician RMA	
5 Jul 1902	7 Sep 1902	Gladys Jane	George & Charlotte	Simms	Gunner RMA	
14 Aug 1902	7 Sep 1902	Nellie Rose	James & Rose	Cake	Acting Bombardier RMA	
23 Jul 1902	7 Sep 1902	Alfred George	Alfred Henry & Ida Jane	Walker	Musician RMA	
28 Dec 1901	9 Sep 1902	Sybil May	Robert Herring & Rhoda Margaret	Cattell	Colour Sergeant RMA	
25 Aug 1902	14 Sep 1902	Jessie	William George & Alice	Arnold	Gunner RMA	

24 Dec 1901	16 Sep 1902	Kathleen Winifred	Henry Herbert & Ellen	**Bury**	Gunner RMA	
1 Sep 1902	17 Sep 1902	Leonard	Edward William & Caroline	**Prior**	Quarter Master Sergeant RMA	121
12 Sep 1902	28 Sep 1902	Emily Jane	Henry & Nellie	**Smith**	Lance Sergeant RMA	
17 Sep 1902	12 Oct 1902	Harry	Henry & Elizabeth	**Stevens**	Sergeant RMA	
23 Sep 1902	12 Oct 1902	Frederick James	Frederick & Fanny Maria	**Jenvey**	Quarter Master Sergeant RMA	
4 Sep 1902	12 Oct 1902	John	John & Mary Jane	**Frain**	Gunner RMA	
1 Oct 1902	19 Oct 1902	John	Sidney Guy & Louisa Caroline	**Dacombe**	Sergeant RMA	
16 Sep 1902	19 Oct 1902	Winifred Emilie	Samuel Longley & Emilie	**Spittles**	Sergeant RMA	
15 Oct 1902	2 Nov 1902	Frederick Horace	Edwin George Thomas & Kathleen	**Tims**	Colour Sergeant RMA	
11 Oct 1902	2 Nov 1902	Annie	William & Annie	**Priddy**	Lance Sergeant RMA	
16 Oct 1902	9 Nov 1902	Arthur John Douglas	William Henry & Eleanor Mary	**Feltham**	Corporal RMA	
14 Dec 1900	9 Nov 1902	Doris Leonie	Frederick Victor & Florence	**Rowe**	Civilian	
11 Oct 1902	23 Nov 1902	Frederick James	Robert & Alice	**Travers**	Gunner RMA	
18 Nov 1902	7 Dec 1902	Lilian May	Joseph & Louisa	**Baits**	Gunner RMA	
9 Nov 1902	18 Dec 1902	Dorothy Wood	John Leonard & Edith Frances	**Homer**	Captain RMA	
27 Nov 1902	4 Jan 1903	Lily Esmeralda	Edward & Arabella	**Mayne**	Lance Corporal Devonshire Regiment	
13 Dec 1902	4 Jan 1903	Alfred John	Robert Amos & Emily Margaret	**Hill**	Boatman Coast Guard	
13 Nov 1902	4 Jan 1903	Mark William	Frederick John & Georgina Grace	**Chivers**	Sergeant RMA	
6 Sep 1902	4 Jan 1903	Margery Edith	Frank & Edith	**Brewer**	Colour Sergeant RMA	
15 Oct 1902	4 Jan 1903	Emily Mayhew	Albert Edward & Jane Bessford	**Cartwright**	Invalid RMA	
21 Oct 1902	4 Jan 1903	Edgar Ernest	Isaac Albert & Sarah Ann	**Wheaton**	Sergeant RMA	
21 Dec 1902	11 Jan 1903	Constance Louise	Thomas Edward & Margaret Mary	**Stevens**	Sergeant RMA	
29 Nov 1902	18 Jan 1903	Percy Douglas	Albert & Sarah Jane	**Gibson**	Superintending Clerk RMA	
17 Dec 1902	18 Jan 1903	Una Emma	George & Eliza	**Boyce**	Sergeant RMA	
8 Nov 1902	1 Feb 1903	Royal	William Edward & Eliza Ann	**King**	Colour Sergeant RMA	
1 Nov 1902	1 Feb 1903	Mabel Beatrice	Frederick Richard & Amelia Ann	**Gold**	Ships Corporal RN	
26 Nov 1902	1 Feb 1903	William	Charles & Elizabeth	**Pitt**	Colour Sergeant RMA	
18 Dec 1902	8 Feb 1903	Sydney Norman	Henry William & Laura	**Lodder**	Corporal RMA	
25 Jan 1903	8 Feb 1903	Joseph Frederick	William & Margaret	**Williams**	Pensioner RMA	
4 Jan 1903	1 Mar 1903	Henry John	Henry & Mary	**Camp**	Corporal RMA	
15 Nov 1902	1 Mar 1903	William James Ernest	Alfred Arthur & Charlotte Adelaide	**Cole**	Gunner RMA	
22 Dec 1902	1 Mar 1903	Albert Edward	Francis William & Mabel	**Baker**	Gunner RMA Fleet Reserve	
7 Feb 1903	1 Mar 1903	Thomas Frederick	Thomas & Mary Ann	**Jefferies**	Gunner RMA	
29 Dec 1902	1 Mar 1903	Enid Price	Arthur Price & Constance Julia	**Hill**	Chaplain RN	122
16 Jan 1903	5 Apr 1903	Owen William	James & Mary Ann	**Jeffery**	Sergeant RMA	

30 Jan 1903	5 Apr 1903	Mabel Mary Hannah	William Charles & Emily	Wall	Sergeant RMA	
31 Jan 1903	5 Apr 1903	Beryl Eileen	Charles & Emily	Dadd	Sergeant RMA	
13 Feb 1903	5 Apr 1903	Joseph Drury	Joseph & Louisa	Tallent	Gunner RMA	
18 Feb 1903	5 Apr 1903	Ivy Edith	Thomas & Harriet	Hoare	Acting Bombardier RMA	
5 Feb 1903	5 Apr 1903	Rose Gertrude	Arthur Edward & Gertrude	Stevens	Gunner RMA	
23 Feb 1903	19 Apr 1903	Basil Lynch	Harry Lynch & Daisie Ellida	Talbot	Major RMA	
10 Mar 1903	3 May 1903	Lilian Alexandra	Louis & Elizabeth Annie	Milner	Bombardier RMA	
17 Apr 1903	10 May 1903	Albert Edward	Ernest & Ellen	Young	Acting Bombardier RMA	
31 Mar 1903	10 May 1903	Lilian Mabel	Herbert Walter & Frances Marion	Thompson	Petty Officer 2nd Class RN	
21 Feb 1903	10 May 1903	Ernest Albert	Ernest & Mary Elizabeth	Spink	Quarter Master Sergeant RMA	
23 Apr 1903	10 May 1903	Dorothy Caroline Martha	William & Miriam	Garwood	Bombardier RMA	
1 Apr 1903	10 May 1903	Reginald	Ernest & Mabel	Child	Sergeant RMA	
4 Apr 1903	10 May 1903	Hilda Louisa	Messenger & Ada	Thorp	Sergeant RMA	
20 Mar 1903	7 Jun 1903	Edith	David Edward & Louisa	Wooton	Gunner RMA	
30 Apr 1903	7 Jun 1903	Percy Charles	George (DD) & Rosina Mary	Perkins	Late Gunner RMA	123
3 Mar 1903	7 Jun 1903	Alfred Ernest	Stephen James & Caroline	Bourner	Gunner RMA	
2 Feb 1903	7 Jun 1903	Nellie Alma	James Charles & Lily Alma	Carter	Gunner RMA	
22 May 1903	23 May 1903	Cornelia Dood Rose	William Thomas & Annie	Joyce	Gunner RMA	124
22 May 1903	23 May 1903	Sarah	William Thomas & Annie	Joyce	Gunner RMA	124
30 May 1903	5 Jul 1903	Dorothy May	Francis William & Rose	Alexander	Sergeant RMA	
18 Jun 1903	5 Jul 1903	James Andrew	James & Alice	Hill	Gunner RMA	
20 Mar 1903	5 Jul 1903	William Leslie	Richard & Maud	Parker	Gunner RMA	
27 Jul 1903	27 Jul 1903	Percy	Leonard James & Emma Louisa	Saunders	Gunner RMA	109
3 Jul 1903	30 Jul 1903	Joan Emma	Humphrey & Emma	Oldfield	Captain RMA	
15 Jul 1903	2 Aug 1903	Lexie Marjorie	Henry & Alexandria	Bishop	Lance Sergeant RMA	
13 Apr 1903	2 Aug 1903	William John	William Charles & Beatrice	Frampton	Gunner RMA	
29 May 1903	2 Aug 1903	Lena Emily	Roland Stephen & Emily	Pottinger	Lance Sergeant RMA	
4 Jul 1903	8 Aug 1903	Doris Kitty	Thomas Arthur & Kate	Baldwin	Corporal RMA	109
3 May 1903	26 Aug 1903	Thomas Richard	Thomas Richard & Lily Maud	Bray	Gunner RMA	109
2 Aug 1903	6 Sep 1903	Gwendoline Emma	Samuel & Annie	Jelley	Gunner RMA	
2 Jun 1903	4 Oct 1903	Gladys Frances Gertrude	Sydney Richard & Edith	Stephens	Lance Sergeant RMA	
13 Sep 1903	4 Oct 1903	Richard	Richard & Minnie James	Newman	Acting Bombardier RMA	
15 Jul 1903	4 Oct 1903	Gertrude Elizabeth	James Peter & Annie Elizabeth	Edwards	Gunner RMA	
24 Aug 1903	4 Oct 1903	Minnicent Beatrix	Richard Charles & Annie Beatrice	Leonard	Gunner RMA	
21 Sep 1902	4 Oct 1903	Florence	William & Edith	Smith-Morgan	Policeman	125
20 Sep 1903	17 Oct 1903	Olive Maud	Charles & Mary	Houghton	Sergeant RMA	109
11 Oct 1903	1 Nov 1903	Reginald George Blyton	George Thomas & Catherine Mary	Tristram	Musician RMA	109
9 Aug 1903	1 Nov 1903	Ernest Walter George	Ernest Walter George & Mary	Stone	Corporal RMA	
8 Sep 1903	1 Nov 1903	Ernest William	Ernest William & Rose	Perring	Colour Sergeant RMA	
10 Mar 1901	1 Nov 1903	Lucy Alice	Alexander & Lucy	Buick	Corporal RMA	

27 Sep 1903	1 Nov 1903	Ernest George	Frank Felix & Alice Lily	**Crowe**	Gunner RMA	
6 Oct 1903	1 Nov 1903	George Charles	Alfred Charles & Sophia Mary	**Burrell**	Lance Sergeant RMA	
1 Oct 1903	1 Nov 1903	Ida Annie	Richard & Annie Elizabeth	**Harriman**	Acting Bombardier RMA	
5 Sep 1903	1 Nov 1903	Eric George	William Benjamin & Ada	**Cooper**	Gunner RMA	
26 Sep 1903	1 Nov 1903	Victoria Constance	William & Bertha	**Wheeler**	Gunner RMA	
14 Aug 1903	1 Nov 1903	Nora Kathleen	Henry Patrick & Emma Jane	**Gardner**	Leading Stoker RN	
	18 Nov 1903	Mary Ann	blank	**Newman**	Blank	126
	18 Nov 1903	Lydia	blank	**Buchanan**	Blank	126
30 Oct 1903	12 Dec 1903	Eleanor May	Robert & Louisa	**Williamson**	Gunner RMA	109
2 Nov 1903	6 Dec 1903	Helen Carrie	William Uriah & Caroline	**Driscoll**	Corporal RMA	
6 Oct 1903	6 Dec 1903	Gilbert Ernest	Caleb & Florence Jeannette	**Warham**	Sergeant RMA	
29 Sep 1903	6 Dec 1903	Frederick George	William James & Elizabeth Rickaby	**Coen**	Sergeant RMA	
4 Nov 1903	6 Dec 1903	Cuthbert John	Cuthbert John & Ethel Rose	**Alexander**	Gunner RMA	
10 Nov 1903	3 Jan 1904	Vincent Augustus	Augustus Wesley & Mary	**Kimber**	Pensioner RMA	
4 Dec 1903	3 Jan 1904	Mildred	Lewis & Emily	**Norris**	Corporal RMA	
1 Dec 1903	3 Jan 1904	Reginald William	George & Alice	**Bullock**	Provost Sergeant RMA	
21 Dec 1903	24 Jan 1904	Doris May	Edward John & Eliza Jane	**Rolls**	Sergeant Major RE	
10 Dec 1903	7 Feb 1904	Thomas Richard	Thomas Richard & Mary Ann	**Wheeler**	Coachman	
18 Feb 1903	7 Feb 1904	Annie Louisa	William & Sarah	**Rogerson**	Sergeant RMA	
17 Dec 1903	7 Feb 1904	Robert Edward Gordon	Charles Henry & Mary	**Dickerson**	Corporal RMA	
5 Nov 1903	7 Feb 1904	Dorothy Ethel	Robert & Emma Eliza	**Spencer**	Corporal RMA	
24 Nov 1903	7 Feb 1904	Maria Mabel	Walter & Emily	**Osgood**	Stoker RN	
28 Dec 1903	7 Feb 1904	Charlotte Catherine	George & Charlotte	**Bone**	Gunner RMA	
10 Jan 1904	21 Feb 1904	Edgar Arthur Richard	Frank George & Alice Lucy	**Chapman**	Licensed Victualler	
8 Feb 1904	21 Feb 1904	George Thomas	William & Margaret	**Williams**	Pensioner RMA	
	9 Mar 1904	Alexander	blank	**Dix**	Blank	17
	9 Mar 1904	Alfred	blank	**Tooley**	Blank	17
	15 Mar 1904	Annie	blank	**Hay**	Blank	17
28 Nov 1903	1 Apr 1904	Roland	Arthur & Nellie	**Height**	Sergeant RMA	109
29 Jan 1904	3 Apr 1904	Ivy	John & Lucy	**Gilliam**	Armourer Sergeant RMA	
15 Mar 1904	3 Apr 1904	Annie Florence	Albert & Annie	**Day**	Sergeant RMA	
24 Mar 1904	10 Apr 1904	Samuel Thomas Murray	Samuel & Elizabeth	**White**	Gunner RMA	
12 Apr 1904	1 May 1904	Helen Lilian	George & Charlotte	**Simms**	Gunner RMA	
6 Apr 1904	1 May 1904	Madeleine	John & Alice	**Wilmer**	Gunner RMA	
22 Sep 1903	1 May 1904	Frederick Joseph	Frederick & Emily	**Salmon**	Sergeant RMA	
5 Apr 1904	22 May 1904	Henry Thomas John	Henry & Florence	**Hugill**	Coast Guard	
4 May 1904	22 May 1904	Arthur William	William Arthur & Martha	**Hunt**	Corporal RMA	
24 Apr 1904	5 Jun 1904	John Turpie Robertson	George & Elizabeth	**Beautyman**	Sergeant RMA	
28 Apr 1904	5 Jun 1904	Ida Cecilia	William & Florence	**Gasson**	Sergeant RMA	
22 Apr 1904	5 Jun 1904	May Caroline	George Thomas & Jane	**Merrick**	Sergeant RMA	
6 Apr 1904	5 Jun 1904	Ronald Leslie	Charles & Agnes Isabel	**Mauser**	Quarter Master Sergeant RE	
29 May 1904	3 Jul 1904	Leonard Charles	Charlie & Gertrude	**Hill**	Gunner RMA	
23 Jun 1904	14 Jul 1904	Edith Mabel	Henry William & Louisa	**Spratt**	Gunner RMA	127
23 Jun 1904	14 Jul 1904	Alfred James	Henry William & Louisa	**Spratt**	Gunner RMA	127

20 Aug 1904	22 Jul 1904	Emily Edith	Edward Wesley & Catherine	Weston	Bombardier RMA	
6 Oct 1904	22 Jul 1904	Edward Pollhill	Edward Wesley & Catherine	Weston	Bombardier RMA	128
25 Jul 1904	7 Aug 1904	Philip	James & Rose	Cake	Acting Bombardier RMA	
15 Jun 1904	7 Aug 1904	William Henry	Herbert John & Flora Annie	Neal	Sergeant RMA	
1 Jul 1904	15 Aug 1904	Richard James Alexander	Richard Vernon Tredinnick & Diana	Ford	Captain & Adjutant RMA	
4 Aug 1904	21 Aug 1904	Ernest	Ernest & Mabel	Child	Sergeant RMA	
28 Jun 1904	21 Aug 1904	Marjory Winifred	George & Elizabeth	Lewis	Sergeant RMA	
25 Jun 1904	4 Sep 1904	John Edward	John & Ethelreda	Crockett	Acting Bombardier RMA	
1 Aug 1902	4 Sep 1904	Francis Robert John	Walter William & Alice Annie	Golding	Corporal RMA	
12 Jun 1904	4 Sep 1904	Florence Norma Edith	Walter William & Alice Annie	Golding	Corporal RMA	
24 Jul 1904	4 Sep 1904	Charles Stanley	George William & Elizabeth	Copeland	Musician RMA	
30 May 1904	4 Sep 1904	Thomas Sidney	Thomas Sidney & Ellen Kathleen	May	Gunner RMA	
7 Aug 1904	2 Oct 1904	Clara Jessie	Richard & Maud	Parker	Gunner RMA	
22 Mar 1904	2 Oct 1904	Sydney Charles	William Richard & Lizzie Amelia	Lavender	Acting Bombardier RMA	
2 Sep 1904	2 Oct 1904	Helen Mary	Thomas & Helen Elizabeth	Clowes	Sergeant RMA	
13 Sep 1904	2 Oct 1904	Edward Charles	Francis Arthur & Sarah	Butt	Gunner RMA	
5 Aug 1904	2 Oct 1904	Florence Elizabeth	John & Clara Elizabeth	Pitchers	Gunner RMA	
20 Jun 1904	9 Oct 1904	Mary Ellen	Frederick George & Sarah Ann	Goater	Lance Sergeant RMA	
1 Aug 1904	9 Oct 1904	Hector Colin	Frank & Jessie Agnes	Ford	Sergeant RMA	
3 Oct 1896	27 Oct 1904	Gladys Louisa	John Frederick & Mary Louisa	Yeoman	Commissioned Boatman	
12 Aug 1898	27 Oct 1904	Edith Rose	John Frederick & Mary Louisa	Yeoman	Commissioned Boatman	
15 Jun 1900	27 Oct 1904	Beatrice Eden	John Frederick & Mary Louisa	Yeoman	Commissioned Boatman	
18 Aug 1904	6 Nov 1904	Stanley Harwin	Henry & Florence Rose	Davis	Lance Sergeant RMA	
26 Sep 1904	6 Nov 1904	Ceciley Emma	Alfred Henry & Ada Jane	Walker	Musician RMA	
17 Sep 1904	6 Nov 1904	Betha Ardwina	William Edward & Eliza Ann	King	Quarter Master Sergeant RMA	
1 Sep 1904	6 Nov 1904	Alfred Basil	Charles & Rosanna Eliza	Bent	Acting Bombardier RMA	
16 Sep 1904	6 Nov 1904	Arthur George	William George & Alice Amy	Arnold	Gunner RMA	
4 Aug 1904	4 Dec 1904	Winifred Kathleen	Douglas William & Kathleen	Lock	Gunner RMA	
15 Jul 1904	4 Dec 1904	Harry Douglas Curtis	Robert Carmichael & Amy Clarice	Wilson	Civilian	
15 Sep 1904	4 Dec 1904	Ivy Hilda	William Robert & Eliza	Scadden	Gunner RMA	
11 Nov 1904	4 Dec 1904	Henry	Alfred & Florence	Statham	Sergeant RMA	
8 Oct 1904	4 Dec 1904	Harry Walter Ernest	William Henry & Eleanor Mary	Feltham	Sergeant RMA	
23 Sep 1904	4 Dec 1904	Sidney William	William Thomas & Ethel Mary	Hawkins	Lance Sergeant RMA	
20 Oct 1904	4 Dec 1904	Violet	William John & Mary Ann	Lee	Gunner RMA	
29 Oct 1904	1 Jan 1905	Constance Irene	Albert Edward & Mabel	Butler	Pensioner RMA	
13 Oct 1904	1 Jan 1905	Elizabeth Maud	Arthur Harry & Jessie Alice	Brothwell	Gunner RMA	
17 Nov 1904	1 Jan 1905	Alfred Valentine	Alfred Valentine & Elizabeth Jessie	Conway	Sergeant RMA	

9 Oct 1904	1 Jan 1905	Daisy Olive Alexandra	George & Bertha	**Clapp**	Pensioner RMA	
29 Sep 1904	6 Jan 1905	Elsie Ruth	Alexander & Annie	**Orr**	Acting Bombardier RMA	109
23 Jan 1905	3 Feb 1905	Cyril Herbert Caygill	Frederick William & Martha Ellen	**Berry**	Lance Sergeant RMA	129
23 Jan 1905	3 Feb 1905	Frederick William Caygill	Frederick William & Martha Ellen	**Berry**	Lance Sergeant RMA	129
7 Nov 1904	5 Feb 1905	Cecil Harry	Albert & Sarah Jane	**Gibson**	Superintendant Clerk RMA	
25 Dec 1904	5 Feb 1905	Grace Ellen	Ernest & Ellen	**Young**	Acting Bombardier RMA	
30 Nov 1904	5 Feb 1905	Caroline Sophia	Stephen & Caroline	**Bourner**	Gunner RMA	
14 Nov 1904	5 Mar 1905	Winifred Hilda May	Robert & Hilda Mary	**Aveley**	Gunner RMA	
11 Jan 1905	5 Mar 1905	Ethel Violet	William & Martha	**Smith**	Civilian	
23 Jan 1905	5 Mar 1905	Norman Victor	William & Bertha	**Wheeler**	Gunner RMA	
20 Nov 1904	13 Mar 1905	William George	Ernest & Ellen Eliza	**Saunders**	Colour Sergeant RMA	109
7 Feb 1905	2 Apr 1905	Arthur William	Charles & Helen	**Atkinson**	Gunner RMA	
28 Oct 1904	2 Apr 1905	Douglas	William & Mary	**Marshall**	Colour Sergeant RMA	
23 Feb 1905	9 Apr 1905	Charles Frederick	Alfred Charles & Sophia Mary	**Burrell**	Sergeant RMA	
2 Mar 1905	9 Apr 1905	Edith	Frederick John & Georgina Grace	**Chivers**	Sergeant RMA	
12 Mar 1905	9 Apr 1905	Evelyn Marian	Philip Christopher & Mary Ann	**Newman**	Gunner RMA	
11 Mar 1905	26 Apr 1905	Winifred Anne	Herbert & Winifred Mary	**Slessor**	Major RMA	
13 Mar 1905	7 May 1905	Eileen Winifred	Richard Charles & Annie Beatrice	**Leonard**	Gunner RMA	
1 Apr 1905	7 May 1905	Charles Henry	David & Elizabeth	**Bullard**	Acting Bombardier RMA	
11 Apr 1905	7 May 1905	Henry Herbert	Henry Herbert & Ellen Martha	**Edwards**	Gunner RMA	
1 Apr 1905	7 May 1905	Lily Sarah	Frederick & Lily Edith	**Tunnicliff**	Corporal RMA	
10 Mar 1905	7 May 1905	Albert Edward	Charles Ernest & Elizabeth Ellen	**Jory**	Naval Pensioner	
	15 May 1905	Lily Stephens	blank	**Barrett**	Blank	17
5 Mar 1905	4 Jun 1905	Dorothy Ada	Thomas & Ada	**Hudson**	Bombardier RMA	
2 May 1905	4 Jun 1905	Edith Minnie	Richard & Minnie	**Newman**	Acting Bombardier RMA	
20 Mar 1905	4 Jun 1905	Winifred Ethel	Edward Charles Grills & Charlotte Agnes	**Brock**	Colour Sergeant RMA	
9 Apr 1905	4 Jun 1905	Mabel Rose	Francis William & Rose	**Alexander**	Sergeant Master Shoemaker	
28 Mar 1905	4 Jun 1905	Marjorie Evelyn	Albert Edwin & Evelyn Annie	**Trayfoot**	Bugle Major RMA	
28 Feb 1905	4 Jun 1905	Lily Ivy	Frank George & Alice Lucy	**Chapman**	Civilian	
26 Mar 1905	4 Jun 1905	Hilda Dorothy	Thomas & Alice	**Layzell**	Gunner RMA	
7 Feb 1882	25 Jun 1905	Edward	Edward & Catherine	**Thomas**	Engine Driver	130
17 May 1905	2 Jul 1905	Frances Mary	George & Sarah Ann	**Boulton**	Sergeant RMA	
26 May 1905	2 Jul 1905	Arthur Howel	Albert Edward & Alice Louisa	**Griffin**	Sergeant RMA	
10 Jun 1905	2 Jul 1905	Winifred Constance	Louis & Elizabeth Annie	**Milner**	Corporal RMA	
28 Dec 1904	2 Jul 1905	Thomas Sheldon	Joseph & Louisa	**Bates**	Gunner RMA	
26 May 1905	2 Jul 1905	Francis Michael Drury	Joseph & Louisa	**Tallent**	Pensioner RMA	

16 Mar 1905	16 Jul 1905	William Augustus	William & Ada Sarah	**Boughtflower**	Sergeant RMA	
3 Jun 1905	16 Jul 1905	Charles Henry	James & Alice Mary	**Penfold**	Gunner RMA	
1 Jul 1905	6 Aug 1905	Adeline Louisa	James & Clara	**Jarrett**	Petty Officer RN	
	6 Aug 1905	Henry Arthur James	Henry Arthur & Mary Elizabeth	**Morgan**	Civilian	
27 Jun 1905	27 Aug 1905	Rose Ella	William & Ada Frances	**Holloway**	Sergeant RMA	
8 Jul 1905	3 Sep 1905	Elsie Madge	Arthur & Mary	**Bishop**	Boatman Coast Guard	
8 Aug 1905	3 Sep 1905	Hilda Alice	Walter William & Alice	**Brown**	Staff Sergeant RE	
16 Aug 1905	3 Sep 1905	Constance Edith	Samuel Thomas & Emma	**Edmiston**	Boatman Coast Guard	
16 Aug 1905	3 Sep 1905	Freda Ethel	John Frederick & Mary Louisa	**Yeoman**	Commissioned Boatman Coast Guard	
10 Aug 1905	3 Sep 1905	Elsie May	William & Emma	**Overbury**	Gunner RMA	
26 Jul 1905	3 Sep 1905	Ada Aminda	William & Florence	**Treend**	Musician RMA	
31 Dec 1904	20 Sep 1905	Arthur Victor	Arthur Clarence & Alice Rosetta	**Head**	Civilian (AB HM Navy)	
30 Jun 1905	1 Oct 1905	Edward Leslie	Albert Edward & Annie Maud	**Broadbent**	Gunner RMA	
22 Aug 1905	1 Oct 1905	Daisy Margery	George & Alice	**Bullock**	Provost Sergeant RMA	
13 Sep 1905	1 Oct 1905	Enid Norrie	James & Hilda Nelly	**McIntosh**	Gunner RMA	
9 Jul 1905	5 Nov 1905	Ernest Henry	Archibald & Gertrude Elizabeth	**Goodwin**	Bombardier RMA	
20 Sep 1905	5 Nov 1905	Alice May	John & Alice	**Wilmer**	Gunner RMA	
1 Oct 1905	5 Nov 1905	Rhoda Winifred	Robert William & Emily	**Bragg**	Able Seaman RN	131
22 Aug 1905	5 Nov 1905	Esther	John William & Harriet	**Osborne**	Acting Bombardier RMA	
25 Sep 1905	19 Nov 1905	Jack Cornelius Andrew	John & Mary Jane	**Flowers**	Drum Major RMA	
17 Jun 1905	19 Nov 1905	Dorothy Gwendoline	Messenger & Ada Louise	**Thorp**	Sergeant RMA	
26 May 1905	3 Dec 1905	Lionel Alan	Frederick George & Louisa Maud	**Deacon**	Quarter Master Sergeant RMA	
19 May 1905	3 Dec 1905	Gertrude May	Richard Daniel & Annie Maud	**Juffs**	Sergeant RMA	
15 Nov 1905	3 Dec 1905	Ethel May	Thomas & Mary Ann	**Jefferies**	Gunner RMA	
26 Oct 1905	26 Nov 1905	Kate	George Herbert & Kate	**Tyrrell**	Bombardier RMA	
23 Nov 1905	17 Dec 1905	Dorothy Edith Winifred	Evan Llewellyn & Ada Elizabeth	**Parry**	Gunner RMA	
9 Nov 1905	24 Dec 1905	Muriel Florence Evelyn	Thomas & Rosina Ada	**Hall**	Acting Bombardier RMA	

Notes to the baptisms

These notes provide any other information recorded by the chaplain and comments of my own. For some private baptisms the chaplain has clearly indicated where the baptism was conducted but in many cases this is not recorded. The register has a column for Place and some chaplains have entered RMA Church here and some just Eastney. Where the baptism was private and the place shown as Eastney it is impossible to know whether the baptism was held at home or in the church.

For the name of the chaplain conducting the baptism please see Appendix A

The text in Upright type is what is written in the register, the text in *Italics* type is my comment.

1   Eliza added by the wish of father on 19 Mar 1868

2   Privately

3   Privately at Cumberland House, Southsea

4   *Place:* Parish Church of Portsmouth Hants *This baptism was entered in the register between 5 Jan and 2 Feb 1869*

5   Private by request

6   4 yrs old

7   aged 16 months

8   6 yrs old

9   aged 21 months

10   Privately, admitted 1 Nov 1868

11   (married adult), RMA

12   Private

13   15 months old

14   Privately. *Place:* Leapold Terr, Southsea, recd at Eastney 2 May 1869

15   Privately. *Entered after 4 October in the register*

16   Privately. *Place:* Southsea. Brevet *is very pale, possibly in pencil*

17   Adult

18   by permission

19   Privately, *Place:* Fort Cumberland, Portsea Is.

20   Place: Southsea (Privately)

21   Place: Fort Cumberland, Privately

22   Privately, sick

23   Privately, since dead

24   *entered in the register after the 19 Aug entry*

25   Place: 6, Highland Terrace, Eastney

26   17 years old

27   *There is a note between 26 May and 30 June 1872 that says -* June 13 – Mawby

28   (Dead) *written after Saley*

29   Married to Gunner Paradise

30   *This is the Mawby baptism omitted from its place in 1872 – see Notes 27 & 61*

31   *Name originally written as William Henry*

32   7 years & 7 months old

33   1 year & 3 weeks

34   9 years & 4 months

35   7 years & 6 months

36   5 years & 8 months

37   3 years & 1 month

38   3 years & 4 months

39   Place: *Southsea*

40   *Chaplain's name also blank*

41   *Ada Ella in GRO Index*

42   *Recorded in the register after 7 July 1877*

43   Adult. wife of Gunner Simms

44   Adult. *Charles* – Sergt

45   *Surname:* Print *deleted* and Kent *overwritten* in pale ink

46   RMA is *crossed-out in Rank* column

47   *Birth date is overwritten, looks like March*

48   Privately. *Listed before 27 Jan in the register*

49   Private. received into church 25 Aug

50   Private. *Entered in the register after 25 Aug*

51   *Mother's name is Armnell in 1881 census*

52   *See second full entry entered the same day*

53   *Crossed-out in pencil –* see next page *– but the next entry for Baggs has a different birth year*

54   Crossed-*out in pencil –* see next page *– but the next entry for Hunt has a different birth month*

55   *Looks like Bailly here but GRO index has Bailey*

56   *Date:* Received March 28. *Note added: Private Baptism see July 2nd 1878. This child was recorded as being baptised privately on 4 Jul 1878 and this second entry refers to him being received into the church*

57   *There is a pencil '?' over the columns for the parents' names and father's rank*

58   *Place:* Eastney Barracks

59   *In same register entry as Harry, annotated Twins*

60   *In same register entry as Sarah Ellen, annotated Twins*

61   *This baptism was entered in Jan 1882 and is annotated omitted from its place in the year 1872. This baptism was omitted from the register in Jul 1872 but added in Apr/May 1873 and then added again here in Jan 1882 – see Notes 27 & 30*

62   Private, child dying

63   *Place:* Fort Cumberland Terrace, Private, child dying

64   *Place:* Bembridge View, Private

65   *Place:* Eastney Barracks, Private

66   *Birth date corrected from 23 Nov*

67   *Omitted from proper date position and added after 28 Oct 1883*

68   Private. Publicly recd into the RMA Church 25 Feb 94

69   Private. child died

70   *Entered into the register out of date order*

71 Private baptism 10 May 1886

72 Adult Baptism. *John Oscar recorded as RN Ship's Steward*

73 Private. Received publicly 31 May 1891

74 Private at RMA Barracks. Publicly recd into the RMA Church 19.6.1892

75 Private. *Place:* 5, Henderson Rd, Eastney

76 Private. *Place:* 9, Agincourt Terrace, Eastney

77 Private. *Place:* 3, St George's Road, Eastney

78 Private. *Place:* 6, Garfield Terrace, Eastney

79 Private at RMA Barracks

80 Private. *Place:* 5, EatonTerrace, Eastney. Publicly recd. 16.7.93

81 Private. *Place:* B Block, MQ Eastney Barracks

82 Private. *Place:* 14, Garfield Terrace, Eastney

83 Private. *Place:* 21, Eastney View, Eastney

84 Private. *Place:* 25, Block A, Eastney Barracks

85 Private. *Place:* 8, Tokar Terrace, Eastney. Recd 11 Oct 96

86 Private. *Place:* 7, Adair Terrace

87 Private. Place: 7, Agincourt Terr. Recd RMA Church 4 Sep 1898

88 Private. Place: Adair Terrace, Died

89 Private. Place: 20, St Augustine Road

90 *This baptism was conducted by Rev W D Barber at St Saviours, Victoria, British Columbia and subsequently added to the RMA baptism register*

91 Private. *Place:* 12, Fort Cumberland Terrace, Died

92 At Registrar Woolwich. *This entry records a birth registration in Woolwich and not a baptism in the RMA Church – see T W Anderson in Chapter 6.*

93 Private. Place: RMA Barracks and in pencil D. D. – *see Note 124*

94 *No date was entered for this baptism but it was entered in the register between 17 May and 14 June 1896*

95 Private. *Place:* 8, Fort Cumberland Terrace

96 Private. *Place:* Married Quarters, RMA Barracks. Recd 26 Sep 1898

97 Private. D. D. – *see Note 124*

98 Private. *Place:* 11, Garfield Terrace. D. D.

99 Private. *Place:* Linchmere Terrace, Eastney. D. D.

100 *Birth year must be wrong, GRO index shows Apr–Jun 1894*

101 *Place:* Private at RMA Barracks. Recd 26 Sep 98

102 *Place:* Private at St George's Terrace, Eastney. D.D. – see Note 124

103 *Noted by Chaplain as being recorded out of chronological order*

104 *Barbara Ursula in GRO index*

105 *Birth and baptism date are the same but no note of it being private*

106 *Edward is recorded tentatively in pencil*

107 *One of two entries for 8 Jan recorded out of date order*

108 *One of three entries for 6 Jan recorded out of date order*

109 Private Baptism *but place not recorded*

110 Twins. *Dorothea and Minnie Agnes*

111   Private Baptism D.D. 30 Jul 1899 *(see note 124) place not recorded*

112   Twins *(William & George)*

113   Private Baptism. Recd into Church 3 Dec 1899

114   Private Baptism *place not recorded* D.D. *(see Note 124)*

115   Baptised Privately. Place: Turiff, Aberdeen 25 Nov 1899. Recd into RMA Church 25 Feb 1900

116   *Birth year in error, presumably 1899*

117   Private Baptism - *place not recorded.* Recd into the Church 24 May 1901

118   Conditional Baptism of Adult. Now wife of Wm Henry Lerwill

119   Adult. *Mother Mary Elizabeth* (now deceased)

120   Private Baptism - *place not recorded.* Recd at RMA Church 11 May 1902

121   Private baptism at RMA Church

122   *This is Rev Hill baptising his own daughter*

123   *D.D. is the naval abbreviation for Discharged Dead*

124   Private. *Place not recorded.* Twin. *Entered in the register out of date order*

125   Adopted by

126   Adult. Married surname

127   Twin. Private. *Place not recorded.* (Edith Mabel & Alfred James)

128   *Birth year must be in error, presumably 1903*

129   Twin. Private. *Place not recorded. (Cyril Herbert Caygill & Frederick William Caygill)*

130   Adult. *Edward jnr* – Gunner RMA

131   of 2, Worsley St

Appendix A
Chaplains' Baptisms List

This table shows the dates of the baptisms performed by each chaplain or minister in chronological order, arranged under the thirteen permanent chaplains. The chaplains' and ministers' names do not appear in the transcriptions in Part Three but they can be established by referencing the date of the baptism in the transcriptions against the dates in this table. Please note that the dates relating to the permanent Chaplains in this table refer to the dates of the baptisms they performed not the dates of posting as recorded in their relevant Navy service record.

Dates	Chaplain	Deputies
22 Jul 1866 to 1 Sep 1867	S Beal	
6 Oct 1867 to 19 Aug 1871	J Cawston	16 Aug 1867 – N H NacGachan 6 Aug 1871 – L Shepherd
3 Sep 1871 to 10 Apr 1875	J S Robson	28 Apr 1872 – R A Corbett 23 May 1872 – J Cawston 26 May 1872 – R A Corbett 13 Jun 1872 – J Cawston 19 Oct 1872 – J Cawston 31 Aug 1873 – C E York 28 Sep 1873 – C Clark 12 Aug 1874 – J Kirkpatrick 27 Sep 1874 to 25 Oct 1874 – M W Bayliss
25 Apr 1875 to 25 Apr 1880	E A Williams	25 Jul to 29 Aug 1875 – J Cox-Edwards 25 Jun 1876 to 30 Jul 1876 – J Sharp 27 Aug 1876 – W E Smith 29 Aug 1876 – J Kirkpatrick 24 Jun 1877 to 26 Jun 1877 – J Sharpe 29 Oct 1877 – J Sharpe 22 Aug 1878 – J Sharp 25 Aug 1878 – J F Falwasser 28 Sep 1879 – J Sharpe
20 May 1880 to 25 Dec 1881	W V Lloyd	2 May 1881 – S C Adam 25 Sep 1881 – J Sharpe 27 Nov 1881 – J S Robson
16 Jan 1882 to 26 Apr 1885	F Davies	10 Apr 1883 – E A Williams 30 Sep 1883 – J Sharpe 30 Dec 1883 – J Sharpe 27 Jan 1884 – J Allcock 28 Jan 1884 – J Sharpe 5 Sep 1884 – W J Harvey 21 Jul 1884 to 14 Sep 1884 – J Sharpe 15 Sep 1884 – W J Harvey 25 Sep 1884 – J Sharpe 26 Oct 1884 – J Sharpe 27 Oct 1884 – W A Shakespear
17 May 1885 to 29 Aug 1889	T F Morton	18 Jul 1885 – F W F Bishop 13 Jun 1886 – W W Parry 24 Apr to 29 May 1887 – W Boyce 14 Aug 1887 – A P Hill 1 Jan 1888 – J Sharpe 1 Aug 1889 – W A Rutherford
29 Sep 1889 to 23 Sep 1894	S Kenah	12 Feb 1893 – G B P Viner

21 Oct 1894 to 26 Sep 1898	C E York	16 Dec 1894 – F Scott 24 Mar 1895 – W Reed 23 Jun 1895 – H A Taylor 30 Jun to 7 Jul 1895 – W Reed 9 Sep 1895 – W D Barber 3 Oct 1895 – W D Barber 3 Nov 1895 – W D Barber 16 Dec 1895 – T W Anderson 19 Jan to 2 Feb 1896 – W Romanis 8 Mar 1896 – O R Hughes 15 Mar 1896 – H A Taylor 14 Jun 1896 – W Romanis 21 Jun to 28 Jun 1896 – H A Taylor 4 Oct 1896 – E J Vaughan 13 Jun 1897 – W Romanis 29 Aug 1897 – W Romanis 26 Sep 1897 – H A Taylor 17 Oct 1897 – W Romanis 2 Jan to 30 Jan 1898 – W Romanis 27 Feb 1898 – H A Taylor 19 Jun 1898 – J N D Hurdon
16 Oct 1898 to 28 Feb 1901	W S Harris	6 Aug to 14 Aug 1899 – E W Evans
3 Mar 1901 to 31 May 1901	W B Atherton	
9 Jun 1901 to 16 Jul 1905	A P Hill	9 Jul 1901 – W S Harris 10 Apr 1904 – E H Good 2 Oct 1904 – L Walker 26 Apr 1905 – G Cotesworth
6 Aug 1905 to 24 Dec 1905	A W Plant	

Appendix B - List of Sources for Parts 1 and 2
Abbreviations

BL   British Library
BNL   British Library Newspaper Library
BNLO   British Library 19th Century Newspaper Library on-line
CHL   Cheltenham Local and Family History Library
COL   City Of London Library Catalogue
GTP   Gateway to the Past Catalogue (on-line, Staffordshire CC)
GRO   General Register Office registers
HAN   Historic Hansard 1803-2005 on-line
HD   Historical Directories at www.historicaldirectories.org
HLSU   Hartley Library, Southampton University
HRO   Hampshire Record Office
ILEJ   Internet Library of Early Journals at www.bodley.ox.ac.uk/ilej/
LGO   London Gazette Online
LGU   www.legislation.gov.uk
LMA   City of London, London Metropolitan Archives
LPL   Lambeth Palace Library
NAL   National Art Library, Victoria & Albert Museum
NAM   National Army Museum
NRO   Norfolk Record Office online catalogue
OUP   Oxford University Press
PCO   Portsmouth Cemeteries Office
PHC   Portsmouth History Centre
PPR   Principal Probate Registry (www.ancestry.co.uk)
RIBA   Royal Institute of British Architects Library
RMHS   Royal Marines Historical Society
RMM   Royal Marines Museum, Portsmouth
RNM   National Museum of the Royal Navy Library, Portsmouth
TDA   The Times Digital Archive, 1785–1985 at http://gale.cengage.co.uk/times.aspx/
TNA   The National Archives
TNAL   The National Archives Library
WSHC   Wiltshire & Swindon History Centre
WSRO   West Sussex Record Office
YPSR   York Probate Sub Registry

Note: The Portsmouth History Centre was formed by the amalgamation of Portsmouth Record Office and the genealogical and naval history collections of Portsmouth Central Library in May 2011.

Chapter 1

1   St Andrew's Church, photograph, CHU 50/4/1, PHC

2   Photo 13/11/16/064, RMM

3   Hampshire Telegraph & Sussex Chronicle, 30 October 1858, page 5, PHC

4   Photo 13/11/13/49, RMM

5   *Post Office Directory of Portsmouth*, 1859, page 111, PHC

6   Portsmouth Evening News, 5 January 1932, page 9, PHC

7   Hampshire Telegraph & Sussex Chronicle, 23 September 1899, page 6 & 24 September 1892, page 5, BNLO

8   Photo of Church bell, ACQ 1976/83, RMM

9   Diocese of Winchester Consistory Court Exhibit Books, 21 M65 C4/18, HRO

10 Portsea Tithe Map & Apportionment Book, 78/1/1 & 78/1/2, PHC

11 White, William, *History, Gazetteer & Directory of Hampshire*, 1859, page 271, PHC

12 Last Will and Testament of William Butcher, 4 March 1874, Probate 5 September 1876, YPSR

13 *Southsea It's Story*, William Curtis, Bay Tree Publishing, Alresford, 1978

14 Portsmouth Times, 16 October 1858, page 4, PHC

15 Proceedings of the Portsmouth and Southsea Commissioners, Oct 1852-Oct 1862, G/ICP 1, item 9, PHC

16 The Times, 7 June 1862, page 4, TDA

17 Portsmouth Times & Naval Gazette, 14 June 1862, page 1, PHC

18 St Simon's Church, Southsea: Conditions and arrangements for erection of church, CHU 50/2B/1, PHC

19 Scrapbook 3, PHC

20 Census 1841, HO 107, piece 415, book 1, folio 65, page 13, TNA

21 Census 1851, HO 107, piece 1658, folio 80, page 1, TNA

22 Census 1861, RG 9, piece 636, folio 31, page 8, TNA

23 Census 1871, RG10, piece 1131, folio 25, page 7, TNA

24 Census 1861, RG 9, piece 641, folio 162, page 17, TNA

25 Ordnance Survey 1:500 scale map, 83.12.23, 1861, with gas company information added, PHC

26 Portsmouth Times & Naval Gazette, 25 November 1865, page 5, PHC

27 Hampshire Telegraph & Sussex Chronicle, 14 February 1866, page 2, PHC

28 Hampshire Telegraph & Sussex Chronicle, 24 February 1866, page 1, PHC

29 Hampshire Telegraph & Sussex Chronicle, 10 March 1866, page 1, PHC

30 Hampshire Telegraph & Sussex Chronicle, 22 December 1866, page 4, PHC

31 Admiralty: Royal Marine Office out-letters, ADM 56/100, page 83, TNA

32 Admiralty In-letters and papers: From Architect, 1866, ADM 1/5979, No 960, TNA

33 Photo 13/11/13/94, RMM

34 Admiralty In-letters and papers: From Architect, 1867, ADM 1/6015, No 68, TNA

35 Ordnance Survey 1:2500 scale map, 84.9, 2nd edition, 1898 (revised 1896), PHC

36 Admiralty In-letters and papers: From Architect, ADM 1/6015, No 569, TNA

37 Admiralty: Royal Marine Office: Out letters general, ADM 56/105, page 248, TNA

38 Admiralty: Royal Marine Office: Out letters general, ADM 56/105, page 217, TNA

39 Admiralty Digests, ADM 12/1286, 71.22, 1895, TNA

40 Admiralty: Royal Marine Office, Letters to Admiralty, ADM 191/32, November 1867, TNA

41 Postcard ca 1907, Dennis Bill collection

42 Photo 13/11/13/50, RMM

43 Postcard E 23, PHC

44 Portsmouth Evening News, 7 November 1987, page 4, PHC

45 Admiralty: Royal Marine Office out-letters, ADM 59/1, items 318 & 1244, 1868-69, TNA

46 Admiralty: Royal Marine Office, Letters to Admiralty, ADM 191/32, December 1867, TNA

47 Admiralty Solicitor, Journals of Proceedings: 1867, TS 38/2, page 482, TNA Admiralty Solicitor: Report Books, TS 6/15/1197, 1967; TS 6/15/2, TS 6/15/4 & TS 6/15/66, 1868, TNA Treasury Solicitors Opinions: War Office: TS 25/2075/ 567-585, 28 February 1868, TNA

48 Admiralty Solicitor, Journals of Proceedings: 1868, TS 38/3, pages 119 & 240, TNA

49 Army Chaplains Act 1868, Chapter 83 (Regnal. 31 and 32 Vict), LGU

50 Admiralty: Out-letters to RMA, ADM 59/2, 10 November 1869, page 626, TNA

51 Photo 13/11/13/90, RMM

52 Portsmouth Evening News, 16 March 1904, page 5, PHC

53 Hampshire Telegraph & Sussex Chronicle, 8 March 1882, page 4, BNLO

54 *Chamberlain's Portsmouth Directory*, 1879, PHC

55 Hayward, Abel & Sons, *A Guide To Portsmouth*, ca 1876, PHC

56 Globe & Laurel, Vol V, 7 June 1898, page 61, RMM

57 Navy Estimates, House of Commons Debate, 30 March 1903, vol 120, cc585-639, HAN

58 Globe & Laurel, Vol IX, 7 May 1902, page 57, RMM

59 Globe & Laurel, Vol XI, 7 April 1904, page 39-40, RMM

60 Hampshire Telegraph & Sussex Chronicle, 21 January 1905, page 2, PHC

61 Portsmouth Evening News, 9 June 1905, page 3, PHC

62 Hampshire Telegraph & Sussex Chronicle, 18 November 1905, page 2, PHC

63 Portsmouth Evening News, 18 November 1905, page 3, PHC

64 Note on the Crinoline Church by Sergeant Major Beale, Arch 17/6/2, RMM

65 Admiralty: Royal Marines Registers of Service, RMA, ADM 159/80, TNA

66 London Gazette, Issue 30732, 7 June 1918, page 6771, LGO

67 Death Registers Index, April-June 1968, Havering, volume 5c, page 27, GRO and Globe & Laurel, Vol LXXVI, August 1968, page 263, RMM

68 Oakley, Captain Derek MBE, RM, *Albert Medals Awarded to Royal Marines*, RMHS Special Publication No 32

69 Photo 13/11/140/007, RMM

70 Photo 13/11/140/058, RMM

71 Photo 13/11/140/011, RMM

72 *HMS Captain* picture, Illustrated London News, 24 September 1870, page 316, RNM

73 Admiralty: Correspondence & Papers, *HMS Victoria* Court Martial, ADM 1/7174, TNA

74 Photo 13/11/140/010, RMM

75 Globe & Laurel, Vol I, 1 July 1893, RMM

76 Globe & Laurel, Vol I, 1 August 1893, RMM

77 Photo 13/11/140/073, RMM

78 Admiralty: Correspondence & Papers, from Admirals Mediterranean, ADM 1/6481, N10,   TNA

79 *HMS Thunderer* after the explosion, Illustrated London News, 25 January 1879, page 1,   RNM

80   Photo 13/11/12/053, RMM

81   Admiralty: Officer's Service Records, ADM 196/61, TNA (Daniel & Shakespear)

82   The Times, 2 January 1879, page 3, TDA

83   The Times, 4 January, 1879, page 6, TDA

84   The Times, 6 January, 1879, page 11, TDA

85   The Times, 7 January, 1879, page 6, TDA

86   The Times, 15 November, 1856, page 1, TDA

87   Census 1881, RG 11, piece 4475, folio 11, page 15, TNA

88   Photo 13/11/140/023, RMM

89   Admiralty: Officer's Service Records, ADM 196/59, TNA

90   Admiralty: Officer's Service Records, ADM 196/66, TNA

91   London Gazette, 20 August 1855, Issue 21765, page 3173, LGO

92   Globe & Laurel, Vol III, 7 March 1896, page 52, RMM

93   Census 1901, RG 13, piece 2326, folio 56, page 5, TNA

94   Photo 13/11/140/020, RMM

95   Globe & Laurel, Vol XX, 7 Mar 1913, page 44, RMM

96   Highland Road Cemetery Registers, PCO & PHC

97   Grave photographs, © Dennis Bill 2013

98   Photo 13/11/12/062, RMM

99   Hampshire Telegraph & Sussex Chronicle, 16 January 1892, page 6, PHC

100 Photo 13/11/140/070, RMM

101 Photo 13/11/12/052, RMM

102 London Gazette, 22 September 1855, Issue 21788, page 3546, LGO

103 London Gazette, 5 March 1858, Issue 22110, page 1339, LGO

104 Hampshire Telegraph & Sussex Chronicle, 15 Apr 1865, page 4, BNLO

105 Hampshire Telegraph & Sussex Chronicle, 21 January 1865, page 4, BNLO

106 Hampshire Telegraph & Sussex Chronicle, 27 November 1886, page 8, BNLO

107 The Times, 3 February 1865, page 12, TDA

108 Out-letters to RMA, 1874-75, ADM 59/7/1005, TNA

109 *Oxford Dictionary of National Biography*, OUP

110 Photo 13/11/140/005, RMM

111 Photo 9/2/F1/12, RMM

112 Admiralty: Officer's Service Records, ADM 196/60, TNA

113 The Times, 12 September 1870, page 12 and 13 September 1870, page 3, TDA

114 Census 1871, RG 10, piece 2788, folio 7, page 8, TNA

115 Census 1871, RG 10, piece 1148, folio 21, page 39, TNA

116 Photo 13/11/140/008, RMM

117 Census 1841, HO 107, piece 272, folio 10, page 6, TNA

118 Census 1851, HO 107, piece 1658, folio 42, page 26, TNA

119 Census 1861, RG 9, piece 643, folio 101, page 22, TNA

120 Census 1871, RG 10, piece 1146, folio 18, page 30, TNA

121 Census 1891, RG12, piece 1696, folio 68, page 16 (son), TNA

122 Bilcliffe, John, *Irreproachable Character – The Award of the Royal Marine Meritorious Service Medal*, Pub No 30, Royal Marines Historical Society, 2005

123 Photo 13/11/140/021, RMM

124 Photo 13/11/140/009, RMM

125 RM Officers Index, RMM

126 Hampshire Telegraph & Sussex Chronicle, 10 October 1896, page 5, BNLO

127 Globe & Laurel, Vol III, 7 November 1896, page 150, RMM

128 Globe & Laurel, Vol V, 7 June 1898, page 61, RMM

129 Globe & Laurel Vol XXIII, 7 May 1918, page 77, RMM

130 Field, Colonel Cyril, RMLI; *Britain's Sea Soldiers, Vol 2*, Chapter XXXI, pages 184-188, Lyceum Press, Liverpool, 1924

131 Hart's Army List 1888, page 401b, PHC

132 Photo 13/11/140/044, RMM

133 Photo 13/11/140/045, RMM

134 Photo 13/11/12/059, RMM

135 Admiralty: Correspondence & Paper, Dublin Castle, 1883, ADM 1/6688, TNA

136 Navy List, 1882, Royal Marines Pay, page 465, RNM

137 RM Museum medal collection, RMM

138 London Gazette, 20 August 1855, Issue 21765, page 3173, LGO

139 London Gazette, 29 August 1854, Issue 21588, page 2666, LGO

140 Globe & Laurel, Vol XXV, May 1918, page 95, RMM

141 Photo 13/11/140/022, RMM

142 Poore family window & plaque photos © Dennis Bill 2013

143 Nares, Capt Sir G S, *Voyage to the Polar Sea*, 1878 (see Bibliography)

144 Coleman, E C, *The RN & Polar Exploration Vol 2*, with the author's permission (see Bibliography)

145 Burial picture, from Coleman, E C, *The RN & Polar Exploration Vol 2*, with the author's permission

146 Hampshire Telegraph & Sussex Chronicle, 1 November 1876, page 4, PHC

147 Photo 13/11/140/061, RMM

148 Globe & Laurel, Vol IV, 7 August 1897, page 88, RMM

149 Photo 13/11/140/006, RMM

150 Photo 13/11/12/082, RMM

151 London Gazette, Issue 24885, 24 September 1880, page 5036, LGO

152 Photo 13/11/140/075, RMM

153 Hampshire Telegraph & Sussex Chronicle, 29 October 1887, p8, BNLO

154 Hampshire Telegraph & Sussex Chronicle, 31 December 1887, p8, BNLO (Beer)

155 Admiralty: RN Registers of Seamen's Services, ADM 188/180, TNA (Beer)

156 Photo 13/11/12/083, RMM

157 Photo of plaque in St Jude's church, © Dennis Bill 2013

158 Admiralty: Officer's Service Records, ADM 196/62, TNA

159 Globe & Laurel, Vol IV, 1897, page 123, RMM

160 St Andrew's Church memorial plaques photo folder, RMM

161 Admiralty: *Royal Sovereign* – Report of Accident, ADM 116/590, TNA

162 Globe & Laurel, Vol VIII, 1901, page 139, RMM

163 *HMS Royal Sovereign* memorial photo © Dennis Bill, 2013

164 Photo 13/11/12/151, RMM

165 Globe & Laurel, Vol III, 7 March 1896, page 52, RMM

166 St Andrew's Church memorial plaques photo folder, RMM

167 Photo 13/11/12/146, RMM

168 Photo 13/11/140/074, RMM

169 Admiralty: Royal Marines, Registers of Service, ADM 159/28, TNA

170 Globe & Laurel, Vol IX, 7 December 1902, page 140, RMM

171 Photo 13/11/140/072, RMM

172 Hampshire Telegraph & Sussex Chronicle, 23 May 1891, page 6, BNLO

173 The Times, 22 May 1891, page 10, TDA

174 Photo 13/11/140/063, RMM

175 Photo 13/11/12/039, RMM

176 Globe & Laurel, Vol VII, 7 August 1900, pages 87 & 96, RMM

177 Photo 13/11/140/014, RMM

178 Photo 13/11/12/147, RMM

179 Hampshire Telegraph & Sussex Chronicle, 7 July 1900, page 4, PHC

180 The Times, 21 October 1902, page 5, TDA

181 Photo 13/11/140/050, RMM

182 Photo 13/11/140/055, RMM

183 Photo 17/2/5/183, RMM

184 Admiralty: In-letters from Marine Office, ADM 1/6077, 1868, TNA
     Admiralty: Out-letters to RMA, ADM 59/1/23, 23 October 1868, TNA
     Admiralty: RMA Out-letters to Admiralty, ADM 191/34, page 222, TNA

Chapter 2

1   Portsmouth Evening News, 16 March 1904, page 5, PHC

2   *Up To Date Pleasure Guide for Portsmouth & Southsea*, 3rd edition, Lang, Southsea, 1893, PHC

3   Herbert, Gilbert, *Pioneers of Prefabrication: the British contribution in the nineteenth century*, Johns Hopkins University Press, 1978, BL

4   Emails: Bill-Herbert, 27-29 July 2009

5   Conway-Jones, Hugh, *William Eassie – A Notable Victorian Contractor*, Journal of the Gloucestershire Society for Industrial Archaeology, 2004, pages 53-58

6   Bristol Mercury, 25 November 1854, page 8, BNL

7   Census 1851, HO 107, piece 1658, folio 680, page 2, TNA

8   The Times, 20 November 1854, page 10, TDA

9   Papers of Sidney Herbert, 1st Baron Herbert of Lea, 2057/F4/64, WSHC

10 The Times, 29 November 1854, page 10, TDA

11 Illustrated London News, 1 September, 1855, page 250, RNM

12 The Times, 4 December 1854, page 10, TDA

13 The Times, 7 December 1854, page 7, TDA

14 The Times, 5 January 1855, page 7, TDA

15 The Times, 24 January 1855, page 10, and 6 January 1855, page 10, TDA

16 The Times, 28 December 1854, page 7, TDA

17 The Times, 22 December 1854, page 10, TDA

18 The Daily News, 7 August 1855, page 5, BNL

19 The Builder, 15 September 1855, page 443, LPL

20 Hampshire Telegraph & Sussex Chronicle, 25 August 1855, page 5, PHC

21 The Times, 14 August 1856, page 7, TDA

22 Hampshire Telegraph & Sussex Chronicle, 3 February 1855, page 5, PHC

23 War Office: Reports, Memoranda and Papers, Report on best system of Hutting, WO 33/2A, 1856, TNA

24 Plans extracted from War Office: Reports, Memoranda and Papers, WO 33/2A at MFQ 1/549, TNA

25 Silver, Christopher, *Renkioi: Brunel's Forgotten Crimean War Hospital*, Valonia Press, 2007

26 For an example see *St John's Church and Parsonage in the Wilderness*, Drawings and Watercolours, 1981-10-43-1 to 3, NAM

27 Colchester Garrison Church at www.camulos.com/garrisonchurch.htm and St John's Orthodox Church at www.orthodoxengland.org.uk/zchurch.htm

28 Hoad, Margaret J & Temple Paterson, Prof A, *Portsmouth & The Crimea War*, Portsmouth Paper No 19, Portsmouth City Council, 1973.

29 Drinkall, Pamela, *A Brief History of Beaumanor Hall and Park*, Leicestershire Education Committee, 1978

30 The Herrick Manuscripts, DG 9/2142, 2148 & 2151, Leicestershire, Leicester and Rutland Record Office catalogue, A2A, TNA

31 Hampshire Telegraph & Sussex Chronicle, 15 March 1851, page 5, BNLO

32 Hampshire Telegraph & Sussex Chronicle, 14 October 1854, page 5, BNLO

33 Riley, R C, *The Houses and Inhabitants of Thomas Ellis Owen's Southsea*, Portsmouth Paper No 32, Portsmouth City Council, 1976

34 Hampshire Telegraph & Sussex Chronicle, 9 August 1851, page 1, BNLO

35 Hampshire Telegraph & Sussex Chronicle, 31 October 1857, page 1, BNLO

36 Hampshire Telegraph & Sussex Chronicle, 9 October 1858, page 8, BNLO

37 Hampshire Telegraph & Sussex Chronicle, 20 September 1856, page 4, BNLO

38 Hampshire Telegraph & Sussex Chronicle, 7 June 1856, page 8, BNLO

39 East, R, *Extracts from the Portsmouth Records*, Lewis, 1891, page 402, PHC

40 Hampshire Telegraph & Sussex Chronicle, 23 April 1859, page 5, BNLO

41 Highland Road Cemetery Registers, PCO & PHC

42 Grave photograph, © Dennis Bill 2013

Chapter 3

1 Hampshire Telegraph & Sussex Chronicle, 30 October 1858, page 5, PHC

2 Ware, Dora, *A Short Dictionary of British Architects*, Allen & Unwin, 1967, TNAL

3 London Gazette: Issue 21303, 23 March 1852, page 893; Issue 21814, 13 November 1855, page 4227; Issue 21818, 23 November 1855, page 4436, LGO

4 *Dictionary of Scottish Architects, 1840-1980*, www.scottisharchitects.org.uk, 2008

5 Census 1861, RG 9, piece 183, folio 64, page 58, TNA

6   www.churchplansonline.org , The Incorporated Church Building Society, Lambeth Palace Library

7   Census 1871, RG 10, piece 1817, folio 22, page 2, TNA

8   *Directory of Norfolk & Lowestoft*, Harrod & Co, 1877, HD

9   Census 1881, RG 11/1949, folio 56, page 1, TNA

10 Census 1891, RG 12/1530, folio 9, page 11, TNA

11 Death Register Index, April-June 1898, Norwich, vol 4b, page 102, GRO

12 *A Short History of the Church and Parish of St Bartholomew's, Southsea*, 1858-1934, Malcolm's Printing Works, 1934, CHU 32/2B/1, PHC

13 Census 1851, HO 107, piece 1502, folio, 103, page 56, TNA

14 Census 1861, RG 9, piece 134, folio 19, page 38, TNA

15 Post Office London Directories, 1853-1861, LMA

16 For example: The Builder, Volume IX, 22 March 1951, page 193 and Volume X, 15 May 1852, page 318, ILEJ

17 London Gazette, Issue 21955, 2 January 1857, page 37, LGO

18 The Times, 15 May 1861, page 11, TDA

19 Census 1851, HO 107, piece 1508, folio 160, page 65, TNA

20 Census 1841, HO 107, piece 353, book 7, folio 50, page 4, TNA

21 Census 1851, HO 107, piece 1973, folio 348, page 4, TNA

22 Post Office Directory of Gloucester with Bath & Bristol, Kelly & Co, London, 1856, HD

23 Cheltenham Examiner, 13 December 1854, CHL

24 Berrow's Worcester Journal, 3 September 1853, page 3, BNLO

25 Cheltenham Examiner, 9 January 1856, CHL

26 The Builder, 3 May 1856, page 245, LPL

27 Illustrated London News, 17 May 1856, page 537, RNM

28 Death Registers Index, October-December 1857, Cheltenham, vol 6a, page 273, GRO

29 RIBA Journal, 30 August 1902, page 461, RIBA

30 The Ecclesiologist, Vol VIII, 1847, pages 107-8, HLSU

31 The Ecclesiologist, Vol XI, 1850, page 47-9, HLSU

32 The Builder, Vol XVI, 29 May 1858, page 380, RIBA

33 The Ecclesiologist, Volume XIV, 1853, page 62, HLSU

34 The Builder, Vol XXI, 18 April 1863, page 281, NAL

35 Building Design, No 280, 9 January 1976, page 24, RIBA

36 The Ecclesiologist, Volume XIX, 1858, page 198, HLSU

37 Baptism Registers, All Saints, Earsham, 26 November 1797, FreeREG

38 *Pigot's London Directory*, 1828-9, LMA

39 *Pigot's London Directory*, 1830; Robsons London Directory, 1831 & 1832; *Pigot & Co Commercial Directory*, 1832-4, LMA

40 The Times, 4 March 1836, page 7, TDA

41 Norfolk Record Office, N/TC/D1/106/2, 3, 5, 6 &7, 307X2, 1832-1842, NRO

42 London Gazette, Issue 20933, 5 January 1849, page 56, LGO

43 The Builder, Volume 1, 18 March 1843, page 70, ILEJ

44 The Times, 15 December 1842, page 2, TDA

45 The Builder, Vol II, 14 September 1844, pages 470 & 471, NAL PP.20.A or ILEJ

46   Darlington, Ida, *The Metropolitan Buildings Office*, The Builder, 12 October 1956, pages 628-632, RIBA

47   Metropolitan Buildings Office, MBO/424, items 1058, 1082, 1216, 1315, 1507, 1520, 1659, 1871 & 1892 (Jan-Mar 1845) and MBO/398, case 50, (Apr 1845), LMA

48   The Ecclessiologist: Vol VIII, 1847, pages 63-64; Vol IX, 1848, page 332; Vol IV, 1845, page 148, HLSU

49   The Times, 8 July 1846, page 7, TDA

50   London Metropolitan Archives, MBO/PLANS/120, LMA

51   The Times, 29 April 1847, page 5, TDA

52   Email: Bill-Hatfield (Eton College Archivist), 14-14 August 2009

53   The Times, 8 September 1845, page 2, TDA

54   Papers of Sidney Herbert, 1st Baron Herbert of Lea; 2057/F8/I M33 & M38, November 1845, WSHC

55   Census 1851, HO107, piece 1493, folio 647, page 5, TNA

56   London Gazette, Issue 20979, 18 May 1849, page 1677, LGO

57   London Gazette, Issue 21119, 19 July 1850, page 2043, LGO

58   London Gazette, Issue 21211, 20 May 1851, page 1348, LGO

59   The Times, 5 September, page 5, 1853 (also 12 September, page 3), TDA

60   Darlington, Ida, *Thompson Fecit*, The Architectural Review, No 740, September 1958, pages 187 188, RIBA

61   Guildhall Library Catalogue, London, A 5.2 Nos 19 & 33, COL

62   Notes and Queries, 4 June 1853, page 545, ILEJ

63   William Salt Library catalogue, M1355 and G95.215.0001, GTP

64   London Metropolitan Archives catalogue: 460:PAU(2):ext; H1:CL & H1:MAR, COL

65   Death Registers Index, October to December 1874, Barnet, vol 3a, page 89, GRO

66   Census 1871, RG 10, piece 1324, folio 124, page 11, TNA

67   London Metropolitan Archives, MBO/424/1316, LMA

68   Herbert, Gilbert, *Pioneers of Prefabrication: the British contribution in the nineteenth century*, Johns Hopkins University Press, 1978, BL

Chapter 4

1   Bilcliffe, John, *Irreproachable Character – The Award of the Royal Marine Meritorious Service Medal*, Pub No 30, Royal Marines Historical Society, 2005

2   Clowes, Sir William Laird, *The Royal Navy: A History – From the earliest times to 1900*, Volume 6, Chapter XLIII, page 204, Royal Comission on promotion and retirement

3   Thompson, Julian, *The War At Sea*, 1914-1918, page 224, Imperial War Museum, Sidgwick & Jackson, London, 2005

4   Field, Colonel Cyril, RMLI; *Britain's Sea Soldiers, Vol 2*, Chapter XXXIII, page 612, Lyceum Press, Liverpool, 1924

5   Globe & Laurel, Volume IV, 7 Apil 1897, Corps Gazette, RMM

6   Trowbridge's Diary, Arch 7/14/5, RMM

7   Photo 7/14/5/10, RMM

8   Field, Colonel Cyril, RMLI; *Britain's Sea Soldiers*, Vol 2, Chapter XXXIII, Lyceum Press, Liverpool, 1924; picture credited to the Graphic newspaper, date unknown

9   Admiralty: In-letters and papers: 1900-1909, ADM 1/7613, TNA

10 Orders In Council for the Regulation of the Naval Service, Vol 2, July 1856-July 1864: Orders bearing on the Royal Navy, 13 May 1859, pages 72-3, RNM

11 Admiralty: Queen's Regulations, Chapter III, Rank and Command, para 137, 1879, RNM

12 Taylor, Gordon, *The Sea Chaplains*, Oxford Illustrated Press, 1978

13 Admiralty: In-letters and papers, From Admirals Channel Squadron, ADM 1/6302, V228, 1874, TNA

14 Navy List 1893: Uniform Regulations for Officers of the Fleet, page 565, RNM

15 Admiralty Digests: ADM 12/1176, 71.22, 1887, TNA

16 Admiralty Digests: ADM 12/1160, 71.22, 1886, TNA

17 Admiralty: Digests and Indexes, ADM 12/1127, Digest 63.3, 1884, TNA

18 Orders in Council for the Regulation of the Naval Service, Vol VIII, No 215, 11 August 1902, RNM

19 Admiralty: In-letters and papers: 1900-1909, ADM 1/7613, TNA

20 Portsmouth Times, 10 March 1866, page 4, PHC

21 King's Regulations and Admiralty Instructions, 1913, Volume 1, page 655, RNM

22 Admiralty: Out-letters to RMA, ADM 59/3/484 & 509, 1871, TNA

23 Admiralty: Chaplains Service Records: ADM 6/440/278 & RN Officers Service Records, ADM 196/68/790, TNA

Chapter 5

1 Admiralty: Officers' Service Records, Vol 5, Chaplains & Naval Instructors, ADM 6/443/301, TNA

2 Census 1891, RG12, piece 2349, folio 90, page 3, TNA

3 National Probate Calendar (Index of Wills and Administrations), 1861-1941, PPR

4 Illustrated London News, 15 August 1857, page 156, RNM

5 Admiralty: Register of Chaplains' Services, ADM 6/440/248, TNA

6 Admiralty: Register of Chaplains' Services, ADM 6/441/12, TNA

7 *Cambridge University Alumni 1261-1900*, Cambridge University Press, at www.ancestry.co.uk

8 Admiralty: Officer's Services register, ADM 196/68/436, TNA

9 *Oxford Dictionary of National Biography*, Oxford University Press, 2004-2010, www.oxforddnb.com

10 London Gazette Extraordinary, Issue 22027, 1 August 1857, page 2683, LGO

11 The Times, 24 August 1889, page 9, TDA

12 Admiralty: Register of Chaplains' Services, ADM 6/440/251, TNA

13 Admiralty: Register of Chaplains' Services, ADM 6/441/14, TNA

14 Admiralty: Officer's Services register, ADM 196/68/439, TNA

15 Census 1841, HO 107, piece 221, book 23, folio 18, page 31, TNA

16 Census 1851, HO 107, piece 1894, folio 530, page 47, TNA

17 Hampshire Telegraph & Sussex Chronicle, 10 March 1900, page 6, BNLO

18 Admiralty: Register of Chaplains' Services, ADM 6/440/346, TNA

19 Admiralty: Register of Chaplains' Services, ADM 6/441/47, TNA

20 Admiralty: Passing Certificates, Naval Instructors, ADM 13/246, 1860, TNA

21 Admiralty Digests, ADM 12/1044, 71.22, 1879, TNA

22 Cheshire Observer, 20 January 1894, page 6, BNLO

23 Admiralty: Register of Chaplains' Services, ADM 6/441/155, TNA

24 The Times, Naval & Military Intelligence, 21 Oct 1902, page 5, TDA

25   The Times, Obituary, 25 May 1835, page 14, TDA

26   Weir, Colin, *The History of Cambridge University Football Club, 1872-2003*, Yore Publications, Harefield, Middlesex, 2004

27   Email: Bill-Dr J A Little, 27 July 2009

28   The Times, 29 November 1875, Football – Oxford & Cambridge, page 6, TDA

29   Lloyds Weekly Newspaper, London, 28 November 1875, page 12, BNLO

30   Eastleigh Borough Council Cemeteries Database at www.eastleigh.gov.uk

31   *Who Was Who*, A & C Black, 1920-2008; online edition Oxford University Press, 2007

32   Navy and Army Illustrated, 28 May 1910, pages 125-126, RNM

33   Grave photographs © Dennis Bill 2012

34   Admiralty: Register of Chaplains' Services, ADM 6/441/163, TNA

35   Lyon & Wingfield, *The Sail and Steam Navy List, All the Ships of the Royal Navy 1815-1889*, Chatham Publishing, 2003

36   Admiralty: Register of Chaplains' Services, ADM 6/440/378, TNA

37   Admiralty: Register of Chaplains' Services, ADM 6/441/66, TNA

38   Admiralty: Passing Certificates, Naval Instructors, ADM 13/246, 1867, TNA

39   *Alumni Dublinenses*, Burtchaell & Sadleir, Dublin, 1935, (Email: Bill-Aisling Lockart, Trinity College, Dublin, 7 July 2009)

40   Admiralty: Register of Chaplains' Services, ADM 6/440/320, TNA

41   Admiralty: Register of Chaplains' Services, ADM 6/441/35, TNA

42   Admiralty: Digests and Indexes, ADM 12/1012, HRH Duke of Edinburgh, 14 September 1878, TNA

43   Admiralty Digests: ADM 12/1062, 71.22, 1880, TNA

44   Admiralty: Out-letters to the RMA, ADM 59/12/235, April 1880, TNA

45   Baner ac Amserau Cymru, 1 July 1896, page 10, BNLO

46   Admiralty: Register of Chaplains' Services, ADM 6/440/388, TNA

47   Admiralty: Register of Chaplains' Services, ADM 6/441/73, TNA

48   Admiralty Digests, ADM 12/1128, 71.22, 1884, TNA

49   Admiralty: Officers' Services register, ADM 196/82/394, TNA

50   Census 1911, RG14 PN5603 RG78PN254 RD90 SD4 ED11 SN103, TNA

51   Census 1901, RG 13, piece 4619, folio 85, page 19, TNA

52   Admiralty: Register of Chaplains' Services, ADM 6/440/236, TNA

53   Admiralty: Register of Chaplains' Services, ADM 6/441/7, TNA

54   Admiralty: Officer's Services register, ADM 196/68/417, TNA

55   Admiralty: Out-letters to RMA, AND 59/4/740 & 768, 1871-2, TNA

56   Admiralty Digests, ADM 12/591, 71.22, 1854, TNA

57   Census 1881, RG 11, piece 870, folio 13, page 1, TNA

58   Census 1871, RG10, piece 907, folio 88, page 21, TNA (Schon)

59   Hampshire Telegraph & Sussex Chronicle, Southsea Visitors, 26 November 1881, page 3, BNLO

60   Admiralty: Register of Chaplains' Services, ADM 6/440/269, TNA

61   Admiralty: Register of Chaplains' Services, ADM 6/441/19, TNA

62   Admiralty: Officer's Services register, ADM 196/68/441, TNA

63   London Gazette, Issue 22142, 21 May 1858, page 2514, LGO

64   London Gazette, Issue 22154, 18 June 1858, page 2955, LGO

65   London Gazette, Issue 22176, 24 August 1858, page 3901, LGO

66   Admiralty Digests: ADM 12/1144, 71.22, 1885, TNA

67   Admiralty: Out-letters to the RMA, ADM 59/8/520, June 1875, TNA

68   Williams, Rev E A, *The Cruise of the Pearl, with an account of the operations of the Naval Brigade in India, 1857-1858*, Naval & Military Press, 2004.

69   Illustrated London News, 20 May 1876, page 501, RNM

70   Illustrated London News, 9 October 1875, page 348, RNM

71   Admiralty: Register of Chaplains' Services, ADM 6/441/99, TNA

72   *Oxford University Alumni, 1500-1886*, database on-line at www.ancestry.co.uk

73   Census 1901, RG13, piece 1002, folio 116, page 35, TNA

74   Admiralty Digests, ADM 12/1406, 71.22, 1904, TNA

75   Globe & Laurel, Vol XVIII, 7 Dec 1911, page 182, RMM

76   Taylor, Gordon, *The Sea Chaplains*, Oxford Illustrated Press, 1978

77   Reverend York memorial plaque photo © Old Royal Naval College, Greenwich

Chapter 6

1   Census 1841, HO107, piece 559, book 24, folio 31, page 13, TNA

2   Census 1851, HO107, piece 2191, folio 102, page 1, TNA

3   Census 1871, RG 10, piece 2934, folio 103, page 12, TNA

4   Census 1881, RG 11, piece 1162, folio 137, page 3, TNA

5   Census 1891, RG12, piece 529, folio 90, page 4, TNA

6   Birth Register, October-December 1895, Woolwich, vol 1d, page 1172, GRO

7   E-mail: Bill - Jacquie Nevins, British Colombia Diocesan Archivist, October 2009

8   *Cambridge University Alumni 1261-1900*, Cambridge University Press, at www.ancestry.co.uk

9   National Probate Calendar (Index of Wills and Administrations), 1861-1941, PPR

10   Census 1861, RG 9, piece 751, folio 99, page 4, TNA

11   Census 1871, RG10, piece 378, folio 56, page 3, TNA

12   Admiralty: Register of Chaplains' Services, ADM 6/440/368, TNA

13   Admiralty: Register of Chaplains' Services, ADM 6/441/57, TNA

14   Census 1901, RG13, piece 4056, folio 130, page 9, TNA

15   GRO Death Register, Jan-Mar 1907, Ipswich, vol 4a, page 680, GRO

16   *Oxford University Alumni, 1500-1886*, database on-line at www.ancestry.co.uk

17   GRO Death Registers, Jul-Sep 1912, Congleton, vol 8a, page 306, GRO

18   Army Lists, various

19   Marriage Registers, October-December 1902, Wantage, vol 2c, page 773, GRO

20   Census 1901, RG13, piece 1103, folio 49, page 1, TNA

21   Admiralty: Register of Chaplains' Services, ADM 6/440/403, TNA

22   Admiralty: Register of Chaplains' Services, ADM 6/441/89, TNA

23   Admiralty: Passing Certificates, Naval Instructors, ADM 13/246, 1871, TNA

24   Navy and Army Illustrated, 28 May 1910, pages 125-126, RNM

25   The Times, 30 March 1926, page 19, TDA

26 Census 1891, RG12, piece 1806, folio 46, page 1, TNA

27 Census 1901, RG13, piece 2445, folio 12, page 1, TNA

28 Census 1881, RG11, piece 1242, folio 91, page 8, TNA

29 Hampshire Telegraph & Sussex Chronicle, Southsea Visitors, 24 Aug 1878, page 3, PHC

30 Admiralty: Register of Chaplains' Services, ADM 6/443/76, TNA

31 GRO Death Registers, Oct-Dec 1931, East Preston, vol 2b, page 503, GRO

32 Census 1881, RG11, piece 980, folio 97, page 20, TNA

33 Census 1891, RG12, piece 528, folio 31, page 53, TNA

34 Admiralty: Register of Chaplains' Services, ADM 6/443/45, TNA

35 Photo from Navy & Army Illustrated, Vol 13, 28 September 1901, page 44, RNM

36 Hampshire Telegraph & Sussex Chronicle, Southsea Visitors, 18 June 1898, page 7, PHC

37 Census 1861, RG09, piece 1695, folio 105, page 39, TNA

38 Marriage Registers, October-December 1868, Catherington, vol 2c, page 257, GRO

39 Admiralty: Register of Chaplains' Services, ADM 6/440/371, TNA

40 Admiralty: Register of Chaplains' Services, ADM 6/441/59, TNA

41 Admiralty: Passing Certificates, Naval Instructors, ADM 13/246, 1866, TNA

42 Census 1891, RG12, piece 873, folio 59, page 23, TNA

43 Census 1901, RG13, piece 1002, folio 45, page 33, TNA

44 Census 1901, RG13, piece 1002, folio 67, page 33, TNA

45 Kelly's Directory, Portsmouth & Southsea, 1896 & 1897, PHC

46 www.cyberhymnal.org/bio/r/o/romanis_w.htm, 2012

47 Kelly's Directory, Portsmouth & Southsea, 1898, page 471, PHC

48 Grave photographs © Dennis Bill 2013

49 Admiralty: Register of Chaplains' Services, ADM 6/440/360, TNA

50 Admiralty: Register of Chaplains' Services, ADM 6/441/51, TNA

51 Admiralty: Passing Certificates, Naval Instructors, ADM 13/246, 1864, TNA

52 Admiralty Digests, ADM 12/1094, 71.11, 1882, TNA

53 Census 1891, RG12, piece 4274, folio 6, page 5, TNA

54 Census 1901, RG13, piece 4853, folio 6, page 4, TNA

55 Census 1911, RG14, PN31213, RG78, PN1788, RD571, SD1, ED5, SN52, TNA

56 The Naval Who's Who, 1917, J B Hayward & Son, 1981, PHC

57 Census 1891, RG12, piece 876, folio 111, page 2, TNA

58 Census 1901, RG13, piece 990, folio 68, page 9, TNA

59 Kelly's Directory, Portsmouth & Southsea, 1892, page 277; 1897, page 124 & 1898, PHC

60 Census 1871, RG10, piece 14, folio 53, page 27, TNA

61 Census 1891, RG12, piece 117, folio 78, page 9, TNA

62 Census 1871, RG10, piece 3750, folio 17, page 25, TNA

63 Census 1881, RG11, piece 1162, folio 45, page 35, TNA

64 Census 1891, RG12, piece 876, folio 133, page 46, TNA

65 Highland Road Cemetery Registers, PCO & PHC

66 Admiralty: Register of Chaplains' Services, ADM 6/440/409, TNA

67 Admiralty: Register of Chaplains' Services, ADM 6/441/88, TNA

68   Admiralty Digest, ADM 12/1006, 71.2, 1877, TNA

69   Birmingham Daily Post, 24 April 1877, page 8, BNLO

70   Census 1881, RG 11, piece 5642, folio 76, page 1, TNA

71   Admiralty: Register of Chaplains' Services, ADM 6/440/327, TNA

72   Admiralty: Register of Chaplains' Services, ADM 6/441/39, TNA

73   Admiralty: In-letters and papers, from Admirals Pacific, ADM 1/5790, Y88 & Admiralty Digests, ADM 12/719, 71.22, 1862, TNA

74   Census 1901, RG 13, piece 5318, folio 154, page 20, TNA

75   Census 1901, RG13, piece 990, folio 68, page 10, TNA

76   Census 1891, RG 12, piece 885, folio 39, page 18, TNA

77   Census 1881, RG 11, piece 1174, folio, 64, page 1, TNA

78   Admiralty: Officers' Service Records, ADM 196/82/368, TNA

79   Census 1901, RG13, piece 1007, folio 114, page 5, TNA

80   Census 1881, RG11, piece 732, folio 108, page 89, TNA

81   Marriage Registers, September-October 1887, Lewisham, vol 1d, page 1504a, GRO

82   Admiralty: Register of Chaplains' Services, ADM 6/443/553, TNA

83   Census 1901, RG13, piece 990, folio 112, page 27, TNA

84   Census 1911, RG14, PN34971, RD640, SD2, ED41, SN9999, TNA

85   Death Registers, July-September 1959, Bournemouth, vol 6b, page 166, GRO

86   London Gazette, Issue 33483, 5 April 1929, page 2274, LGO

Chapter 7

1   Out-letters to RMA, Kassasin Casualties, ADM 59/15, pages 43 & 54, TNA

2   Photo 17/7/9/61, RMM

3   RM Ranks Index, RMM

4   Census 1861, RG 9, piece 3951, folio 1, page 22, TNA

5   Census 1871, RG10, piece 5779, folio 146, page 30, TNA

6   Census 1881, RG 11, piece 2534, folio 46, page 27, TNA

7   *With Full & Grateful Hearts, A Register of Royal Marine Deaths 1914-19*, RMHS, 1991

8   Admiralty: RM Registers of Service, ADM 159/27, TNA

9   Commonwealth War Graves Commission database, on-line

10   War Death Navy All Ranks Indices (1914 to 1921), year 1915, volume RN, page 467, GRO

11   Admiralty: RM Registers of Service, ADM 159/23, TNA

12   Census 1911, RG14 PN5594 RD90 SD4 ED2 SN199, TNA

13   Grave photographs © Dennis Bill 2013

14   Admiralty: RN Officer's Service Records, ADM 196/61, TNA

15   Globe & Laurel, Vol XXIV, 7 Feb 1917, page 36, RMM

16   RN Cemetery Haslar Burial Records, PHC

17   Birth Registers, July-September 1869, Ludlow, vol 6a, page 520, GRO

18   Census 1901, RG13, piece 991, folio 6, page 4, TNA

19   Census 1911, RG14 PN9571 RD188 SD6 ED15 SN20, TNA

20   Census 1871, RG 10, piece 1828, folio 12, page 14, TNA

21   Census 1901, RG 13, piece 990, folio 122, page 1, TNA

22   Census 1911, RG14 PN5686 RD93 SD1 ED8 SN257, TNA

23   Census 1911, RG14 PN23811 RD464 SD ED110 SN280, TNA

24   War Death Navy All Ranks Indices (1914 to 1921),year 1916, volume RN, page 1466, GRO

25   Admiralty: RM Registers of Service, ADM 159/32, TNA

26   Admiralty: Naval Courts Martial & Boards of Enquiry, Loss of HMS Natal, ADM 178/122, TNA

27   Globe & Laurel, Vol XXIII, 7 Feb 1916, page 28, RMM

28   Photo 2/10/5/73, RMM

29   Admiralty: RM Registers of Service, ADM 159/30, TNA

30   London Gazette, Issue 30424, 12 December 1917, page 13013, LGO

31   Holloway, S M, *From Trench and Turret, Royal Marines' Letters and Diaries 1914-18*, Constable, London, 2006, PHC

32   Admiralty: RM Registers of Service, ADM 159/31, TNA

33   Admiralty: RM Registers of Service, ADM 159/22, TNA

34   Admiralty: RM Registers of Service, ADM 159/28, TNA

35   Census 1891, RG 12, piece 1887, folio 35, page 8, TNA

36   Admiralty: RM Registers of Service, ADM 159/24, TNA

37   War Death Navy All Ranks Indices (1914 to 1921), volume RN, page 3107, GRO

38   Admiralty: RM Registers of Service, ADM 159/22, TNA

39   Census 1911, RG14 PN5541 RD90 SD2 ED20 SN89, TNA

Chapter 8

1   Admiralty: RN Officer's Service Records, ADM 196/137, TNA

2   Bacon, Admiral Sir Reginald H S, *The Dover Patrol, Vols 1 & 2*, Hutchinson, London, 1919

3   Humphreys, Roy, *The Dover Patrol 1914-18*, Sutton Publishing, 1998

4   O'Moore Creagh, Sir & Humphris, E M, *The Distinguished Service Order 1886-1923*, J B Hayward & Son, London, 1978

5   London Gazette, Issue 29436, 12 January 1916, page 547, LGO

6   Blumberg, General Sir H E, *Britain's Sea Soldiers*, Swiss & Co, Devonport, 1927, PHC

7   London Gazette, Issue 27426, 18 April 1902, page 2599, LGO

8   London Gazette, Issue 27428, 25 April 1902, page 2759, LGO

9   *Who Was Who*, A & C Black, 1920-2008; online edition Oxford University Press, Dec 2007

10 Sutherland, James, *The Distinguished Service Order 1924-2008*, Savannah Publications, London, 2009

11 War Office: Recommendations for Honours and Awards (Army), Middle East 1941-43, WO 373/29, TNA

12 London Gazette, Issue 35908, 18 February 1943, page 863, LGO

13 Death Registers, May 1986, Richmond upon Thames, vol 14, page 1569, reg 586, GRO

14 War Office: Service Medal & Award Rolls Index, WW1, WO 372, TNA, ancestry.co.uk

15 London Gazette, Issue 29890, 4 January 1917, page 209, LGO

16 London Gazette, Issue 29886, 1 January 1917, page 25, LGO

17 Hampshire Chronicle, 12 September 1964, page 11, HRO

18 London Gazette, Issue 30450,1 January 1918, page 25, LGO

19 War Office: Service Medal & Award Rolls Index, WW1, WO 372, TNA, ancestry.co.uk

20   Admiralty: RM Registers of Service, ADM 159/33, TNA

21   London Gazette, Issue 29635, 22 June 1916, page 6213, LGO

22   Globe & Laurel, Vol LXVI, Jun/Jul 1958, page 151, RMM

23   Globe & Laurel, Vol LXVI, Oct/Nov 1958, page 255, RMM

24   Portsmouth Evening News, Death Announcements, 1 April 1958, PHC

25   Admiralty: RM Registers of Service, ADM 159/27, TNA

26   Admiralty: RM Registers of Service, ADM 159/89, TNA (WJC junior)

27   Admiralty: RN Officer's Service Records, ADM 196/98, TNA

28   Personal Papers, ARCH 10/12/C, (Coen senior), RMM

29   London Gazette, Issue 30581, 16 March 1918, page 3395, LGO

30   Globe & Laurel, Vol LXXXV, July-August 1976, page 259, RMM (WJC junior)

31   Highland Road Cemetery Registers, PCO & PHC

32   Grave photographs © Dennis Bill 2013

33   Admiralty: RM Registers of Service, ADM 159/28, TNA

34   London Gazette, Issue 29752, 15 September 1916, page 9088, LGO

35   Photo from The Sheet Anchor, Summer 2004, Royal Marines Historical Society, RMM

36   National Probate Calendar (Index of Wills and Administrations), 1858-1966, PPR

37   Death Registers, April-June 1933, St George Hanover Square, vol 1a, page 450, GRO

38   London Gazette, Issue 29422, 1 January 1916, page 22, LGO

39   London Gazette, Issue 30077, 18 May 1917, page 4876, LGO

40   London Gazette, Issue 30693, 21 May 1918, page 5982, LGO

41   London Gazette, Issue 31092, 1 January 1919, page 26, LGO

42   London Gazette, Issue 29886, 1 January 1917, page 41, LGO

43   Admiralty: RM Registers of Service, ADM 159/30, TNA

44   London Gazette, Issue 30424, 12 December 1917, page 13013, LGO

45   Admiralty: RM Registers of Service, ADM 159/24, TNA

46   Admiralty: RN Officer's Service Records, ADM 196/97, TNA

47   London Gazette, Issue 27353, 10 September 1901, page 5935, LGO

48   London Gazette, Issue 27359, 27 September 1901, page 6308, LGO

49   Census 1881, RG11, piece 2031, folio 31, pages 11 & 12, TNA

50   Globe & Laurel, Vol VII, 7 December 1900, page 140, RMM

51   Globe & Laurel, Vol XXII, 7 November 1915 page 203, RMM

52   Birth Registers, April-June 1868, Chippenham, vol 5a, page 58, GRO

53   RM Museum medal collection, RMM

54   Photo 10/2/D1/26, RMM

55   London Gazette, Issue 29940, 13 February 1917, page 1574, LGO

56   Globe & Laurel Vol XII, 7 May 1905, page 57, RMM

57   Death Registration, July-September 1944, Greenwich, vol 1d, page 602, GRO

58   Death Register, April-June 1944, Dartford, Vol 2a, Page 1070, GRO

59   London Gazette, Issue 31092, 1 January 1919, page 38, LGO

60   London Gazette, Issue 31534, 3 September 1919, page 11110, LGO

61   Photo 14/9/3/10, RMM

62 RM Ranks Index, RMM

63 Admiralty: RM Registers of Service, ADM 159/26, TNA

64 Admiralty: RN Officer's Service Records, ADM 196/99, TNA

65 Globe & Laurel, Vol VI, Jul 1899, page 222, RMM

66 Globe & Laurel, Vol XXVII, May 1920, page 71, RMM

67 Navy & Army Illustrated, 29 July 1899 page 447, photo credited to "Cribb, Portsmouth", RMM

68 Abbott, P E, *Recipients of the DCM, 1855-1909*, Hayward & Son, 1975

69 Globe & Laurel, Vol IV, 7 December 1897, pages 134-5, RMM

70 Field, Colonel Cyril, RMLI; *Britain's Sea Soldiers, Vol 2*, Chapter XXXIII, Lyceum Press, Liverpool, 1924

71 Photo 13/11/13/78, RMM

72 Admiralty: RN Officer's Service Records, ADM 196/97, TNA

73 London Gazette, Issue 31604, 17 October 1919, page 12783, LGO

74 Trowbridge's Diary, Arch 7/14/5, RMM

75 London Gazette, Issue 27159, 30 January 1900, page 600, LGO

76 London Gazette, Issue 27173, 13 March 1900, page 1710, LGO

77 Navy & Army Illustrated, 7 May 1898, page 160, RMM (photo) and www. melik.org.uk

78 Admiralty: RM Registers of Service, ADM 159/23, TNA

79 London Gazette, Issue 27188, 1 May 1900, page 2756, LGO

80 Globe & Laurel, Vol XIX, 7 December 1912, page 191, RMM

81 Census 1901, RG 13, piece 13, folio 108, page 35, TNA

82 Census 1911, RG 14 PN355 RD3 SD5 ED18 SN207, TNA

83 Death Registers, April to June 1943, Wandsworth, vol 1d, page 405, GRO

84 London Gazette, Issue 27094, 30 June 1899, page 4074, LGO

85 London Gazette, Issue 27077, 5 May 1899, page 2889, LGO

86 Death Registers, July-September 1904, Portsmouth, vol 2b, page 295, GRO

87 Letters, Arch 11/12/4, RMM

88 He was baptized in St Mary the Virgin, Petworth on 23 August 1874, www.familysearch.org

89 Census 1881, RG 11, piece 119, folio 83, page 19, TNA

90 Census 1891, RG 12, piece 905, folio 162, page 32, TNA

91 Census 1901, RG 13, piece 990, folio 133, page 25, TNA

92 War Office: Royal Hospital Chelsea: Soldiers Service Documents, WO97/4047/102 & WO 121/223/1, TNA

93 Globe & Laurel, Volume IV, 7 August 1897, Corps Gazette, RMM

94 Hampshire Telegraph & Sussex Chronicle, 22 April 1899, page 8, BNLO

95 Photo 10/2/T1/10, RMM

96 Admiralty: RN Officer's Service Records, ADM 196/63, TNA

97 London Gazette, Issue 31099, 1 January 1919, page 113, LGO

98 Bilcliffe, John, *Irreproachable Character – The Award of the Royal Marine Meritorious Service Medal*, Pub No 30, RMHS, 2005

99 Globe & Laurel, Vol XII, 7 Aug 1905, page 86, RMM

100 Globe & Laurel, Vol LVIII, November 1950, page 300, RMM

101 Scarlett, R J, *The Naval Good Shooting Medal 1903-1914*, The London Stamp Exchange, 1990

102 Chichester & Southdown Observer, Death Announcements, 16 September 1950, WSRO

103 Admiralty: RM Registers of Service, ADM 159/22, TNA

104 Census 1911, RG14 PN5541 RD90 SD2 ED20 SN72, TNA

105 Admiralty: RM Registers of Service, ADM 159/20, TNA

106 Census 1901, RG 13, piece 987, folio 91, page 2, TNA

107 Census 1911, RG14 PN5498 RD90 SD1 ED20 SN360, TNA

108 Death Registrations, October-December 1938, Gosport, volume 2b, page 796, GRO

109 Globe & Laurel, Vol LXVI, Jun/Jul 1958, p 151, RMM

110 Death Register, October-December 1929, Cheltenham, Vol 6a, Page 441, GRO

111 Admiralty: RM Registers of Service, ADM 159/34, TNA

112 1901 Census, RG 13, piece 5328, folio 122, page 15, TNA

113 Death Register, January-March 1967, Surrey SW, Vol 5g, Page 568, GRO

114 Census 1881, RG 11, piece 1162, folio 139, page 8, TNA

115 Census 1891, RG 12, piece 4482, folio 24, page 41, TNA

116 Census 1911, RG 14 PN32780 RD594 SD3 ED23 SN342, TNA

117 Death Register, April-June 1890, Swansea, vol 11a, page 457, GRO

118 Death Register, July-September 1935, Nantwich, vol 8a, page 352, GRO

119 Census 1911, RG14 PN12529 RD269 SD269 ED4 SN45, TNA

120 Globe & Laurel, Vol LIX, March 1951, page 87, RMM

121 Personal Papers, ARCH 10/2/G, RMM

122 Admiralty: RM Registers of Service, ADM 159/85, TNA

123 London Gazette, Issue 39732, 30 Dec 1952, page 29, LGO

124 Death Registers, April-June 1981, South Glamorgan, volume 28, page 1978, GRO

125 Admiralty: RM Registers of Service, ADM 159/21, TNA

126 Census 1911, RG14 PN15325 RD325 SD3 ED31 SN82, TNA

127 Death Registers, April-June 1937, Gloucester, Vol 6a, page 404, GRO

128 Portsmouth Evening News, 10 April 1931, PHC

129 Globe & Laurel, Vol 1931, page 152, RMM

130 Census 1871, RG 10, piece 1148, folio 79, page 43, TNA

131 Census 1881, RG 11, piece 1162, folio 101, page 23, TNA

132 Birth Register, January-March 1839, Portsea Island, vol 7, page 146, GRO

133 Death Register, January-March 1931, Portsmouth, vol 2b, page 876, GRO

134 Admiralty: Correspondence & Papers, *HMS Thunderer* casualties, ADM 1/6481/N10, TNA

135 Census 1901, RG 13, piece 2386, folio 8, page 7, TNA

136 Census 1911, RG 14 PN14939 RD319 SD4 ED12 SN62, TNA

137 Death Registers, January to March 1934, Bristol, vol 6a, page 143, GRO

138 Census 1901, RG 13, piece 264, folio 98, page2, TNA

139 Census 1911, RG14 PN1315 RD15 SD2 ED25 SN32, TNA

140 Census 1911, RG14 PN7276 RD132 SD2 ED31 SN65, TNA

141 Death Registers, April-June 1936, Bournemouth, vol 2b, page 900, GRO

142 Census 1841, HO 107, piece 677/4, page39, TNA

143 Census 1881, RG 11, piece 716, folio 96, page 21, TNA

144 Census 1891, RG 12, piece 504, folio 89, page 44, TNA

145 Census 1901, RG 13, piece 532, folio 48, page 17, TNA

146 Census 1911, RG 14 PN2646 RD28 SD3 ED5 SN98, TNA

147 Birth Registers, January-March 1841, Marylebone, vol 1, page 174, GRO

148 Marriage Registers, January-March 1901, Greenwich, vol 1d, page 1045, GRO

149 Death Registers, April-June 1926, Greenwich, vol 1d, page 863, GRO

150 Birth Registers, October-December 1841, Bedford, vol 6, page 23, GRO

151 Census 1851, HO 107, piece 1752, folio 273, page 6, TNA

152 Census 1881, RG 11, piece 295, folio 76, page 19, TNA

153 Census 1901, RG 13, piece 1494, folio 39, page 24, TNA

154 Globe & Laurel, Vol III, 7 November 1896, page 153, from Hackney Express & Shoreditch Observer, 17 Oct 1896, RMM

155 Globe & Laurel, Vol XXI, 7 May 1914, page 85, RMM

156 Globe & Laurel, Vol L, February 1942, page 31, RMM

157 Globe & Laurel, Vol LXIV, April 1956, page 86, photo attributed to Wright & Logan, Southsea, RMM

158 Census 1911, RG14 PN110 RG78 PN4 RD2 SD1 ED23 SN50, TNA

159 Milton Cemetery Registers, PHC & PCO

160 Census 1911, RG14 PN5608 RD90 SD4 ED16 SN383, TNA

161 Census 1901, RG 13, piece 4448, folio 121, page 27, TNA

162 Census 1911, RG 14 PN2838 RD517 SD2 ED1 SN225, TNA

163 Globe & Laurel, Vol XXXV, June 1927, page 146, RMM

164 Census 1861, RG 9, piece 642, folio 187, page 15, TNA

165 Census 1881, RG 11, piece 1154, folio 6, page 5, TNA

166 Census 1891, RG 12, piece 867, folio 50, page 12, TNA

167 Census 1901, RG 13, piece 985, folio 45, page39, TNA

168 Census 1911, RG 14 PN5523 RD90 SD2 ED2 SN38, TNA

169 Death Registers, April-June 1869, Portsea, vol 2b, page 284, GRO

170 Kingston Cemetery Registers, PHC & PCO

171 Census 1911, RG14 PN5558 RD90 SD2 ED37 SN18, TNA

172 Death Registers, January-March 1946, Portsmouth, vol 2b, page 882, GRO

173 Birth Registers, October-December 1873, St George's Hannover Square, vol 1a, page 355, GRO

174 Census 1881, RG 11, piece 103, folio 109, page 60, TNA

175 Census 1911, RG 14 PN5541 RD90 SD2 ED20 SN339, TNA

176 London Gazette, Issue 27293, 12 March 1901, page 1759, LGO

177 Admiralty: Miscellaneous Medal Roll, ADM 171/61, page 604, TNA

178 Admiralty: Roll of Naval War Medals, Royal Marines, NCOs & Men, She-Z, ADM 171/171, page 291, TNA

179 Globe & Laurel, Vol LIX, April 1951, page 120, RMM

180 Death Registers, January-March 1951, Portsmouth, vol 6b, page 747, GRO

181 Census 1891, RG 12, piece 797, folio 103, page 3, TNA

182 Census 1901, RG 13, piece 917, folio 102, page 1, TNA

183 Census 1911, RG14 PN2355 RD26 SD5 ED70 SN248, TNA

184 Death Registers, July-September 1930, Rochford, vol 4a, page 589, GRO

185 Admiralty: RM Registers of Service, ADM 159/25, TNA

186 Admiralty: RN Officer's Service Records, ADM 196/64, TNA

187 Death Registers, January-March 1938, Winchester, vol 2c, page 197, GRO

188 Census 1911, RG 14 PN4141 RD51 SD3 ED14 SN169, TNA

189 Service and personal papers, ARCH 10/2/W, RMM

190 Census 1901, RG 13, piece 339, folio 98, page 22, TNA

191 Census 1911, RG 14 PN6950 RD128 SD5 ED23 SN52, TNA

192 Birth Registers, July-September 1860, Peterbro, volume 3b, page 206, GRO

193 Marriage Registers, July-September 1882, Portsea, volume 2b, page 744, GRO

194 Death Registers, January-March 1933, Droitwich, volume 6c, page 282, GRO

195 Admiralty: Roll of Naval War Medals, Royal Marines, NCOs & Men, She-Z, ADM 171/171, page 528, TNA

196 Marriage Registers, January-March 1913, Brentford, volume 3a, page 114, GRO

197 Death Registers, January-March 1912, Chelsea, volume 1a, page 493, GRO

198 Photo 2/7/6/232 (extract), RMM

199 Census 1901, RG 13, piece 1549, folio 42, page 1, TNA

200 Census 1911, RG 14, PN9279 RD186 SD1 ED8 SN3, TNA

201 London Gazette, Issue 31182, 15 February 1919, page 2361, LGO

202 Globe & Laurel, Vol LXIX, October/November 1961, page 338, RMM

203 Death Registers, July - September 1961, North Bucks, volume 6a, page 383, GRO

204 London Gazette, Issue 31452, 12 July 1919, page 8943, LGO

205 Census 1911, RG 14 PN369 RD3 SD5 ED32 SN117, TNA

Chapter 9

1 Photo 13/11/140/011, RMM

2 Census 1881, RG 11, piece 772, folio 91, page 9, TNA

3 Census 1901, RG 13, piece 5330, folio 100, page 7, TNA

4 Census 1911, RG14 PN34972 RD640 ED Vessels SD 9999, TNA

5 Census 1871, RG 10, piece 1147, folio 56, page 6, TNA

6 Census 1901, RG 13, piece 1005, folio 100, page 28, TNA

7 Census 1871, RG 10, piece 1142, folio 44, page 33, TNA

8 Census 1891, RG 12, piece 869, folio 138, page 14, TNA

9 Census 1901, RG 13, piece 1006, folio 109, page 8, TNA

10 Census 1911, RG14 PN5580 RD90 SD3 ED20 SN70, TNA

11 St Mary's Church, Portsea, Marriage Registers, 1894, CHU 3/1D/92, PHC

12 Admiralty: RM Registers of Service, ADM 159/20, TNA

13 Kingston Cemetery Registers, PHC & PCO

14 Admiralty: In-letters & Papers, Courts Martial, 1893, *HMS Victoria*, ADM 1/7174, TNA

15 Census 1901, RG 13, piece 979, folio 43, page 28, TNA

16 Globe & Laurel, Vol XXXI, March 1924, page 44, RMM

17 National Probate Calendar (Index of Wills and Administrations), 1858-1966, PPR

18 Admiralty: RM Registers of Service, ADM 159/24, TNA

19 UK Incoming Passenger Lists 1878-1960, BT 26, page 614, item 103, TNA

20 Census 1911, RG 14 PN5473 RD89 SD1 ED10 SN260, TNA

21 Cullimore Memorial photo from *www.roll-of-honour.com* by permission of Martin Edwards

22 RM Ranks Index, RMM

23 Personal papers, ARCH 11/12/4, Arch 3/19/1 & Arch 2/7/6, RMM

24 Birth Registers, April-June 1869, Clifton, vol 6a, page 103, GRO

25 Highland Road Cemetery Registers, PCO & PHC

26 Census 1891, RG 12, piece 723, folio 111, page 32, TNA

27 Census 1901, RG 13, piece 989, folio 9, page 11, TNA

28 Marriage Registers, April-June 1909, Portsmouth, volume 2b, page 1074, GRO

29 Census 1911, RG 14 PN5559 RD90 SD2 ED38 SN233, TNA

30 Census 1911, RG 14 PN3962 RD47 SD2 ED36 SN9999, TNA

31 RM Museum medal collection, RMM

32 Admiralty: Ships' Ledgers, Vanguard, 1875 Jan-Sept, ADM 117/994, TNA

33 Census 1881, RG 11, piece 998, folio 131, page 37, TNA

34 Census 1891, RG 12, piece 0049, folio 10, page 12, TNA

35 Census 1901, RG 13, piece 0487, folio 45, page 42, TNA

36 Census 1911, RG 14 PN2242 RD26 SD3 ED22 SN53, TNA

37 Death Registrations, April-June 1903, Wandsworth, vol 1d, page 359, GRO

38 Census 1851, HO 107, piece 1731, folio 527, page 13, TNA

39 Census 1861, RG 9, piece 405, folio 91, page 6, TNA

40 Census 1881, RG 11, piece 1162, folio 145, page 18, TNA

41 Census 1891, RG 12, piece 3725, folio 112, page 28, TNA

42 Census 1901, RG 13, piece 3717, folio 136, page 5, TNA

43 Death Registers, January-March 1922, Dewsbury, Vol 9b, page 833, GRO

44 Globe & Laurel, Volume XXIX, March 1922, page 39, RMM

45 Census 1901, RG 13, piece 988, folio 58, page 4, TNA

46 Census 1911, RG 14, PN 5275, RD 81, SD 3, ED 1, SN 10, TNA

47 War Office: Soldier's Documents, WW I, WO 363/K475, TNA

48 War Office: Service Medal & Award Rolls Index, WWI, WO 372/11, TNA

49 The Companies of the Royal Garrison Artillery, The role of the Heavy Battery, www.1914 1918.net

50 Birth Registers, July-September 1870, Portsea, vol 2b, page 447, GRO

51 Death Registers, October-December 1870, Portsea, vol 2b, page 293, GRO

52 Census 1861, RG 9, piece 4441, folio 37, page 35, TNA

53 Census 1871, RG 10, piece 1148, folio 75, page 36, TNA

54 Census 1881, RG 11, piece 1161, folio 121, page 16, TNA

55 Census 1891, RG 12, piece 1765, folio 73, page 27, TNA

56 Census 1901, RG 13, piece 2135, folio 61, page 15, TNA

57 Death Registers, July-September 1910, Tiverton, vol 5b, page 223, GRO

58 Globe & Laurel, Vol XX, 7 Feb 1913, page 31, RMM

59 Census 1871, RG 10, piece 1966, folio 33, page 9, TNA

60   Census 1881, RG 11, piece 2056, folio 59, page 10, TNA

61   Census 1891, RG 12, piece 1609, folio 103, page 18, TNA

62   Marriage Registers, July-September 1866, Portsea, volume 2b, page 6/7, GRO

63   Marriage Registers, July-September 1878, Alderbury, volume 5a, page 295, GRO

64   Death Registers, January-March 1877, Warminster, volume 5a, page 107, GRO

65   Death Registers, October-December 1894, Warminster, volume 5a, page 77, GRO

66   Nares, Capt Sir G S, RN, KCB, FRS. *Narrative of A Voyage To the Polar Sea*, Sampson Low, Marston, Searle & Rivington, London, 1878.

67   Birth Registers, July-September 1847, Selby, volume 23, page 555, GRO

68   Census 1871, RG 10, piece 5779, folio 73, page 5, TNA

69   Census 1881, RG 11, piece 1162, folio 111, page 43, TNA

70   Census 1891, RG 12, piece 3663, folio 138, page 13, TNA

71   Census 1901, RG 13, piece 4193, folio 134, page 20, TNA

72   Census 1911, RG 14 PN27129 RD501 SD1 ED12 SN381, TNA

73   Admiralty: Medal Rolls, Arctic Medal 1875-6, ADM 171/61, TNA

74   Globe & Laurel, Vol XXIX, Aug 1922, page 120, RMM

75   Death Registers, April to June 1922, Hunslet, vol 9b, page 632, TNA

76   Census 1891, RG 12, piece 2054, folio 4, page 2, TNA

77   Census 1901, RG 13 piece 2473, f olio 64, page 5, TNA

78   Census 1911, RG 14 PN15632 RD336 SD1 ED1 SN30, TNA

79   Death Registers, October-December 1919, Ross, volume 6a, page 529, GRO

80   Ambler, John, *The Royal Marines Band Service, Volume 2*, RMHS Special Publication 37, 2011

81   Death Registration, May 1993, Dover, vol 5631A, entry 258, GRO

82   The Blue Band, Volume 29, No 3, December 1976, pages 119 & 165-6, RMM

83   Photo 15/10/5/35, RMM

84   Thompson, Julian, *The Imperial War Museum Book of The War at Sea 1914-1918*, Sidgwick & Jackson, 2005 (Letter from Engineer Lieutenant Shrubsole)

Appendix C - Bibliography and Internet Links
Bibliography

Herbert, Gilbert, *Pioneers of Prefabrication: the British contribution in the nineteenth century,* Johns Hopkins University Press, 1978

Silver, Christopher, *Renkioi: Brunel's Forgotten Crimean War Hospital*, Valonia Press, 2007

Hoad, Margaret J & Temple Patterson, Prof. A, *Portsmouth and the Crimean War*, Portsmouth Papers No19, Portsmouth City Council, 1973

Riley, Dr R C, *The Growth of Southsea as a Naval Satellite and Victorian Resort*, Portsmouth Papers No16, Portsmouth City Council, 1972

Bayley, C C, *Mercenaries for the Crimea*, McGill-Queen's University Press, Montreal & London, 1977

Brooks, Richard & Little, Matthew, *Tracing Your Royal Marine Ancestors*, Pen & Sword Family History, 2008

Pappalardo, Bruno, *Tracing Your Naval Ancestors*, PRO (TNA), 2003

Cock, Randolph & Rodger, N A M, *A Guide To The Naval Records In The National Archives Of The UK*, University of London, 2008

Sweetman, John, *The Crimean War,* Osprey Publishing, 2001

Kerr, Paul, *The Crimean War,* Boxtree, 1997

Blumberg, General Sir H E, KCB, *Britain's Sea Soldiers: A Record of the Royal Marines During The War 1914-1919,* Swiss & Co, Devonport, 1927. Reprinted as RMHS Special Publication No42, Royal Marines Historical Society, 2014

Field, Colonel Cyril, RMLI; *Britain's Sea Soldiers*, Lyceum Press, Liverpool, 1924

Fraser, E and Carr-Laughton, L G, *Royal Marine Artillery*, Royal United Service Institution, 1930

Brooks, Richard, *The Royal Marines – 1664 to the present*, Constable, London, 2002

Brooks, Richard, *The Long Arm Of Empire: Naval Brigades from the Crimea to the Boxer Rebellion*, Constable, London, 1999

Smith, Peter C, *Per Mare Per Terram, A History of the Royal Marines*, Balfour, 1974

Bilcliffe, John, *Irreproachable Character – The Award of the Royal Marine Meritorious Service Medal,* Pub No 30, RMHS, 2005

Ambler, John, The *Royal Marines Band Service, Volume 2*, RMHS Special Publication 37, 2011

Clowes, Sir William Laird, *The Royal Navy: A History – From the earliest times to 1900*, Chatham, 1996 (reprint)

The Naval Who's Who 1917, J B Hayward & Son, 1981 Winfield, Rif & Lyon, David, The Sail and Steam Navy List, All the Ships of the Royal Navy 1815-1889, Chatham Publishing, 2003

Hill, Richard, *War At Sea In The Ironclad Age*, Cassell, 2002

White, Colin, *The End of the Sailing Navy: Victoria's Navy*, Kenneth Mason Publications Ltd, 1981

Hough, Richard, *Admirals In Collision*, Hamish Hamilton, London, 1959

Preston, Antony and Major, John, *Send A Gunboat!*, Longmans, Green & Co Ltd, London, 1967

Warlow, Ben, *Shore Establishments of the Royal Navy*, Maritime Books, 2000

Hampshire, Arthur Cecil, *They Called It Accident*, William Kimber, 1961

Regan, Geoffrey, *The Guinness Book of Naval Blunders*, Guinness Publishing Ltd, 1993

Taylor, Gordon, *The Sea Chaplains*, Oxford Illustrated Press, 1978

Thompson, Julian, *The Imperial War Museum Book of The War at Sea 1914-1918*, Sidgwick & Jackson, 2005

Humphreys, Roy, *The Dover Patrol 1914-18*, Sutton Publishing, 1998

Bacon, Admiral Sir Reginald H S, *The Dover Patrol, Vols 1 & 2*, Hutchinson, London, 1919

Nares, Capt Sir G S, RN, KCB, FRS. *Narrative of A Voyage To the Polar Sea*, Sampson Low, Marston, Searle & Rivington, London, 1878.

Williams, Rev E A, *The Cruise of the Pearl, with an account of the operations of the Naval Brigade in India, 1857-1858*, Naval & Military Press, 2004.

Coleman, E C, *The Royal Navy and Polar Exploration, Vols 1 & 2*, Tempus, 2007

Churchill, Winston S, *The River War*, Longmans, Green and Co., London, 1902

O'Moore Creagh, Sir & Humphris, E M, *The Distinguished Service Order, 1886-1923*, J B Hayward & Son, London, 1978

Sutherland, James, *The Distinguished Service Order, 1924-2008*, Savannah Publications, London, 2009

Bate, Christopher K & Smith, Martin G, *For Bravery In The Field, Recipients of the Military Medal*, Bayonet, 1991

Fevyer, W H, *The Distinguished Service Medal, 1914-20*, J B Hayward & Son, Suffolk, 1982

Fevyer, W H, *The Distinguished Service Medal, 1939-46*, Hayward; London, 1981

Abbott, P E, *Recipients of the DCM, 1855-1909*, Hayward & Son, 1975

Walker, R W, *Recipients of the Distinguished Conduct Medal, 1914-20*, Midland Medals, Birmingham, 1981

Walker, R W, *Citations of the Distinguished Conduct Medal, 1914-20*, Naval & Military Press, 2007

Honours and Awards, Army, Navy & Air Force 1914-20, Hayward, 1979

With Full & Grateful Hearts, A Register of Royal Marine Deaths 1914-19, Royal Marines Historical Society, 1991

Bid Them Rest In Peace, A Register of Royal Marines Deaths 1939-1945, Royal Marines Historical Society, 1992

Oakley, Captain Derek MBE, RM, *Albert Medals Awarded to Royal Marines*, RMHS Special Publication No 32

Scarlett, R J, *The Naval Good Shooting Medal 1903-1914*, The London Stamp Exchange, 1990

Holloway, S M, *From Trench and Turret, Royal Marines' Letters and Diaries 1914-18*, Constable, London, 2006

Maloney, Senan, *The Phoenix Murders: Conspiracy, Betrayal and Retribution*, Mercier Press, Dublin, 2006

Corfe, Tom, *The Phoenix Park Murders, conflict, compromise and tragedy in Ireland, 1879-1882*, Hodder & Stoughton, 1968

Weir, Colin, *The History of Cambridge University Football Club, 1872-2003*, Yore Publications, Harefield, Middlesex, 2004

Internet Links

Here are a few of the web sites that I have found helpful:

www.royalmarinesmuseum.co.uk

www.nmrn-portsmouth.org.uk/ - National Museum of the Royal Navy

www.pdavis.nl/index.htm - Don't be put off by the home page, there is much more to this excellent site than a personal history of William Loney RN and the free frigate simulator. Click on 'Search this site', enter a ship name (19th century) and all, or at least much, will be revealed. From any ship page you can navigate to other ships' pages alphabetically. An excellent resource, especially if you haven't got easy access to the Navy Lists.

www.pbenyon.plus.com/Naval.html - Late 18th, 19th and early 20th Century Naval History and ship details, another excellent site

www.melik.org.uk (Nile Gunboats)

www.battleships-cruisers.co.uk - history, ship details, photos and prints of the world's navies

www.historyofwar.org/articles/wars_crimean.html - Crimean War

www.firstworldwar.com

www.lsars.pwp.blueyonder.co.uk/rolls.htm - Life Saving Medal Rolls and Citations (Royal Humane Society)

www.naval-history.net

www.ams-museum.org.uk - Army Medical Services Museum

http://wellcomelibrary.org - Wellcome Library, Hospitals: Military & Naval

www.cwgc.org - Commonwealth War Graves database with photos

www.roll-of-honour.com – war memorial database with photos

http://cwrs.russianwar.co.uk/cwrsentry.html - Crimean War Research Society

http://www.cityoflondon.gov.uk/things-to-do/london-metropolitan-archives/Pages/default.aspx London Metropolitan Archives

www.1914-1918.net - The Long, Long Trail; The British Army in the Great War

www.ancestry.co.uk - Cambridge University Alumni 1261-1900, Cambridge University Press, and Oxford University Alumni, 1500-1886, database on-line

www.ukwhoswho.com - online edition of Who's Who 2012 and Who Was Who, A & C Black, 1920-2008; Oxford University Press

http://specialcollections.le.ac.uk/cdm/landingpage/collection/p16445coll4/hd/ - Historical Directories of England & Wales, University of Leicester

www.bodley.ox.ac.uk/ilej/- Internet Library of Early Journals

My Crinoline Church web site is at – **www.thecrinolinechurch.org.uk**

My own family history website is at – **www.dennisbillfamilyhistory.co.uk**

Index

Civilian Clergy

Civilian Personnel